TRANSLATING MOUNT FUJI

Translating Mount Fuji

Modern Japanese Fiction and the Ethics of Identity

Dennis Washburn

Columbia University Press • New York

Columbia University Press
Publishers Since 1893
New York   Chichester, West Sussex
Copyright © 2007 Columbia University Press
All rights reserved

The publication of this book was supported through funds provided by the author's research professorship at Darmouth College. The Press wishes to express its sincere gratitude to the anonymous donor who generously established this professorship.

Portions of some of the chapters in this book are revisions of materials previously published in *The Journal of Japanese Studies* and *Monumenta Nipponica* and by the Publications Program of the Center for Japanese Studies at the University of Michigan. The author wishes to acknowledge and thank these organizations for granting permission to use these materials.

Library of Congress Cataloging-in-Publication Data
Washburn, Dennis C. (Dennis Charles), 1954–
    Translating Mount Fuji : modern Japanese fiction and the ethics of identity /
Dennis Washburn.
        p.   cm.
    Includes bibliographical references and index.
    ISBN 0–231–13892–X (cloth : alk. paper)
    1. Japanese fiction—1868—History and criticism. 2. Japanese fiction—Edo
period, 1600–1868—History and criticism. 3. National characteristics in
literature. 4. Nationalism and literature—Japan. I. Title.
    ∞
PL747.57.N287W37 2006
895.6'3409—dc22
                                                                    2006010406

Columbia University Press books are printed on permanent
and durable acid-free paper.
Printed in the United States of America

c 10 9 8 7 6 5 4 3 2 1

CONTENTS

PREFACE

THIS VOLUME EXPLORES the relationship between the representation of ethical values in selected works of prose fiction and the discourse on identity in Japan. The individual essays each exemplify particular aspects of this relationship, but they all touch in varying degrees upon a number of more general, interconnected themes: the crucial role that the notions of autonomy and authenticity have played in debates over the sources of culture-defining values, the hybrid quality of modern Japanese society and the role of cultural translation in the formation of the ideas of nation and subjectivity, and the instability of the spatial and temporal horizons of the ethics of identity.

Because portions of some of the essays contain previously published material, I feel it is important at the outset to acknowledge the advice and suggestions of reviewers and colleagues who took the time and trouble to seriously engage my readings. In addition, reflecting back on the manner in which this volume came together, I believe it may be helpful to present a brief explanation of the general considerations that guided my choice of subjects and the approaches I adopted in my discussions of them.

In certain respects, this volume is a continuation of an earlier monograph, *The Dilemma of the Modern in Japanese Fiction*. In that study, I focused mainly on the question of how attempts to define the modern through a synthesis of Western and Japanese cultural forms affected the development of narrative conventions of voice and perspective. For many writers, the aim of achieving a synthesis, and thereby becoming modern, was liberating in that it opened up new possibilities for artistic expression. However, this liberation came at a high price, since it threatened to displace older representational forms that were perceived as culturally unique. Many writers sensed they were caught in a historical trap: to be modern and Japanese was a paradoxical state in which they were compelled to reject their cultural past. The creation of a new cultural identity, then, was inevitably associated with a profound sense of loss.

The present volume is a survey that continues to look at developments in modern narrative conventions, but with a different focus on the question of how those conventions reflect shifts in the sources of belief in ethical values that enable an individual to define his or her proper place in society. My survey is, of course, not an exhaustive one, given the complexity of the question. It is an open-ended history leading to conclusions that are at times more suggestive than definitive. The challenge confronting a broad survey of literary history is similar to the problem a cartographer faces when trying to make an accurate map. To account fully for every topographical or physical detail, a map would have to be the same size as the area it is mapping. This is the goal toward which all mapmaking gestures, but the task remains at least impractical, if not impossible. In the case of literary studies, to create an exhaustive map of reading requires a survey of the field, and yet to pursue such a strategy in good faith also requires an admission of the selective, idiosyncratic nature of the project.

Few works illustrate the limits and paradoxes that arise when we contemplate the ideal of a perfect map of reading as cleverly and incisively as Jorge Luis Borges's short story "Pierre Menard, Author of the *Quixote.*" Cast in the form of a critical essay, Borges's story is a faux literary history. The narrator, who has worked to establish the definitive bibliography of the published poetry, essays, and fiction of Pierre Menard, draws our attention instead to Menard's unfinished work, which consists of the ninth and thirty-eighth chapters of the first part of *Don Quixote*, as well as a fragment of chapter 22.

Menard's unfinished *Quixote* was not intended to be an updated version or adaptation of the original story, which would have been a somewhat easier project to undertake, nor was it meant to be a simple, mechanical copy of Cervantes's masterpiece. Instead, Menard wanted to produce independently "a few pages that would coincide—word for word and line for line—with those of Miguel de Cervantes."[1] What made Menard's conception of his *Quixote* uniquely impossible was his decision to take a purely synchronic approach to the task. He considered employing a diachronic approach: to study the language thoroughly, to experience the religious and political events and recover the ethical consciousness of Cervantes's Spain,

to forget all of European history between 1602 and 1918—in short, to try
to *be* Miguel de Cervantes. However, of all the impossible ways of writing
Quixote, Menard concluded that the diachronic was too easy: "To be, in
some way, Cervantes and reach the *Quixote* seemed less arduous to him—
and consequently less interesting—than to go on being Pierre Menard and
reach the *Quixote* through the experiences of Pierre Menard."[2]

To give us a better sense of Menard's work and his achievement, the narrator then briefly compares and analyzes two passages for us. The first is
from Cervantes: "truth, whose mother is history, rival of time, depository
of deeds, witness of the past, exemplar and adviser to the present, and the
future's counselor." The second is from Menard: "truth, whose mother is
history, rival of time, depository of deeds, witness of the past, exemplar and
adviser to the present, and the future's counselor." For the narrator, the difference between these passages is obvious. He dismisses Cervantes's lines
as "a mere rhetorical praise of history." They are an empty flourish that
pale before Menard's more accomplished version. The narrator explains the
difference as follows: "History, the *mother* of truth: the idea is astounding.
Menard, a contemporary of William James, does not define history as an
inquiry into reality but as its origins. Historical truth, for him, is not what
has happened; it is what we judge to have happened. The final phrases...
are brazenly pragmatic."[3]

The narrator is able to read a completely different meaning into Menard's *Quixote* because of Menard's historical consciousness. The irony is
that the narrator's own project of assessing an unfinished and impossible
work is as idealized as the work itself. Indeed, he gets so caught up in the
fancy of his critical judgment, which finds Menard's version subtler and
more richly ambiguous (even if it suffers from the affectations of a deliberate archaism), that he begins to detect traces of Menard's style in passages
by Cervantes. In the end, however, he concludes of both *Don Quixote* and
of Menard's project that "there is no exercise of the intellect which is not,
in the final analysis, useless."[4] And though the narrator sees nothing new in
the way Menard confirms this nihilistic truth, he is struck by the determination Menard derived from that truth. At the very least, as a result of his
determination, Menard may be credited with unintentionally enriching the
art of reading by the new techniques "of the deliberate anachronism and the
erroneous attribution."[5]

The project of Borges's perfect reader was utterly self-enclosed and synchronic, and so despite Menard's nearly superhuman determination, his

Quixote remained unfinished and outside the official canon of his works. By imagining such a perfect and hopelessly impossible literary project as the work of a perfect reader who effectively rewrites the classics, Borges's story also exposes the motivations and methods of literary critics and historians who, by merely invoking the presence of a particular cultural conscious- ness, can read vastly different meanings into the same words. We possess what we read as much as we are possessed by it, and there is no way out of this hermeneutic circle.

The narrator's conclusion that intellectual pursuits are ultimately futile is a difficult one to challenge, since it points to the ultimate relativism and emptiness of the values we use to justify critical assessments. Rather than accept this position as an argument against criticism and literary history, however, I see it as a perverse encouragement, if for no other reason than that it keeps us focused on the relative historical position of writers and their fascination with the project of taking possession of and reauthoring the past. If the significance of Menard's hidden life work were simply that an ideal reader is ideal because of the impossibility of his project, then I would not claim any privilege of place for my own readings of Japanese literature. What I can claim, however, is that the open-ended approach of a survey compensates analytically for its selectiveness and idiosyncrasy by making explicit the hermeneutic conundrum Borges playfully brings to the surface in his story. A historical survey of works, no matter how limited, constantly displays in the dialectical relationships it establishes the fundamental read- ing strategies—diachronic and synchronic—available to us.

As a matter of critical methodology, it is hard to imagine anyone (in- cluding, to go back many decades, proponents of the New Criticism) who would not eschew an exclusively synchronic approach as being too narrow, aestheticized, and blind to the cultural and historical values that shape liter- ary artifacts. And yet as Borges's narrator concludes, a synchronic approach may not be wholly without merit after all. Is it not fundamentally misguided to read literary texts—and here I refer to texts that are presumed to have an overtly aesthetic function—as historical evidence of ethical values that de- fine a particular cultural epoch? Reading a fictional narrative for what it can tell us about history or about ethical consciousness runs the risk of serious- ly distorting our interpretation of that story by subordinating its aesthetic aims. Readings that do not address the charm of a piece of writing, the reasons for its affective appeal in the present, tend to divide criticism into opposing tasks of appreciation versus analysis. Thus, while a diachronic approach may provide critical distance and perspective by helping us to step back from the manipulative and seductive allure of the rhetoric of a text, it may also lessen our ability to know what it is like to read in the manner of those who were susceptible to the pull of the text precisely because they were blind to assumptions prevailing in their culture at a specific historical moment—assumptions now obvious to us.

The essays that make up my survey are primarily concerned not with establishing a historical ordering or linkage among texts—in any case, I cannot avoid possessing the works and authors I have chosen to discuss by bringing them in proximity to one another in this book—but with considering how the perception of historical linkages among literary works is a source of imaginative power for individual authors. It seems on the face of it that a survey history of the discourse on values, identity, and literary practice should at minimum attempt to take into account the antihistorical impulses that shaped that discourse—impulses that arose out of an ethically motivated if thoroughly problematic desire to transcend history. By suggesting a general development of ideas and discursive forms, a survey provides a way to keep before us the possibilities for critical play between diachronic and synchronic strategies and for reading without unduly separating form and context.

This justification raises an entirely different issue regarding the appropriateness of reading fiction to get at a history of the ethics of identity. Why take up topics such as autonomy and authenticity, national identity and ethical consciousness, through a study of literature? Why not circumvent the problem raised by the aesthetic claims of literary texts and examine these topics in a way that is more direct and definitive in a disciplinary sense? To put the question even more bluntly: When it comes to questions of ethical values, why profess Japanese literature at all?

This question is disconcerting because there is no readily persuasive response to it. If the point of professing literary studies is aesthetic knowledge, as opposed to historical or anthropological knowledge, then approaches that favor the self-enclosed study of rhetoric are the only game in town. It is my sense, however, that there is a widely held assumption that criticism ought to do more—that it ought to fill in all the details that allow us to experience the atmosphere of another era or place. Yet even if criticism achieves such a vaguely lofty aim, what sort of knowledge does it actually produce? Do close readings of fiction produce knowledge (at least aesthetic knowledge) or mere affect? Is the stimulus of criticism, which can make the reading experience richer for us by opening up or enlarging other views of the world, no different from that provided by good chocolate and red wine?

The suspicion that there may be no persuasive response to these questions arises from the challenge to literary studies presented by the prestige of the sciences as a knowledge-producing institution. The success of the sciences in explaining the world is seen to derive from its rigorous methodologies and its stress on observable and testable outcomes. Consequently, a near obsession with developing "literary theory" has come to dominate contemporary conceptions of reading. The very term "literary theory" strikes me as a marvelous curiosity. Theory denotes knowledge of the principles and methodologies of a discipline, which is how it is used in the phrase "literary theory," but the word also denotes a principle or set of hypotheses verified or at least potentially verifiable by their taxonomic rigor and predictive capability. The epistemological claims of the word theory seem at best inapplicable and at worst irrelevant to the knowledge that may be achieved by professing literature.

Perhaps, by clinging to the conviction that there is some intrinsic worth to professing literary studies, we can dismiss as a kind of navel gazing the question of what knowledge criticism produces. Unfortunately, the appeal to intrinsic value, the self-evident belief that we are somehow better off for our encounter with literature and art, does not get us very far, either as a disciplinary justification or even as a starting point for critical analysis. To say that something has intrinsic worth is to appeal to a kind of aesthetic religiosity—an appeal that is anathema to critical discussion, because it places art beyond the scope of any kind of analysis. Of course, the invocation of intrinsic worth may have practical value as a kind of mystifying counter to the arguments of those less sensitive types who dismiss the teaching of Japanese literature as exotic esoterica that can never be central to the core mission of the academy—a mission, I would note, that is usually defined, in a breathtaking example of circular reasoning, as the preservation and extension of values embodied in the institutions of American higher learning. If we set aside the utilitarian function of this kind of justification of criticism, however, it is clear that the appeal to intrinsic worth relies upon a universal notion of cultural value that does not justify the study of Japanese literature as a particular historical or aesthetic phenomenon, but instead justifies a way of thinking about the world that gives us an excuse to find a place for Japanese literary studies in our own institutions.

A different defense of literary studies looks beyond notions of intrinsic worth to appeal to values that are asserted to be central to the production of knowledge. For example, the subject I profess is sometimes justified on the basis of values such as tolerance for the local and for diversity, values that explicitly challenge and critique the social and political institutions that foster the idea of intrinsic worth, which in turn underpins assertions of national literary canons and core curricula. Unfortunately, such a defense is rendered incoherent by apparently competing claims. On one side, the study of Japanese literature is justified by a humanistic universalism that discovers common elements of rhetoric or experience across cultures. On the other side, the study of Japanese literature as a means to understand larger social and historical developments is justified by virtue of its parochialism, the uniqueness of a tradition that affirms a decentering of cultural values. Although these justifications have different emphases, they locate the sources of the heuristic value of the literature of Japan in either comparative or universalistic terms set by ideological agendas in the American academy—agendas that are in fact external to the cultural contexts that have determined the history and the place in history of Japanese literature. Reading Japanese literature, then, becomes an exercise in self-reflection, possessing value only to the extent that it reflects our own assumptions back at us. The self-reflective tendency exemplified by notions such as intrinsic worth or diversity highlight the circularity of our critical language. It is just this circularity that, when we consider issues related to values and identity, makes the question "Why profess Japanese literature?" seem at once laughably trivial and plausibly serious.

The fact that we could even conceive of such a question reveals a number of assumptions that go to the heart of the essays that follow. The structure of the arguments surrounding the question—indeed, the very form of the question itself—is an indication of a deep fissure at the core of modern ethical consciousness. Although values are often taken as the foundation of specific cultural identities, they presuppose or require, even within an avowedly parochial context, a pretense of universality and objectivity. Reacting to the prestige of scientific models for producing knowledge, literary studies as a field is strained by its ambivalent appeal to values arising out of local conditions and to the notion of the universality of values. Celebrating or performing what is authentic to a particular culture provides access to knowledge about that culture, but it also exposes just how relative and indeterminate our knowledge may be.

This problem seems especially intractable when we try to justify the value of an object of study like Japanese literature. I raise the question, then, not only as a way of getting at the main topic of this book, which is the relationship between the justification of values and narrative form, but also as a way to lay out the methods and assumptions involved in my readings. Certainly, we could just dismiss all this as a contrived contretemps that willfully ignores the idea that critical reading should as a matter of course engage all sides of questions about values—the aesthetic and the historical, the intrinsic and the analytical. Yet the image of common sense that this attitude projects is a chimera that merely provides a brief respite from the anxiety that arises when we attempt to find solid ground for justifying our belief in values. Simply setting the problem aside under the pretense of moving toward a fully objective approach—a view from nowhere—does nothing to address or resolve the tortured dialectic of reading revealed in our critical terminology.

The survey approach I have adopted for this volume is a tacit acknowledgment that there is no way to fully resolve the dialectic of reading. This does not mean, however, that I consider my work an abnegation of critical and ethical responsibility. As I mentioned above, I believe a survey makes transparent the turbulent process of reading both diachronically and synchronically. Keeping that process in front of us, making us always aware of its presence, is one way to keep us alive to the significance of the breach in modern ethical consciousness and the dangers of denying or effacing history and politics. In this regard, my approach is an endorsement of the notion put forth by Martha Nussbaum that "the best ethical criticism, ancient and modern, has insisted on the complexity and variety revealed to us in literature, appealing to that complexity to cast doubt on reductive theories."[6] The knowledge we achieve through the study of literature, however imperfect or incomplete, derives from the effort to engage and recover the consciousness of writers in the past toward their own efforts to represent values and identity in fictional narratives.

TRANSLATING MOUNT FUJI

INTRODUCTION
Real Identities

IN HIS ACCEPTANCE SPEECH for the 1994 Nobel Prize in literature, Ōe Kenzaburō attempts to capture the history of Japan's experience of modernity in a single word, "ambiguity." By "ambiguity" he does not mean the aestheticized vagueness or inscrutability that has so often been invoked as the stereotyped essence of Japanese conceptions of beauty. To the contrary, "ambiguity" is described by Ōe as anything but beautiful. It is for him a "scar" or a "disease" that resulted from his nation having been torn by its contradictory desires to emulate the modernity of the West while preserving the traditions of Asia.

Ōe locates in Japan's ambiguous position in the world the fundamental cause of the violent crimes committed during its wars of aggression in Asia, the degradation of its environment through the uncontrolled application of technology, and the spiritual emptiness of its material culture. By enumerating the terrible costs of ambiguity, Ōe presents a political and moral critique of modern Japanese history to justify his views concerning the power and necessity of art—a purpose he makes explicit when he draws a clear distinction between his aesthetic vision and that of the only other Nobel laureate in literature from Japan, Kawabata Yasunari. Whereas Kawabata's 1968 speech, "Japan, the Beautiful, and Myself," was an attempt to define a uniquely Japanese aesthetic, Ōe tries instead to establish a broader, more critically informed context for understanding recent literary developments. In his view, the response to ambiguity, especially among the writers of his own generation, is best characterized not by Kawabata's aestheticism but by a heightened ethical consciousness that creates a sense of mission. Building upon his notion of ambiguity, he argues that the writers most sincere in their awareness of a mission were the "postwar school" who came onto the literary scene deeply wounded by the catastrophe of war yet full of hope for a rebirth. They tried with great pain to make up for the atrocities committed by Japanese military forces in Asia, as well as to bridge the profound gaps that existed not only between the developed nations of the West and Japan but also between African and Latin American countries and Japan. Only by doing so did they think that they could seek with some humility reconciliation with the rest of the world. It has always been my aspiration to cling to the very end of the line of that literary tradition inherited from those writers.[1]

Ōe's summary of postwar Japanese literature is based upon an overpowering moral awareness that the forces of modernization and war guilt have disfigured his culture. The pressures of modernization created a deep anxiety about the authenticity of Japanese identity, while the shattering experience of defeat and guilt made even more urgent the search for values that could give meaningful purpose to being Japanese. For Ōe, the ambiguity of identity, the apparently unsettled meaning of values, and the difficulties faced by individuals forced to create their own ethical universe are not mere abstractions but defining experiences for his generation.

Ōe sees himself as coming at the end of a unique postwar tradition, but the paradox revealed in his notion of ambiguity places his views within a much larger history of the ethics of identity.[2] Over the last two centuries, the discourse on identity in Japan has been dominated by a tendency to invoke moral and aesthetic values as a way to represent what it means to be authentically Japanese. To place Ōe within this discourse does not ignore or distort his critical view of that discourse, nor does it diminish his individual achievements as an artist and the genuine courage he has shown throughout his life in defending his political and moral principles. Yet for all that, it is fascinating that a writer so acutely aware of history and so driven by a sense of moral mission should fall back on the notion of authenticity to justify his belief in what he calls the "wondrous, healing power of art"—a power that makes it possible to achieve something of genuine moral worth.[3]

Ōe's moral justification for art is one he shares with many other Japanese writers and intellectuals, even those whose political views are fundamentally opposed to his. It is motivated by a sense of urgency concerning the question of identity, a question born in part from outside pressures on Japan and in part from the heightened awareness of and sensitivity to cultural difference that arose when Japan ended its policy of limiting contact with the outside world in the nineteenth century. The perception that Japan was opening itself up to the world reflected the extent of the awareness of difference—not just between Japan and foreign cultures, but also between Japan and its own past—that was largely responsible for a fundamental shift in ethical consciousness. If the grounds upon which belief in values was justified could be seen to vary from culture to culture or from epoch to epoch, then values could no longer be taken as natural or universal, but as constructed and relative. Consequently, the notion that values held by a particular culture may still be viewed as inviolable and true for that culture came to hold considerable appeal as a counter to the destabilizing effects of ethical relativism. What mattered was not so much the need to account for cultural difference—a condition that was an accepted fact—as the need to discover the stable essence of culture itself. If what was authentic to Japan could be enunciated, then it would provide stable grounds for justifying belief in those moral and aesthetic values that define Japanese identity.

The emergence of a consciousness of the created nature of values occurred just when Japan began actively reengaging the global political economy. The emphasis on authenticity as a reason to believe in the new conception of national identity was engendered in Japan through the challenge presented to long-held systems of value, which may be classified generally as aretaic ethics, by the consequentialist and deontological systems that had begun to assume a dominant position in the imperialist cultures of the West.

Aretaic ethics posit ideals, the virtues, that are largely determined and justified by social norms or religious authority external to the individual. The individual's responsibility is to develop his or her character to its full potential by cultivating virtues and making them habitual, thus bringing personal behavior in line with the expectations of the community.

In contrast, the determination and justification of value in consequentialist and deontological ethics is made on the basis of factors internal to the individual, in particular the faculties of reason and moral intuition that enable the analysis of the relative merits of outcomes or the discovery of universally applicable rules of conduct. The effect of the shift in emphasis away from externalized ideals toward an internalized process of judgment as the means to justify belief in values is apparent in the dominant place that the concepts of autonomy and authenticity came to hold in the ethical consciousness of modern Japan. These concepts have been especially important in establishing a connection between the reasons given for the belief in particular cultural values and the definition of cultural identity. The shift toward a more internalized process of judgment and justification has emphasized the importance of autonomy, of ethical free will, in determining the worth of an object or deed. The notion of authenticity seeks to counterbalance the relativism implied by the idea of autonomy in order to reestablish external, absolute grounds for belief in values.

The push and pull between autonomy and authenticity has largely determined the parameters of the discourse on identity within the literary cultures of modern Japan. Notions of individual rights and responsibilities and conceptions of subjectivity and selfhood within a modernizing society were filtered through a lens created by the unshakable assumption that there existed an essential Japanese identity defined by unchanging values that transcend history and mere politics. Because the essence of this identity was believed to lie beyond the reach of temporally bound understandings, it resisted reduction to the exigencies of language. What emerged from the discourse on identity, then, was an ethical consciousness divided—or, to use Ōe's term, rendered ambiguous—by its recognition that the desire to create a stable modern identity was an act of betrayal, one displacing Japan from its cultural origins. By the phrase "ethical consciousness" I refer to an awareness of the historical process by which belief in moral and aesthetic values is established. Awareness of the created, fictive nature of values has always been implicit in insistent assertions of the authenticity of the defining characteristics of Japanese identity. The coexistence of these contradictory moods—anxiety over the stability of values and confidence in an ineffable essence of identity—has been among the most distinctive characteristics of modernity in Japan.

The Discourse on Values and Identity

The literary critic Maeda Ai analyzed the connections between the terms of the discourse on identity and the source of ethical values in late nineteenth-century Japan, and concluded:

> The new moral orthodoxy that the Meiji state demanded was the so-called cult of success [or careerism—*risshin shusse shugi*].... And a major issue for the people of Meiji was how to systematize the energy of those

who had suddenly risen to prominence. That was accomplished rather quickly by patching together Confucian ethical consciousness with a vulgarized utilitarianism.[4]

Maeda argues that the hybridity of the culture of the Meiji period (1868–1912) gave rise to a sense of unease with regard to issues of identity—an unease that came to be associated inextricably with the conditions of modernity. The effort to define identity in nationalist terms required not only the establishment of new grounds for justifying belief in previously accepted values, but also the development of modes of representation that would make those values relevant and useful to the new political regime. The effect of this reevaluation, however, was to raise doubts about the trustworthiness of received moral and aesthetic norms and destabilize the ontological ground of Japanese identity, rendering it a ghostly phantom that seemed to remain forever out of reach.

Miyake Setsurei (1860–1945), a journalist and cultural critic, provides a vivid example of this tendency in his 1891 tract "Shinzenbi Nihonjin" ("Truth, Goodness, Beauty, and the Japanese"), when he confronts the problems involved in defining the essence of identity:

What is it about the question, "Who are the Japanese?" The people who ask it are Japanese, and naturally know that they are Japanese. And the people who are asked are also Japanese and know they are Japanese. But when we raise the question, "Who are the Japanese?" we are all dumbfounded and can't respond. Who are the Japanese? The people of Japan. And who are the people of Japan? I know I ought to be able to answer the question, but then somehow I forget the answer. The Japanese. The people of Japan. When we mull over the question silently, the meaning of those phrases flickers clearly before the eyes like some phantom. But when we open our mouths to answer, the phantom suddenly disappears.[5]

The maddening elusiveness of an answer to the question Miyake poses was for him not a problem of identity per se—after all, he is sure there is a Japanese identity, and he knows intuitively what that means. The vagueness of being Japanese was instead an ideological false echo, a problem of representation that occurred because of the inadequacy of language. This problem was no small matter, for the ability to enunciate a commonly shared sense of identity was considered a necessity for Miyake's generation, who sought a way to justify modernization and cope with the upheaval caused by the enormous political, economic, and cultural changes that were transforming Japan. Given the stakes, Miyake felt compelled to equate cultural identity with those ethical values he deemed crucial to the formation of the modern nation state. The approach he developed to represent identity was to enunciate a specific set of duties that individuals were morally obligated to perform for the nation.

Miyake's notion of identity was rooted in a radical reassessment of both the language of values and the wider discursive fields that establish the reasons behind judgments of right and wrong, good and bad. Under the pressure created by internal political and economic transformations from the mid-eighteenth century onward, and by more direct interactions with Western cultures beginning in the mid-nineteenth century, the ideal of national identity was vigorously promoted first as a bulwark against the encroachment of foreign empires and then as an ideological tool to establish the legitimacy of Japan's own empire. The effort to enunciate and thus create Japanese identity was widespread—carried out not simply as a top-down mandate of political or cultural elites, but as an expression of popular sentiment.[6] As a consequence, even though the task of pinpointing the precise characteristics and values that define Japanese culture has proven stubbornly open-ended, the ideological structure and rhetorical patterns of the discourse on identity have remained largely consistent over time.

The apparently insubstantial quality of national identity is what drove men like Miyake to address the question of identity so obsessively. One of the dominant tendencies among intellectuals during the early part of the Meiji period was to measure Japan's progress toward modernization by the broad standard of Western civilization. At the time of the Restoration, a number of leading writers and intellectuals held the position that the best way to foreclose the possibility that Japan's modernization would result in cooption by the West was to embrace Enlightenment values of rationalism and individual autonomy as the foundations of the new state. The ideals of the Enlightenment, *keimō shisō*, were the guiding spirit behind the founding of the *Meirokusha* (the 1873 Society), a group that promoted changes in customs and education.

Members of the *Meirokusha* were convinced that institutional reform and the achievement of civilization and enlightenment (*bunmei kaika*) required a new moral consciousness. To help forestall or at least ameliorate the uncomfortable possibility that Japan might be found wanting or inferior by such a standard, the concept of a universal civilization shared by all people was embraced at the time by a number of leading intellectuals. For example, the concept of a universal civilization underlies the bold assertion at the very beginning of *An Encouragement of Learning* (*Gakumon no susume*, serialized between 1872 and 1876), which states that there are no innate status distinctions separating people: "It is said that heaven neither creates one person above others nor one person below others."[7] The author of this enormously influential work, the educator Fukuzawa Yukichi (1834–1901), promoted the idea that all people are equal legally and politically. The only thing that distinguished them, in Fukuzawa's view, was the degree of their educational attainment, which had a major ethical role to play in the development of good character. "It is only the person who has studied diligently, so that he has a mastery over things and events, who becomes noble and rich, while his opposite becomes base and poor."[8]

Fukuzawa's equating of material success and good character was not motivated solely by idealism, but reflected political realities insofar as it was presented as a means to help justify the Meiji oligarchy's dismantling of the Tokugawa-era caste system. What is most interesting about his emphasis on personal autonomy is that he uses the concept to argue, by analogy, that the same principle applies to nations. "Modern-day Japan as well cannot compare in wealth and strength with the nations of the West. But by reason of the inherent rights of nations, Japan is not the least inferior. If the day comes when Japan suffers injustice from without, we should not fear to take on the whole world as our enemy."[9]

Japan may have been equal in idealistic terms, but Fukuzawa knew very well that Japan was in a precarious position, in the face of Western imperial power. The harsh reality of nineteenth-century geopolitics left many intellectuals and political leaders in a quandary over what direction Japan should take. Fukuzawa thought that only the most radical kind of social reform would suffice, so he made the remarkable call for a change in consciousness among the Japanese people, arguing that the way to ensure Japan's national independence (*ikkoku dokuritsu*) was for its citizens to cultivate individual independence (*isshin dokuritsu*).[10] He based his call on the argument that the nation can only gain stature and independence after individuals have achieved a full measure of subjectivity by internalizing the process of evaluative judgment. To support his stance, Fukuzawa had to disguise the universalist claims of Western ideas about the individual and the nation by making those claims truly universal—that is, by asserting that they belong to no particular place or individual. Such a claim, however, effaced the particularities of Japanese culture, and so to make his universalist position palatable, he turned to utilitarian notions of value. For Fukuzawa, Japan could gain its rightful and unique place among the nations of the world only by diligently seeking knowledge (*chishiki*) and the reason or logic (*dōri*) that inheres in all things.

As Fukuzawa used them in his treatise, the words knowledge and reason were empty placeholders that provided a means to reference the idea of a universal culture. Beyond that function, the terms lacked specificity, in part because of Fukuzawa's desire to avoid subordinating Japanese cultural values to those of the West. A significant component of Fukuzawa's encouragement of learning was his early advocacy of the adoption of Western cultural forms, especially political and legal notions of contracts. He also admired the advancement of Western science, not so much because of the technological breakthroughs it enabled, but because it was a sign of the spirit of independence (*dokuritsu no kiryoku*) without which he believed the outward forms of modern society are meaningless.[11] But Fukuzawa was also sensitive to the need to temper his call for the adoption of Western forms with a universalist claim that truth and knowledge are not bound temporally or spatially. Writing in the 1870s, he had a clear vision of Japan's national interests, and he was a realist when it came to understanding Japan's geopolitical situation. In his view, the way to realize those interests required a universalist notion of civilization, which in pragmatic terms aligned Japan with the Western world.

Even though it seems clear now why Fukuzawa's universalism did not address directly the specific question of the nature of Japanese identity, the vagueness of the call for a new ethical consciousness left the position of the Westernizers open to attack. Because Fukuzawa did not enunciate specific Japanese cultural values, which would establish the imaginary boundaries of national identity, even the most ardent supporters of Westernization had serious reservations about the applicability of foreign ideas and cultural forms to Japan. The adoption of Western forms came to be viewed in increasingly ambivalent terms, as both a help and hindrance to the rise of the new ethical consciousness that would provide the moral foundation for the modern state. Fukuzawa insisted upon the importance of providing a moral justification for modernization, which he enumerated as a list of duties to the nation, but he was reluctant to take the idea of individual autonomy and the spirit of independence too far, for fear of crossing the policies of the oligarchy. When the People's Rights Movement gained momentum in the 1880s, he kept silent about the radical implications of the proposals he made in early Meiji.[12] His caution may perhaps explain the generality with which he insisted that his fellow Japanese develop a spirit of independence in order to define national identity.

Throughout the 1870s, there was growing unease that sweeping social changes might potentially uproot the values that gave significance to being Japanese. Nishi Amane (1829–1897) tried to negotiate between the positions of the modernizers and the traditionalists in two works: *Hyakuichi shinron* (*New Theory of the Hundred and the One*, 1874) and a set of essays titled *Jinsei sanpōsetsu* (*An Account of Three Human Treasures*), which appeared in 1875, in the *Meiroku zasshi*, the journal of the *Meirokusha*. Influenced heavily by Mill and Kant, Nishi on the one hand insisted that government should not be involved with moral education, which pertains to matters of individual character and judgments of the good, but should be concerned with matters of law as they relate to individual rights and responsibilities in a secular state. On the other hand, he was alarmed that a long tradition of moral education was being displaced by modernization, and so he stressed the need for public morality to balance the increasing emphasis on individualism.[13] His formulation of a public realm of ethical discourse that could act as a balance to the modern emphasis on autonomy and subjectivity drew primarily on principles derived from Japan's (and Asia's) own traditions of moral philosophy.[14]

The effort to recover an older discursive grounding for contemporary values created a projection of the past onto the present. To that extent, Nishi's ideas were in line with general trends in the political discourse of the Meiji oligarchy, which in its own way had projected onto the present an image of Japan's imperial past, with its claims of mythic inviolability and historical continuity, to legitimize the modern state. Projecting the past onto the present in this manner allowed for the gradual emergence of a cultural synthesis. But if that synthesis was seen as an achievement, as a sign of progress toward civilization, it was also regarded as an expedient, transitional phase on the way to realizing Japan's identity. The modernizing policies of the early Meiji state, by dismantling the political economy of the old regime, continuously posed a problem because it raised the specter of cultural cooption. Universalist pretensions and strivings for modern civilization came to be severely criticized as just another form of acquiescence to the colonial ambitions of the West. Yet critics of the modernizers could not simply ignore the obvious sources of the military and economic power of some Western nations, nor could they easily respond to the claim that such power was a mark of moral superiority—a claim that always lurked behind even the most virulently racist justifications for colonial empire. The fear of cooption and the sense that there was a need for new grounds for legitimizing power in a modern state were among the key motivating forces behind discussions of the nature of national identity.

The ambivalence of attempts to clarify what it meant to be Japanese and what constituted the mission of the modern state is evident in the hybrid approach taken by Nishi, who, in the process of using received ethical terms to translate Western ideas, fused Neo-Confucian and utilitarian ethics.[15] His attempts to salvage elements of the Neo-Confucian tradition and to encourage the development of an ethical consciousness for the sake of creating a new public morality typified the main rhetorical tendencies of the Meiji discourse on identity.

The attractiveness of a hybrid approach to answering the question of identity is apparent when we consider how it inflected even the arguments of those intellectuals who resisted the notion that there is a universal civilization toward which Japan must progress. To return to the work of Miyake Setsurei cited above, he advocated a more vigorous nationalist position, going so far as to help organize a group, the *Seikyōsha* (Society for Political Instruction), to promote his ideas in the political sphere. The journal of this society was titled *Nihonjin* (*The Japanese People*), suggesting just how central the concern with identity was in his ethical conception of the nation and of Japan's mission and responsibility in the world.

Miyake, following Western theories of race, stressed the antiquity of the Japanese people and their origins in Asia.[16] This was not a point most exponents of a notion of global or universal civilization would have disputed, but his particular emphasis is important to note here. The proponents of modernization looked upon Japan's place in Asia as one of geographical and historical happenstance. For Japan to find its place in the world, to redefine itself, it had to break away from a backward, unenlightened, and uncivilized Asia. Like Miyake, most nationalists did not dispute that Japan had to situate itself in a global political economy that transcended Asia. Even so, they insisted that Japan's global role was not as important as its regional position. For Miyake, the construction of national identity could only be rooted in and justified by the values that emerged out of Japan's historical development prior to the Meiji era—a development determined largely by set conditions such as geographical location, climate, and the continuity of institutions that promoted what he saw as uniquely Japanese values.[17] He argued that Japan could fulfill its international role both as a global power equal to Western nations and as a regional power working to civilize and enlighten the rest of Asia only by being true to its distinctive cultural characteristics.[18]

Miyake did not reject Western culture as such, and he readily acknowledged the current superiority of Western science and technology, though he was confident that in the twentieth century Japan would draw even.[19] However, like many of his contemporaries, he was oblivious to the specific historical circumstances that led to the creation of those institutions in the West, viewing science as somehow an acultural phenomenon. Separating technology from values allowed Miyake to buttress his opposition to the idea that Western modernity represented a universal standard, the ultimate goal in the teleology of civilization. The abilities of each nation and race, he argued, were superior in some ways and inferior in others.[20] The realities of international politics, especially the threat of imperialism, made it imperative that a nation examine the best of its own culture and supplement it with selective borrowing from others.

The assertion that modern identity may be defined by reclaiming—or even just recalling—the values that inhere in Japan's cultural traditions is on its face compelling. The affective power of Miyake's appeal to tradition may be difficult to appreciate now, but it is crucial to understanding the radically nationalist turn Japan later took in the 1920s and 1930s. The problem for proponents of tradition is deciding what it means, what values it represents. Miyake's catalogue of Japanese virtues, captured succinctly in the title of his tract, is so broad that it acts as a placeholder in a way similar to Fukuzawa's use of the words truth and knowledge. Truth, beauty, and goodness—all are surprisingly free-floating in Miyake's account, though the very sweeping quality of his usage may help explain why the stock of terms used to denote culture-defining values remained relatively stable before and after the Meiji period, even if the usage of these terms did not.

Miyake's nationalistic view of identity is no more specific than Fukuzawa's call for a new ethical consciousness. Miyake may assert that certain virtues inhere in every individual in Japan, but like Fukuzawa, he has to externalize those virtues, defining them as a set of concrete responsibilities that help define national identity. Japan had a responsibility to take the lead in spreading knowledge about Asia. Japan also had a responsibility to promote righteousness in the world by strengthening itself economically and militarily in order to confront Western imperialism. This particular view, of course, was widely shared, and became a cornerstone of Japan's justification of its policies in Asia through World War II. Finally, Miyake saw his nation as having a special duty in terms of aesthetic values, and he argued forcefully that the Japanese should nurture their distinctive sense of beauty.[21]

Miyake tightly binds aesthetics to his project of defining Japanese identity through domestic and international political responsibilities. The connection may seem surprising or even forced, because there is a general sense that the realm of aesthetic goods is separate from or at best a subset of the realm of moral goods. But his emphasis on the connection was a rhetorical strategy to facilitate a concrete enunciation of national identity. The justification for the new state and for the formation of modern Japanese identity was driven largely by the terms of Western science and political philosophy, and so any effort to recover pre-Meiji ideas on ethics and governance to forestall intellectual cooption by the West was reactive and belated, since the source of values was always located in some other place or time. In the realm of aesthetics, however, many Japanese believed they could claim values that were unique and independent from those of the West. Emphasizing the idea that tastes naturally vary across cultures and that differences in artistic temper are a natural condition like race and climate allowed them to brush aside relativism in order to create a space for culture-defining values. Even more important, they could claim that Japan was in many ways a superior culture: not only the most advanced nation of Asia, serving as the steward and guardian of a larger aesthetic tradition that included the cultures of India and China, but also a country willing to learn from the West while maintaining the ability to appreciate the beauty of its own artistic forms and ceremonies.

Miyake's brand of aestheticized nationalism eventually became a dominant view. An important proponent of the claim that a distinctive aesthetic sensibility defined Japanese identity was Okakura Kakuzō (1862–1913), an art historian, critic, and in the West, a popularizer of Japanese aesthetics, who shared many of the views on Japan's role in the world espoused by his contemporaries. Although he wrote in English for an American readership in 1904, at the time of the Russo-Japanese War, the rhetoric of his defense of Japanese culture in his book *The Awakening of Japan* is strikingly similar to that employed by Miyake. He begins by stressing the unique characteristics of the Japanese people as a way to understand their recent success:

Our sympathizers have been pleased to marvel at the facility with which we have introduced Western science and industries, constitutional government, and the organization necessary for carrying on a gigantic war. They forget that the strength of the movement that brought Japan to her present position is due not less to the innate virility which has enabled her to assimilate the teachings of a foreign civilization than to her capability of adopting its methods. With a race, as with the individual, it is not the accumulation of extraneous knowledge, but the realization of the self within, that constitutes true progress.[22]

Okakura suggestively echoes Fukuzawa's conception of a spirit of independence, but he does so, thirty years after Fukuzawa's tract, as an explanation for Japan's achievements. He interprets the success of Japan's drive to great power status not as part of the process of creating a new ethical consciousness, but as the outcome of a spirit or moral intuition unique to the Japanese people. His equation of Japanese identity with a traditional moral and aesthetic intuition puts him squarely in the camp of writers such as Miyake. What sets his views apart is that Okakura is writing after the victory in the Sino-Japanese war, after the repeal of the unequal treaties, and during the first flush of Japan's military victories in the Russo-Japanese War. As a consequence of these events, his confidence in his sense of self—that is, his sense of national identity—is higher, and his claims are more assertive.

By 1904, many of the early supporters of modernization, with its implied acceptance of the universality of Western culture, had become disillusioned and angered by the racism and ethnocentrism of the West. Tokutomi Sohō, a journalist whose publication *Kokumin no tomo* (*Friend of the People*) was a major organ shaping public opinion, wrote with asperity about the Western world's refusal to regard Japan as an equal.[23] Japan's military victories over China and Russia convinced many intellectuals that their nation had come of age. The imperialist threat from Europe, while still pressing, no longer appeared quite so overwhelming, and the ardor for possessing the products of European culture, even among people like Fukuzawa and Tokutomi, was cooled by the criticism that such things represented a faddish, empty materialism. In such an atmosphere, the notion of a universal culture lost some of its luster. The idea was not entirely discredited, however, but persisted in the generally held view that Japan should be part of the Western world—if not in cultural terms, then at least in its economic, diplomatic, and military endeavors. This form of aestheticized nationalism grew increasingly influential by the end of the nineteenth century, and it is picked up in Okakura's vigorous, confident defense of Japan's policies in the Korean peninsula and Manchuria.

This confidence is expressed in Okakura's aggressively gendered language. The phrase "innate virility," for example, calls forth an image of righteous manliness to assert that Japan no longer occupied an uncertain, subservient (i.e., feminized) position vis-à-vis the West. In Okakura's mind, identity is linked both to specific actions and policies and to an assumed virtue—in the sense that manliness was synonymous with ethical development—that taken together establish the ground of modern Japanese identity. The nationalist pride that Okakura shared with contemporaries such as Miyake and Tokutomi is further expressed by his claim of Japanese superiority (or at least priority) over the other cultures of Asia. He writes that while the Japanese are grateful to the West for what it has taught them, the authentic source of Japanese inspiration is the cultures of Asia:

> Great as was the difficulty involved in the struggle for a national reawak-ening, a still harder task confronted Japan in her effort to bring an Oriental nation to face the terrible exigencies of modern existence. Until the moment when we shook it off, the same lethargy lay upon us which now lies on China and India. Over our country brooded the Night of Asia, enveloping all spontaneity within its mysterious folds.[24]

Why did Japan succeed where the other older, formerly great cultures of Asia failed? Okakura, like Miyake, sees the source of that success as what he calls "the reincarnation of Old Japan."[25] Again, the wording here is consciously chosen not only to recall Asian traditions but also to get around the thornier problem of concretely defining national identity. What, exactly, constitutes "innate virility"—or "Old Japan"? For Okakura, the answer could be found in a catalogue of past virtues—and in making this claim he is at pains to stress that for the Japanese people aesthetic and moral values are inseparable.

> In the thoroughness and minutiae of our preparations for war, [the Western observer] will recognize the same hands whose untiring patience gave its exquisite finish to our lacquer. In the tender care bestowed upon our stricken adversary of the battle-field will be found the ancient courtesy of the samurai, who knew "the sadness of things" and looked to his enemy's

wound before his own. The ardor that leads our sailors into daring enter-
prises is inspired by the Neo-Confucian doctrine which teaches that to
know is to do. The calmness with which our people have met the exigencies of a national crisis is a heritage from those disciples of Buddha who
in the silence of the monastery meditated on change.

All that is vital and representative in our contemporary art and literature is the revivified expression of the national school, not imitation of
European models.[26]

This checklist of past virtues—patience, benevolence, courtesy, propri-
ety, sensitivity, courage, wisdom, quiescence, sincerity—is longer and more
detailed than Miyake's catalogue, but the strategy of explaining Japan's success after the fact, by projecting the past onto the present, was not new
with Okakura. It was and still remains a key tendency of the ethics of identity—one that tries to define identity in terms of traditional values but is
ultimately caught up in the self-referential circularity of the terms denoting
those values.

Despite his show of confidence, Okakura is unable to shake off fully the
anxieties that accompanied and in some ways defined Japan's modernization. Stung by racially motivated alarm in the West of an impending Yellow
Peril, he dismisses Western concerns with the reassurance that Japan is a
peaceful culture. He goes on to further counter this concern by pointing to
what Asians refer to as the White Disaster, the threat of Western racism
and power that has forced Japan to pursue its current foreign policies. His
unease, however, runs deeper than policy conflicts, and he gives voice to
the fear that the virtues defining what it is to be Japanese may be overrun
by the tide of Western ideas, tastes, and material culture. If they are overcome, he argues, it will not be the fault of the West so much as the fault of
Japanese who blindly run after the fads and fashions of the West and forget
themselves in a rush toward what he calls "occidentalism."[27]

There is, of course, an obvious and audacious contradiction in this concern. If the virtues that brought Japan to a position of dominance in Asia
and to the point of claiming equal status with the West are inherent to
the culture and innate characteristics of Japanese identity, then why should
he be anxious that they would be overwhelmed, especially in the realm of
art? Apparently, Okakura did not recognize or perhaps did not care about
this contradiction. What mattered was that the material success of Western
cultures had to be confronted, if for no other reason than to counter the

threat the West posed to the freedom and sovereignty of non-Western cultures. Moreover, Western assertions of inalienable, essential values, no matter how self-serving of Western claims of material and moral superiority, provided a model for the construction of national identity. For this reason, the apparent inability or unwillingness of men like Miyake and Okakura to acknowledge the expedient quality of their definitions of national identity suggests just how difficult it was to isolate the essential characteristics of being Japanese. It also points once again to the effect of the anxiety many Japanese felt in the face of the perceived threat from the West. The spirit of independence Fukuzawa called for required a liberation from the past, even though the past was widely assumed to be the source of values. It is no oversimplification of recent history to see in the contradictions engendered by the discourse on identity an important cause of the modern pathologies of aggressive nationalism, racism, and chauvinistic ethnocentrism.

Looking back over the history of Japan during the first half of the twentieth century, it seems that there was no way to easily resolve these contradictions. The aesthetically powerful appeal to a common identity was one way to relieve the individual from the burden of a modern ethical consciousness, which demanded skepticism over belief and the struggle for independence of spirit over the comforts of conformity. Appeals to the modern concept of nation—embodied in redefined terms such as the national essence (*kokutai*), the people (*kokumin*), and even the Japanese language (*kokugo*)—made it possible to establish identity based on a model of civilization that claimed universal validity while still remaining distinctively parochial. It allowed for Japan's embrace of modern science and technology in the name of progress and for its global drive for colonies and empire in the name of its unique national mission. The language employed by Fukuzawa, Nishi, Miyake, and Okakura reveals a discursive shift that justified the adoption of Western cultural and institutional forms through the translation of traditional values—solidarity, harmony between ruler and people, loyalty, filial piety, righteousness, martial prowess—into an idiom that also defined the nation (*koku*) and its interests.

What made this discourse viable was the assumption of cultural authenticity, of an irreducible essence to Japanese identity that defied reduction to language precisely because it did not need to be defined. As Tokutomi put it, "To live in present-day Japan and talk about present-day Japan appears to be a useless exercise, just as it would be to convince a horse that it is a horse, or to stand in front of a mountain and argue that it is a mountain."[28] To return to Miyake's image, Japanese identity is an elusive phantom because to be Japanese is to possess an essence, a consciousness or spirit, beyond the grasp of language and the power of rationality. The consciousness of Japanese identity can be observed only through actions that exemplify values—that point to the essence and sustain it. The effort of intellectuals to define Japanese identity was reflected in the translations of traditional values into language that was broadly intelligible and manipulable by a modern state. As with any form of translation, this effort was analytic rather than synthetic, meaning that any enunciation of national identity could only be rendered true by definition—that is, by virtue of circular reference rather than verification.

The emphasis on the rhetoric of authenticity that emerged during the nineteenth century largely determined the structure of the discourse of identity well into the twentieth. It is reflected most apparently in the virulent strains of nationalism that regarded Western culture as largely or totally incompatible with Japan's national essence—an idea that eventually came to dominate cultural and political discourse in the 1920s and 1930s. A mission to purify the corrupt modern world through the aggressive promotion of its superior cultural values defined Japanese identity.[29] The appeal of the rhetoric of authenticity was not limited, however, to the extreme right. It exerted an especially powerful attraction on those who still held that Japan was part of Asia, and even on intellectuals who had doubts about the conceit of Japan's uniqueness or about its ability to maintain a traditional ethical consciousness. An example of the strangely ecumenical appeal of authenticity is provided by the work of Kobayashi Hideo, one of the most influential literary critics of the twentieth century.

In his famous 1933 essay, "Literature of the Lost Home," Kobayashi argues that Japanese culture was collapsing in a distinctive way best exemplified by modern literary history. Modern Japanese literature was made possible only by the influence of the West, and yet the reach of that influence through translations was so great that by the 1930s it was no longer possible for Japanese readers to distinguish what originated in the West and what did not.[30] His description of the state of Japanese culture comes off as a kind of fortunate fall:

> Can we fear that anything remains to be taken away, we who have lost our feel for what is characteristic of the country of our birth, who have lost our cultural singularity? Is it any consolation to think that those writers of a preceding generation, for whom the struggle between East and West

figured crucially in their artistic activity, failed to lose what we have suc-
ceeded in losing?[31]

What exactly has been lost remains undetermined, and what is characteristic of "the country of our birth" is never defined in anything other than
self-referential terms. Kobayashi is no more capable of breaking free of the
circularity of the discourse on identity than Fukuzawa, Okakura, or Miyake.
The most striking thing about this essay is its emphasis on a sense of loss
as the defining characteristic of modern Japanese culture. Kobayashi makes
his most important ideological move on just this point, for the sense of
loss provides its own compensation by making the Japanese cosmopolitan,
enabling them to understand the literature of the West. Kobayashi's assertion rests on the assumption that Japan is now part of a universal culture;
it has reached the end that prompted the call for a new ethical consciousness made by Fukuzawa and other early proponents of modernization. Still,
in making this assertion Kobayashi employs rather protean language. His
rhetoric finds common ground with the language used to describe identity
by overtly accepting that there is an essence that has been lost as the result
of global historical transformations. At the same time, although he shares
the assumption of an authentic, mythic Japanese identity, his embrace of a
consciousness of loss and of the idea of the universal, inevitable progress of
modernity presents a clear challenge to nationalist ideology.

The circularity of his rhetoric is laid bare in Kobayashi's final comment
in the essay: "History seems always and inexorably to destroy tradition. And
individuals, as they mature, seem always and inexorably to move toward its
true discovery."[32] Kobayashi neatly captures the paradox of identity without
resolving it. This is hardly surprising since, for Kobayashi, paradox and anxiety are the two modes of thought, deriving from a sense of loss, that define
modern consciousness. The expression of a coherent sense of national identity relies on a language of values, sentiments, and traditions that is ultimately
divorced from historical realities. In "The Anxiety of Modern Literature," he
observes that "we go into the streets full of anxiety. Nothing exists out there
that we can call 'the city' or 'society' with any certainty. Strangely, each and
every thing necessary for a city or a society lies right before our eyes: the
railway station, the post office, buildings, and factories. But we have no stable
belief in what exists behind them, the strings that make them run."[33]

Kobayashi goes well beyond the naïve nationalism of Miyake Setsurei
in that he recognizes the fictive nature of the language of values. And yet

his rhetoric continues to echo Miyake in crucial ways. The breach between language and values that created the anxious suspicion that modern identity is a phantom, always there and always out of reach, was certainly acknowledged during the Meiji period. But the breach was never healed, and the elusive intangibility of Japanese identity became, by Kobayashi's time, its own distinguishing characteristic—an utterly self-referential receptacle for belief. Kobayashi, to rework a phrase from Wallace Stevens, lived in an old chaos of the Meiji sun, caught in the thrall of nineteenth-century longings for an ontological core at odds with the material realities—the rail stations, post offices, and factories—of modern society. "Language can be reductively simple," Kobayashi dryly observed, "while the facts of reality are complex." To reconcile language and reality, "we need to look back and examine the self. My own limited experience instructs me that my mistakes and misperceptions came not from an excess of feeling but from an excess of thinking, or from an ideology that took no account of the self and others. In other words, the obstacle to seeing the true shape of things is not feeling as such, but feeling under the control of ideology."[34]

Kobayashi recognized the forces exerted upon him as a consequence of his historical position, and so he knew there could be no escaping the effects of ideology. But his knowledge was enmeshed within a set of assumptions and expressed within a structure of thought that, though more sophisticated than Miyake's, still replicated the key patterns of the discourse of identity that emerged during the late nineteenth century. Unable to escape the trap of history, to get to a state of feeling without ideology, he chose to embrace his awareness of that trap as the distinctive essence of modern identity. Culturally, politically, and spiritually, Japan was seen to occupy an imagined third space between the West and Asia—a space that, by making room for both cultural authenticity and universalist aspirations, precluded any resolution of the divided ethical consciousness that emerged in modern Japan. As a result, many intellectuals and artists were haunted by doubts as to whether the hybrid condition of being modern and Japanese could ever be a real identity.

Authenticity and Cultural Hybridity

The seductive power of the concept of authenticity, as it was employed in discussions of moral and aesthetic values, derived from the desire to stabilize the meaning of identity and render it more tangible. The desire was kindled in part by the encounter of the Neo-Confucian system of aretaic or virtue ethics with the claims of deontological and consequentialist ethics, which were perceived in Japan as radically different grounds used to justify Western political and legal institutions. The cult of success, which was one outcome of this encounter, was a significant phenomenon in that it pointed to a change in ethical consciousness in which individual autonomy becomes a fundamental value.

The Meiji-era shift in ethical consciousness paralleled developments in Western cultures. Charles Taylor has traced out the history of these developments, and his narrative centers on the inextricable relationship between the concepts of autonomy and authenticity discussed briefly above.[35] In Taylor's view, the modern emphasis on autonomy constituted a fundamental shift in the view of ethical intuition, starting with the inception of the Romantic movement in the late eighteenth century. The conception of ethical intuition—the ability to comprehend right and wrong or appreciate beauty and truth—dominant prior to the eighteenth century was rooted in the belief that humanity possessed an innate moral sensibility. To know values, then, was to be in touch with that inner sensibility or intuition. What changed in modern times is that being in touch took on independent moral significance.[36] That is, the notion that autonomy is vital to evaluative judgments became a key feature of modern ethical consciousness.

This change carried with it a heavy burden, which is reflected in the emergence of authenticity as an important element in modern ethical consciousness. As Taylor notes,

> in a flattened world, where the horizons of meaning become fainter, the ideal of self-determining freedom comes to exercise a more powerful attraction. It seems that significance can be conferred by *choice*, by making my life an exercise in freedom, even when all other sources fail. Self-determining freedom is in part the default solution of the culture of authenticity, while at the same time it is its bane, since it further intensifies anthropocentrism. This sets up a vicious circle that heads us toward a point where our major remaining value is choice itself.[37]

Giving priority to individual judgment raises the specter of ethical relativism, making it difficult to reconcile the modern emphasis on autonomy with the claim of individual duty to the state or community that was at the heart of the discourse on identity in Japan and elsewhere. To rely increasingly on the subjective consciousness of the individual is to risk losing the certainty that values are reliable, that they transcend the individual and history. The concept of authenticity was invoked as a reaction against the loss of an absolute grounding for values implied by the appeal to individual autonomy. The invocation of an authentic Japanese culture resulted in an outward displacement of consciousness, a move to find timeless embodiments of values that could serve as externalized exemplars for both the individual and the nation.

Taylor's overview of the concepts of subjectivity and selfhood and his history of the notion of authenticity provide a comparative framework between the experience of Japan and that of Western culture. Even so, the changes in ethical consciousness in nineteenth-century Japan cannot be explained entirely by reference to Taylor's historical overview of the idea of authenticity in the West.[38] Moreover, it is important to point out that Taylor himself unabashedly embraces the aim of trying to recover authenticity as a value.[39] A perhaps unintended consequence of his effort is that he gives us a description of modern ethical consciousness not only through his historical account, but also through his own reliance on the circularity of the rhetoric of authenticity. Consider, for example, the language of the following statement:

> If authenticity is being true to ourselves, is recovering our own "sentiment de l'existence," then perhaps we can only achieve it integrally if we recognize that this sentiment connects us to a wider whole. It was perhaps not an accident that in the Romantic period the self-feeling and the feeling of belonging to nature were linked. Perhaps the loss of a sense of belonging through a publicly defined order needs to be compensated by a stronger, more inner sense of linkage.[40]

The language of this statement carries echoes of the discourse of writers like Kobayashi, who, as we have seen, articulated both the appeal and the dangers of authenticity. This common element of their discourse enables both Taylor and Kobayashi to make trenchant observations on the history of modern consciousness, but their observations are circumscribed by an ill-defined, ineffable, quasi-religious notion of the spiritual dimensions of individual subjectivity.

Taylor's views on subjectivity and authenticity illustrate an important aspect of the culture of authenticity, which is its spiritual, quasi-religious appeal as a kind of panacea for the anxieties of the global culture of modernity. Theodor Adorno, writing about Germany, has analyzed this appeal as a function of what he termed the "jargon of authenticity." His description of the characteristics of that jargon is illuminating in that it focuses on its empty aesthetic appeal. The jargon is

> a trademark of societalized chosenness, noble and homey at once—sublanguage as superior language.... While the jargon overflows with the pretense of deep human emotion, it is just as standardized as the world that it officially negates; the reason for this lies partly in its mass success, partly in the fact that it posits its message automatically, through its mere nature. Thus the jargon bars the message from the experience which is to ensoul it. The jargon has at its disposal a modest number of words which are received as promptly as signals. "Authenticity" itself is not the most prominent of them. It is more an illumination of the ether in which the jargon flourishes, and the way of thinking which latently feeds it.[41]

Adorno's analysis of the rhetoric of authenticity builds upon a Marxist critique of the fetishism of commodities. Turning values and the conception of essential cultural traits into objects for consumption and political suasion disrupts the ability to express the relation between language and truth. The "ether" that the word authenticity reveals is a kind of absolutism that seeks to conceal or at least subordinate the difference between reflective judgment of values and values themselves. Making authenticity the starting point for discussions of identity is one way to overcome the self-consciousness required for reflection. The result, as Trent Shroyer puts it, is that the rhetoric of authenticity shares with contemporary advertising—especially political advertising—the pretense that idealized forms are somehow real: "Just as the mass media can create a presence whose aura makes the spectator seem to experience a nonexistent actuality, so the jargon presents a gesture of autonomy without content."[42]

As was the case in Germany, in Japan the term authenticity itself was rarely invoked. In fact, there is no single dominant term in the discourse used specifically for the concept, which is instead expressed by reference to specific values exemplified by such terms as *iki* (a soulful, manly chic), *aware* (sensitivity to the pathos of the world), or *makoto* (sincerity), or by concrete spaces and objects such as the anonymous sculpture of ancient Japan, examples of *shinden* architecture and classical landscape gardens,

Korean-inspired pottery, or the *furusato* (ancestral village or home)—all of which gestured toward an ideal condition of apprehending without thought, feeling without ideology.[43] Nonetheless, the protean character of the concept of authenticity—its linguistic and ontological malleability—made it an effective ideological tool. So much so that it could co-opt the appeal to freedom and subjectivity by presenting itself, to borrow Shroyer's phrase, as a gesture of autonomy.

The injunction to be true to one's self in matters of ethical judgment maintains the autonomy of the individual as the source for any objectively grounded determination of what is right, but it does so in a strangely convoluted way. Being true to oneself, or finding one's real identity, is an ethical imperative based on the assumption that there is an objective, even absolute truth for each individual. The wording of this imperative demonstrates the struggle with ethical relativism by virtue of its effort to have it both ways, that is, to maintain an emphasis on autonomy while trying to hold onto something absolute, something beyond the individual and obliquely comprehended in the transcendent, oceanic feelings stirred by a connection with nature, the sacred, or the nation, all of which provide more stable sources of belief in culture-defining values.

In the case of moral sentiments, autonomy demands that the individual stand by his or her ethical convictions even when those convictions are not in agreement with the rules or dictates of the community at large. However, the atmosphere created by the invocation of authenticity preempts this stand. To be authentic is also to trust one's convictions, even against the community, not because those convictions are grounded in subjective, rational judgment, but because they originate in a moral intuition that is natural, essential, and transcendent: that is, not because the individual is objectively right on the facts of the matter, but because the individual is heroically in touch with the true sources of values that the community has forgotten or corrupted.

The discourse on modern identity in Japan discloses the hybridity of the categories of self and individual in which Western conceptions came to co-exist with indigenous ideas of socially constructed selfhood.[44] In reaction to this disclosure, the concept of authenticity worked to conceal the hybridity of modern culture under the cloak of the belief that identity could be traced to mythical or natural origins. This belief was useful to nationalist ideologies because it facilitated the construction of idealized forms—the Japanese nation, the Japanese people, even the Japanese language—that were materially and spiritually expedient. It is more than a little ironic, then, that the rhetoric of authenticity, which seeks to conceal the central characteristic of modern Japanese culture, should perform such a central and overt narrative function in histories of modern Japan.

A striking example of this narrative function is provided by a collection of essays titled *Japanese Thought* (*Nihon no shisō*), published in 1961. Written by the noted intellectual historian Maruyama Masao, *Japanese Thought* became a foundational work in postwar modernization theory. Maruyama's motive for this book was not to go back and correct earlier definitions of Japanese identity, but to explore the reasons why prewar constructions of identity collapsed and, more important, why they had led to the catastrophe of war and defeat. The essays occasionally exhibit a tendency to ignore contingencies and see these failures as inevitable—a blind spot that extends to an uncritical acceptance of Western cultural and institutional forms as the standards for both the history of modernization and the concept of subjectivity.[45] For all that, the book gives a coherent depiction of modern ethical consciousness in Japan, showing how deep and persistent the rhetoric of authenticity remained during the postwar period and bringing new life to the concept of a universal culture of modernity.

In the final essay of the collection, "De aru koto to suru koto" ("Being and Doing"), Maruyama identifies the reason for Japan's failure in the war as his nation's inability to fully modernize. By modernize, he means quite clearly the achievement of full autonomy for individuals. He sets out this thesis by adopting the strategy of compiling a series of concrete examples to make his point. The first example is the legal principle of prescription (*jikō*), which holds that the right of ownership is lost if an individual fails either to make a claim of ownership or to demonstrate the right of ownership. Maruyama sees that same principle embedded in both Article 12 of the postwar constitution, which states that "the freedom and rights guaranteed by this Constitution must be maintained by the unceasing efforts of the Japanese people," and in the declaration of Clause 97, that fundamental human rights are the outcome of humanity's long struggle to obtain freedom. At the heart of these statements is a notion of process, the concept that rights and freedom can only exist if one performs them.

This notion informs Maruyama's understanding of the system of democracy and the notion of freedom and autonomy.

While we are busy claiming that our society is free and worshiping the very notion of freedom, before we know it, in reality, freedom becomes just an empty phrase. Freedom is not something that just lies there, like some object we have set down. It can be protected only by actually making use of it. To put it another way, freedom can only come into being by our striving to become free.[46]

Maruyama's position, that autonomy and democratic systems can never really be but are realized only in the process of their becoming, has clear echoes of Adorno's critique of the jargon of authenticity. The danger for values, for freedom and democracy, is that they become subjected to the self-interests of individuals and groups and fetishized (Maruyama uses the word *busshinka*).[47] The process of consciously bringing about, of doing, defines the modern ethical consciousness for Maruyama. He explicitly ties this quality to consequentialist notions of outcomes and to the process of rational evaluation. He observes that the dynamic of the modern spirit (*kindai seishin*), which "dismantles status societies, redefines idealism as nominalism, puts all dogmas through the sieve of experimentation, and challenges the practical function and efficacy of the authority that has circulated 'inherently' in various fields of politics, economics, and culture," originates in "the relatively important shift from the logic and values of *being* to the logic and values of *doing*."[48]

Maruyama does not claim that the logic and values of "doing" are necessarily superior or even operative in all cases, nor does he claim that modern ethical consciousness has entirely supplanted what he calls the ethics of "being." The mingling of these modes of thought are, in his view, what makes it possible for Japan in 1961 to seem both hypermodern (*kakindai*) and nonmodern (or antimodern, *hikindaiteki*).[49] The hybridity of Japanese culture explains, in Maruyama's view, certain aspects of Japan's recent history, especially its struggles over national identity and the ultimately destructive policies that emerged out of that struggle.

Maruyama extends his analysis by contrasting the ethical consciousness of Tokugawa Japan with that of modern Japan. Tokugawa Japan was a society based on an ethics of "being" and, as such, was characterized by two major tendencies. The first was an externalization of the grounds on which belief in moral and aesthetic values was justified. In the highly stratified status society of the Tokugawa period, social norms and values were absolute within a class, though there was something of a sliding scale of norms between classes. Maruyama stresses that the justification for accepting those values and norms depended on factors—social status, family lineage, inherited occupation, or birthplace—that were assumed to be natural and fixed beyond the control of the individual. In such a society, the exercise of free will and reason in the questioning of belief in values could not take place. The second tendency was an absence of public morals (Maruyama suggestively uses the mixed English-Japanese term *paburikku na dōtoku*), a term he uses to refer to the rational and impartial rule of law that governs relationships among strangers in society. Japan's ethical consciousness before the nineteenth century thus in Maruyama's opinion lacked a fully developed concept of autonomy, was arbitrary in its application of rules and its imposition of judgments, and was based on principles exterior to the individual subject.

Maruyama's language in this essay prefigures the historical overview of the ethics of authenticity set forth by Taylor, and it echoes the rhetoric of writers from the Meiji period up through the period of World War II. The instability associated with the notion of autonomy—an association that existed, in Maruyama's view, only because of the failure to fully realize autonomy in Japan—was a catalyst for the search for authentic values. But Maruyama also recognized that the circular, self-justifying nature of the concept of authenticity ultimately provided unstable grounds for defining national identity. He ends his essay with a critique of modern culture's tendencies to turn the classics (*koten*) into a fetish fundamentally devoid of meaning and to assert the existence of intrinsic values as a means to counter the politicization of modern culture.[50]

Translation Culture and the Ethics of Identity in Japanese Fiction

The appeal of the concept of the classics, or of a cultural canon, depends upon the assertion that the concept represents something authentic, a claim always rendered true by definition. Awareness of such blatant circularity is apparent in a number of the most salient conditions of the culture of modernity in Japan: its self-consciousness with regard to its own project of actualization; its obsession with cultural borrowing and the threat of marginalization; its simultaneous rejection of the immediate historical past and chauvinistic embrace of mythic national origins; its creation of a national language, which embodied and promoted Japan's cultural uniqueness; and the triumph of a radical, fundamentally conservative ideology, with its revisionist invention of Japan's cultural traditions. The discourse on identity emerged out of these conflicted conditions as a direct response to changes in social organization, economic production, and ideological formation.

Maruyama was struck by how the hybrid quality of the ethics of identity in modern Japan was manifested in narrative terms, and he made a strong association between the development of narrative subjectivity in fiction and notions of authenticity and political autonomy.[51] His association is based on a reading of the history of literary practices, which had sought since at least the early Meiji period to make connections between social modernization and new narrative forms. As we have seen, the connection between the hybridity of ethical consciousness and literary practices was observed by Kobayashi as well, who identified it in different terms by referring to modern Japan as a translation culture.[52] The function of literary narrative within the discourse on identity was not solely an instrumental one, in which the development of subjectivity in narrative had to precede, in order to make intelligible, the notion of political autonomy. Rather, the connection between literary practice and concepts of autonomy and authenticity was both instrumental and metaphorical—the emergence of modern literature standing in for the emergence of a modern ethical consciousness.

The dual function of literature as both instrument and metaphor for modernization is most obvious in the practice of translation. The translation and adaptation of cultural forms from the West was considered a necessity for the revitalization and preservation of Japanese identity. This belief was held even in the face of the potential cost of the alienation caused by the displacement of established modes of representing commonly shared values, which came to be identified as the tradition or the canon only with the passage of time. The price of creating a cultural synthesis, an idea expressed early in the Meiji period by the image of a new, enlightened Japan, was by no means the simple inconvenience of developing a different vocabulary to describe Japanese identity. The process of cultural translation raises inescapable questions about the accuracy of representation and the epistemology of cultural and ethical norms even as it attempts to reconcile cultural and linguistic differences to get at something universal and essential.

Concerns about originality and belatedness that accompanied the process of translation mirrored and reinforced the significant changes in ethical consciousness revealed in the interplay between the notions of autonomy and authenticity. Efforts to formulate the ontological core of Japanese identity raised the problem of how to reconcile an understanding of national identity derived from a belief in the existence of a unified, pure culture with the recognition of the hybrid quality of modern ethical consciousness. To talk about either a shared ethical consciousness or shared cultural myths required a reconsideration of narrative forms and metaphorical language. This was achieved in large part through a process of translation that facilitated the shift from an aretaic ethics, which Maruyama referred to as the ethics of being, to the consequentialist and deontological ethics that Maruyama referred to as an ethics of doing. The major transformation that occurred in Japan may be described as a translation of the idioms of an exteriorized, traditional ethical consciousness into an interiorized, modern mode of belief and evaluation.

The presence of the mediating barrier of the language of a translation signifies the absence or displacement of an original cultural form, thus raising the concern that the reader is blocked from a full and authentic understanding of the original. It does not matter whether we are dealing with a translation of a form from outside Japan or from the indigenous culture, for in both cases a translation acts as a trace of difference and even cultural marginalization. For that reason, an examination of the relationship between cultural translation and the imaginative representation of ethical values in fictional narrative provides a more complete picture of the anxieties produced by modernization and represented by the rhetoric of authenticity.

The translation of moral concepts and sentiments into a commonly shared and intelligible idiom was crucial to enabling the symbiotic relation between the development of narrative subjectivity and the notion of political autonomy. In this regard, it is important to keep in mind the point noted above that the vocabulary of virtues and values that appears in the work of writers from the nineteenth century onward has remained relatively stable and continuous. What changed, in response to new social and economic conditions, was not so much the definition of the terms of values as the nature of the belief in those values. In the context of developments in literature and the arts, this change was apparent in the emphasis placed on the belief in the integrity of the artist and in essential canons of taste.

The gradual devaluation of certain forms of literary practice that dominated prior to Meiji is a judgment reflecting strong historical biases that have to be taken into account in considering the connection between narrative forms and the hybrid quality of modern ethical consciousness. Beginning in the late nineteenth century, there was a growing sense that the canon of cultural values, and the canon of literary works seen as best representing those values, was in need of reformation. Canon reformation was a vexing issue, because it involved both a reassessment of the cultural past and an appropriation of the past—a retrieval of values that arose as an outcome of a new understanding of the tradition.[53] The standardization of the Japanese language—or more precisely, the creation of a national language—became an important part of the process of canon reformation. In that respect, the modernization of the Japanese language was not driven merely by material considerations (that is, it was not simply the outcome of economic, military, or educational needs), but was driven in large part by the desire to discover an idiom appropriate to express a new constellation of standards and tastes. Older and newer forms may have existed side by side, but for the most part, literature came to be viewed, like other cultural products, in terms of the Meiji myth of enlightenment—that Japan was moving toward a higher, advanced stage of civilization. At the same time, the effort to create a cultural synthesis through a reformation of canon and language was self-marginalizing, since it required negotiating the acceptance of standards and tastes that had the potential to be deeply alienating. How can standards and tastes be accepted as norms when they act as a sign of foreignness—that is, when they appear translated and not authentic?

Kobayashi was justified in seeing in the history of modern literature an analogy to wider cultural changes. The antinomy that marks the ethics of identity in Japan, the condition that Ōe has termed ambiguity, is exemplified in the literary culture by the repeated attempts of different writers at different times to come to some satisfactory resolution to the question raised immediately above. These attempts took the form of opposing impulses to introduce the rhetorical forms of foreign literatures and to recover or preserve elements from the past—impulses that instantiated the widespread concern about authenticity and the hybrid nature of a culture of translation. The literary works discussed in the essays that follow describe this antinomy in more specific detail, but they are not presented as a complete account of the role the concepts of autonomy and authenticity played in the ethics of identity. Instead, they demonstrate the persistence of a deeply rooted anxiety about the effects of a divided ethical consciousness, and explore the ways that anxiety has generated a remarkable tradition of artistic experimentation and achievement.

1
Ghostwriters and Literary Haunts

T HE SOURCES OF THE language of values and the rhetoric of authenticity
in Japan from the Meiji Restoration to the present may be traced back
to developments dating from the eighteenth century. During the latter half
of the Tokugawa period (1600–1868), the project of uncovering the origins
of the Japanese language became a near-obsessive concern for a number of
key intellectual movements, most notably National Learning (*kokugaku*).
Although scholars of this movement did not imagine "nation" (*koku*) either
in the spatial sense of the political and class boundaries that took shape
in Meiji Japan or in the social sense of a unified ethnic or racial category,
their search for a pure language and culture, which they believed existed in
the distant past, had a decisive effect on modern representations of nation
and identity.

The Tokugawa conception of Japanese as a culturally unifying language
made it possible to imagine the existence of a common identity as well.
However, as Naoki Sakai has observed, the unity implied by a shared ethnic
identity was divorced from the social order that existed at the time because
a pure Japanese language, the source of Japan's ethnic communality, existed
only in antiquity. As Sakai puts it:

> Ethnic unity was always projected into the past, into antiquity. In this
> sense, a certain reification of an anonymous collectivity, which social ac-
> tion establishes, had already taken place, but it was not directly equated
> to the existing order. This ethnic identity came into being primarily as a
> loss, as that which had existed a long time ago but was no longer avail-
> able. Thus, Japanese was born into eighteenth-century discourse long
> dead; Japanese was stillborn.[1]

Since a pure language (and culture) could be inferred from research but never actually recovered, the discovery of nation and folk in an imaginary original language was also a discovery of loss. And the sentiment of loss, as Maruyama Masao has argued, was responsible for the consciousness of crisis that emerged in the nineteenth century.[2] The effect of a sentiment of loss is seen most immediately in the idea of authenticity, which not only arose as a means to compensate for the threat of cultural relativism, but also served as a palliative for the anxiety of loss, drawing affective power from the implied, nostalgic hope of a return to a lost unity of language and identity.

The sense of loss of a shared past was radically transformed during the nineteenth century by the obsession with discovering an authentic identity for the present. Increased emphasis on the autonomy of the subject, a heightened historical awareness, and an interiorization of the sources of belief made it seem possible for the past to be projected onto the present, for original identity and language to be recovered. At the same time, anxieties over external threats made efforts to enunciate a national identity seem a necessity. The eighteenth century's sense of loss became less a phantasm of linguistic research and more an immediate problem with real-world consequences that gave the discourse on identity a more virulent nationalist quality.[3] Pre-Meiji conceptions of cultural and ethnic identity thus provide a point of reference from which to gain a better sense of the evolution of the concepts of autonomy and authenticity as they relate to the modern ethics of identity.

Few works of the eighteenth century are as preoccupied with the distant past, exhibit such a profound sense of loss, and assume such a close connection between values and identity as *Ugetsu monogatari* (*Tales of Rain and the Moon*). Published in 1776,[4] this collection of nine ghost stories was composed by Ueda Akinari (1734–1809) at a time when he was involved in a number of literary and intellectual pursuits as a doctor, a scholar of National Learning, and a *haikai* poet. These pursuits placed Akinari at the center of some of the most important intellectual and literary movements of his day, and their presence is apparent in the language and structure of *Ugetsu*, a work written with the aim of recovering, if only fleetingly in the realm of fiction, the undivided ethical consciousness that characterized the authentic culture of the past.

Given his interest in the ethical consciousness of ancient Japan, why did Akinari choose to write fantastic tales about the supernatural—a choice that on its face suggests that he believed in the primacy of the value of literature for its own sake? Why did he compose his stories in the manner of adapted fiction, *hon'an shōsetsu*? Why did he develop a style that combined elements of both elegant and vulgar idioms and paid particular attention to historically accurate detail? These questions point to the most salient feature of *Ugetsu*, its hybrid form, language, and aims. Akinari's fiction was the product of a complex set of interests, and it is important to note that during his lifetime he never publicly acknowledged his authorship of *Ugetsu*.[5] This decision, though not at all an unusual practice at the time, indicates a deeply ambivalent attitude about the value of fiction. He was willing to use ghost stories as a means to explore questions of values and identity, yet the view held by the preeminent scholar of *kokugaku*, Motoori Norinaga (1730–1801), that the practice of fiction was autonomous and not bound by moral considerations, was never seriously challenged by Akinari. The method of composition of his masterwork is evidence that his primary concern was working toward a synthesis of art and morals.

Kokugaku and the Subordination of Morals to Art

Kokugaku arose in avowed opposition to Neo-Confucianism and to all other foreign systems of thought. Its methodologies and the structure of its ideology, however, were indebted to an earlier Neo-Confucian scholarly movement, *kogaku* (ancient learning).[6] *Kogaku* scholars, who established a systematic approach to the study of ancient Chinese texts, brought together the rationalism implicit in their empirical linguistic research with an antirational, fundamentalist tendency to accept the authority of the ancient past in all areas of intellectual inquiry, especially the ethical authority of the ancient sage-kings of China.[7] By stressing research into the past, they encouraged the growth of nativist movements that adapted *kogaku* to an examination of Japan's ancient history and literature.

The primary aim of *kokugaku* research was to recover the linguistic origins of Japanese. This research was empirical insofar as it was based on the observation of linguistic changes over time. Yet underlying the *kokugaku* project was an acceptance of the belief that ancient society was characterized by an absolute correspondence between words and the objects, thoughts, and actions they signified. Only with the passage of time, as the original meanings of words were forgotten or as new systems of thought were introduced, did the original unity of word and world begin to break

apart. *Kokugaku* research sought to move between and reconcile the intellectual poles created by what was perceived to be the corruption of the
language, and thereby recover authentic culture and with it the ethical consciousness of the Japanese people.

Kokugaku scholars viewed the importation of foreign doctrines, Confucianism in particular, as one of the major causes of this linguistic rup-
ture. That assumption, however, did not result in an outright rejection of
Neo-Confucianism, which remained deeply embedded in *kokugaku* beliefs
and practices. This apparent contradiction may be attributable in part to
the pressure exerted by official Tokugawa support of Neo-Confucian doctrine, which few individuals were willing or able to challenge. Another
explanation is that *kokugaku* scholars did not sense that contradiction,
since they were engaged in an ideological adaptation of *kogaku* practices
to a Japanese context. Consequently, *kokugaku* scholars carried forward a
number of Neo-Confucian assumptions: belief that improving the present
depends upon an understanding of the past; belief in the limits of human
knowledge; acceptance of the past as the source of ethical authority, with
the major difference being that scholars like Kamo no Mabuchi (1697–
1769) and Norinaga naturalized that authority by turning to texts like the
Manyōshū (compiled between 752 and 772) and *Kojiki* (712) instead of the
Confucian classics; and an acceptance of a historical approach to the study
of ancient texts.

These assumptions had important ramifications for Akinari in that they
came to serve as the basis for justifying the study of literature. Maruyama
notes:

> The natural human sentiments that Sorai released from the fetters of
> moral rigorism moved, as one might expect, in the direction of "refined
> tastes and literary talents." The Ken'en's reputation for putting literature
> above everything else was not completely unmerited. Just as Sorai reject-
> ed moralistic restrictions in politics and history, he insisted that literature
> should be independent of ethics.[8]

Sorai's work led to a reevaluation of critical standards that decoupled literature from the normative values of Confucian or Buddhist doctrines and liberated the study of literature in general from the narrow interpretive frame-
works that had previously held sway. This idea later found its most famous
critical formulation in the concept of *mono no aware*, which Norinaga iden-

tified as the underlying aesthetic principle of *Genji monogatari* (*The Tale of Genji*). Norinaga argued in his study *Genji monogatari tama no ogushi* (*The Tale of Genji: A Small Jeweled Comb*) that "because the novel [*Genji monogatari*] takes as its main purpose the understanding of what it means to be moved by things [*mono no aware o shiru o*], it often follows that tendency and turns its back on the teachings of Confucianism and Buddhism."[9]

Akinari's research on Japan's early literature suggests that he concurred with this approach to literary studies. Indeed, one of the turning points in his life was his shift toward *kokugaku* activities around the time he began composing *Ugetsu monogatari* in the late 1760s. Under the influence of Katō Umaki (1721–1777), who had been a disciple of Kamo no Mabuchi, Akinari began to focus his work on the study of words and texts. His undertook investigations of poetic devices, such as the *kireji* (literally, "cutting words") *ya* and *kana* and *makurakotoba* (pillow words), and engaged in a famous debate with Norinaga over the reliability of the text of the *Kojiki* and over the presence of a final nasal syllabic *-n* in ancient Japanese.[10] Although he located his ideals in the past and saw the present as having diverged or regressed from those ideals, Akinari did not blame foreign influences, and he rejected the xenophobic leanings of Mabuchi and Norinaga.[11] He did agree with them that ancient society held pure values, but he did not believe it possible to recover that purity, and his disagreement with Norinaga over the indisputable truth of Japan's myths led him to adopt the relativist position that different ages have different characteristics.[12] Still, Akinari deferred to the authority of the past, and in that respect he is very much in general agreement with both Neo-Confucians and fellow *kokugaku* scholars.

Akinari's views are on full display in his short study of *Genji monogatari* titled *Nubatama no maki* (*Black-Jewel Scroll*), written under the pseudonym Muchō. The preface dates this work to 1779, and explains that it is a translation into modern language of a treatise written by Sōchin, who lived in the late years of the Muromachi period (1392–1573). Sōchin is devoted to the study of *Genji*, having copied the work in its entirety twenty-four times. One night, while working on yet another copy, he falls asleep over the manuscript and dreams that he is walking along the strand at Akashi. He meets Kakinomoto no Hitomaro, the great *Man'yōshū* poet, and they begin discussing *Genji monogatari*. Sōchin wonders if Murasaki Shikibu herself had once strolled along this same beach, given how her work so vividly describes the place. Hitomaro replies:

[*Genji monogatari*] has always delighted people because it recreates so completely and interestingly the world as it was then. Yet the book is mere empty words of trifling value. The officials of the capital thought of such writing as nothing more than playing with beautiful phrases. Since it was quite natural for them to set down things just as they were, it is extremely foolish now to take such idle pastimes for the wisdom of the world.[13]

Hitomaro notes Murasaki's ability to capture reality in her words, but he is unwilling to praise her for something that came naturally, that was not the product of the artistic imagination.

Sōchin then questions Hitomaro about the value of fiction. Even though fiction is treated in China as "empty words" containing no truth, the ideas of an author, whether grieving over the world, lamenting the decline of the state, or criticizing high officials, may still express, even if only in a vague, roundabout way, the realities of the present.[14] Such ideas contain a measure of truth, Sōchin asserts, citing as support the so-called *monogatari ron* (theory of the tale) that appears in the "Hotaru" ("Fireflies") chapter of *Genji*. There Genji sets forth the argument that fiction performs a moral function by instructing in the manner of *hōben*, the expedient teachings of Buddhism, or by providing important details of the past not contained in historical chronicles.

In rebuttal, Hitomaro insists that Sōchin is in error because he holds a divided conception of fiction, considering it either a diversion that allows for the expression of human emotions or a representation of the real world that serves as a means for moral instruction. He asserts that this divided conception did not exist in Japan in the ancient days. Instead, "there was no theoretical distinction between fiction and reality. There was but one tradition recorded in their writings."[15] That tradition was lost because with the passage of time "the meanings of ancient words became obscure. Confucian and Buddhist teachings, as well as the doctrine of *yin* and *yang*, were taken up, leaving only shallow things."[16] To make this situation worse, according to Hitomaro, later interpretations appeared so that the original tradition, customs, and outlook of Japan gradually became confused. Early *waka*, an expression of natural emotions, and ancient fiction, a pastime that also gave vent to natural feelings, were thus misread.

In *Nubatama no maki*, Akinari argues that the ethical consciousness of ancient Japan was pure, honest, and sincere—values reflected in the original language, which made no distinctions between fiction and reality or between aesthetic and moral purpose. That unity represented the ideal toward which all political, scholarly, or literary activities should strive. While Akinari did not believe it possible to effect a return to the past, his efforts were aimed at trying to recover something of the ancient ethical consciousness through the study of language. As a *kokugaku* scholar, he took an empirical, historicist approach that established the autonomy of literary practice. All the while, he maintained as a fundamental article of faith an intuitive belief in the authenticity and authority of the past. These warring assumptions, which underpinned his scholarship, were not anomalous in the late eighteenth century, and they indicate that the divided ethical consciousness of the late nineteenth century did not emerge *ex nihilo*.

Authenticity and Adaptation:
The Uncanny Art of Ghostwriting

The notion of authenticity that justified *kokugaku* belief in the ethical authority of the past is expressed in *Ugetsu* by using the supernatural as a metaphor for the mythic unity of language and consciousness. Although the rationalism of its methods led some *kokugaku* scholars to dismiss belief in the supernatural as superstition, others, including Akinari, viewed the supernatural as part of a continuum of reality that intersected human experience of the world. To speak of the supernatural as a metaphor for authenticity is not to say that the supernatural had only metaphorical significance for Akinari. Though the unity of language and consciousness of the past was now for the most part inaccessible, that did not make it any less real. The experience of the supernatural, even if in fleeting encounters with the uncanny, was proof of an authentic state of being that was the source of moral and aesthetic values. This belief led Akinari to turn his attention to writing ghost stories, which he adapted to the worldview represented by *kokugaku*.

Akinari consciously asserted his relationship to the literary past and readily acknowledged his debts to both the Chinese and Japanese traditions in the preface to *Ugetsu monogatari*:

Lo Kuan-chung wrote *Shui hu chuan*, and subsequently monstrous children were born to three generations of his descendants. Murasaki Shikibu wrote *Genii monogatari*, and subsequently she descended into hell. It is thought that their suffering was punishment for having led people astray with their fictions. Yet when we look at their works we see in them an abundance of strange and wondrous things. The force of their words draws near the truth; the rhythm of their sentences is mellifluous and lovely, touching the heart of the reader like the reverberations of a koto. They make us see the reality of the distant past.

As for myself, I have a few stories that are nothing more than products of idleness in an age of peace and prosperity. But when the words come tumbling from my lips, they sound as queer and inauspicious as the raucous crying of pheasants, or the roar of dragons. My tales are slipshod and full of errors. Accordingly, those who thumb through this volume are not expected to mistake my jottings for the truth. The good thing is that I shall avoid the retribution of descendants with harelips or noseless faces.[17]

Akinari contrasts his approach to fiction, which claims to understand the pleasures of literature, to the values of overly serious moralists. The achievement of writers like Lo and Murasaki is that their works have the power to elicit powerful emotional responses that bring the reader near the truth. However, Akinari is not advocating formal realism. He is clearly more attracted to the stories of Lo and Murasaki because they tell of "strange and wondrous things" without limiting themselves to the merely plausible. This is an early formulation of the idea he later explored more fully in *Nubatama no maki*, that fiction has nothing to do with reality. The choice of the phrase *shin ni semari*, "drawing near the truth," emphasizes that a distance remains between literary language and the real world. As it is used here, it indicates both a consistency of the text with reality—the truth of what is said—and an ability to convince the reader that the text is consistent with reality—the credibility of its manner of saying. The verisimilitude of great literature is an aesthetic effect produced by the fleeting illusion that reality is unified with the figural language of text.[18]

The preface asserts that literature must be understood according to its particular laws and methods, not according to a predetermined reading based on an external set of values. Akinari's argument clearly shows his debt to *kokugaku* notions of the autonomy of literary practice, and it follows naturally from that point that he looks to the authority of the literary language of the past for his models. He praises Lo and Murasaki by stressing that the affective quality of their language is the mechanism by which truth is revealed. This suggests that the emotional response elicited by fiction is somehow entwined with the real world.[19] His assessment that the works of Lo and Murasaki "make us see the reality of the distant past" foreshadows the notion he later put forth in *Nubatama no maki*, that in the past fiction and reality were not distinguished because ethical consciousness was not divided. Also, Akinari's emphasis on the correctness of past models leads him to humbly state that his own work is defective.

Akinari's humility is double edged, for he pokes fun at Confucian and Buddhist criticisms that *Shui hu chuan* and *Genji monogatari* are dangerous moral deceptions. The tradition of this type of reading gave rise to legends about how both Lo and Murasaki were punished for writing so well.[20] That Akinari took an ironic view of those legends is suggested by the name he used for the preface, Senshi Kijin, "the eccentric with clipped fingers." When Akinari was five, he contracted smallpox, and an infection caused two of his fingers, one on each hand, to atrophy, leaving him noticeably deformed. Like the pseudonym he used for *Nubatama no maki*, Muchō (the Crab), Senshi Kijin is a self-mocking reference to his crippled hands.[21] This choice of names was a sly way for Akinari to place himself in the tradition of Lo and Murasaki. For in rejecting the moralists he is proclaiming the value of literature and of his own position as one of the deformed descendants of Lo.

The impact of *kokugaku* on Akinari's conception of *Ugetsu* is apparent in his acceptance of the authority of the past, which assumed the existence of a pure, authentic ethical consciousness, and his assertion of the autonomy of literary practice. More important, that impact is evident in the practice of adaptation, which is his primary method of composition. Each of the stories is literally a pastiche, with Akinari borrowing not simply the plot outlines from Chinese and Japanese sources, but even minute details of characterization or description.[22] This method of composition may perhaps call into question the originality of the author, though it is more likely that even with an annotated text the modern reader will not be able to sense the extent or quality of the borrowing. More troublesome than the potential misunderstanding of Akinari's creativity is the possibility that the modern reader will not see the debt, and consequently will not read the work within the context of the literary tradition it is consciously invoking. The verisimilitude of the stories is a function of the degree to which they remain true to literary types and conventions familiar to the reader. Originality, which in any case was not an overriding value in Akinari's poetics, is more a function of the degree of variation.

The process of adapting elements of *kokugaku* discourse on morals and art to Akinari's source works left its marks throughout the collection. For example, the opening tale, "Shiramine" ("White Peak," the name of a mountain in Shikoku), is a retelling of the historical events of twelfth-century Japan from the perspective of the ghost of an exiled emperor, Sutoku. In the course of the story, Sutoku reveals that the cause of the upheavals of the late Heian Period (792–1185) that eventually led to a government by military overlords was a curse he placed on his rivals.[23]

"Shiramine" begins with an account of a journey taken by the famous poet-priest Saigyō. This prologue includes many place names found in Saigyō's poetry that had become *utamakura* (place names that convey the essence of culture in the very invocation of the landscape) and that poetry serves as a narrative frame for the tale.[24] On his journey, Saigyō visits Shiramine, where he goes to the neglected gravesite of the former emperor to pay his respects. During the night, as he says prayers before the tomb, he is moved to compose a poem. His recitation of this verse calls forth the ghost of Sutoku, who offers a poem in reply.[25] After Sutoku reveals his ill will and the curse he has placed on his enemies, he shows himself to be a demon king who commands *tengu*, demons that are half-bird, half-human.

Akinari's adaptation introduces a number of new elements into the source works that emphasize the position and power of the poet Saigyō. First, though the ghost tells the primary story, it is the poetry of Saigyō that brings forth the spirit and makes the narration possible. Second, Saigyō engages the ghost in debate, boldly questioning Sutoku's rationale for the Hōgen Disturbance in 1156, the succession dispute that led to Sutoku's exile. The story moves from poetic to ethical discourse, and Saigyō becomes a mouthpiece for nativist ideology. Although a Buddhist priest, he begins by asking Sutoku if he really believed that he was not going against the teachings of the native gods of Japan (*ama no kami no oshie*; i.e., the traditional account of imperial descent from the sun goddess Amaterasu) when he rebelled.[26] The ghost is angered by this question and defends his actions on Confucian grounds, claiming that while his father, Toba, was alive he was a filial son. He then cites Mencius's claim that rebellion is justified if it represents the will or mandate of Heaven,[27] and chastises Saigyō for turning away from Confucianism and abandoning his family to follow the selfish path of personal enlightenment through Buddhist practices.[28]

Saigyō reminds Sutoku that, as emperor, he need not look to China for examples of proper action. He points to the filial behavior of the sons of Emperor Honda, Ōsasagi and Uji. They did not fight over the succession, but tried to give way to each other. Although Uji was the first imperial prince to embrace Confucianism, the ancient kings of Japan did not need Confucius to comprehend ethical behavior, as it was immanent in them.[29] Saigyō then remarks that the full work of Mencius has never reached Japan because the native gods will not permit the importation of such a dangerous foreign doctrine and call up storms to wreck all ships that try to bring the book. The imperial line, having descended from the gods, is inviolable, and thus the ethics of rebellion espoused by Sutoku do not pertain to Japan. Saigyō eventually persuades the ghost that his actions were wrong.[30]

The narrative idiom of this part of the story is strikingly different from that of the poetic travelogue. The vocabulary of Saigyō's argument is anachronistic, since it relies on the authority of older poetic and dramatic traditions to buttress a kokugaku-inspired interpretation of history. By emphasizing Sutoku's personal responsibility in allowing a foreign doctrine to obscure his native ethical consciousness, the story gives a radically different explanation for the ultimate causes of the disasters that overtook the imperial court during the second half of the twelfth century. This interpretation of history drives the adaptation of the source works for "Shiramine" and confirms the priority and authenticity of an essential Japanese ethical consciousness. That consciousness in turn finds its figural representation in both the language of Saigyō's poetry, which for Akinari derives its power from the use of utamakura, and in the imperial line.

The priest placates the ghost by reciting another poem, but there is nothing he can do to stop the course of history.[31] Saigyō's poem foreshadows the building of a proper memorial to appease Sutoku, which was undertaken by Emperor Go-Shirakawa in 1191, and the eventual worship of the exiled emperor as a god. Poetry is thus used as a structural device to create a narrative frame, and it is used to suggest that poetry, in both a literal and a figurative sense, has the power to call forth and appease ghosts, to bridge the past and present.

The fifth story in the collection, "Buppōsō" ("The Bird of the Three Treasures"), provides a more explicit example of the importance of kokugaku concerns to the process of adaptation. The result is an unusual ghost tale centered on a philological analysis of a classical poem. Muzen, a contemporary poet, encounters the ghosts of Toyotomi Hidetsugu (1568–1595) and his retinue on Mt. Kōya. Like the ghost of Emperor Sutoku, the spirit of Hidetsugu is vengeful. The period of his rule as *kanpaku* (chancellor) was a reign of terror that ended in 1595, when he was forced to commit suicide by his uncle, Hideyoshi, the de facto ruler of Japan.

Muzen and his son have come to Mt. Kōya to worship, but having stayed too late to attempt to descend the mountain, they choose to spend the night in prayer and meditation. Muzen explains the significance of the sacred mountain to his son, and recounts the miracles performed by the temple's founder, Kūkai. As he finishes his account, they hear a *buppōsō*, a bird whose cry was identified with the Three Treasures of Buddhism.[32] It was often associated with Mt. Kōya, and according to Muzen, no one before had ever been certain of hearing it. He takes this as an auspicious sign that heralds salvation, and recites two poems for his son's benefit. The first is a *kanshi* (a poem in Chinese) by Kūkai.[33] The second is a *waka*, a Japanese lyric by Fujiwara Mitsutoshi (1210–1276).[34] Muzen is then inspired to produce his own allusive verse in the seventeen-syllable *haikai* (nonstandard) form he favors.

Tori no ne mo	The cry of a bird
himitsu no yama no	in the thick undergrowth
shigemi kana	of the mountain of mysteries.[35]

Hidetsugu's party appears, and Muzen and his son withdraw. As the ghosts assemble and begin to eat and drink, Hidetsugu calls for Satomura Jōha (1524–1602), a renowned master of linked verse. Hidetsugu has a deep interest in antiquity, and he asks the poet a number of questions. As the discussions proceed, one of the warrior-ghosts cites the following *waka* by Kūkai:

Wasurete mo	Lest you forget, traveler,
kumiyashitsuran	you should not drink
tabibito no	the poisonous waters
takano no oku no	of the Tama River
Tamagawa no mizu	in the recesses of Takano.[36]

This warrior asks why Kūkai, whose virtue gave him extraordinary powers, did not simply purify the stream. Jōha explains that the poem appears in the seventeenth imperial anthology, the *Fūgashū* of 1349, prefaced by the following explanation (*kotobagaki*): "A river called the Tamagawa runs along the road to the shrine in the recesses of Takano. Because poisonous insects cover the surface of the water, the following poem was composed to keep those who read it from drinking from this stream."[37] He then recounts some of Kūkai's exploits, and maintains that because of the great priest's powers, the *kotobagaki* does not seem to be truthful. Furthermore, Jōha continues, the word *tama* in Tamagawa means "jewel," and he cites various usages to show that it was meant to praise the purity of the stream. He concludes that the *kotobagaki* was a later, mistaken addition to the poem, which should actually be understood to mean that although pilgrims to the shrine in the recesses of Takano may have forgotten this stream, they will be struck by its purity and instinctively scoop up the water and drink.[38]

The company is impressed with Jōha's philological erudition, and they lavish him with praise. Then, during a brief lull, the cry of the *buppōsō* is heard again. Hidetsugu is delighted, and calls for a poem by Jōha. He declines, telling his lord that a traveler who can compose in the currently popular mode of *haikai* is present. Muzen is called forward. He approaches, trembling, and is asked to repeat the poem he composed earlier. In his fright he begs to be excused, claiming that he has forgotten it. Jōha urges him on, and so Muzen asks about the identity of the nobleman, and remarks that he thinks the banquet is a strange affair. Jōha then identifies every member of the group and tells Muzen, "You and your son have been granted a wonderful audience. Now quickly recite the poem you composed earlier."[39]

The design of the story follows the order and language of the poems recited earlier by Muzen to his son. The sequence moves from the staid formality of Kūkai's *kanshi*, to the sparse elegance of a classical *waka*, to the modern stanza by Muzen, which seeks to echo its ancient models. The fact that Muzen has been granted "a wonderful audience" indicates that his art has the power, like the poetry of Saigyō, to conflate past and present, mundane and supernatural. However, Muzen seems a diminished figure when compared to the great Heian poet. Lacking Saigyō's courage and enlightenment, Muzen is unable to recite his poem. He scribbles it out and one of the warriors reads it. Hidetsugu is pleased, and asks someone to cap the verse. The ghost of Yamada Sanjūrō produces the following link:

[*Tori no ne mo*	[The cry of a bird
himitsu no yama no	in the thick undergrowth
shigemi kana]	of the mountain of mysteries.]

Keshitaki akasu   Offering incense, the dawn breaks.
mijika yo no yuka   An altar on a short summer's evening.[40]

Just as Hidetsugu begins to offer his praise, one of the retainers shouts, "It is the hour of the Asura! I hear the demons coming to meet our lord. Arise!"[41] The spirits turn blood red and rise up in a fury. Hidetsugu does not like the fact that he has shown himself to humans, and tells his retainers to take the two men with them into battle. The older retainers intervene and protect the men.[42] The ghosts disappear and Muzen and his son fall into a faint. They awake the next morning, offer prayers, then hurry back to the capital. Later, when Muzen passes by the mass grave of Hidetsugu and his family, the *Chikushōzuka* (Mound of Beasts), he thinks, "Even in the day-time it's frightening."[43]

The appearance of the supernatural is transformed by Akinari's presentation of the historical development of poetry. Read in that context, Jōha's arguments are not a pedantic exercise, but draw together the various elements of the tale—the poetry, the setting, the allusions to Kūkai and to Hidetsugu—and connect them with the *haikai* world of Muzen. It is implied that Muzen's poetry is a falling off from the past, but it still belongs in the tradition, and its composition is called forth by the affective pull of the strange cry of a bird, a figure of natural, unaffected beauty that also heralds salvation. By bringing the poetic past alive in the present, this reading of Japan's literary tradition, inspired by *kokugaku* methods, results in an adaptation that makes possible an aesthetic rendering of a sense of horror.

A third example of the way in which *kokugaku* ideas shaped the adaptation of Akinari's source material is provided by "Hinpukuron" ("A Dialogue About Poverty and Wealth"), the final story of the collection. Disputation plays an important role in many of the stories, but for the most part, it takes place within the context of some more important incident. In "Hinpukuron," the argument *is* the story, and Akinari moves most completely to the language of *kokugaku* as his literary medium to achieve a synthesis of past and present concepts of morals and art.

The setting is the province of Mutsu, and the hero is a man named Oka Sanai, a warrior in the service of Gamō Ujisato (1556–1595). Akinari's hero is based on a real-life warrior, also known as Okano Sanai, who fought for Gamō and for the Uesugi clan. He appears in a number of books that served as sources for "Hinpukuron," the most important being *Okina-*

gusa, a miscellany compiled by Kamisawa Sadamoto (1710–1795). Sanai also figures briefly in the *ukiyo-zōshi, Seken tekake katagi* (Character Sketches of Worldly Mistresses), that Akinari wrote just before composing *Ugetsu*. Apart from his courage, Sanai was best known for his love of money,[44] and "Hinpukuron" opens with a consideration of his character. He is an accomplished warrior, but his acquisitiveness is repellent to others. Sanai derives pleasure not by viewing the moon or cherry blossoms, but by going to his storehouse and counting out his pieces of gold. The general opinion of him changes, however, when Sanai finds out that one of his servants has secretly managed to set aside a *koban*, a small ingot of gold. He calls the man before him and gives him a short lecture. The power of wealth, Sanai asserts, far exceeds the power of weapons, and therefore a warrior must not waste money, but save it. Extremely pleased that the servant has saved beyond what was expected of him, Sanai rewards the man with ten *ryō* of gold and a sword. From that day on people started thinking of Sanai not as a miser, but as "merely eccentric."[45]

The night of the incident with the servant, Sanai is awakened by a tiny old man. His unexpected visitor is the spirit of the gold that Sanai has managed to accumulate. Pleased with the treatment accorded the servant, the spirit has come to share his thoughts. Much of what he says Sanai agrees with, as if he were of one mind with the spirit. Indeed, the little man is almost as much an emanation of Sanai's mind as he is the spirit of gold.

The dialogue consists of three main sections. In the first part, the spirit sings the praises of wealth. The second part is Sanai's defense of poverty. The final section presents the major argument, which is that the accumulation of wealth or the failure to do so has nothing to do with moral behavior. The spirit of wealth has to be respected because it is different from the spirit of man. A wealthy man in an act of generosity, for example, may loan his money without proper security, and thereby lose everything, and a person whose behavior is beyond reproach may never gain wealth, no matter what good deeds he performs. In the end, the best way to deal with wealth or poverty is the way of the sages of antiquity, whose purity of heart made them carefree as to whether or not they gained wealth. "The person who acts according to his opportunities will live frugally, save, and work hard, and his house will flourish of its own accord. I know nothing of the Buddhist teaching about previous lives, nor do my ideas have any connection with the Confucian idea of the will of Heaven. I travel in a different realm."[46]

The way to wealth is a practical art that requires learning and experience to master. Since the hollow theorizing of Buddhism and Confucianism cannot explain it, how does one learn this practical art? By looking to the way of the ancient sages, who made no distinctions between moral and immoral wealth, but who took it or left it according to the opportunities accorded them by Heaven. Each activity of human life has its own reasons and its own proper place. The spirit of gold argues that wealth and poverty must be understood on their own terms, and since this argument is the core of the supernatural encounter, it implies that the narrative itself cannot be reduced to interpretations based on totalizing ethical systems.

Kokugaku ideology makes its presence felt in Akinari's literary art both in the opinions on language and ethics found in the tales and in the way those views transform the structure of the source works. The art of adaptation— more literally, in the case of *Ugetsu*, the art of ghostwriting—is shaped by the impulse to seek out and recover the original unity between language and the world, to give equal weight to the autonomy of artistic representation and the authenticity of essential values. The practice of adaptation situates *Ugetsu* within a complex of critical ideas that generally shaped the development of fiction in mid-Tokugawa Japan and continued to exert influence well into the Meiji period, even after many writers had rejected the literary practices and assumptions of Tokugawa writers.

Akinari asserted the independence of literary practice from overly moralistic interpretations while extolling both the ethical and aesthetic values of the past. The supernatural tale is the means by which he expressed these competing aims. Throughout *Ugetsu*, the representation of ethical values reflects *kokugaku* assumptions about language and the source of those values, and the most frequently recurring theme deals with the consequences (that is, the supernatural encounters) that arise from a lack of moral discipline or from an extraordinary display of moral discipline. The moral theme thus becomes a narrative motif with a decidedly aesthetic function. When the desire for either autonomy or for authentic values is strong enough, the result is a form of haunting.

Autonomy and the *Bunjin* Ideal

The emphasis placed on the authority of the past in *kokugaku* ideology had a major influence on Akinari's conception of the artist, who is represented in *Ugetsu* as a kind of interpreter playing out variations on established themes. Since an author draws upon a familiar tradition, the interest of his stories lies in the quality of the variation (or adaptation). The ability of an artist to access the past through the tradition brought the present into at least fleeting contact with something real, which Akinari represented as an encounter with the supernatural, the realm where ethical consciousness and language merged with reality.

For all the importance *kokugaku* assumed in his life from about the time he began writing *Ugetsu* in 1768, it must be stressed that Akinari's scholarship was not the sole source of his conception of the artist. As noted above, Akinari was deeply involved in a number of other important intellectual pursuits. He was a student of Chinese medicine, a writer of popular fiction, and a poet. His efforts to create a synthesis of art and morals was motivated by a desire to emulate the ideal of the literatus (*bunjin*), which had been naturalized from Chinese models largely by painters and the practitioners of *haikai* poetry.

At the heart of this ideal was a tension created by competing claims of traditionalism and self-expression—a tension reflected in the ambivalent ideological structure of *kogaku* and *kokugaku*, which promoted empirical methodologies while holding absolute belief in the authority of the past. The appeal of traditionalism was in part the outcome of the commitment of literati to orthodox morality. It was the expression of the values of a particular class committed to transmitting a conservative ideology. Neo-Confucian developments in Ming China contributed to this conservatism by seeking to recover the true teachings of the past. Consequently, the literature of the period often attacked the shortcomings of the present age, and sought proper models to prescribe the correct way of writing, which led to a preference for editing and anthologizing.[47]

Balancing this traditionalism was an emphasis on self-cultivation. This did not imply unbridled freedom, but within the constraints imposed by traditionalism, some leeway was permitted through eclectic styles and personal interpretation. Operating strictly within the canons of taste that defined the literati class, it was possible for the individual to give expression to his personal understanding of those canons. As Joseph Levenson has observed regarding literati painters in China, by late Ming times "the end of the approved painter was the demonstration of his mastery of means. Style became a counter in an artist's game of self-display, while gentry-literati-officials and their set were the self-appreciative few who recognized the rules and knew the esoterica."[48] Expression of the self was tied to knowledge of the tradition and to a concern with style and structure, but it did not depend on technical proficiency alone. Technical proficiency was the concern of the craftsman. For the literati, connoisseurship and amateurism were far more important. Connoisseurship was the bridge between personal preference and established canons. It defined the individual in relation to the tradition.

Because for the most part Japanese literati shared the worldview of their Chinese counterparts (accepting the dual claims of traditionalism and self-cultivation), it would be misleading to portray the *bunjin* as a significantly more varied class. Nonetheless, some general differences between Japanese and Chinese literati should be noted. First, the educational and social background of the Chinese literati was generally more uniform, due to the institutional and economic support provided by the examination system of the bureaucracy. Moreover, there were a number of social constraints that tended to make Chinese literati relatively more uniform in outlook. As Robert Hegel notes, "this phenomenon was a function of seventeenth-century China's Confucian legacy of attention to social roles, models, and responsibilities.... The discernible limits of individualism among the elite as a consequence of this tradition likewise tended to curb the extent to which eccentric behavior could go."[49]

The relative lack of both institutional support and class identity among Japanese literati is evident in the greater commercialization of *bunjin* culture. This phenomenon is partly attributable to the growth of the publishing industry in Japan over the course of the eighteenth century, though it was not merely the tangible products of literary practice that were merchandised. Many poets set themselves up as masters of their own schools and lived off the proceeds of their teaching. Akinari, who made very little from his own writing, deplored such activities himself,[50] but it was perhaps inevitable that the *bunjin* turned to art to make a living, since they lacked official status and support. Mark Morris notes that the Chinese "who considered themselves *wenjen* had the education and income to make artistic amateurism a viable stance."[51] For most Japanese literati, life was a different matter: "However much a Japanese *bunjin* might admire his Chinese *wenjen* predecessors' ideal of multitalented amateurship, a *bunjin* like [Yosa] Buson had to put one or another of his talents to work in the cultural marketplace."[52]

The lack of uniformity among the *bunjin* as a class is also manifested in the proliferation of schools of literature or art that grew up around master artists, as part of the commercialization of literati culture. This phenomenon helped accelerate the vernacularization of the tastes and practices of literati culture, which earlier had been invested with the sacred aura of secret teachings. This trend was most apparent in the world of *haikai* poetry.

Akinari himself was an active *haikai* poet, and many of his literary interests centered on relationships he established through poetry circles. His most famous relationship was with the poet-painter Yosa Buson (1716–1783), a literary friendship that seems to have been based on a sense of mutual admiration.[53] Buson's aesthetics were likely an important influence on Akinari when the latter composed *Ugetsu*, though Buson's most explicit statement of his understanding of the principles of *haikai* did not appear until the preface to a collection of verse titled *Shundei kushū* (1777). The preface is in a question-and-answer format, with a disciple interrogating Buson. The first question is "what is *haikai*?" It receives the following reply: "*Haikai* is that which values detachment from the vulgar while using vulgar language. Using the vulgar to be free of the vulgar, the rule of detachment is very difficult. *Haikai* is like the rule of detachment in Zen, when Priest So-and-So asks about the sound of one hand clapping."

Because detachment from the vulgar, which is likened to a form of enlightenment, is so difficult to attain, the disciple next wants to know if there is a quick way to achieve it. Buson replies that the student must study Chinese poetry—a point that confuses the disciple, since it seems counterintuitive to abandon *haikai* and study *kanshi*. Buson insists, however, that the study of literature is the only way to achieve detachment from the vulgar. He urges his pupil "to become friends with" the four great *haikai* masters of the past and to become well acquainted with nature:

> Enjoying the calm spirit of natural scenery, making elegance your state of mind—these are as the beginning of things. Close your eyes and struggle to write a poem. When you have the verse, open your eyes. Soon you will leave the poets of the past behind, and without knowing how, you will be transformed into an immortal. Spellbound, you will tarry by yourself awhile. In time the fragrance of the flowers will waft on the breeze; the moonlight will float on the water. You are in the realm of *haikai*.[54]

One of the most interesting propositions here is Buson's acceptance of the vernacularization of language for the purpose of art. The notion that vulgar language has value only when it is used within a context created by a literary consciousness is a reworking of earlier ideas about composition that governed the efforts of Chinese literati, especially compilers like Feng Meng-lung (1574–1646). The artist must study the classical models of the past, for it provides the *bunjin* with a sense of discrimination. The model for Buson's argument here is the ideal of connoisseurship, in which the *bunjin* strives for self-cultivation and detachment through a complete understanding of the canons of taste.

A third important idea expressed by Buson in this preface has special significance for Akinari. *Haikai* is achieved not only by studying models of the past, but also by observing and studying the natural world. By virtue of observation the poet is able to discriminate, to understand an elegant state of mind, and thereby transform to achieve unity with nature like a Taoist immortal. The artist has special powers to access both the natural world and the supernatural—an affective theory of poetics that moves between the poles of intellectualism and intuitionism that formed the defining boundaries of the literati ideal of mid-Tokugawa Japan.

The literati ideal plays a key role in the process of adaptation in several stories in *Ugetsu*. For example, in "Asajigayado" ("A Hut Amid Tangled Grasses"), the qualities that make possible the supernatural encounter, the loving devotion and feminine piety of the heroine, Miyagi, are equated with her aesthetic sensibility. The plot is rather simple. Miyagi's husband, Katsushirō, is a lazy young man who squanders his inheritance. He is forced to leave his beautiful wife in their home village of Mama, in the province of Shimōsa, and seek his fortune in the capital. Though he promises to return soon, he meets with a number of mishaps that keep him away for seven years. After such a long period, during which his home province is swept up in the turmoil of war, Katsushirō is certain his wife is dead. However, he journeys back to find out what has become of her and finds his home much as he remembered it. He is surprised to find Miyagi, who has grown old and haggard from grief at her husband's long absence, still waiting for him, but her love is so strong that she forgets her bitterness at once, and they spend the night together. The next morning Katsushirō wakes up to find himself in the ruins of his house. He discovers his wife's grave nearby and realizes that he has slept with her ghost.[55]

"Asajigayado" relies heavily upon poetic allusion to create a variation on an archetypal motif in Japanese literature, the longing of an abandoned woman. The title of this story alludes to a poem in the "Kiritsubo" chapter of *Genji monogatari*.[56] Other instances of poetic allusion serve to construct the narrative by invariably emphasizing the motif of yearning. For example, when Miyagi and Katsushirō say their farewells on the eve of his departure, she quotes lines from poems in the *Kokinshū* (947 and 387) to give voice to her grief. He tries to comfort her, and promises to return by the autumn. He seals that promise with a line from a poem in the "Matsukaze" chapter of *Genji monogatari*.[57] When he fails to come back by the promised season, Miyagi again uses poetry to express her sorrow.

Mi no usa wa	There is no one
hito shi mo tsugeji	to convey my sorrow.
ausaka no	Cock crowing at Osaka barrier,
yū zuke tori yo	let him know
aki mo kurenu to	that autumn is nearly past.[58]

Later, on the morning when he realizes Miyagi is dead, Katsushirō vents his grief by quoting the last words of a famous poem by Ariwara no Narihira.[59] He then discovers her final work on her grave:

Saritomo to	Deceived by my longing heart,
omou kokoro ni	which thought he would return,
hakararete	how have I continued
yo ni mo kyō made	even to this day
ikeru inochi ka	to live in this world?[60]

Miyagi's poem is a variation on a verse by Fujiwara Atsutada, which appears in book 11 of the fourth imperial anthology, the *Goshūishū* (1086). This suggests she has a rather remarkable knowledge of the courtly tradition. But Akinari's decision to assign to her a poem that makes this poetic allusion underscores the intent of his adaptation, which is to associate the appearance of the virtuous feminine ghost with the realm of aesthetics. This point is driven home by the stark contrast in style between Miyagi's final poem and the memorial verse Katsushirō composes in reply.

When Katsushirō subsequently learns the details of her death, how she fought off suitors and preserved her chastity and devotion to him to the end of her life, he is moved to compose a final poem of farewell in the faltering, clumsy manner of an uncouth rustic:

Inishie no	Did they yearn
Mama no Tegona o	in olden days

kaku bakari	for Tegona from Mama
koite shi aran	the way I yearn for you?
Mama no Tegona	Ah, Tegona from Mama![61]

Katsushirō's poem compares the story of his beloved wife with that of a story in *Man'yōshū* about a woman named Mama no Tegona who killed herself when she could not have the man she loved.[62] The narrator ends by commenting on Katsushirō's clumsy, countrified poem: "He was not able to scratch even the surface of his emotions, and yet it could be said that his work had more true feeling [*masarite aware nari*] than the poems of people who are much more skilled at versifying."[63]

It may seem odd that the story ends with an assessment of Katsushirō's verse, but the plainness of his style alludes to the earliest and by implication most authentic poetic tradition represented by the *Manyōshū* . The poem conveys true emotion not mediated by rational thought or aesthetic calculation. Because it is sincere and heartfelt, the poem emulates at least the spirit that produced great works in the past. The borrowing and poetic allusion throughout the story establish a context in which the mysterious, lyrical beauty of Miyagi, which is both an ethical and an artistic ideal, can be expressed. Katsushirō's verse cannot compete with those classic works, but by recovering the affect—if not the elegance—of the language of the past, his poem and the supernatural moral and aesthetic virtue it memorializes capture a sense of authenticity that makes it worthy of the tradition.

The ability of an artist to initiate an encounter with the supernatural by recovering the original unity of words and reality is also a central element of the story "Muō no rigyo" ("Carps Inspired by a Dream"). The most immediate source for Akinari was probably a story entitled "Hsueh lu-shih yu fu cheng hsien" ("Hsueh the Archivist Takes the Form of a Fish and Proves the Miraculous"), which is found in Feng's anthology *Hsing-shih heng-yen.* That story is in turn based on a tale from a T'ang collection, the *T'ai-ping kuang-chi* (*Chronicles of the Great Peace*) titled "Hsueh Wei," after its eponymous hero. Hsueh Wei is an archivist who falls ill in the second year of the Ch'ien-yuan Era (759). He appears to die, but because his chest is still warm, his family postpones the funeral rites. After twenty days, he revives and tells the story of how his spirit wandered from his body and was transformed into a carp. He was caught by a fisherman and eaten by the officials with whom he worked, at which point his spirit returned to his human body. Throughout this narrative, the minute details observed by Hsueh Wei when he was a carp, such as the game of chess being played by the magistrates, the peach eaten by one of the officials, and the words spoken by various people, are used as evidence to prove the truth of his extraordinary account.

"Muō no rigyo" is virtually identical to this story, but where Akinari varied the account he did so in a way that emphasized literati values. In this case, the variation is achieved through the portrait of the hero, Kōgi, who is given a very different background from the character in the Chinese source work. The tale is set in the Enchō period (923–931), while Kōgi is a priest at the Miidera. He is also a painter whose skill is widely acclaimed. He paints only fish, and frequently goes out onto Lake Biwa to observe and sketch, often paying fishermen to free the fish they have caught. Akinari prefaces the main story with the following anecdote: "One time, as he was putting all his skill and heart into a painting, Kōgi fell asleep; and in his dream he entered the river and played with the various kinds of fish. When he awoke he at once painted the fish exactly as he saw them. Hanging the painting on his wall he titled it himself, calling it "Muō no rigyo" ["Carps Inspired by a Dream"]."[64]

Kōgi's artistic method is ostensibly realistic—he paints things as he sees them—but it is a realism of a different order, inspired by his dream vision. His moral actions, exemplified by his efforts to save the lives of fish, carry over into his attitude toward his own paintings of his favorite fish, the carp, which he is reluctant to give up, because they have a life of their own. The reason behind his attitude, he jokes, is that "I couldn't possibly give away fish raised by a priest to Philistines who would take their lives and eat them."[65]

One year, Kōgi falls ill and the story of his miraculous transformation unfolds almost exactly like its source work. "Muō no rigyo" concludes with the following coda:

> Kōgi recovered after this and lived to a ripe old age. When he was approaching death, he took his many paintings of carp and scattered them on the lake. Whereupon the carp that had been painted leapt off the silk scrolls and sported in the water. For this reason his paintings were never handed down. His disciple, Narimitsu, inherited his master's art and gained renown. Once he painted a rooster on a sliding door in the Kan'in Palace, and a live rooster, seeing the painting, scratched at it. So it is written in old tales.[66]

Narimitsu's skill is said to have been great enough to fool a rooster into mistaking a painting for a live object. But there is also a strong hint here that

Narimitsu's art has fallen off the standard set by his master. Kōgi managed to break down the distinction between representation and reality. His world was one in which the two were unified, so that painted fish were easily capable of swimming off the silk and into nature. The truly miraculous transformation portrayed in the story is the one achieved by art and the artist. By shifting the emphasis of his models from the mere realism of circumstantial detail to the artistic spirit that brings life and truth to the story, Akinari has created a metaphor for the process of art, his own "carp inspired by a dream."

The eighth story, "Aozukin" ("Blue Hood"), presents another striking portrait of the literati ideal. It bears many resemblances to the short religious tales found in *setsuwa* collections such as the *Nihon ryōiki* and the *Konjaku monogatari*, and borrows elements from two common types of Buddhist *setsuwa*: the miraculous deeds performed by a priest and the explanation of the founding of a particular temple.[67]

The hero of the tale, the priest Kaian Zenji, visits the village of Tomita on a pilgrimage. He hears the story of a local priest, an enlightened man who fell in love with a young boy. His obsession became so great that when the boy died he refused to give up the body. Unable to watch the corpse decay, the priest went insane and devoured it, eventually turning into a flesh-eating demon who terrorized the province. Upon hearing this story, Kaian resolves to save the man.

The following day, he goes up to the temple where the demon-priest lives. The setting is eerily dilapidated, and when Kaian calls out asking for shelter, a single monk, as withered as a dead tree, emerges from the sleeping quarters and advises him to go back to the village.[68] Despite the warning, Kaian asks to stay, and is left on his own. Around midnight, under a beautiful moon, the demon-priest reemerges, ready to devour Kaian. But Kaian's holy virtue and grace render him invisible, and the demon-priest, after searching here and there in a frantic, crazy dance, collapses in the garden.[69]

The next morning, the demon-priest recognizes that Kaian is a living Buddha, confesses his evil, and asks to be taught the way to salvation. Kaian gives him a *kōan*, a Zen riddle, in the form of the following two verses:

Kō getsu terashi shō fū fuku	Upon the inlet the moonlight shines. The wind in the pines blows.
Eiya seishō nan no shoi zo	The clear scenery of a long autumn night. For what purpose does it exist?[70]

He places a blue hood, the symbol of the Sōtō Zen priesthood, on the demon-priest's head, and commands him to sit and meditate on the meaning of the verses. He then leaves the temple.

A year passes. The trouble around Tomita has stopped, but the villagers are still afraid to go to the temple to see if the demon-priest is dead or alive. When Kaian returns, he goes up the mountain and finds the demon-priest chanting in a voice so muffled it is like the murmuring of a mosquito. He recognizes the chant as the *kōan* and screams, "Well? What is its purpose?"[71] He strikes the demon-priest on the head with his stick, and instantly the body disappears, leaving only a skeleton and a blue hood. Kaian's fame spreads, and the narrative ends by noting that the temple flourished and still exists today.[72]

The tale of the demon-priest could be interpreted as a simple moral fable illustrating the evil effects of lust and the workings of karmic retribution. However, the specific act that Kaian performs to save the demon-priest— that is, the offering of two lines of poetry—is an adaptation of the *setsuwa* form that infuses the moral fable with a recognition of the supernatural qualities of art. In this respect "Aozukin" bears a marked resemblance to "Muō no rigyo." Kōgi, who has accrued great merit through his good works, desires to experience the life of a carp. His wish is directed away from himself, and when it is granted, his metamorphosis is auspicious until he gives into temptation and experiences the horror of being eaten. Yet even though it does not end well, Kōgi's vision of himself as a carp expresses his dream of life and salvation. In contrast, the desire of the demon-priest is directed inward, and its obsessive quality leads to the much greater horror of consuming human flesh. But in "Aozukin," art and salvation are joined again in the form of the poem-riddle. The obsessive desire of the demon-priest is directed toward the path of enlightenment, as he focuses singlemindedly on the poems.

Miyagi's haunting, Kōgi's singleminded vision, and the demon-priest's obsession transport them to realms beyond normal human existence, not only as a ghost, a fish, or a demon, but also as individuals who achieve salvation. These transformations call to mind the state of detachment that Buson describes as the ultimate goal and essence of *haikai* aesthetics, and that connection is suggested by the register of the language in each of these stories. The rustic descriptions of emotions in "Asajigayado," the mundane language of the circumstantial detail of "Muō no rigyo," and the simplicity of the *setsuwa* form each set off the elevated language associated with both the supernatural and *haikai* aesthetics. The structure of "Aozukin," in which Kaian first hears the tale and then enters into the world of that tale, and in which a poem provides both the instrument of salvation and the narrative frame marking the beginning and end of the progress to enlightenment, points to Akinari's belief that art can transcend mundane experience and allow us to apprehend the sublime—an aesthetic state that, to borrow Edmund Burke's sense of the word, inspires both terror and spiritual awe.

The Culture of Adaptation

Akinari's practice of adaptation, especially of Chinese materials, seems strange in light of his connection with the nativist school of *kokugaku*, which studied ancient Japanese language as a way to get back to an authentic culture free of the taint of Chinese spirit (*karagokoro*). Akinari, however, was far less xenophobic than many of his peers, and since he considered the practice of literature autonomous and separate from the realm of morals, there was no reason for him to have been bothered by his debt to foreign literature. Indeed, the fact that he did not try to disguise more thoroughly his literary debt indicates that he did not consider the recognition of Chinese elements in his works an especially significant problem. His view of the artist as an interpreter of the tradition suggests an interest not so much in emulating or repeating the specific ideas or rhetorical devices he found in his models as in experimenting with the different narrative possibilities inherent in them. Shigetomo Ki has argued that with *Ugetsu*, Akinari

> strikes a new attitude not previously seen. For the first time he shows a tendency *to try to directly examine human beings and human relationships*; and it is by that tendency that we know he has been guided by *pai hua* fiction. It is normal in *pai hua* fiction for the author not to question the form, asking whether it is a miraculous tale or a ghost story, but to concentrate on dramatization and structure, and to forcefully indicate his worldview, or his view of humanity.[73]

The use of continental sources for fiction was a well-established practice by the time Akinari began composing his ghost stories. As early as 1666, Asai Ryōi (d. 1691) brought out *Otogibōko* (*A Charm Doll*), which was based on *Chien-teng hsin-hua*. By the early decades of the eighteenth century, interest in Chinese fiction was greatly stimulated by the activities of *kogaku* scholars. Okajima Kanzan (d. 1727), who had worked as an interpreter at Nagasaki, returned to Edo in 1705 and began teaching Chinese to Ogyū Sorai and other intellectuals. In 1727, just before his death, he published the initial section of a localized version of the *Shui hu chuan*. This was not so much a translation as a glossing of the Chinese original so that it was more accessible to Japanese readers. Another portion of the novel appeared in 1759, and other men carried on with this type of work. The *San yen* (c. 1620), a collection of 120 tales in three anthologies compiled by Feng Meng-lung, and the *Chin-ku ch'i-kuan* (*Wonders of the Past and Present*, c. 1640), an anthology of previous Ming anthologies, were among the most influential of the works to be either glossed or translated.

By the middle of the eighteenth century, adaptations of Chinese source works appeared that more thoroughly naturalized the original texts. In 1749, Tsuga Teishō (1718–1795?) published *Kokon kidan hanabusa sōshi* (*Strange Tales Old and New: A Wreath of Heroes*), a collection of nine stories in five volumes, eight of which were based on tales from Feng's collection. Teishō reworked the stories, setting them in the Kamakura and Muromachi periods, but perhaps the most significant aspect of the work is its style. In his preface, Teishō remarks that in an effort to echo the stylistic qualities of his Chinese models, with their mix of vernacular and classical elements, and to separate his work from other *sōshi*, which he thinks are entertaining but vulgar, he has chosen to write using what he terms an "elegant" style.[74]

Teishō's stories were widely imitated. Takebe Ayatari, for example, recast the *Shui hu chuan* into a native form, publishing *Honchō suikoden* in 1773. Akinari was also influenced by Teishō's work, as the use of Chinese fiction in *Ugetsu monogatari* makes apparent, and he even copied the format of *Hanabusa sōshi*, by dividing his nine stories into five volumes.[75] Chinese fiction thus had an important impact on the development of Tokugawa fiction in general and on *Ugetsu* in particular.

The Ming novels and anthologies adapted by Japanese writers did not arise from the popular tradition, but were products of literati culture. The popular tradition in China was certainly vibrant, nurtured by an urban culture and expanding social and economic conditions similar to those that later helped shape *chōnin* (townsman) culture. As would be the case in Tokugawa Japan, the reading audience in Ming China increased, and distinctions that might be likened to classes of readership subsequently appeared, with the levels and types of reading material growing more diversified. The authors and readership of the sophisticated works of Ming fiction, which were by and large the works that served as models for writers like Akinari, constituted a literary elite.[76] One of the characteristics of this group of literati was a tendency to use colloquial language or popular literary conventions within a framework provided by the classical idiom of their education.[77]

Given the great diversity of styles to be found among the numerous works of *pai hua* fiction, their most important influence on Japanese fiction was the general tendency to break styles into the two broad categories of classical (or elegant) and vernacular (or vulgar). This distinction became widespread in Japan in the early eighteenth century, when it was used by students of Chinese fiction, scholars like Sorai, to distinguish the classical and vernacular components of Ming fiction, and it was later used by nativist Japanese critics to distinguish between the classical idiom of the Heian Period and the colloquial language of their own day.[78]

The classical idiom provided one way to invoke the authority of the past and place the colloquial within a traditional context, and the vernacular idiom provided a means to create variations on the classical idiom and place the old within a new context. A broad correspondence with the aims and methods of *kokugaku* is apparent here, in the sense that as a literary approach, this method of adaptation seeks justification for itself in a kind of neoclassical invocation of an ideal past. The transmission of the ideology of Ming Neo-Confucianism was facilitated not only by similarities in the social realities and cultural assumptions of China and Japan, but also by the importation of literary models that bore the stamp of that ideology.

The accepted practice of mixing elegant and vulgar registers of language explains the hybrid quality of the literary style of *Ugetsu*, and this mixed style was a crucial rhetorical feature of Akinari's practice of adaptation, which shaped other elements in the narratives, such as plot, perspective, and characterization. A vivid example of the effects of Akinari's hybrid style is provided by the second story of the collection, "Kikuka no chigiri" ("Chrysanthemum Oath"). The main source for this tale is the Chinese story "Fan Chu-ch'ing chi-shu ssu-sheng-chiao" ("Fan Chu-ch'ing: A Meal of Chicken and Millet, a Friendship of Life and Death"), which relates the exemplary friendship between characters named Fan Chu-ch'ing and Chang Shao.[79]

Akinari's adaptation starts with his main characters. Akana Sōemon, who is based on Fan Chu-ch'ing, served as a teacher of military strategy to En'ya Kamonnosuke (d. 1486), a historical figure who was lord of Tomita Castle. Because Sōemon was a loyal and trusted adviser, En'ya sent him on a secret mission to Sasaki Ujitsuna in Ōmi province. While Sōemon was in Ōmi, Amako Tsunehisa (1458–1541), the previous lord of Tomita Castle, who had been dismissed for plotting an insurrection, attacked the castle and killed En'ya. Sōemon urged Ujitsuna to retaliate, but Ujitsuna did nothing. Sōemon slipped away from Ōmi and tried to go back to Izumo. On the way, he stopped in the town of Kako in Harima province, where he fell ill and was nursed back to health by Hasebe Samon, a poor but honest scholar-physician based on the Chang Shao character.

Their friendship deepens to the point where Sōemon agrees to become Samon's adoptive older brother. Soon after making that bond, Sōemon sets out for Izumo, promising to return on the ninth day of the ninth month, the day of the Chrysanthemum Festival. Upon returning to Izumo, he finds everything changed. No one remembers En'ya, and even Sōemon's cousin, Akana Tanji, has shifted allegiance to Tsunehisa. Sōemon cannot abide the situation, and using his promise to meet Samon as an excuse, he asks for permission to set forth. His request is denied, and Tanji places him under house arrest. Unable to keep his vow, he kills himself so that his spirit can make the journey back to Kako and visit Samon.

Apart from these details of the plot, Akinari's source work also provided the figurative language used to describe the virtue of loyalty that is the basis of the friendship between Samon and Sōemon. "Fan Chu-ch'ing" begins with the following poem:

When you plant a tree, do not plant the weeping willow.
When making friendships, do not choose fickle companions.
The purple willow cannot withstand the blasts of autumn wind.
A fickle friend is easily made, and just as easily lost.
You may not realize it, for yesterday a letter arrived saying he thinks
    of you.
But when today you meet, he does not acknowledge you.
A fickle friend is not even as good as a willow, which lasts longer.
For every time the spring breezes blow,
The branches of the willow will at least sway again.[80]

Akinari adapts this verse to create a narrative frame in his opening lines:

> Do not plant the verdant willow of spring in your garden. Do not form friendships with fickle people. The willow effortlessly grows thick, but cannot withstand the first blasts of autumn. A fickle person easily makes friends, but just as quickly will cut you off. And even though the willow will always blossom again in the spring, a fickle friend, once he has cut you off, will never call a second time.[81]

The fact that Akinari made such prominent use of his Chinese source as a narrative frame suggests that he was interested mainly in exploring the moral ideal of friendship, and except for the addition of historical detail to naturalize the account, "Kikuka no chigiri" does not alter the core plot of "Fan Chu-ching." Nonetheless, Akinari's use of a hybrid style transforms the structure of the source tale in significant ways. For example, the scene on the day when Samon is waiting for his friend's return is considerably longer than it is in Feng's version, and the sense of impatience is more palpable. Samon makes his preparations and assures his mother that Sōemon will be true to his vow. The repetition and tedium of his actions is given further emphasis by the scenes he observes on the street outside his door:

> The weather was clear that day, the cloudless sky seemed to stretch out forever, and groups of travelers passed by, talking about this and that. "Today's the day so-and-so is going to the capital. It's fortunate he has this kind of weather. It's a sign he'll make good profit." A warrior, who was past fifty, turned to his companion, a man of about twenty dressed in the same fashion, and said, "The seas would be calm on a day like this. If we had taken an early morning boat at Akashi we would have been at Ushimado by now. Young men are so timid, and they squander their money." The young samurai replied, "When our lord went to the capital he crossed from Azukijima to Murotsu by boat. But I heard from a friend that they ran into trouble, so when you think about it, anyone would be hesitant to cross there. Don't be angry. When we get to Uogabashi I'll treat you to some soba." They passed by while he was pacifying the old man. Then a packhorse driver lost his temper, and gruffly rearranging the saddle he shouted, "You goddamn nag! Can't you keep your eyes open?"[82]

This description of apparently random incidents draws the story out, delaying the resolution of the plot. The style, which is the colloquial idiom of the *ukiyo-zōshi*,[83] provides a familiar, ordinary context. It establishes a narrative ground that highlights the crucial moment of the ghostly encounter, which is described in language infused with poetic allusion.

> Thinking he might yet come, Samon stepped outside the door to take a look. The stars of the Milky Way twinkled coldly. He felt sad, as if the moon were shining on him alone. He could hear the howling of a watchdog somewhere. The sound of the waves seemed to draw near to where he stood. When the moon disappeared behind the rim of the mountains and it was completely dark, Samon thought, "He won't be coming now." He closed the door and was about to go inside when suddenly something caught his eye. There was a man among the misty shadows who seemed to have come drifting on the wind. Thinking it strange, he took a closer look and found that it was Akana Sōemon.[84]

This passage has less of the colloquial familiarity and vulgarity of the earlier daytime scene because it is consciously allusive. The image of the moon that conjures Samon's loneliness is a well-worn poetic conceit, as is the mention of the sound of the waves, a reference to the "Suma" chapter in *Genji monogatari*.[85] The contrast in the language serves as a prelude to the moment when Samon finally gives up. His disappointment seems to confirm for us that Sōemon is one of those fickle friends we were warned about at the beginning of the story. Just when Samon's sense of isolation and disappointment is confirmed, however, Sōemon appears. And just when he feels joy that his faith in his friend is justified, Samon learns the truth. This constant undercutting of expectations produces a sense of uncertainty and suspense. Neither Samon nor the reader know if Sōemon is a true friend until the proof of his extraordinary virtue, his ghost, appears. The moral admonition about fickle friends that frames the story does not lose its validity, but is transformed by the tension of the contrasting styles of language into an aesthetic narrative element that generates a mood of foreboding and suspense.

The use of this mixed style is extended in the last section of the story when the discursive practices of scholars of Neo-Confucian teachings or of *kokugaku* are suddenly introduced into the narrative. On the day after the ghostly visitation, Samon leaves for Izumo to gather his brother's remains.

When he arrives, he goes directly to Tanji's house and starts lecturing him on the virtue of loyalty.[86] At this point in the narrative, almost at the very end of the tale, we finally learn Samon's true purpose. Finishing his lesson, he suddenly draws his sword, kills Tanji, and escapes. Tsunehisa, impressed by this example of brotherly devotion, does not give chase. The story closes with a reprise of the moral warning, "Ah! One must not make friends with a fickle person!"[87]

Samon's learned disquisition functions as both a moral lesson and a plot device that lulls Tanji and the reader into a false sense of complacency, which is then shattered by the act of revenge. The structure of the tale's ending forces the reader to focus not on Samon's moral reasoning but on the beauty of his act, and admire it as Tsunehisa does. The rhetoric preceding the climactic moment radically transforms the model story, by suggesting that the supernatural encounter endows Samon with genuine moral and aesthetic authority, and justifies his actions.

Similar examples of the narrative effects generated by the hybrid quality of Akinari's style are present in "Kibitsu no kama" ("The Cauldron of Kibitsu"). Akinari's adaptation of his primary source, "Mu-tan teng-chi" ("The Peony Lanterns") from *Chien-teng hsin-hua*,[88] begins by paraphrasing a passage from a secondary source, *Wu tsa tsu*: "A jealous wife is difficult to control, but as you grow old you will understand her value."[89] The narrator does not agree with this, and proceeds to list the various calamities suffered by men with a jealous wife. The only way a husband can avoid such disasters is to be virtuous and educate his wife. The narrator cites *Wu tsa tsu* again: "To tame a bird requires spirit; to control a wife requires the husband to be manly."[90] This idea, the narrator claims, is certainly true.

Akinari once again uses an aphorism as a narrative frame. In "Kibitsu no kama," however, the story does nothing to contradict the truth about the dangers of a jealous wife. The plot follows the pattern of a love triangle—dissolute husband, suffering wife, beautiful courtesan—that figures so prominently in Tokugawa fiction and drama. Shōtarō is a young man whose drinking and sexual indulgence has outraged his parents, who are determined to mend his ways by finding him a good wife. They arrange a marriage for him with Isora, an especially good match because her father is head priest at the Kibitsu Shrine. An oracle at this shrine, a singing cauldron, warns against the marriage, but the warning is ignored and the prophecy comes true when Shōtarō meets a prostitute named Sode. This dalliance distresses Isora and angers Shōtarō's father, who confines his son at home. Shōtarō escapes with Sode, and they find refuge with one of her relatives, Hikoroku. Isora dies of grief, and when Sode dies soon after, Shōtarō suspects that she was killed by Isora's jealous spirit.

From the moment the lovers arrive at the home of Hikoroku, the narrative perspective begins to shift. Up to the point in the story where Shōtarō escapes, the narrative is in third-person perspective. Once Isora has been deserted, however, Shōtarō's view of events begins to dominate. He visits Sode's grave every night, and one autumn evening, he notices a new grave next to hers. A woman mourner comes to say a prayer, and they offer mutual condolences. In the course of their conversation, the woman tells him that the new grave is that of her lord, whose widow, a beautiful woman, continues to live in a desolate hut nearby.

Shōtarō, showing again his true nature, is aroused by this story and goes to visit the young widow. "Standing by a moss-covered well, Shōtarō peeked inside the house through the slight opening in a door covered in Chinese paper, and saw the light of a lamp flickering in the breeze, and a black lacquered shelf. He wanted to see more."[91]

The setting and the stolen glimpse or *kaimami* are reminiscent of the beginning of many literary love affairs. The allusive language of this scene sets up the vivid description of the ghostly encounter that follows. Shōtarō, anticipating only a romantic interlude as he is shown into the room where the woman is waiting, is shocked when he encounters instead the angry, emaciated ghost of Isora, and falls to the ground in a faint.

When he wakes up, he finds himself in a meditation hall that had long stood on the spot. He rushes home and seeks the help of a famous diviner, who tells him Isora's spirit is not appeased and that he must protect himself. Because spirits wander the earth for forty-nine days after death, the diviner calculates that the danger will last for another forty-two days. He writes ancient Chinese characters on Shōtarō's body and gives him slips of vermilion paper covered with special charms, to be pasted on all the doors and windows of the house. Shōtarō spends the next forty-one nights listening in terror as Isora's vengeful spirit tries to get into his room. When the final evening of his ordeal arrives, Shōtarō takes special care. After hours of waiting, the night sky lightens, and in his joy he tells Hikoroku to meet him outside. Just as Hikoroku goes to open his door he hears a scream so terrifying it knocks him over. He grabs an axe and rushes out to aid his friend, but he cannot find him. A late moonrise has deceived them.

Wondering what could have happened, and trembling in awe and fear, he picked up a lantern and looked around. There, on the wall beside the door, warm blood flowed, trickling down into the earth. Yet neither corpse nor bones were to be seen. Then, by the moonlight, he caught sight of something underneath the eaves. Raising his lantern, he saw a man's topknot dangling. There was nothing else. No pen can ever do justice to the sense of amazement and horror.[92]

Words cannot represent reality in this case, and the oblique description of the conclusion leaves the reader in a state of suspense and hesitation. We share with Shōtarō the dread of a ghostly presence that remains unseen in its demonic manifestation. Then, through Hikoroku, we indirectly witness the ending, and are left with the grisly traces that suggest the fury behind Shōtarō's destruction.

The shifts in perspective are a crucial aesthetic effect in "Kibitsu no kama," and are created by mixing classical narrative conventions with a more colloquial type of descriptive language. Initially, the perspective of the story encourages the reader to identity with the plight of Isora, but once she loses her human qualities, that identification (and with it the narrative perspective) shifts to her husband. This is not to say that he is somehow redeemed morally, but by presenting things through his perspective, we end up identifying with his horror and anxiety, and the question of his moral guilt gives way to the rhetorical logic of the supernatural tale. Isora's haunting is a self-inflicted punishment for Shōtarō: the pangs of the guilt he has felt from the moment Sode became sick. The structure of the tale, with its perspectival shifts, functions as a metaphor for Shōtarō's psychic and physical demise. As the story draws to a close, we are given a kind of double perspective on events through Hikoroku. On the other side of the thin wall from Shōtarō, Hikoroku vicariously identifies with the horror his friend endures, and allows the reader to vicariously encounter the supernatural.

Sophisticated use of perspective is an especially important element as well in "Jasei no in" ("The Serpent's Lust"), the longest story in the collection. Akinari makes the fantastic encounters with the supernatural depicted in this tale familiar on one level by providing some mundane rationalizations, but the effect is a narrative complicated by the text showing and denying the existence of the supernatural multiple times.

Akinari drew on two main sources: the story "Pai Niang-tzu yung chen Lei-feng-ta" ("The White Serpent Is Forever Subdued Under Thunder-Peak

Pagoda"), from Feng's *Ching-shih t'ung-yen*, and the Nō play *Dōjōji*. His key adaptation is the depiction of the protagonist, Toyoo, a young man who has lost control over his life. The narrator tells us that Toyoo "had a kindly disposition, enjoyed refined and elegant things, but had no practical skills to make a living."[93] Takesuke, his father, does not think highly of his youngest child. Afraid to give him his inheritance lest he lose it, and unwilling to risk the shame of giving him up in adoption lest he prove an embarrassment, Takesuke decides to let the situation run its course, in the hope that Toyoo will become a scholar or a priest. He figures that Tarō, his oldest son, can always look after his younger brother, and so he "does not try to forcibly discipline" Toyoo.[94]

It is clear that Takesuke is neglecting his moral duties. This not only sets the stage for what is to follow, but also suggests that the cause of subsequent events lies as much with internal qualities of character as with supernatural forces. The plot is set in motion when Toyoo meets by chance a young widow, Manago. His affair with Manago is a sign of a lack of moral discipline, a flaw suggested by a dream in which he acts out his sexual desire for her. His lack of control over himself and external events is further emphasized by a repetition of the plot. Toyoo is twice beguiled and nearly destroyed by Manago's beauty. The first time that she tempts him he agrees to exchange vows. In gratitude, she makes a present of a valuable sword, which turns out to have been stolen. Toyoo comes close to losing his life when he is arrested as a thief, and only the act of exposing Manago as a supernatural being saves him from punishment.

Shamed by his conduct, Toyoo moves away to his sister's home. There he again meets with Manago and her maidservant, Maroya. What follows is a remarkable scene, heavily indebted to "Pai Niang-tzu," in which Manago proceeds to turn the narrative on its head.[95] She first convinces Toyoo that she is really human by pointing out that she appears among crowds in the daytime, wears normal clothes, and casts a shadow in the sun. When Toyoo lists the evidence against her, including her supernatural escape from the magistrates, she explains it as merely a trick suggested by Maroya, and blames her former husband for the theft of the treasures. As she weeps, her demeanor is so gentle and vulnerable that not only Toyoo but also his sister and brother-in-law take pity and accept her story. They even tell her that "after hearing Toyoo's story we were convinced there are many frightening things in the world. But such things don't really happen in this day and age. These feelings that have led you here from afar are truly pitiable, and so we shall let you stay, even though Toyoo may not consent."[96] Manago's behavior is so proper that Toyoo again falls in love, and at the urging of his relatives, promises to marry her. He is saved only by the intervention of a venerable old priest, who recognizes the true serpent forms of Manago and Maroya.

After this second misadventure, Toyoo's parents try to help him by arranging a desirable marriage with a woman named Tomiko. Just when Toyoo feels he is finally safe, Manago appears a third time as a vengeful, jealous spirit who possesses his human bride. At each important point in the story, Toyoo is tricked into accepting things as they appear, not as they really are. The result is an extremely complex structure created by the mechanism of denying what has been previously presented as the truth. Toyoo's initial erotic fantasy is shown to be an illusion when Manago is exposed as a supernatural being. She then rationalizes what happened, and gives an entirely new reading to events. This story is in turn denied when we learn that she is really a serpent. Toyoo attempts to break this pattern of repetition by marrying Tomiko, but this shattering of the plot proves to be a false ending when Manago possesses his bride. The continuous use of false leads and false climaxes is a reflection of the state of mind of the hero within the structure of the narrative. Because Toyoo is concerned with finding his true self and with learning the true circumstances surrounding his affair, the focus shifts to the question of narrative truth. "Jasei no in" is designed to create the sense both of Manago's obsessiveness and of Toyoo's helplessness.

The style and structure of the story internalize key elements of the ghost story, so that the reader more fully identifies with Toyoo and his feelings of suspense, wonder, and dread. Moreover, Manago's temptations take on an allegorical quality—they stand in for the weaknesses of the protagonist's character—and thus give the reader a deeper sense of his state of mind. Akinari's adaptation suggests this allegorical reading through its depiction of the progress of Toyoo toward the moral ideal of manliness, of control over himself and his environment. The method of adaptation, however, imparts a sense of ambivalence, because the style fuses archetypal, allegorical figures with sharply individuated ones.

This ambivalence reflects the tension between traditionalism and self-cultivation, between the appeal of the authenticity and authority of antiquity and the desire for individual expression, rationalism, and the autonomy of literary practice that was the defining feature of Akinari's aesthetics. The same tension permeates the structure of ideology and methods of all the major influences on Akinari—*kokugaku*, the literati ideal of *haikai* aesthetics, and the mixed stylistic practices of Chinese vernacular fiction. Rather than attempting to resolve that tension, Akinari exploits its rhetorical potential for creating sensations of suspense and horror. By giving priority to aesthetic concerns in the process of adaptation, Akinari precludes an interpretation of the tales from a single vantage point, and thus denies the kind of absolute interpretation that a reductive reading based on totalizing moral values would otherwise demand.

Ugetsu Monogatari and Modern Ethical Consciousness

The rhetorical features of *Ugetsu* outlined above have led some scholars to classify *Ugetsu* as a *yomihon*. This term, which means literally "a book for reading," defines a literary genre and a publishing format. Most other forms of Tokugawa popular fiction relied as much upon pictures as upon text for their appeal. Because it did not utilize the picture-text format as much as other genres, was usually printed in runs of no more than two thousand copies, and was more expensive than other types of books, it is reasonable to conclude that a *yomihon* was aimed at a relatively more literate and sophisticated readership.[97]

Strictly speaking, *Ugetsu monogatari* is not a *yomihon*. The exhaustive classification of fictional types that included *yomihon* developed after *Ugetsu* was published. Nonetheless, even though contemporaries of Akinari did not refer to *Ugetsu* as a *yomihon*, it seems likely that they read it as an important milestone in the history of the development of the form. Ōta Nampo, for example, looked upon Tsuga Teishō's *Kokon kidan hanabusa sōshi* as the ancestor of the *yomihon*, while Bakin made a claim for Takebe Ayatari's *Honchō suikoden*.[98]

Whether or not we label it a *yomihon*, the recognition that works like *Ugetsu* exhibited distinctive characteristics identified as the origins of the form provides further evidence of a common concern among late Tokugawa scholars and literati with achieving a unity of morals and art by recovering the lost cultural spirit—the authenticity—of Japanese antiquity. Asō Isoji has noted some of the features of *yomihon* that reflect that concern. The form is not naturalistic but "stands upon a moral foundation, and assumes a viewpoint that elevates humanity and sees value in human life." At the same time, the *yomihon* is romantic literature and is not intrinsically religious or moral writing. Because it is a hybrid form, "the *yomihon* obtained a new and unusual structure that bridges past, present, and future. Transcending the present world, it attempts fantastic description."[99]

Asō's analysis, though distorted by an urge to read *yomihon* authors as 1950s postwar humanists, captures the ambivalent aims of the form. In its obsessive preoccupation with language it was, compared with other types of publications, self-consciously literary: "In the *yomihon* language takes center stage and stands before us. The narration of incidents and affairs gives language the principal role as far as possible, and words hold sway. We are struck by the magic of the language and by a singular type of feeling emanating from the words."[100] The synthesis of a moralistic outlook and an aesthetic approach goes beyond the didactic notion that literature must promote good and chastise evil—a notion summed up by the phrase "*kanzen chōaku*." The ideal of a unity between representation and reality instead points to a complex ethical consciousness shared by the writers of *yomihon* and their readership.

Reading *Ugetsu* as part of the literary lineage that produced *yomihon* is helpful in broadening the historical context of its composition. Akinari chose to adapt colloquial ghost stories in *Ugetsu* in an attempt to reconcile his beliefs in the autonomy of literary practice, which was based on a historical awareness of cultural difference, and in the authenticity of traditional values, which was based on a faith in the ethical authority of the past. Ethical problems are central to the nine tales, for it is the breaking of a moral code or in some cases the strict adherence to a code of behavior that creates the possibility for a supernatural encounter. However, none of these stories is limited to a narrow didacticism, and Akinari often uses his ethical arguments to serve rhetorical functions. In some cases, he uses them to help create suspense or surprise, and in other cases, the moral element of the story provides the means by which Akinari can present his variation of the source work. In all the stories, the moral concerns are transformed so that they produce not a didactic statement but an aesthetic effect.

Even though the autonomy of literary practice was a widely held assumption in late Tokugawa Japan, that autonomy did not free the individual writer from the authority of his tradition. Indeed, in a paradoxical way it bound the Tokugawa writer ever more tightly to the tradition as the source of values.[101] This paradox is reflected in the clear setting out of the historical context in all the tales in *Ugetsu*. The concern with establishing a connection to the past reveals an ethical consciousness that subsumes judgments beneath a more relativistic understanding of all human activities, including the practice of literature, according to the particular laws appropriate to them.

The relativism implicit in Akinari's historical consciousness was part of the trend in fiction toward a particularization of form and content that resembles in broad outline the developments that gave rise to the modern European novel.[102] Ian Watt has tied the appearance of the novel in Europe to what he identifies as a tendency from the Renaissance onward for "individual experience to replace collective tradition as the ultimate arbiter of reality."[103] Given the belief in the authority of the past in moral or aesthetic matters that prevailed during the Tokugawa period, Akinari's concern with history is not exceptional. It indicates that he shared what Maruyama referred to as the divided ethical consciousness typical of Neo-Confucian and *kokugaku* ideology—an awareness of the past as a lost ideal, and an understanding that language, customs, and values inexorably change over time.[104] As a result, despite the conventional praise of Tokugawa rule as a time of peace and prosperity that closes *Ugetsu*, the Japan that emerges out of this collection is truly a haunted landscape. Marked by a consciousness of loss and longing, Akinari's masterwork was situated within (and contributed to) a deeply conflicted discourse about nation and cultural identity that was never resolved. Instead, the discourse itself was eventually adapted, in the radical transformation of Meiji society, to represent the agendas of the modern imperial state.

2

Translating Mount Fuji

I N HIS 1908 NOVEL *Sanshirō*, Natsume Sōseki imagines the following conversation between the eponymous hero and his mentor, Professor Hirota.
Sanshirō has recently arrived in Tokyo from his provincial home on the
southwestern island of Kyushu to study at university. He and another student, a character named Sasaki Yōjirō, need to find lodgings, and one day
as they are wandering around the city with Hirota they come across a house
that seems appropriate for them. When Yōjirō goes in to inquire about it,
Sanshirō and Hirota are left to themselves for a few moments.

"How do you like Tokyo?"
"Well..."
"Just a big, dirty place, isn't it?"
"Hmmm..."
"I'm sure you haven't found a thing here that compares with Mount
Fuji."
Sanshirō had completely forgotten about Mount Fuji. When he re-
called the Mount Fuji he had first seen from the train window, having
had his attention called to it by Professor Hirota, it had indeed looked
noble. There was no way to compare it with the chaotic jumble of the
world inside his head now, and he was ashamed of himself for having
let that first impression slip away. Just then Hirota flung a rather strange
question at him.
"Have you ever tried to translate Mount Fuji?"
"To translate...?"
"It's fascinating how, whenever you translate nature, it's always transformed into something human. Noble, great, or heroic."

Sanshirō now understood what he meant by translate.

"You always get a word related to human character. For those poor souls who can't translate into such words, nature hasn't the slightest influence on them when it comes to character."

Thinking there was more to come, Sanshirō listened quietly. But Hirota cut himself off at that point.[1]

Lifting this passage out of context may make this brief interlude seem rather quirky. Sōseki presents the reader with an off-the-cuff, rambling exchange that serves primarily as a means to represent the flow of real-life experience in the narrative. The representation of incidents and quotidian details as if they are somehow accidental or uncalculated is a key technique of narrative realism. *Sanshirō* makes consistent and coherent use of that technique, creating the illusion that the conversation cited above is somehow a contingent, even aleatory incident stumbled upon by the reader.

Of course, there is nothing random about the creation of this scene. The exchange between Hirota and Sanshirō refers back to the circumstances of their first meeting, which is related in the opening chapter. Their chance encounter takes place on the train bringing Sanshirō to Tokyo for the first time. Because they are strangers meeting on the way, they do not formally introduce themselves to each other. Only later does Sanshirō discover that the man he met is Professor Hirota, and the coincidence strikes him as "farfetched."[2] The narrative goes out of its way to stress the randomness of their meeting and how unlikely it was, and this artful honesty offers a way to preserve the rhetorical logic of realistic fiction by calling our attention to a plot device that, because of its dependence on timing and coincidence, seems like a holdover from the more melodramatic techniques of late Tokugawa fiction.[3]

Because formal realism strives to conceal the lack of contingency in fiction, that is, to disguise the fact that seemingly random events are the product of willfully imposed artistic choices, it is noteworthy that Sōseki seemed almost driven to draw attention to the artifice that sustained his literary output. His short, decade-long career as a novelist was in fact distinguished by a remarkable openness to literary experimentation. Because Sōseki has come to occupy an almost unassailable position in the modern canon, the daring of his works may not be so obvious now. Yet from the time he began to devote himself heavily to writing fiction in 1905, his willingness to experiment is evident in the hybridity of the style and narrative modes he developed.

Sōseki's representation of the seemingly spontaneous chitchat of these two characters tightly and carefully binds this brief scene into the rhetorical structure of the novel as a whole. The scene not only adds to the accumulation of details out of which the story and its themes emerge, but it also acts as a rhetorical supplement, by introducing the notion of translation as a metaphor for Sanshirō's experience of coming of age in modern Tokyo.

The metaphor of translation situates Sōseki's novel in a historical moment when the discourse on identity was framed by the perception that Japan had become a translation culture. The limiting force of this perception is evident in the question Hirota puts to Sanshirō: "Have you ever tried to translate Mount Fuji [*Kimi, Fuji-san o hon'yaku shite mita koto ga arimasu ka*]?" Hirota doesn't ask him if he has ever tried to describe the mountain, which is what the adjectives he chooses in his subsequent remarks suggest. The word Sōseki chooses, *hon'yaku*, means translation, not description. The word is distinct from *hon'an*, which refers to adaptation in the sense of altering the conception of an original work in order to localize it. This distinction is noteworthy because Sōseki has his character Hirota argue that translation seeks to render the ultimate natural symbol of Japanese identity in terms of qualities of human character that exemplify aesthetic and moral values.

What is even more striking than the strange wording of the question, which Sōseki overtly calls to our attention by having Sanshirō refer to it as an *igai na shitsumon*, a strange (or unexpected) question, is the fact that Sōseki was able to imagine one of his characters asking it in the first place. Where did such a question come from, and what does it say about the writer who penned it and the historical context of its composition? The question evokes a number of concerns related to the historical development of various understandings of the constitutive elements of the culture of modernity. Specifically, Hirota's language and attitude in this passage, and in fact throughout the novel, is a parodic reflection and critique of the Meiji discourse on the ethics of identity.

The use of the word "translation" in the question is highly calculated, in that it makes explicit reference to the nature of Meiji-era culture, which was defined by its preoccupation with the paradox of how to translate the material culture of Western modernity into Japan without losing the essence of cultural identity. The fact that the object of the question is Mount Fuji suggests the desire to preserve Japanese identity by locating its source not merely in nature, but in a metaphorical nature that provides an authentic and unalienable ground that justifies belief in traditional ethical values.

At the time of their first meeting on the train to Tokyo, Sanshirō and Hirota observe a foreign couple, whose presence serves as one reason for their striking up a conversation in the first place. After remarking how beautiful foreign women are, Hirota tells Sanshirō:

> "We Japanese are sad-looking things next to them. We can beat the Russians, we can become a first-class power, but it doesn't make any difference. We've still got the same faces, the same feeble little bodies. You just have to look at the houses we live in, the gardens we build around them; they're just what you'd expect from faces like this.... Oh yes, this is your first trip to Tokyo, isn't it. You've never seen Mount Fuji. We go by it a little farther on. It's the finest thing Japan has to offer, the only thing we've got to boast about. The trouble is, of course, that it's just a natural object. It's been sitting there for all time. We certainly didn't make it." He grinned broadly once again.
>
> Sanshirō had never expected to meet anyone like this after the Russo-Japanese War. The man was almost not a Japanese, he felt.
>
> "But still," Sanshirō countered, "Japan will start developing from now on at least."
>
> "Japan is going to perish," the man replied coolly.[4]

This is a heady brew of sentiments—a mixture of national pride and scorn at the delusions of nationalism, of trenchant skepticism and feelings of inferiority and self-loathing. Although Sanshirō's initial nationalistic reaction is to see Hirota as somehow lacking the qualification to be Japanese, the professor in fact embodies the vexed condition of Meiji cultural identity, which was characterized, to paraphrase Antonio Gramsci, by pessimism of the intellect and optimism of the will. Hirota is a modern man who possesses the skeptical consciousness that allows him to see through the pretensions and parochial follies of his age. That same worldly consciousness, however, also cuts him loose from his culture, renders him spiritually homeless, and leads him on a search for stable values.

Hirota's conception of Mount Fuji reveals his skepticism, his obsession with individual autonomy, and his questioning of authority—attitudes that are given fuller development as the novel unfolds. Sanshirō, being a naïve provincial, a stock literary figure at the beginning of the story, has never encountered such worldly attitudes so directly. Yet as radical and iconoclastic as Hirota appears to Sanshirō, the older man's attitudes also give evidence of a deep ambivalence and conservatism. This aspect of his character comes to the surface when he implies that traditional values of character are crucial and that they are in danger of being lost in modern Japan. This ambivalence is further apparent in Hirota's assertion that those who cannot translate, who have lost touch with the literal, physical ground of values in Japan represented by Mount Fuji, lack the language of virtue and are therefore cut off from identity. Hirota—perhaps Sōseki himself?—is scornful of the attempt to evoke traditional values, and yet he avails himself of the tradition as a means to represent his ideas. He sarcastically pronounces Mount Fuji to be the only thing Japan has to boast about as a way to belittle the Japan that blindly strives to be the equal of the Great Powers.

Read within the historical contexts that produced the Meiji discourse on identity, Sōseki's ability to conjure up Hirota's strange question—"Have you ever tried to translate Mount Fuji?"—is more readily comprehensible. The question, by its own logic, indicates the autonomy that the individual can potentially exercise in defining nation, values, and identity, and in this way carries considerable significance for the novel's story of self-discovery and socialization. At the same time, the question suggests that Mount Fuji, by virtue of its sheer natural presence, is authentic and does not symbolize false, transient, or parochial values.

Mount Fuji holds metaphorical power for Hirota precisely because it is not manmade, but is the inviolable and universal symbol of Japanese identity.[5] He seeks to transform that power into values that accommodate his skeptical consciousness, so that he may resist those who translate—or more precisely, mistranslate—Mount Fuji as a chauvinistic symbol of nation. His view and the personal motives behind it, which Sōseki lays out for the reader over the course of his novel, point to the significance translation had as an act productive of national identity and as a metaphor for the paradox of that identity. If translation was seen as a necessary process in the formation of conditions that promoted modernity, then it was also viewed as a process that threatened the destruction, through hybridization, of the purity and authenticity of Japan. The cultural synthesis fostered by a coercive state was successful in the sense that it encouraged a widely accepted if tenuous notion of national identity. But even though the state's narrative of what was real attempted to disguise its own contrivance, it could not completely conceal the spiritual fissures created by the drive for modernization.

In this respect, Hirota's question about translating Mount Fuji is a crystallization of the contradictory forces pulling at Sanshirō, and at Sōseki's narrative, as the younger man tries to find his way and himself in the modern world of Tokyo. Hirota's own ambivalent attitude about his position in modern society perhaps explains why the matter-of-fact wording of his question seems so peculiar. He equates values of character, the basis of national identity, with Mount Fuji, a symbol of order, beauty, and permanence, in order to provide a reason to believe in them. Given that Fuji is a dormant volcano, its use as a symbol in this manner is ironically apt. For Hirota's notion of translation, his peculiar effort to fuse symbol with reality, is seismically unstable. The effort to translate a symbol into authentic values does not provide absolute grounds for belief in those values, but merely renders the symbol a contextless, empty receptacle for ideology. The metaphorical power of translation, as Hirota uses the word, derives from its close association with the master narrative of Japan's modernity. That is, the metaphor of translation stands in for the antinomy of modern consciousness, a condition that may be traced to the historical moment of the founding of the Meiji state.

Translation as Metaphor

On April 6, 1868, one day after Katsu Kaishū and Saigō Takamori had negotiated the surrender of Edo, members of the pro-imperial forces presented the young Meiji emperor with a document for promulgation that set out a list of goals and ideals retroactively justifying the Restoration and charting the future course of modernization. This document, known as the Charter Oath, promised sweeping institutional and ideological changes. The Charter Oath has received a considerable amount of attention as the ideological foundation of the Meiji state, but it will be useful to review its contents here as a document of the culture of translation.

> *Gokajō (no) goseimon to chokugo*
> An imperial oath and rescript in five articles
>
> (1) *Hiroku kaigi wo okoshi banki kōron ni kessu beshi.*
> We shall convene councils far and wide and decide all state affairs by public discussion.
>
> (2) *Shōka kokoro wo hitotsu ni shite sakan ni keirin wo okonafu beshi.*
> People of high and low station will be of one mind and shall vigorously carry out the governance of the nation.

(3) *Kanbu itto shomin ni itaru made kaku sono kokorozashi wo toge hito*
     kokoro wo shite umazarashimen koto wo yō su.

It is necessary that aristocrats and samurai, and even the common people,
achieve their own respective aspirations with singleness of purpose and
that the people/individuals will take care not to become discouraged.

(4) *Kyūrai no rōshū wo yaburi tenchi no kōdō ni motozuku beshi.*

We shall do away with corrupt customs of the past and be grounded on a
public morality that is universal.

(5) *Chishiki wo sekai ni motome ooi ni kōki wo shinki su beshi.*

We shall seek knowledge in the world and greatly invigorate/encourage
the foundations of imperial rule.

Wagakuni mizou no henkaku wo sen toshi Chin mi wo motte shū ni sakinji
tenchi shinmei ni chikahi ooi ni kō [or kono] kokuze wo sadame banmin
hozen no michi wo tatan to su shū mata kono shishu ni motozuki kyōryoku
doryoku seyo.

As our nation undergoes an unprecedented reform I myself shall precede
the people and swear to the deities of heaven and earth that we shall establish these great principles/plans for the nation and set out on the path
of peace and security for all the people, and that the people/masses will,
on the basis of these intentions, cooperate and strive [to achieve them].

Article 1 vaguely gestures at the language of a constitutional monarchy,
by calling for the establishment of deliberative councils so that government
policy would be decided by at least taking into account a limited notion of
the popular will. Article 2 hints at a moderate leveling of society by asserting that all classes of people should work together to carry out the manage-
ment of state affairs. Article 3 reads like a "pursuit of happiness" clause,
since it promises that all people, commoners as well as officials, will be free
to follow their own calling in order to avoid social discontent. Article 4 is
the most sweeping of the promises, in that it calls for a break with the corrupt customs of the past, referring to the notion of the arbitrary exercise of
political and judicial authority, and the formation of a kind of government
justified by its reliance on universal principles of governance located in "a
public morality."

Although the Charter Oath translates some elements of the rhetoric of
eighteenth-century Western political philosophy into the founding docu-

ment of Meiji Japan,[6] there is a disconnect between those elements and their ideological function, which disrupts the master narrative that the oligarchy promoted to explain the Meiji Restoration. Article 4 states this disjuncture explicitly. The new rulers of Japan in 1868 set out to justify their claims to authority by breaking with the past on narrowly moral grounds: moral insofar as their reason for rule was the reformation of customs, and narrow insofar as they present an almost exclusively instrumental justification for the break with the past. The language of this oath is a fusion of Neo-Confucian and utilitarian ethics, which allowed the oligarchs to make a claim for a universal ethics that could be represented in Japan by the figure of the emperor. They saw themselves as starting out on a new path while already possessing the ideological image, in their figuration of the emperor, to justify political and economic changes. The dual character of this justification is the source of the idea that the Restoration was a conservative revolution. The oligarchy's master narrative stressed a temporal continuity of events, a simultaneous overthrow and return that sought to conceal the foreign elements of the political discourse of the Charter Oath beneath the assertion of the radical (i.e., rooted) nativism of the Restoration.

Taken together, these articles make for a rather shrewd translation of the principles of life, liberty, and the pursuit of happiness, which in turn makes any attempt to trace out the origins of the original rhetoric referenced by the Charter Oath problematic. It would be misguided to see in the reformulation of Western principles a failure of translation, since that would ignore the impact of nativist ideology, separating it from the economic and political contexts that provide reasons for believing in the values associated with the institution of imperial rule and embodied in the figure of the emperor.

If the force of imperial ideology is demonstrated by the disconnect between rhetoric and intention, then the narrative of the Restoration as a conservative revolution perhaps overcorrects, downplaying too much what was truly new about the event. The Charter Oath's promises of social leveling and representative government were certainly not favored by the oligarchs, and even those like Itō Hirobumi, who later grudgingly accommodated those promises in the 1880s in response to the demands of the People's Rights movement, did so within a highly authoritarian framework. Even though there were many in 1868 who believed that a move toward constitutional monarchy was inevitable and desirable, such pragmatism was merely one of several competing attitudes, and it is not at all clear that the promises made in Articles 1–4 were meant to be adopted institutionally along the lines of emerging liberal democratic societies in the West. And yet, to repeat, ideology does seem to matter in a minimally instrumental way. Even if the Charter Oath made promises that were vague or unlikely to be implemented, its rhetoric accommodated not just the story of a conservative return to an authentic, legitimate realm, but also the story of progress toward a new enlightened civilization. The odd bivalence of the language of the Charter Oath created by the process of translating Western political concepts gave aid and comfort to both those who promoted the transformation of Japan toward a universal culture and those who resisted the concept of a universal culture in favor of nationalist aspirations.

Nowhere is the bivalence of the rhetoric of the Charter Oath more apparent than in Article 5, which can be termed the translation clause. Article 5 pledges to "seek knowledge in the world and greatly invigorate/encourage the foundations of imperial rule." The notion of knowledge (*chishiki*) should be understood here as being instrumental or technical. There was an established, institutional tradition of translating knowledge in this sense from the eighteenth century.[7] Moreover, knowledge refers to technical knowledge because, as we saw in Article 4, the oligarchs looked for culturally neutral grounds to justify imperial rule—that is, they assumed technical knowledge possessed a universal applicability that would support their notion of public morality. The twist in Article 5 occurs with its statement that the end for which knowledge is employed, as a universal instrument of legitimization, is the parochial one of imperial rule.

The rhetoric of Article 5 strains under the weight of the idea of cultural exchange that appears to originate in and decisively influence the progress of Japan's modernization. The contradictory assertions of this final promise are that everything is translatable, that everything can be reduced to universal, immutable laws, but that the essence of culture is not translatable—a form of chauvinism manifested as a belief in uniqueness. These assertions appear to share an underlying assumption that particular ethical or aesthetic values are interchangeable—or at least overlapping and any differences that arise are more an outcome of the manner in which belief in those values is justified. The style or form of justification is thus crucial in apprehending the reason why similar-looking goods—the catalogue of virtues that continued in force before and after the Meiji Restoration—are in fact quite different.

As noted in the introduction, the vocabulary of the catalogue of ethical values remained relatively stable during the Meiji period. It was instead the grounds on which belief in those values was justified that were subject to contestation. The source of that conflict is neatly summed up in Article 5, which states modernity's view of cultural exchange: everything is translatable, but the essence of culture is not. This strained conception of cultural exchange is reflected in the ethical consciousness promoted by the Meiji state, especially in its formation of imperial ideology through documents such as the Imperial Rescript on Education. This document, promulgated in 1889, took effect in 1890 at the same time as the Meiji Constitution, in a move to balance the establishment of a government based on the unsettling principle of the rule of law with the reassurance that new institutions were based on authentic cultural values.

> Know Ye, Our subjects:
>
> Our Imperial Ancestors have founded Our Empire on a basis broad and everlasting, and have deeply and firmly implanted virtue; Our subjects ever united in loyalty and filial piety have from generation to generation illustrated the beauty thereof. This is the glory of the fundamental character of Our Empire, and herein also lies the source of Our education. Ye, Our subjects, be filial to your parents, affectionate to your brothers and sisters; as husbands and wives be harmonious, as friends true; bear yourselves in modesty and moderation; extend your benevolence to all; pursue learning and cultivate arts, and thereby develop intellectual faculties and perfect moral powers; furthermore, advance public good and promote common interests; always respect the Constitution and observe the laws; should emergency arise, offer yourselves courageously to the State; and thus guard and maintain the prosperity of Our Imperial Throne coeval with heaven and earth. So shall ye not only be Our good and faithful subjects, but render illustrious the best traditions of your forefathers.
>
> The Way here set forth is indeed the teaching bequeathed by Our Imperial Ancestors, to be observed alike by Their Descendants and the subjects, infallible for all ages and true in all places. It is Our wish to lay it to heart in all reverence, in common with you, Our subjects, that we may attain the same virtue.
>
> The 30th day of the 10th month of the 23rd year of Meiji. (October 30, 1890)[8]

The argument of the rescript, which replicates the oligarchy's master narrative of modernity, may be summarized as follows: The source of all virtues is the imperial line. Two of these virtues, loyalty and piety, create the nation by uniting the Japanese people spiritually and historically. These virtues are linked to another key value, beauty; the intuitive, timeless apprehension of beauty is the source of learning. The argument then circles back on itself with its assertion that the goal of education is the inculcation and habituation of virtues. The abruptness of this turn is softened by the recitation of a comfortingly familiar catalogue of virtues that ends, not insignificantly, with the ideals of obedience to the state and self-sacrifice. By teaching these virtues, education reveals the truth, which is universal, infallible, and embodied by the figure of the emperor.

In its effort to translate a claim for the political legitimacy of a modern authoritarian state into the idiom of traditional, authentic values, this document makes a number of significant moves. First, it co-opts the argument of Fukuzawa and other proponents of modernization that education must play a key role in the cultivation of autonomy, that spirit of independence identified as vital to the formation of modern subjectivity. It accomplishes this by asserting that even though education may be the instrument by which modern consciousness is inculcated, its source lies in the eternal virtues of loyalty and filial piety. Second, it co-opts the notion of the rule of law, and by extension, the modern conception of ethics enunciated in the Meiji Constitution, by embedding that notion within a catalogue of traditional virtues. The tension created by the ethical relativism that inheres in the idea of the autonomous subject is resolved by claiming that modern culture is no more than an extension of authentic values. The Rescript on Education is a remarkable example of the way the concept of authenticity can become a gesture of autonomy.

The ideological formation of the Rescript on Education may seem blatant or even clumsy now, but it too is an extraordinarily shrewd political document. If translation erases parochial culture by presuming a common interpretative scheme, then the Rescript suggests that such a presumption meshes well with the master narrative of modernity. Like the Charter Oath, the Rescript on Education strives to preserve the essence of culture, represented by the twin fictions of traditional values and the imperial line, in the face of the universal applicability of the principle of the rule of law. The document tries to compensate for the erasure of culture, a historical process symbolized by translation, by appealing to the myth of authentic culture and collapsing the distance between past ideals and the realities of a modernizing state. Yet the imperial mythmaking that reframes Neo-Confucian ethical values and sentiments has nothing to do with an aretaic ethical system, since it assumes that the cultivation of virtues relies more on discovering and naming the essential values of the Japanese nation, which are immanent and inherited, than on internalizing virtuous habits and building character. And it makes that assumption in order to render invisible and thus uncontested its aim of making its catalogue of virtues support the apparatus of an authoritarian state.

The act of translating modern political ideas by means of traditional ethical terms did not simply naturalize those ideas; it also altered the significance of the terms by inscribing the foreign and the modern onto them. Even the most powerfully coercive political documents that defined national identity in terms of authentic values could not escape the paradox created by the hybridity of translation. For that reason, Hirota's observation of the tendency to translate Mount Fuji in terms of traditional virtues of character cannot be read apart from the ethical consciousness embedded in the founding myths of the Meiji culture of translation. To understand the full implications of Hirota's question, then, requires a consideration of how the practices of translation in Meiji Japan connected developments in literary form to the ideological use of translation as a metaphor for the experience of modern life.

Translatability and the Erasure of Culture

In his treatise *The Book of Tea*, Okakura Kakuzō makes the following observation:

> Translation is always a treason, and as a Ming author observes, can at its best be only the reverse side of a brocade,—all the threads are there, but not the subtlety of colour or design. But, after all, what great doctrine is there which is easy to expound? The ancient sages never put their teachings in systematic form. They spoke in paradoxes, for they were afraid of uttering half-truths.[9]

Though he seems to simply repeat the old adage, "traitor translator," something else is going on here. The reference to a Ming sage places the origin of the idea in the East, not the West (i.e., the Italian phrase "*Tradutore, traditore*"). This fits with the general aim of Okakura's own ideological project, which is to assert equal status for Japanese arts. The notion of translation conveyed by the image of Chinese brocade becomes a metaphor for appropriation, for claiming or asserting the cultural priority of indigenous values. The metaphor of translation operates as both a cognitive state and a literary device.[10] Put another way, the metaphor of translation is bivalent in force, as in the example of Article 5 of the Charter Oath, in that it stands in for the formation of ideology and its figuration in text.

To translate is, as Okakura notes, to recognize difference, to acknowledge and embrace otherness while obliterating it at the same time.[11] Translating heightens the historical awareness of the parochial nature of particular languages, which in turn makes manifest issues of originality and influence, of how true the translation is to the original. This happens because the very presence of the translation mediates the original text it makes intelligible. As a mediation of something assumed to be authentic, translation can be justified only if it maintains the pretense that it is accurate and sincere in its attitude toward the original.[12]

Of course, translation is so fundamental to cultural exchange that the self-contradictory nature of the process can seem like an analytical illusion, something that is there only when you think about it. Then again, this illusory quality precisely describes the status of translation as a metaphor for the problem of identity in Meiji Japan. A translation exposes its own foreignness as it comes into being, thereby annihilating its primary objective of achieving a synthesis of language and thought. All translation is a move, however limited, toward universal comprehensibility, but one that highlights the culturally and temporally bound nature of language, calling into question the ability of words to accurately transcribe the world.[13]

Although the classical ideal of translation is transparency,[14] the process of translation also highlights the inseparability of style and substance and the difficulty of conveying precise meaning. Octavio Paz has argued that all language is already a translation, and so the effort to be true to the spirit of a text is always doomed, because there is double displacement; the struggle to reconcile style and content is always already a problem of translation in the original text, and that struggle is simply brought out in the open by the act of rendering the text into another language.[15]

A translation carries with it the specter of cultural erasure, even as it serves to instantiate fundamental differences across cultures. As both a marker and creator of difference, translation, which otherwise is thought of as an instrument of cultural exchange, was implicated by artists and intellectuals in Japan in the ideological conditions that gave rise to the divided ethical consciousness of modernity. Just as the claim for the priority of autonomy in ethical judgment engendered a counterclaim for the authenticity of particular cultures, so the universalizing process of translation carries with it a counterbalancing assumption of the uniqueness and originality of cultures, implying that there is something genuine beneath the surface of language.

Translations are viewed in some histories of Meiji culture almost as a separate category of literature. Thinking of it as a subgenre is odd, but it nevertheless points to the significant role translation played in the effort to create a modern cultural identity in Meiji Japan.[16] Okakura's statement asserts that translation is a mediating barrier between a reader and the foreign text, which by its presence raises questions about authenticity. Moreover, the project of translation threatens to change the native culture, displacing readers from their own cultural origins. The anxiety that Meiji culture was caught in this predicament had important implications for representing the ethical values that defined Japanese identity.

The difference between the modern anxiety of cultural borrowing and eighteenth- and early nineteenth-century attitudes about originality and adaptation is striking. Akinari's method of composition in *Ugetsu* made no effort to hide his literary debts. In contrast, the conflicted position of those Meiji writers who wanted to emulate Western practices while maintaining or reestablishing a connection to their native literary traditions left no space for Akinari's more openhearted position. The strong nationalist positions of some *kokugakusha* gained in influence during the second half of the nineteenth century in part because of the perception that the flood of outside influences would overwhelm Japanese culture. As a consequence, translation, which was strongly promoted by the state for both pragmatic and ideological reasons, carried with it a stigma that was ironically less pervasive in the late Tokugawa, when the volume and content of translations were more strictly controlled.

Compounding this stigma for translators in early Meiji was a lingering bias against writing fiction in general among some intellectuals, who thought of it as a superfluous and frivolous activity.[17] Official emphasis and support had long been given to translating materials deemed to have a practical function, a view challenged neither by anti-Western factions, who wanted to strengthen Japan to resist the colonial powers, nor by modernizers, who wanted to promote deeper ties to global culture. The priority given to translating works of practical or technical importance also followed practices developed in the *Rangaku* (Dutch Learning) tradition, which had been officially recognized by the Tokugawa regime. Given this history, it was difficult even for some modernizers to reconcile completely their misgivings about fiction with the prestige accorded the novel in Western cultures.

This was certainly the case with Oda Jun'ichirō (1851–1919; pen-name Niwa Jun'ichirō), whose severely abridged translation of Bulwer-Lytton's novels *Ernest Maltravers* and *Alice* was published in 1878 under the title *Karyū shunwa* (*A Romance* [literally, "spring tale"] *of Cherries and Willows*). This translation holds an important place in standard histories of modern literature as a breakthrough in terms of the choice of material and the importance attached to Oda's efforts at the time.[18] Bulwer-Lytton's novels were popular in England at the time Oda traveled and studied there. More important, his novels reflected the nineteenth-century transition in the West from traditional to modern moral and literary domains—the same kind of transition from aretaic to consequentialist ethics, from melodramatic to realistic narrative modes, that Japan was experiencing. Oda recognized the hybrid quality of Bulwer-Lytton's novels, which inspired him largely because of their relevance to Japan's own cultural transformation. In a brief postscript to his translation, Oda makes clear his belief in the heuristic value of the novels in the process of creating the New Japan of the early Meiji period. At the same time, he downplays the foreignness of the originals to his readership by comparing them to romances such as *Shunshoku umegoyomi* (*Plum Calendar of Spring Colors*, 1832–1833) by Tamenaga Shunsui (b. 1789).[19]

By reading the source works in terms of an established pre-Meiji form and by presenting an abridged translation of the main elements of plot and character, Oda's work now seems closer to an adaptation, a *hon'an*, than a translation. At the time of publication, however, the work was advertised and accepted as a translation. Oda's choice, then, was two novels he felt demonstrated the value and desirability of modern Western notions of self-determination within a familiar romantic and melodramatic mode comprehensible to his readership. The specific readers he had in mind were educated men, and he saw his project as a means of enlightening them about conditions in the West. His purpose was as much edification as entertainment, and so he employed a somewhat simplified Sinitic style appropriate to the level of literacy of his target audience. As a result of this decision, even though Oda's contemporaries generally praised *Karyū shunwa*, his efforts had little impact on the long-term development of a modernized literary style and did little to change the opinions of some that fiction was an essentially frivolous pursuit. Oda himself certainly recognized the limitations of his project. In 1883, he brought out a new version of the work, in which he simplified his style in part by reducing the number of Chinese characters and by adding more glosses. He tells us in a preface that the goal of his translation was the edification of women and children, a change in purpose that illustrates the sometimes contradictory positions—acceptance of the need for translations versus doubts about the value of fiction—that translators sometimes held with regard to their own work.

The lasting impact of a translation like *Karyū shunwa* was a symbolic one—the fact that the task was seen as worthy at all began a gradual shift in attitudes toward the role of fiction as a marker of national progress toward enlightenment and civilization. The practical effects of Oda's methods are much harder to discern, since the fundamental transformation of the rhetoric of fiction by the vernacularization of the literary language did not begin until several years after Oda's work appeared, with the translations and fiction of writers such as Futabatei Shimei, Uchida Roan, and Mori Ōgai in the 1880s. Nevertheless, Oda's work is a historically important one, because it demonstrates the fluidity of attitudes toward the status of translation and its deep-rooted association with the ideological formation of the modern nation.

The eventual emergence of a vital subgenre of translation literature was a function of a more general trend toward marketing foreign cultures and integrating Japan into an international culture of print capitalism. However, the modernization of literary culture was not accomplished simply by introducing new publishing technologies or methods of dissemination. Creating the desire for a modern national literature—for that matter, creating the idea of a modern national literature—had to precede technological changes, in order to motivate their adoption. The change in consciousness that came with the production of a desire for foreign literature had a material impact in that it made the application of new forms of print media viable. A change in tastes promoted material innovations, which in their turn continued to shape tastes.

The rise of translation literature was also instrumental in the emergence of modern Japanese as a standardized international language. A brief overview of translation practices both pre-Restoration and during the first two decades of Meiji provides a starting point for examining this particular impact. One question that immediately arises is why was there an explosion of translation activity around the time of the Restoration. The obvious answer is the lifting of the isolation policy of the old regime, though we must be careful is assigning such an instrumental cause, since the availability of translated texts during the Edo period was limited but not especially rare. Indeed, some translations were given official sanction. More than previous limits on availability, the underlying cause of the Meiji translation boom was that the lifting of the isolation policy made the material presence of foreign cultures more immediate. In spite of its longstanding importance to Japan, China never exerted the kind of physical presence in Japan that the Western powers did from the mid-nineteenth century on. Even the King of Holland, trying to protect his own nation's interests, made use of that presence when he urged Japan in 1844 to open and modernize in order to ward off the threat posed by Western imperialist powers.[20] The Opium War in particular had awakened Chinese intellectuals such as Wei Yuan to the dangers of their own ignorance of the West. He wrote, "those who want to control the foreign barbarians, must begin by exhaustively studying the conditions of the barbarians. And those who wish to study these conditions must begin by creating a translation bureau and read the writings of the barbarians."[21]

Japanese officials took his warning seriously. From the outset of its more direct encounters with the West, the increasing need for translations was connected with the apprehension of material threat. The contradictory impulses to emulate and resist the West became entwined with the domestic justification for the oligarchy's rule. The materially driven need for translation was an important condition for the creation of the translation culture of modern Japan, but this need by itself is not sufficient to explain the boom in translation activity. There also had to be the means to enable the growth of a market for translations. Advances in publishing technologies, the adoption of the institution of mandatory education, which increased literacy, and the practice of translation as it had evolved during the second half of the Tokugawa period provided the means. In addition, the study of Chinese texts and the work of Nagasaki interpreters, especially those who created the scholarly specialty of *Rangaku*, had laid some of the groundwork that could be exploited in the new economy of print media.

Sugimoto Tsutomu has argued that the notion of *hon'yaku* as an object of study arises in mid-Edo, most notably with the publication of Sugita Genpaku's translation from the Dutch of a work of anatomy, *Katai shinsho* (published 1774).[22] The concept of the translator as a specialized professional emerges soon after, and the *Rangakusha* Udagawa Genshin (1769–

1834) included the term *hon'yakuka* (translator) in a list of professions he compiled for the government. The official recognition of translation was a direct response to the activities of Nagasaki interpreters, linguists, commercial agents, and medical specialists, who compiled numerous grammars and dictionaries in the late eighteenth and early nineteenth centuries. For example, Nishi Zenzaburō (great-grandfather of Nishi Amane) compiled a Dutch-Japanese dictionary using a Dutch-French dictionary as a model. Nakano Ryūho translated works on astronomy by Keill and part of Kaempfer's *History of Japan*, in which he introduced the word *sakoku* to describe the policy of national isolation. Sugita Genpaku called Ryūho the finest interpreter of his time, and Ryūho's influence was extended through several of his disciples: Yoshio Gennosuke, who compiled one of the most widely used Dutch-Japanese dictionaries of the period and who later assisted Phillip von Siebold when he came to Japan in 1825; Yoshi Shunzō, who ran an academy, the Kanshōdō, in Owari, and who authored the work *Yakki* (*Principles of Translation*); and Baba Sajūrō, who worked in the Astronomy Observatory in the Calendrical Bureau in Edo in 1808, and who in 1811 became the head official in the Translation Bureau.

Because of *bakufu*-supported work and other types of activities (*hon'an shōsetsu* or medical research), the institutional means of undertaking translations were already highly developed by the time of the Restoration, so that when the need for an increased volume of translation arose, certain principles of practice and elements of vocabulary were already available. This is not to suggest that the transition was smooth or easy. There was considerable need for more people trained not only in foreign languages but also in technical fields. Moreover, knowledge of the history of foreign (mainly Western) cultures that were the models for modernization was required to fully comprehend the cultural underpinnings of political principles and scientific methods. For that reason, some of the most important translations were in fields like international law, such as Shigeno Yasutsugu's *Bankoku kōhō*, an 1870 translation of Henry Wheaton's *Elements of International Law*.

Katō Shūichi observes that Meiji translations of Western concepts relied on four methods.[23] First, translators used terms from earlier *Rangaku* translations, most especially in the case of terms from the natural sciences. For example, anatomical terms such as *shinkei* and *monmyaku*, which are still in use, were carried over from Genpaku's *Katai shinsho*. The reason for reliance on earlier efforts was the familiarity of both usage and Chinese characters, which provided a degree of signification that transcription in katakana could not. Second, they used terms from earlier translations of Chinese. For example, in 1869, when Mizukuri Rinshō began his translation of the French Civil Code, he had no available options for rendering fundamental terms such as obligations (*gimu*) and rights (*kenri*, which had actually been coined earlier in an 1866 dictionary compiled by Satow and Ishibashi), so he turned to the Chinese translation of Wheaton's *Elements of International Law*. Third, translators made use of classical Chinese vocabulary. For example, they expanded the sense of terms such as *jiyū* (liberty, which took on a broader political sense) and *bungaku* (general studies, which came to mean literature). Finally, translators created neologisms (one of the most famous being *kojinshugi* for the concept of individualism) to fit the demands of their work.

Katō's analysis is perhaps overly schematic, since the process of standardizing vocabulary, which depended on trial and error, took many decades. Translations in early Meiji tended to exhibit a highly Sinitic style (*kanbuntai*), marked by conciseness and a reliance on elements of classical rhetoric that were recognizable to readers familiar with the conventions of *kanbun*. There were of course important exceptions, such as Fukuzawa, who tried to write and translate colloquially for a mass audience, but for the most part, early Meiji translations were marked by the established hybrid practice known as *kanbun no yomikudashi*, reading Japanese as though it were Chinese—a practice that was already a kind of translation. This style was gradually displaced, beginning in the mid-1880s, by the experimentation that marked the development of a standard form of written, colloquial Japanese.

Like items of vocabulary and style, the general principles of translation also exhibit both a debt to Tokugawa translation practices and a changed worldview that made translation seem a new and vital activity. For example, in the preface to *Katai shinsho*, Genpaku identifies three methods of translation: *hon'yaku*, which refers to what we understand as direct or literal translation; *giyaku* (MJ *iyaku*), which refers to loose or free translations and close in sense to the notion of adaptation; and *chokuyaku* (MJ *on'yaku*), which in this case refers not to literal translation but to transliteration.[24] These observations have a familiar ring for modern readers, since they echo the dialectic between the original text and the translated version at the heart of most theories of translation. That dialectic is carried over into Meiji theories, as exemplified by the ideas of Morita Shiken (1861–1897).

Morita was a disciple of Yano Fumio (1850–1931), who had called for a more thorough classification of all scholarly activities in Eastern culture as a way to emulate the rationalistic, scientific West,[25] and this rage for the order of classification is apparent in Morita's rules for translation, "Hon'yaku no kokoroe." This essay, which appeared in 1887 in the *Kokumin no tomo*, was written during a period of important literary developments, which included the publication of Futabatei's translations of Turgenev and of his own novel *Ukigumo* (*Drifting Clouds*), and the accelerating momentum of the *genbun'itchi* movement, the effort to fuse the old literary style with current vernacular usage.

Morita complains about the difficulties of translating that arise because of the use of ornamental terms from Chinese. For him, the use of such well-worn literary devices is acceptable to the extent that they are familiar, but since they only suggest general correspondences in meanings, they tend to lose the intent or "feel" of the original. He calls for an abandonment of this practice in favor of more literal translation, which requires a shift to Western idioms. In support of his position, he cites as an example of a good translator of Chinese the *kogaku* scholar and official Ogyū Sorai (1666–1728), who had argued against the practice of *kanbun no yomikudashi* in favor of looking at the original text to get more directly at its meaning.

Starting from this example, Morita warns against using inappropriate techniques when translating Western languages into Japanese. He proposes four rules: (1) don't mix in old terms, poeticisms, or adjectives not in the original; (2) use correct characters and words that don't have culturally determined meanings; (3) when ideas are expressed in set phrases or idioms, go ahead and use a similar set phrase in Japanese; and (4) choose neutral words and phrases, preferably in a conversational style that avoids peculiarities and mannerisms.[26] Morita reiterates the methods noted by Genpaku, and yet his rules, which seek a neutrality of style, seem far less ideologically neutral than Genpaku's more straightforward account. The aim of accuracy is a given for both men, but Morita is far more concerned with achieving translation that is invisible by erasing anything that smacks of parochialism, which would expose the contrivances of translation. For Morita, the ideal translation does two things: it transparently renders foreign texts into Japanese, and it re-creates Japanese itself as a cosmopolitan language of modernity.

Morita's aims, not surprisingly, align almost exactly with the attitudes toward translation in evidence in the foundational documents of the Meiji state. However, the availability of certain linguistic resources and practices that facilitated the translation boom of early Meiji was not enough to convey the kinds of information the oligarchy desired to propagate in order to transform the national polity and secure its own legitimacy. Direct contact with the Western world was necessary to be able to train people in the use of European languages, but such contact could never take place in a cultural vacuum. As is apparent from Katō's analysis above, the method of reading Chinese as Japanese, which powerfully influenced the work of translators, had a long history, but no such tradition apart from the relatively recent emergence of *Rangaku* existed for working with Western languages. This lack motivated writers and educators to seek a standard national language, a necessary precondition for the transformation of literature.

One of the early exponents of this move was Mori Arinori, who in 1872, in a letter to William Whitney of Yale, proposed the adoption of English as the national language. He writes:

> The necessity for this arises mainly out of the fact that Japan is a commercial nation; and also that, if we do not adopt a language like that of English, which is quite predominant in Asia, as well as elsewhere in the commercial world, the progress of Japanese civilization is evidently impossible. Indeed a new language is demanded by the whole Empire. It having been found that the Japanese language is insufficient even for the wants of the Japanese themselves, the demand for the new language is irresistibly imperative, in view of our rapidly increasing intercourse with the world at large.[27]

There is a fascinating conceptual leap here that seeks to span the gap between the demands of international commerce and the progress of Japanese civilization. Mori's proposal takes the uneasy tension in the language of Article 5 of the Charter Oath to an extreme. Mori distinguishes between *Nihongo*/Japanese as a language-in-use of a parochial tradition (tradition in this case equated with the premodern) and *Kokugo*/English as a national language of modernity in order to avoid the problem of translation altogether—a solution that merely throws into relief the extent to which Meiji understandings of the dialectical nature of translation were equated with the dilemma of modern identity. The linguistic self-erasure that is an inherent aspect of translation is replicated in the wider cultural erasure that occurred during Meiji, as the oligarchs attempted to resituate Japan in the

geopolitical order while redefining the meaning of the past and its significance to the formation of national identity.

Translation and Coming of Age

Reading the exchange between Hirota and Sanshirō in light of a sampling of
Meiji-era views of translation, the ideological sources of the scene become
more apparent, in part because these views give us some sense of the discursive connection between translation and modernity that enabled Sōseki
to imagine the question he has Hirota put to Sanshirō. Moreover, this discursive connection, translation as a metaphor for modernity, helps to situate the passage within the larger rhetorical structure of *Sanshirō*. That is,
Hirota's question ties the metaphor of translation to the larger aim of the
novel, which is to depict the struggle of a young man coming of age in a
modern world—the sense of wonder and marvel, of confusion and conster-
nation experienced as a consequence of his encounter with the new, with
cultural change and difference.

The rhetorical connections created by the metaphor of translation between this brief episode and the rest of the novel play out in a number of
ways. First, the scene helps develop incrementally some key questions that
confront the characters over the course of the story. How does an individual
adapt to, or translate, modern experience? How does one go about finding one's place in the world? How do the past and its values determine the
way individuals experience the present? Second, it serves to reiterate the
closeness of the relationship between Hirota and Sanshirō, by bringing us
back to their first, accidental meeting on a train. The coincidence is striking
enough to give a sense that their relationship was somehow foreordained
and thus a worthy subject of interest for the reader. Third, the presence of
two literary modes, which the text consciously draws to our attention by
combining the realistic quality of their banter with the melodramatic device
of a coincidence, points to the contradictory ideological forces that tug at
both characters, affecting the nature of their interaction and furthering the
development of their characters.

Hirota's cynicism gives him a worldly or at least world-weary air, but the
attitudes he evinces in the passage also expose just how incomprehensible
and threatening the modern world is to him. He is capable of witty paradox,
as his question about Mount Fuji makes clear, but he gives neither Sanshirō

nor the reader any substantive insight into that paradox. In that respect, Hirota, for all the vivid, realistic detail used to establish his quirky personality, is a kind of stock figure, an ineffective intellectual who in spite of his critical view of society remains for the most part passive and unable to engage the world. Insofar as he feels out of his time and displaced by the processes of modernization, Hirota shares traits common to a large number of fictional characters in late Meiji Japan. Significantly, the source of his passivity is a divided consciousness created by his own understanding of the place of the individual in modern society.

Hirota's ideas about the individual attract the sympathy and curiosity of Sanshirō, but they also provide a double-edged model for the younger man. On the one hand, Hirota insists that the autonomy of the individual outweighs all other considerations, even the nation—a lesson he tries to impart to Sanshirō during their first meeting on the train to Tokyo. He advises the young man that Tokyo is bigger than his hometown of Kumamoto, and that Japan is bigger than Tokyo. "Even bigger than Japan, surely, is the inside of your head. Don't ever surrender yourself—not to Japan, not to anything. You may think that what you're doing is for the sake of the nation, but let something take possession of you like that, and all you do is bring it down."[28] On the other hand, Hirota's advice to Sanshirō, to be true to himself, is qualified later in the novel by an admonition against unbridled individualism. During a conversation in which Sanshirō reveals that his mother is pressuring him to come back home and get married, Hirota tells him that he ought to heed her wishes.

> Young men nowadays are too self-aware, their egos are too strong—unlike the young men of my own day. When I was a student, there wasn't a thing we did that was unrelated to others. It was all for the Emperor, or parents, or the country, or society—everything was other-centered, which means that all educated men were hypocrites. When society changed, this hypocrisy ceased to work, and as a result, self-centeredness was gradually imported into thought and action, and egoism became enormously overdeveloped. Instead of the old hypocrites, now all we've got are out-and-out rogues.[29]

Hirota gives voice to one of the great anxieties about modernization. The importance of individual autonomy to the creation of modern culture was recognized, but autonomy was also seen as a threat to the authority of the state, which appealed to traditional ethical values to suppress that threat. Of course, the projection of power raised the question of what limits need to be placed on the actions and behavior of individuals. Hirota's advice is not unreasonable—his balanced sensibleness is one reason Sanshirō looks up to him—but the difference in his views, one advocating the autonomy of the individual while the other warns against egoism, indicates that for all the worldliness of his understanding of the contradictions of his age, he has been unable to find a way to overcome his own conflicted consciousness of modernity.

The sense that Hirota is wise but ineffective is not just the effect of contradictory statements—he recognizes that his own views echo the trap Japan finds itself in as a result of modernization—but is imparted to the reader in a number of other ways. Whenever Sanshirō looks at the professor, he is reminded of a Shinto priest with a Westerner's nose. That uneasy, comical combination provides the outward image of Hirota's complicated personality traits, which include an unworldliness of bearing that is hard to reconcile with his worldly critical attitudes.

A number of the other characters look at Hirota as impractical, even irresponsible,[30] and he sees himself torn between two impulses: the urge for quiescence, for a withdrawal from the world in imitation of the traditional scholar, and the desire for the active, engaged life of a Western intellectual. He believes his predicament started in his formative years at college, a period that witnessed the promulgation of the Meiji Constitution. In a scene late in the novel, Sanshirō visits Hirota, interrupting a nap during which the older man dreamed he met a young girl he had glimpsed only once twenty years earlier. In the dream, he asks her why she has not changed at all, and wonders to himself why he has changed. The girl explains that she has not changed because that moment was the favorite time of her life, and that he has changed "because you wanted to go on changing, moving toward something more beautiful." He replies, "You are a painting." She answers, "You are a poem."[31]

Hirota's self-image is that of an idealist who is also a confirmed bachelor, but his dream hints at desires he has never acted upon, suggesting that he is somehow emotionally stunted. When Sanshirō asks him when he saw the girl, he relates the following memory:

"The promulgation of the Constitution took place in 1889, the twenty-second year of Meiji. The Minister of Education, Mori Arinori, was assassinated before he left for the ceremonies. You wouldn't remember. Let me see, how old are you? Yes, you were still an infant. I was in College. A bunch of us were supposed to participate in the funeral procession. We left school with rifles on our shoulders, assuming we were to march to the cemetery. But that wasn't it. The gym instructor took us over to Takebashiuchi and lined us up along the street. We were supposed to 'accompany' the Minister's coffin to the cemetery by standing there. It amounted to nothing more than watching the funeral go by.... Finally the procession came, and I guess it was a long one. An endless number of rickshaws and carriages went past us in the cold. In one of them was the little girl. I'm trying to bring back the scene, but it's too vague, I can't get a clear picture of it. But I do remember the girl. Even she has gotten less distinct as the years have passed, and now I rarely think of her. Until I saw her in my dream today, I had forgotten all about her. But back then the image was so clear, it was as if burned into my mind."[32]

Hirota's deeply personal memory of this fleeting moment is set against larger historical events, which give the memory greater significance. The references to the Constitution, a document that embedded the ethical imperatives implied by the rule of law within an authoritarian institutional structure, and to the assassination of Mori, whose liberalizing reforms of the educational system also sustained the power of a conformist society, leave no doubt as to the conflicted state of the culture that nurtured Hirota's sensibilities. Being a man of a transitional generation, Hirota lacks the language of emotional autonomy that would enable him to make sense of the desires he associates with the trivial event of glimpsing the girl. Sanshirō immediately romanticizes this memory, assuming it is the reason Hirota never married—a notion Hirota dismisses out of hand, hinting that some people are incapable of marriage because they are emotionally crippled by circumstances.

To support his point, he gives a hypothetical example of a mother who, on her deathbed, confesses to her son that she was unfaithful, that the man he thought was his father was not, and that he should seek out the help of his real father after she is gone.[33] This hypothetical "for instance" is presented to explain why some people cannot marry, but its inclusion in the narrative at this point creates the suspicion, voiced by Sanshirō, that Hirota is talking about his own mother, who died the year after the promulgation of the Constitution. Hirota is a man who recognizes the importance of being true to oneself, of fulfilling one's dreams and individual desires, but he is incapable of acting on his own knowledge, because of the times in which he was born and raised. Hirota sees himself as an individual formed by a major historical transition, and thus not at home in the world of the past or the present.

This attitude is in part responsible for his marginalization at the university. He loses out on a chance for promotion and is even subjected to a harsh and unjust attack on his character, for supposedly encouraging one of his students to write an essay, "The Great Darkness," supporting his promotion.[34] As it turns out, Sasaki Yōjirō wrote the essay, but in an article attacking Hirota it is erroneously attributed to Sanshirō. Sasaki apologizes and Hirota shrugs the affair off, but not before he vents his anger and shock, stating that "the day a man starts up a movement on my behalf without consulting me, it's the same as if he were toying with my existence. Think how much better you'd be having your existence ignored. At least your reputation wouldn't suffer." This statement deepens Sōseki's portrait of a character unable to act either to promote his beliefs or protect their integrity. On the whole, Sōseki presents Hirota to us with a light, comic touch, and he makes him an endearing figure to the other characters. At the same time, Hirota is a prototype for the darker, brooding figures of Sensei in *Kokoro* and Kenzō in *Michikusa* (*Grass on the Wayside*). He is admirable in a way, but also a potentially damaging exemplar for his protégé.

Sanshirō in fact seems doomed to become as marginalized and conflicted as his mentor—an identification or doubling of characters that illustrates the narrative effect of the mix of melodramatic and realistic modes that Sōseki employs. The formal realism of the novel is a function of the detail with which Sōseki depicts Sanshirō's consciousness of his own desires and his longing for self-fulfillment. Such details create the illusion of an autonomous character acting on his fictional world. But Sanshirō lacks the personal resources needed to fulfill his desires, and the conflation of his character with Hirota suggests a dependence on fate and circumstance more typical of melodramatic fiction. Sanshirō's reaction to Yōjirō's essay tells us much about his character. He knows that the essay is empty rhetoric, and that Yōjirō has used him financially and is manipulating Hirota's situation. But being a "country boy," he cannot give precise expression to his feelings of suspicion and dissatisfaction.[35] The other characters remark on Sanshirō's naïve, innocent, passive personality throughout the novel. Sanshirō himself recognizes that his world and the real world are aligned in the same plane but do not touch each other.[36]

Sanshirō lacks Hirota's worldliness, but his dreaminess at least means he is not judgmental toward others. Such openheartedness would be an attractive trait were it not for a character flaw, his cowardice, which makes his passiveness so dominant. This cowardice is on display for us at the very beginning of the novel, when he meets a woman on the train to Tokyo. She asks him to help her find an inn at a stopover in Nagoya, but when they are mistaken for a couple, they end up sharing a room. Sanshirō has no time to protest—a rather extreme display of passivity—and he and the woman spend the night together. However, he does not take advantage of the situation, even though they share the same bedding, and the following morning the woman calmly remarks, "You're quite a coward, aren't you?"[37]

Sanshirō is of course stung by the remark, which to him exposes twenty-three years (his age) of weakness, and as he regretfully mulls over the lost opportunity, he thinks that no one, not even his mother, could have so unerringly struck home about his character. As it turns out, he is not quite correct in that statement, for after he arrives in Tokyo, he receives a letter from his mother, which gives him some backhanded parental advice: "You have been cowardly since childhood. This is a terrible disadvantage, and it must make examinations very trying for you.... You ought to get one of those Tokyo doctors to make you something you can take regularly to screw up your courage. It just might work."[38]

The novel goes out of its way to develop the character of Sanshirō as fully individuated, but like his mentor, he is ineffective and out of place in the real world. As his character unfolds to the reader, it becomes clear that the episode when Hirota asks him about translating Mount Fuji is an integral piece of the novel's larger mosaic of characterization and actions. Its importance lies in the way it contributes to a pattern of figurative language that likens the notion of translation to the process of learning—learning in the sense not only of Fukuzawa's notion of *gakumon*, of formal studies, but also of the development of personality through experiencing the world. Hirota's metaphorical conception of translation establishes the discursive, figurative frame in which all of Sanshirō's character traits and desires are played out for us.

A short time after the conversation about translating Mount Fuji, Sanshirō receives a letter from his mother. After reading it, he falls into a reverie in which he imagines three worlds for himself. The first is the hometown where his mother lives. This is a world of the premodern past, a dream world that is tranquil and drowsy, a place of retreat and warm nostalgia. He does not want to live there unless he fails to find a place in modern Tokyo and his situation becomes desperate. Still, it is a place he thinks of with nostalgia whenever he hears from his mother.

The second world is the academy, a mossy brick building where obscure, poverty-stricken scholars live peacefully, unengaged and unrecognizable to one another in the dim light of a fantasy reading room. Although Sanshirō is an indifferent student, anxious about the fact that the unfortunate men of the academy, like Hirota, know nothing of real life, he is reluctant to leave this world, which he is just beginning to experience and savor.

The third world is one of material success and fame, filled with electric lights, silver spoons, champagne, laughter, and beautiful women. He sees himself as qualified to join this world, even as a necessary part of it. Yet it also seems unattainable to him, closed off for reasons he does not fully comprehend.[39]

The desire to be modern versus the yearning to retreat from the chaos of modernity into a nostalgic past, the desire to be a master of the universe, imposing one's will on the material world, versus the yearning for the authenticity of the life of the mind and the spirit—Sōseki has cleverly refracted the competing values and jumbled desires of Meiji culture through the daydream of his young protagonist. The ideal for Sanshirō would be "to bring his mother from the country, marry a beautiful woman, and devote himself to learning."[40] This ideal is rather ordinary, even mediocre, but it still has meaning for Sanshirō, because he is so deeply invested in the dream. What matters to him is the process of realizing his desires, and it is here that we see the impact of his conversation with Hirota.

> The only drawback to this scheme was that it made a mere wife the sole representative of the entire vast world number three. There were plenty of beautiful women. They could be translated any number of ways. (Sanshirō tried out the word "translate" as he had learned it from Professor Hirota.) And insofar as they could be translated into words relating to character, Sanshirō would have to come into contact with as many beautiful women as possible to enlarge the scope of the influence derived from the translation and to perfect his own individuality. To content himself with knowing only a wife would be like going out of his way to ensure the incomplete development of his ego.[41]

This rather charming inner monologue shows to advantage Sōseki's skill at bringing his characters to life, and in setting up what is to follow, it also suggests the care with which Sōseki structured his narrative. For much of Sanshirō's progress in the novel is set out as small episodes of learning or failures to learn, which involve moments of translation. Most of these are passing references made in connection with some academic, often obscure subject. For example, at one point, several of the main characters discuss how to translate the line "Pity's akin to love," which appears in a stage version of Aphra Behn's novel *Oroonoko*. Yōjirō renders the line in the style of a popular song, producing a much longer Japanese version: "When I say you're a poor little thing, it only means I love you." As might be expected, Hirota is appalled by the tawdriness of the result.[42]

A second example is provided by the scene at a dinner party, during which Nonomiya, a scientist and young colleague of Hirota, ends up explaining in detail the apparatus and methods of his experiments intended to measure the pressure of light. The incomprehensibility of Nonomiya's statements is translated into a more accessible literary idiom when Hirota contrasts the work of scientists with that of writers of the naturalist school.[43]

A third example occurs in a scene where Sanshirō is out drinking with fellow students. Yōjirō uses the phrase *de te fabula*, which is incomprehensible to Sanshirō and left unexplained at that point in the text.[44] The phrase reappears in connection with a new foreign word Sanshirō encounters in his readings, *hydriotaphia*, the title of a book he borrows from Hirota. Yōjirō guesses the word means something similar to *de te fabula*, but "Sanshirō saw an enormous difference between the two. *De te fabula* was a phrase that called for dancing. Just to learn *hydriotaphia* was a time-consuming effort, and saying it twice caused one's pace to slacken. It sounded like a word the ancients had devised specifically for Professor Hirota's use."[45] He goes to Hirota to return the book and ask him the meaning of the word, but Hirota is napping when he arrives. As it turns out, Hirota does not know either, but the encounter leads immediately into the crucial episode when Hirota reminisces about the girl he saw in his dream.

Taken separately, these examples and other passages like them are minor elements of the work, but their accumulative effect is important. They provide a degree of specific detail and add a comic, occasionally satiric tone that enhance Sōseki's broad representation of university life and contribute to the realistic feel of his narration. More important, all of these references help to set the stage for the key experience Sanshirō undergoes in the novel, which is his first encounter with the emotion of love. The object of his desire is a beautiful young woman named Satomi Mineko, and their relationship is consistently framed within the metaphor of translation.

As important as their relationship is to the story of Sanshirō coming of age, it takes up surprisingly little space in the novel. The work is tightly structured but highly anecdotal and episodic. Moreover, even though Mineko and Sanshirō are attracted to each other, nothing much really happens between them because Sanshirō comes into Mineko's life just a little too late and because he is too timid to pursue her aggressively. Their relationship begins with a couple of chance meetings, in which they are never properly introduced, and even after they become acquainted, their interaction is limited to a few conversations, many quite brief and in the company of others.

Before he knew who she was, Sanshirō had seen Mineko from a distance. Soon after his arrival in Tokyo, he feels isolated and afraid, and goes for a walk near the pond on the campus of his university. When he sees her he is struck by her beauty, but also by a sense of discord and contradiction that she should be there at the university. Sanshirō, of course, carried this sense of contradiction with him to Tokyo. Just before he caught sight of Mineko for the first time, he was about to leave the calming atmosphere of the campus grounds and go back to his room to write to his mother. The scene, as Sōseki lays it out for us, is thus the first intimation of the three worlds that form the basis of Sanshirō's deepest dreams and desires: the premodern world of his hometown and his mother, the safe but unreal world of the university, and the alluring but frightening world of material success, individual self-fulfillment, and sexual awakening.

Mineko is one of the beautiful women who stand at the center of that third world of his dreams. She is the kind of woman he wants to "translate" as a way to cultivate his character and develop the full potential of his ego. This does not happen, and their relationship is finally reduced to a single translated phrase: "stray sheep." These words first come up in the novel when Sanshirō and Mineko, accompanied by Hirota, Nonomiya, and Nonomiya's sister Yoshiko, go on an excursion to Dangozaka to see the chrysanthemum doll festival. Along the way, they see a lost child, and discuss if they should help the child find a police box. Hirota notes rather tartly that everyone assumes that someone else will help so that they can avoid any responsibility. Although they express concern, they do nothing, and someone else eventually does help the child. The brief scene with the lost child seems like an incidental detail, but it sets up the following scene.

In the crush of people, Mineko gets separated from the others, and when Sanshirō catches up to her, she tells him she wants to leave. She seems momentarily disoriented and says that she is not feeling well. Sanshirō does not know what he should do; he is not really sure if she is ill, and Mineko is in no mood to talk with him. They continue walking until they come to a thatched house near a small stream. The scene is lovely, and Mineko opens up until Sanshirō breaks the mood by voicing his concern that Hirota and Nonomiya are probably looking for them. She tells him that they are grown up, so it doesn't matter if they are lost, but when Sanshirō begins to fret that they are lost and that the others will be looking for them, Mineko sees through him and recognizes his cowardice. She tells him that if the others try to find them, "All the better for someone who likes to avoid responsibility." Sanshirō does not catch her drift, asking if she means Hirota or Nonomiya. But the rhetorical punch of her silence makes it clear that the person avoiding responsibility is Sanshirō. He asks if she is feeling better and suggests they return to the others.

Mineko looked at him. He had started up, but now he sat down again. It was then that Sanshirō knew somewhere inside that this girl was too much for him. He felt, too, a vague sense of humiliation accompanying the awareness that he had been seen through.

Still looking at him, the girl said, "*Maigo* [lost child]."

He did not respond.

"Do you know how to translate that into English?"

The question was too unexpected. Sanshirō could answer neither that he knew nor that he did not know.

"Shall I tell you?"

"Please."

"*Stray sheep*. Do you understand?"

Sanshirō never knew what to say at times like this. He could only regret, when the moment had passed and his mind began to function clearly, that he had failed to say one thing or another. Nor was he superficial enough to anticipate such regret and spit out some makeshift response with forced assurance. And so he kept silent, feeling all the while that to do so was the height of stupidity.

He thought he understood the meaning of *stray sheep*, but then perhaps he did not. More than the words themselves, however, it was the meaning of the girl who used them that eluded him. He looked at her helplessly and said nothing. She, in turn, became serious.

"Do I seem forward to you?" Her tone suggested a desire to vindicate herself. He had not been prepared for this. Until now she had been hidden in a mist that he had hoped would clear. Her words cleared the mist, and she emerged, distinctly, a woman. If only it had never happened!

Sanshirō wanted to change her attitude toward him back to what it had been before—at thing full of meaning, neither clear nor clouded, like the sky stretched out above them. But this was not to be accomplished with a few words of flattery.

"Well, then, let's go back," she said without warning. There was no hint of bitterness in her voice. Her tone was subdued, as if she had resigned herself to being someone of no interest to Sanshirō.[46]

The word Mineko translates, *maigo* (lost child), refers to the little girl they had seen earlier at Dangozaka. In representing the English words "stray sheep," however, Sōseki elects to use the *kanji* for "lost" (*mayou*, the first character in the compound word *maigo*) and "sheep" (*hitsuji*), which he then glosses in katakana as *sutorei shiipu*. At first, it may seem that Sōseki wanted to avoid the jarring insertion of foreign, romanized text, but his choice of translated word is even more complex and distancing. Mineko's translation uses an unusual combination of characters that are glossed in a script that announces the foreignness of the word every bit as much as romanized script. In an odd way, the English becomes more pronounced because of the multiple layers of signification. No wonder Mineko loses Sanshirō, though the narrative makes it clear that he is of course lost well before Mineko translates the word *maigo* for him.

Is she calling him a lost child, merely recalling the earlier incident, or is she calling herself a lost child? The vagueness of the utterance makes it plausible that all three meanings are intended. The notion that Sanshirō is a stray sheep has already been established, while Mineko is presented as a young woman cut adrift and free-floating in society. In the eyes of a young man like Sanshirō, she possesses the allure and vivaciousness of a modern woman who has a degree of autonomy unthinkable before the Meiji period. Yet the same freedom that makes her seem coquettish, available, and, in Hirota's opinion, reckless, also makes her frightening to him. The misogyny of Hirota and Sanshirō is a manifestation of their own weaknesses, but in projecting a licentious image upon her, they also reveal that, for her part, Mineko is a wistful, sad character. She is a modern woman insofar as she does not want to marry if she cannot choose for herself. But in the hybrid culture of late Meiji, where traditional attitudes still strongly persist, her attitudes make her a lost sheep who does not possess true freedom and cannot act on her own desires—a condition as conflicted and unfulfilled as Hirota's and Sanshirō's.

The full significance of the translation, "stray sheep," is not revealed until the end of the novel. A short time after the Dangozaka excursion, an up-and-coming painter named Haraguchi, who works in Western-style forms, particularly portraiture, decides that he will do a formal painting of Mineko for an exhibition. The creation of this painting takes place over the last part of the novel, one of a number of episodes woven together to fill out the representation of Sanshirō's world. The novel is not strongly plot driven; there are no great, earth-shattering events that bring the story to a clearly defined conclusion. Instead, a number of small incidents and crises—Yōjirō borrowing money from Sanshirō, who then has to borrow money from Mineko; the failure of Hirota to be promoted and the damage to his reputation caused by Yōjirō's clumsy essay; the production of a Japanese version of *Hamlet* that Yōjirō is involved with; Sanshirō's brief illness from influenza—form an ordinary backdrop against which Sanshirō's relationship with Mineko passively plays itself out.

During his convalescence, Sanshirō learns, first from Yōjirō and then from Nonomiya's sister Yoshiko, that Mineko is getting married. Her fiancé, Yōjirō notes, is the same man who had also sought Yoshiko's hand in marriage. Yoshiko is deeply hurt by this turn of events, but despite the mild undercurrent of sexual tension that exists between her and Sanshirō, he views her as slightly odd, and she is never quite able to attract his attention or interest. One Sunday, six days after Yoshiko's visit, he decides to call on Mineko. Yoshiko, who has been living with Mineko's family, greets him instead, and tells him that Mineko has gone off to church. This is the first time Sanshirō has heard that Mineko is a Christian. Her religion is completely foreign to Sanshirō, who has never been inside a church—a fact underscoring just how little he understands her life. He goes to the church with the intent of paying back the money he owes her, and as he waits outside, he can hear Mineko's voice singing with the congregation. The singing stops and Sanshirō looks up at some clouds that now have deep associations for him. "Once, he had looked at the autumn sky with Mineko. That had been upstairs at Professor Hirota's. Once, he had sat by a little stream in the fields. He had not been alone then, either. *Stray sheep. Stray sheep.* The clouds looked like sheep."[47]

When the service ends, they engage in a brief, awkward conversation. She quietly accepts the money he is returning to her, and as she puts away her handkerchief, he catches the scent of her perfume, *Heliotrope*, which recalls for Sanshirō an earlier memory of Mineko and brings him back to the words "stray sheep." After she confirms that she is getting married, Sanshirō is no longer able to talk with her. She stares at him for a moment, then releases an almost inaudible sigh. Touching a slender hand to her rich eyebrows, she murmurs, "For I acknowledge my transgressions, and my sin is ever before me."[48] The wistfulness of this scene tinges the end of their relationship, such as it was, with a romanticism appropriate to a story of young, unrequited love.

Sanshirō and Mineko's final exchange, however, is not without a hint of impending darkness and sad regret. Mineko's Christianity is a revelation that suddenly casts her previous actions in a different light. She is Westernized to a far greater degree than Sanshirō, and that quality, which before was marked in the narrative mainly by her facility in English, is apparent at the end in her radically different ethical consciousness. Her sense of guilt over her own desires and her struggle to control them are an assertion of a sense of autonomy that is still out of place for a woman in her society. Her prayer of repentance at the end explains why her translation of *maigo*, "lost child," as "stray sheep" is not a mistranslation, but, with its use of a Christian image, a perfect description of the guilt and perplexity she feels over who she is: a woman caught in the moral and spiritual limbo created by the hybrid culture of late Meiji Japan.

And how does Sanshirō translate Mineko's translation? As soon as he finishes speaking with her, Sanshirō goes back to his room to find a telegram from his mother, asking when he plans to leave Tokyo for a visit to his hometown. Sōseki goes out of his way to remind the reader of the incompatibility of the worlds that Sanshirō dreams about, but that small detail determines how we read Sanshirō's translation in the very short chapter that ends the novel. Haraguchi's finished portrait is on display at a gallery called the Tanseikai. We learn that Mineko is now married, since she visits the exhibition with her husband on the day after the opening. On the Saturday following the opening, Hirota, Nonomiya, Yōjirō, and Sanshirō visit. Sanshirō is still evidently torn by his feelings of regret over Mineko and is clearly unhappy about his companions' superficial banter over the merits of the work. The novel closes with Yōjirō asking Sanshirō what he thinks of the title of the painting, "The Girl in the Forest." Sanshirō says that it is no good, and when Yōjirō asks him for a better alternative, he does not reply, but merely thinks "Stray sheep. Stray sheep."[49]

By using this translated phrase at the conclusion of the novel, Sōseki achieves at a stroke a sense of perfect ending that provides the satisfaction of a completely realized formal structure without closing off the open, developing quality of Sanshirō's character. Instead, the novel leaves us to ponder what exactly Sanshirō names with his title for the painting. He is certainly identifying Mineko, but the meaning of "stray sheep" is now also a projection onto the painting of his own unrealized desires. All of the rhetorical elements of the novel come together at the very end in a translated phrase that conflates once and forever the stories of Hirota and Sanshirō and gives us a glimpse into the young man's fate. In Hirota's dream of meeting the young girl he saw only briefly twenty years earlier, he called her a "painting," an unchanging image of his ideals that can never threaten to upset his world because it is not real, is not flesh and blood, poses no possibility of loss, and demands no emotional commitment or sense of responsibility. For Sanshirō, Mineko is now reduced to a painting as well, and her transformation into an idealized form that represents his unrealized dreams is a form of misogyny, an expression of his fear of women that blocks him from taking responsibility or even from acting according to the dictates of his desires. His disgruntled, private retitling of the work gives the translation "stray sheep" a new significance that has an effect on the development of his character. It does not change his cowardice or his passiveness, but rather reinforces these traits of character by giving him a sense of loss, of being lost. It justifies his suspicion that ultimately he has no control over—and is thus not responsible for—the forces that determine the course of his life.

The mix of melodramatic and realistic elements by which Sōseki brings his plot and characterization to a conclusion was a recurrent feature of much of his fiction. When the quest for self-realization is blocked by factors beyond the control of a character, as it is for Sanshirō, the narrative mode tends toward melodrama. One of the defining elements of melodrama is timing—being too early, too late, or coincidental—and timing is equated with luck, with a lack of control and autonomy. Apart from externalities— the use of deus ex machina, the presence of luck—melodramatic narratives also tend to rely on externalized character types rather than interior character development, implying that even personality traits are not subject to autonomous control but are contingent. Again, we see this melodramatic tendency at work in the portrayal of Sanshirō as a particular archetype of modern capitalist culture, a young man of rural upbringing who comes to the city to make his way in the world.

As important as these older elements are to Sōseki's conception, the primary literary mode of *Sanshirō* is not melodrama. Sōseki provides more than enough background detail and incident to individuate his protagonist and show that he is no mere archetype. The realistic representation of the interior development, especially the moral education of the main character, is most evident where the plot turns on the subjective choices made by Sanshirō. The development of his character and identity is in part a matter of chance and circumstances beyond his control, but because Sanshirō is so conscious of his circumstances, it is also an exercise of will, of learning to represent, or as he puts it, to translate his open-ended, private experience to himself and others.

The tension inherent to the process of translation, the struggle between the desire for communion with society and the anxiety of self-erasure, is at the center of the Meiji discourse on identity. Immersion in that discourse, especially in the anxious, turbulent, and heady years immediately following the Russo-Japanese War, enabled Sōseki to conceive of Hirota's question. Meiji conceptions of translation are reflected in literature in both the hybridity of narrative form and as a dominant metaphor employed by the state to legitimize its power and represent a master narrative of modernization. The state and its disciplining institutions had no choice but to tolerate, even exploit, the notion of autonomy, but it worked to constrain that notion, by translating it into the ethical values of pre-Meiji Japan. The result was a series of metaphorical constructions—the self-made individual, the youth coming of age, the evolution of nations, the state as family—that conveyed a definition, however tautological, of modern cultural identity. Of all these metaphorical constructions, the young man coming of age proved an exceptionally potent one, signifying the vulnerability, potential, and awakening of both the individual and the state.

The metaphorical meanings of translation extended to the realm of literature, in the argument over the place of fiction in modern society. The claim that fiction was an expression of individual will and creativity, and thus a sign of modernity, was countered by the longstanding idea that fiction was not a legitimate form of expression because it strayed beyond the boundaries established by earlier ethical discourses on the individual and society. By the close of Meiji, a legitimate role for fiction in shaping the discourse on autonomy and the individual was recognized, as Sōseki's stature attests. The public role of literature, however, continued to be circumscribed, in that it was viewed as a sphere separate from political action. In such a society, it was possible to begin to find oneself, as Sanshirō does, and still be lost.

3
Manly Virtue and Modern Identity

THE HYBRIDITY OF THE fiction of Akinari and Sōseki is an effect of the
process of transforming certain ideological tendencies—to define individual or national identity in terms of ethical values, to assume that historical consciousness and subjective experience are vital to knowledge—into
textual figures. For Akinari, the representation of ideology in *Ugetsu* was
accomplished through the practice of adaptation, which invoked the power
of present language to recover the haunting, lost ideal of the undivided ethical consciousness of the past. For Sōseki, the figuration of ideology in his
novel *Sanshirō* was achieved through the metaphor of translation, which
conflated the individual experience of a young man coming of age with the
historical narrative of the emergence of a modern nation.

The perceived connection between subjectivity and modern culture
that gradually emerged during the late Tokugawa and early Meiji periods is
manifest in the literary movements and narrative modes (naturalism, confessional literature, *roman a clef*, and the I-novel) that address the ideological formation of the self as a problem of both theme and form. Certainly
Sanshirō, with its experimental realism and coming-of-age story, exemplifies this aspect of modern literary history. But perhaps the Meiji-period
novel that most directly and transparently explores the relationship between ideology and the figuration of selfhood in text is *Seinen* (*Youth*, 1910),
by Mori Ōgai (1862–1922).

Seinen is also a hybrid narrative, a Japanese *Bildungsroman* that trans-
poses a German narrative model onto native conventions for representing
the ideal of manly virtue. The subject matter of a *Bildungsroman* is the
realization of the protagonist's identity through his integration into society
and its values.[1] Or, to take Hegel's blunter definition, the genre is all about

a young male protagonist who, in the course of the story, gets his girl and a position in the world, marries, and becomes a philistine just like everyone else.[2] Since Ōgai could at times come across in his writing as striving and irritatingly confident (in contrast to Sōseki's occasional fits of brooding fastidiousness), it is tempting to conclude on the basis of Hegel's definition that the *Bildungsroman* was the perfect narrative form for him to choose. Personality tics aside, it is clear that the background of the author—the four years he spent in Germany and an early literary career built in large part on translations of German literature and philosophy—was an important factor in his decision to exploit the literary possibilities offered by the *Bildungsroman* and explore the question of how to achieve a sense of selfhood and identity in a period of immense social upheaval.

The personal confrontation with a moral dilemma or crisis, the danger posed by that crisis to the development of the self, and the need to be able to discriminate wisely between authentic and illusory values are important narrative signposts in marking the progress of the personal development of the protagonist in a *Bildungsroman. Seinen* shares the general trajectory of narrative movement dictated by this interior quest, but what distinguishes this work is the equation of the search for identity with the achievement of manly virtue. Manly virtue is the ultimate value toward which the education of Ōgai's young protagonist, Koizumi Jun'ichi, is directed; it is the social norm that defines—or closes off—the open-ended conception of the autonomous individual.

Because it may be misleading to apply Western critical terminology to a work from a non-Western tradition, it is important to consider the issue of how Western expectations and critical terminologies are brought to bear on readings of Japanese fiction before examining in more detail the ways Ōgai adapted the *Bildungsroman.* The cultural specificity of the values that gave rise to and found expression in the *Bildungsroman* may make it appear inappropriate, at first sight, to apply the term to works in the Japanese tradition. Yet certain qualities of this narrative form seem relevant to developments in modern Japanese fiction, especially the growing crisis of representation of real identities that accompanied the Meiji cultural synthesis. As Martin Swales puts it, "the self-consciousness of the Bildungsroman, its discursiveness and self-reflectivity, its narrative obliqueness, its concern for the elusiveness of selfhood, its dialectical critique of the role of plot in the novel—all these things are not merely German (that is provincial) excesses; they are the staple diet of the modern novelist's unease in respect of the form he has inherited."[3]

These features of the *Bildungsroman* point to the wider underlying struggle between the need to assert autonomy as one of the defining features of modern conceptions of selfhood and the need to express that autonomy within a conventional cultural frame of reference. The struggle at the heart of the *Bildungsroman* not only applies to the specific case of *Seinen*, but also serves as an analogue to more general tendencies in Meiji fiction. During the eighteenth and nineteenth centuries, when the *Bildungsroman* emerged, the German tradition diverged from the broad trend toward expansive works of formal realism occurring in British, French, and Russian literature. The fact that Meiji fiction moved in a direction similar to that taken by German fiction—that is, toward a highly self-conscious fiction obsessed with the question of identity and skeptical of the act of narrating—cannot be taken as an indication of any decisive German influence. Though it is tempting to attribute similarities in narrative developments in Japan and Germany to the notion that they were late modernizers, such a dubious argument levels significant historical and cultural differences. For one thing, it ignores the fact that Japan was on the cultural periphery of the West. For another, many of the most important narrative experiments of mid-Meiji literature are attempts at formal realism, not rejections of it. Finally, even in the West, formal realism hardly constituted a monolithic narrative mode, and so the sources of Western literary influence are neither direct nor clearly cut. Instead, the skepticism, self-consciousness, and interiority of much late Meiji fiction are responses to the sense of severe cultural marginalization and belatedness Japan experienced in the face of Western imperialism.

The term "Japanese *Bildungsroman*" describes a particular instance of the general phenomenon of a conscious embrace of hybridity in modern Japanese literary forms, and in the case of *Seinen*, the term is accurate, insofar as it broadly captures the fundamental elements of the novel. However, the term is also so sweeping that it raises a troubling question about the accuracy of crosscultural classifications. The operative term describes a Western form and emphasizes the fact that *Seinen* is a modification or variant, which implies that our final appraisal of the work must ultimately appeal to Western standards. The term is therefore double-edged: not only does "*Bildungsroman*" call attention to the hegemony of Western standards, but even "Japanese" signifies a conception of nation that reinforces Japan's position on the periphery of modern culture and the myth of its unique status.[4]

As we have seen with both Akinari and Sōseki, adaptation and experimentation do not necessarily have to give privilege of place to foreign cultural forms. The prose fiction of modern Japan, beginning with examples of Tokugawa adaptations of Chinese literature, illustrates the complexity of the interactions between competing modes of narrative representation. Narrative types and conventions common in the literature of Japan before its encounter with the West first coexist with Western types on a relatively equal footing and then, during the ongoing experiments of the period, are conflated with Western forms.

The adaptation or localization of a narrative form like the *Bildungsroman* clearly indicates the extent of Western cultural influence, but recognizing such influence is only part of the critical equation. During the process of adaptation, the author, even one in a highly marginalized culture, exerts a strong degree of control, by shifting the narrative to a representational mode familiar to the native culture, in effect reversing the cultural flow.[5] The author either centers the standards of his own culture in a strong work by claiming universality for his or her mode of representation, or, as in most cases, relativizes the standards of the central culture, by shifting them to a local context. It is this latter type of adaptation that occurred in the composition of *Seinen*. Ōgai was preoccupied with the problems of influence and literary classification, and he made them central elements in his story of a young writer coming of age. He consciously crafted an argument about the social roles and responsibilities of an author—an argument that has aesthetic, political, and moral dimensions. By presenting competing narratives of artistic selfhood, both foreign and native, he reveals the ethical sources of the most fundamental of all cultural classifications, self-identity.

Representations of Self and the Problem of Closure

Since the publication of Ian Watt's *The Rise of the Novel*, it has become a critical commonplace to view individual, subjective experience, as opposed to communal experience, as the crucial determinant of verisimilitude. The move toward fictions of interiority, privacy, and sincerity was the result of the gradual breakdown of a commonly shared public rhetoric that began with the Reformation, with its vernacular challenge to the linguistic authority of the classical languages and the growth of a large, middle-class reading public. A greater reliance on individual experience and autonomy as the primary source of epistemological authority gradually emerged over the seventeenth and eighteenth centuries, and with it, a more private, personal mode of representation.[6]

The problem that arises with this shift in mode is that the scale and significance of narrated experience is diminished. Even though the knowledge arrived at through narratives of personal experience is hard-won and thereby credible, such experience lacks the universal validity to which public rhetoric aspires. The result is that even in novels of a highly interior nature (*Clarissa*, for example), there is a tendency to try to legitimize the authority of private experience both by grounding it in circumstantial detail and by providing an epic sweep to the psychological dimensions of the narrative. The modern novel thus developed with an inherent formal contradiction— a manifestation of the divided ethical consciousness of modernity—that requires some qualification of the notion that the distinctive feature of the form is merely a shift in favor of particularity of experience and a private mode of representation. The novel in general struggles to create the illusion of a narrative voice that is unique, but that also acts as an absolute point of epistemological reference. Since the novel can only suggest the presence of such a voice, a pure narrative of self-realization in which the self is wholly grounded in personal experience is impossible.

The formal contradiction of the novel is apparent when traditional modes of representation are employed to relate the unique experience of the individual. One of these modes is the quest narrative, the story of a search that provides the structures and archetypes of the epic, the romance, and the picaresque. The search may be to prove one's individual worth, or it may be to aid the community, or it may be for transcendental, spiritual knowledge, but whatever form the search takes, the quest narrative is grounded in the passage of the individual from a formless, developing entity to a being recognized as a true individual, by virtue of having been integrated into established roles—that is, by virtue of learning the cultural and spiritual values of the social group. This type of story achieves dramatic force by depicting the struggle between the desire to realize the unique qualities and potential for growth of the protagonist and the recognition that the ultimate goal of the protagonist's quest for experience, knowledge, and self-realization is to come to some reconciliation with social norms—the great, limiting realities of marriage, family, or social roles. The overly precise axiom that assures us that tragedies end in death and comedies end in marriage creates a false dichotomy, for in both cases, the most salient structural feature is that they end. However much we may want to create a self-centered narrative, the rhetorical logic of the novel demands closure.

The problem of formal closure is present in all types of narrative that aim for the construction of a sense of selfhood: namely, the autobiography, the confession, and the *Bildungsroman*. The rhetorical key to these forms is that the emphasis they place on an individual's experience and development must be given some form of epistemological authority; that is, narrated experience must seem at once unique and representative. Yet the emphasis on the experience of the individual implies a potential for ongoing change and development that creates an open-ended structure foreclosing the gratification of a narrative resolution—a possibility played to brilliant comic effect in *Tristram Shandy*. In order to approach a pure representation of individual experience, it is necessary to resist closure, to struggle against the rhetorical limitations of narrative. The challenge to achieving verisimilitude when narrating a quest for self-realization is to make the development of the self seem inevitable, even as the narrative attempts to sustain the illusion of open-endedness, of other possible outcomes.

The widespread use of the conventions of the confession, the autobiography, and the first-person narrative points to the importance attached to this challenge throughout the long history of Japanese prose narratives, both before and after the Meiji Restoration. Especially over the past century, the large number of first-person narratives suggests a heightened awareness in the Japanese tradition of the difficulties encountered in defining the self in a society where social norms have been unsettled. The weakening of the authority of communal values in Meiji Japan by the ideal of the self-made man opened up broader opportunities for self-expression, but that freedom created new constraints in the form of intelligibility. Extreme social change and the fragmentation of public modes of discourse left authors fewer common resources with which to contextualize the more interiorized personal language of narratives of self-identity. This helps explain why many modern artists looked to the authority of the classics to justify the appropriation of older, familiar modes of representation.[7] In many first-person narratives, the protagonist often engages in behavior that challenges social norms not so much because the quest for self-definition is aimed solely at individuation, but because the narrator wants to shift the locus of communal values, to open up an imagined social space that can accommodate a more individuated sense of self.

There is no simple explanation for why the awareness of the limitations of narrative form should be so persistent in modern Japanese literature, but an important element of modern culture, the anxiety created by the break-down of received notions of self-identity and of the place of the individual in the social order, is a reasonable starting point from which to try to reach an understanding of this phenomenon. By way of comparison with the situation in Japan, postmedieval European society managed to reduce the anxieties about death, judgment, and the failure of the old order specific to the culture of the Middle Ages by applying relativistic and quantitative principles, which gave it a greater sense of control over time. Moreover, by appealing to practical reason, the modern West was able to create more flexible social boundaries, manifested in such legal instruments as wills, contracts, and insurance, and consequently to create a confidence that man could exert more control over the future.[8] As William Bouwsma has argued, however, these developments were purchased at the price of a different form of anxiety.

> Even more troubling consequences have come from the need of the individual to adapt to unpredictable circumstances and the changing expectations of others. The needs of survival in a problematic world have tended to alienate the public from any true self for the sake of a social self. Thus, the relations between the boundaries of self-definition and any stable center of the personality have tended to become themselves problematic, and this has been the source of a peculiarly burdensome kind of anxiety in the modern world. Even the artist, his task no longer to discover and illuminate immutable truths but to create some relative cosmos from the chaos that surrounds him, may feel more terror than exuberance as he considers the contingency and fragility of his work.[9]

The opportunity to narrate one's self into being is potentially paralyzing, for its limitlessness robs the literary artist of the formal boundaries that permit self-definition. This paradox shapes the narrative voices and perspectives central to the autobiography, the confession, and the *Bildungsroman*, and raises a number of questions about these forms. Can a life still in progress, that is not yet "ended," be reduced to narrative form? Is it possible to posit even a teleology of identity as it is relived through narrative? Doesn't the attempt to reduce the personal, incomplete self to narrative undermine the epistemological authority of particular experience, by making the self a rhetorical (fictional) construction? In even the most brutally candid confession, is not the flesh-and-blood individual, however unique or alienating his or her experiences, transformed into a marble image, a person whose autobiography becomes everybody's autobiography? In the face of these questions, narratives of the search for selfhood attempt to create the illusion that the growth of the individual survives the closure of the text and continues beyond the narrative, like Dante's rose, in a limitless exfoliation. Ihab Hassan summarizes this paradox as follows:

> Therefore, isn't autobiography a labor of self-creation no less than of self-cognizance or self-expression, itself a quest rather than the record of a quest? Isn't it a mask, the mask of an absent face that becomes actually the face we show and others see? Hence, doesn't autobiography affect the real, dying subject, as if words could change the life they presume merely to describe?
>
> Put another way, isn't autobiography shifty in that a first person present (I, now) pretends to be a third person past (he/she, then), and in the process alters both characters? Or is it rather that we all continually live in a dimension that is not wholly past, present, or future, but a blend of them all, a dimension that autobiography simply makes explicit, rendering it into speech?[10]

Although Hassan's observations are limited to the autobiography, his characterizations of the conventions of the quest narrative, with its attendant tension between public and private voices, are no less applicable to other narratives that deal with a search for self-definition, including the *Bildungsroman*. Georg Lukács saw the *Bildungsroman* (he specifically points to Goethe's *Wilhelm Meister* as his prime example) as a form that "steers a middle course between abstract idealism, which concentrates on pure action, and Romanticism, which interiorizes action and reduces it to contemplation."[11] Accordingly for Lukács, the *Bildungsroman* deals with the "reconciliation of the problematic individual driven by deeply felt ideals with concrete social realities."[12] Wulf Koepke expands on this definition by noting that most studies of the form look upon the growth of the protagonist through his experiences in a psychological light. The young hero "sets out on his life's journey as an adolescent with many youthful dreams, aspirations, and illusions, and his experiences lead him to a healthy realism, to the abandonment of such dreams as illusions. It is to a high degree a process of acculturation, of adapting to existing societal structures."[13]

The tension between private experience and communal values noted by both Koepke and Lukács is a trace left by the process of adapting the narrative conventions of the quest to the *Bildungsroman*. This is a common feature of the form, and, as was noted above, an important element in *Seinen*. Before looking at the *Bildungsroman* in a Japanese context, however, there is one final aspect about the meaning of the term that limits its usage and must be addressed. The term *Bildungsroman* is culturally specific, and refers first and foremost to a genre peculiar to eighteenth- and nineteenth-century German literature. The word *bildung* suggests the developmental process in the growth of an individual and the collective cultural and spiritual values of a specific historical epoch: namely, the values of the eighteenth-century German middle class.[14] As long as the term is used with its heuristic meaning clearly in mind, there seems to be no reason preventing us from talking about non-German *Bildungsroman*. Even so, to claim as a *Bildungsroman* any narrative that deals with the growth of a young man into adulthood is to make the term so inclusive as to be nondescriptive.

Because of this limitation on the usage of the term, the reading of *Seinen* that follows focuses mainly on two issues. First, the structure of the narrative is distorted by the irreconcilable aims of the quest. The attainment of selfhood, a developmental process in which the presentation of the life of the protagonist is open-ended, must be achieved through social norms that, by making a claim to universality, require formal closure. Second, following Lukács's analysis, the theme of such a narrative is not the achievement of self-realization, but an acknowledgment that such an achievement is impossible. That is, the theme is reconciliation to the impossibility of complete self-expression as the private individual moves to conform to public values.

This theme has possessed great appeal in Japan, judging from the sheer number of coming-of-age stories, I-novels, and confessional narratives that have been produced over the past century. The source of this appeal to those writers and intellectuals who were vexed by the intangible ghostliness of Japanese identity was the theme's potential to resolve the question of identity by subordinating the individual to socially acceptable and histori cally determined values.

Manly Virtue and the Quest for Selfhood

A socially defined concept of selfhood is at the heart of the Japanese mode of the quest narrative Ōgai adapted. This mode is a quest in which the development of the individual moves toward an ethical code of behavior embodied in the Japanese words *masurao* and *masuraogokoro*. The word *masurao* is extremely ancient, and conveys the basic meaning of "man," but usually in a hortatory sense, such as a strong, heroic, or magnificent man. The word *masuraogokoro* also appears very early in Japanese literature, with much the same meaning as *masurao*.[15] The words denote a socially determined concept of masculinity, the proper, ideal role for which every man should strive. In a narrow sense, they are close in meaning to the modern Japanese word *otokorashii*, "manly." However, the term *otokorashii* is not an exact synonym, because it does not convey as strongly certain ideological and ethical assumptions that adhere to the word *masuraogokoro*.

One of the most famous literary uses of the word appears in the story "Jasei no in" ("The Lust of the Serpent") in *Ugetsu monogatari*. As discussed above, the protagonist, Toyoo, falls under the erotic spell of a supernatural being, Manago, whose true form is serpentine. In the course of the story she twice bewitches him. He escapes both times, but her true form is revealed to him only after the second episode, when an elderly priest breaks her spell. The following day Toyoo brings some gifts to the priest, who then gives the following warning: "This beast is lustfully attracted to your good looks and entwines herself around you. You will be charmed again by her false appearance and will have no manly spirit [*masuraogokoro nashi*]. From now on, if you have manliness and properly calm your heart, you will not need the power of an old priest to drive away this evil creature. By all means control your passions."[16] Toyoo tries to heed this warning, and his parents arrange a marriage for him. Yet he cannot free himself entirely from the serpent's power, and after he marries a woman named Tomiko, Manago returns to haunt him by possessing his bride.

In many respects, "Jasei no in" is a prototype for the *Bildungsroman*. Toyoo, who is a second son, is depicted as a feckless youth with fine aesthetic sensibilities, but with no practical skills to make his way in the world. As a result, his frustrated father decides to do nothing to discipline him, allowing his son to "live as he wishes."[17] From the point of view of Neo-Confucian ethics, this attitude is irresponsible, because it severs Toyoo from the social and moral systems that would provide guidance. Toyoo is free to act out his individual desires, but that freedom threatens to lead him astray in his attempt to create a social role and identity for himself. He is, as a consequence of his father's decision to cut him loose from the norms that would give him a sense of selfhood, susceptible to the erotic temptations provided by the false beauty of Manago—he literally loses himself in her sexuality—and his story becomes a quest to find his social and ethical identity. This quest is an interior one, and although Manago represents a real and very dangerous external threat, Toyoo's susceptibilities are made evident for us by the erotic dream he has about Manago before he goes to visit her the first time.[18] The ethical framework of the story, as the old priest later enunciates it, makes it clear that the real problem for Toyoo lies within himself.

The result of this interiority is a story that is self-reflective and highly self-conscious. Returning to some of the central features of the *Bildungsroman* listed above, we see that "Jasei no in" shares a large number of them. At the heart of the story is the problem of the elusiveness of selfhood, and the narrative is extremely discursive as it sets out the ethical problem confronting the protagonist. The demon that torments Toyoo is represented as an external threat, and thus the interior development of his sense of moral control, the development of the boundaries of his self-identity, is dealt with in a highly oblique manner. The plot reversals—the first unmasking of Manago, her subsequent convincing Toyoo that she is really human, the second unmasking that reveals her true essence, and her final appearance as a demonic spirit possessing Toyoo's bride—call into question the reliability of our understanding of the world, by constantly creating false endings that lead to a sense of open-ended personal development for the protagonist and thus an open-ended narrative structure. The uncertainty and suspense appropriate to the narrative structure of a supernatural horror tale perfectly matches the protagonist's anxiety and his own ongoing search for selfhood. Finally and most importantly, the very notion of selfhood is determined by values specific to mid-Tokugawa culture, so that we see in "Jasei no in" the same kind of narrative tension, typical of the *Bildungsroman*, between the passions of the unformed self and the attempt to integrate the individual into the social norms exemplified by the ethical ideal of manliness.

The conventions of the quest mode are adapted to the search for identity in the *Bildungsroman*, and Ōgai both understood and followed his model carefully. Ōgai's treatment of narrative elements such as characterization, plot, and structure translates the conventions of the quest for manly virtue into a modern mode of representation that relates that quest to the protagonist's search for ethical knowledge and for a viable social identity. By depicting the dangers of erotic passion and false love as a central problem in the quest for selfhood, *Seinen* touches on the nature of individual identity specifically in terms of the individual's responsibility to others—terms reminiscent of the language used by Miyake and Okakura to define Japanese identity.

The search for selfhood in *Seinen* is an interior one, and it moves across a literary-intellectual landscape. The central problem confronting the protagonist, Koizumi Jun'ichi, who wants to be a writer, is that he has no firm conception of selfhood toward which he can direct his search. He is merely the unformed, developing character type denoted by the title of the novel, *Youth*. Because his ambition to be a literary artist is vague, Jun'ichi believes he must set out to learn what constitutes not only literature but also the autonomy of the author. This is an uncertain proposition, and so uppermost in the process of his education is the issue of individualism. More specifically, he must learn the ethical limitations that define the individual, even in a modern society where selfhood is increasingly understood in open-ended terms that cut the individual loose from traditional value systems.

As mentioned above, the autonomy provided by an open-ended concept of identity is a double-edged sword for the writer, since it flies in the face of those conventions, literary and ethical, that provide narrative closure and the boundaries of selfhood. Thus it is no accident that Ōgai chose to make his protagonist a young man who wishes to become a writer. The figure of the writer or artist was for Ōgai, as it was for many of his contemporaries, symbolic of the new man in Meiji Japan, of the possibilities and dangers confronting the individual in a society no longer grounded in traditional social and ethical systems of values. Accordingly, much of the narrative in *Seinen* is constructed of dense literary and philosophical debates about the nature and role of the individual and the artist. These debates are included not just for their content, that is, for the purpose of the formation of a concept of selfhood and identity, but also for their aesthetic, figurative function.

The literary dimensions of Jun'ichi's education, and by extension the careful planning of the narrative structure, are made clear to us from the beginning. The representation of his character is similar to that of Sanshirō, in that it is initially established in almost exclusively spatial terms. Jun'ichi is a young man who has come from the provinces to the center of Japan's new culture, Tokyo, to gain the kind of experience that will make him a modern author. He seems in many ways a complete innocent. He does not speak the dialect of Tokyo and has to rely on his knowledge of literary texts for his understanding of the language of the new Japan.[19] The quest to author himself, again very much like the story of Sanshirō coming of age, is represented by the device of having him find his way around the modern metropolis. Jun'ichi's perambulations around Tokyo—an activity that also appears prominently in a number of other stories by Ōgai—are quite literally a way of finding his place, in both senses of the word, in the modern world.

His initial contacts in the big city are two people from his native province: Seto Hayato, a young man who also wants to become a writer, and Ōishi Roka (Kentarō), an established writer to whom Jun'ichi considers apprenticing himself. Jun'ichi is an innocent, but he is not without personal resources, and his native sense of discrimination appears early on, when he avoids any kind of serious friendship with Seto. He sees Seto as a dangerous type, a young man who has lost all ethical bearings, and he goes so far as to dismiss Seto as a "Bohemian," in response to a warning by another friend, Ōmura Shōnosuke.[20] Similarly, his relationship with Ōishi never develops very far. During his initial meeting, in fact, he is kept waiting an inordinate amount of time while the older man is being interviewed by a journalist. Although the situation is a humorous one, Jun'ichi finds Ōishi very strange and his actions incomprehensible.

Jun'ichi is not a *tabula rasa* at the outset, but has brought a set of traditional values from his home province that serve as a point of reference to guide him over the course of his education. To a certain degree, his education is a matter of confirming those native values, and in terms of the narrative, the plot strategy of giving Jun'ichi an independent as opposed to an empty mind is important to the sequence of arguments about the individual that serve as the basis for Jun'ichi's education. Two literary possibilities are presented to the hero and eventually rejected by him. The first is the view of the artist presented by Ōishi. During the course of his interview with the journalist, which Jun'ichi listens to as a passive bystander, Ōishi gives an explanation of his approach to art. When the journalist, Kondō Tokio, cites critics who praise Ōishi for writing true confessions with a "serious [genshuku] attitude," comparing him to St. Augustine and Rousseau, the following exchange takes place:

> "That's very kind of them. But since the studies of present-day scholars, not to mention the writings of people of long ago, are such a bother, I haven't read them. However, I have heard that when St. Augustine was a young man he led a dissipated life, and that after he became a Christian he changed completely and wrote his confession as a fanatical priest. And as for Rousseau, he confessed that he had a child with a woman who was not his wife. The child was too much trouble to raise, so they placed it in

an orphanage. But he was a shy, awkward man by nature, and later, when he was serving in the Italian legation, he was taken to a place with some very beautiful women, but ended up trembling violently, unable to do anything, right? The characters I write about do wanton things. They go to prostitutes. Do the critics really say that's so great?"

"Yes, they say it's important. Your characters may go to prostitutes, but the critics praise their attitude, the way they reflect on the act of buying a whore as they are doing it, as serious."

"Then are they saying that a person who doesn't buy a whore can't be serious?"

"No, they're saying there are bigoted men who would never do such a thing. And there are those who, even though they may buy a whore, disguise the fact and pretend they know nothing about it. Those hypocrites have a meager inner life. They don't understand anything about art. They can't write novels. They don't have the means or the material to write a confession. They have no way to pose a serious attitude."

"Hmm. Do the critics say that there are people who can understand art and be creative without being bigoted and without covering things up in pretty phrases?"

"No one can say for certain whether there is such a godlike person or not. However, the object of criticism isn't God, it's man."

"So everyone buys a whore, then?"

"You shouldn't tease me."

"I don't tease."[21]

Ōishi's diffidence in the face of Kondō's reading of his work stems from his resistance to equating self-reflection with seriousness. He is preoccupied with autonomy, with the freedom of choice that allows him to pursue his desires. In denying the past—especially his debt to earlier confessional writers—and in writing about sexuality, Ōishi seeks to free the conception of art from the dead hand of tradition and put the individual and his immediate desires at the center of his representation of selfhood. For that reason, he tries to distance himself from Kondō's praise of seriousness, because that reading of his work puts the ideal of seriousness before the experience of the artistic self. This is not to say that in Ōishi's view, as presented here, seriousness is not a value. His position is that of the Japanese naturalists—a position heavily indebted to the Western Romantic notion of the solitary self as the source of artistic inspiration—in that it seeks to fuse life and art and thereby make the artist the arbiter of values who defines the ideal of selfhood.

Jun'ichi is quickly disillusioned with this view of the artist, which, in collapsing what it takes to be the artificial distinction between real life and rhetorical life, makes no allowance for anything beyond the day-to-day experience of the artist. The goal of Ōishi and by implication the naturalists is to meld life and art, not to elevate life to art. The result as Jun'ichi sees it is an extreme reduction of art to the mediocrity of life. On his second visit to Ōishi, Jun'ichi brings up his desire to become a poet and write novels, even though he expects that Ōishi will dismiss him by telling him that poets are born, not made. Ōishi, however, does not say if his desire is good or bad, but rather explains his own method of writing (Ōishi is quoted indirectly throughout the following passage):

> There is no method of training, no method of practice. There is only the effort to write. Practice may be a necessity if you want to write in the classical style, but Ōishi himself could not do that sort of thing. Even in the sentences he did write, there were probably mistakes in the use of *kana*. He did that sort of thing carelessly. In short, he said it was the state of his mind. Beyond that, in any case it wasn't a very productive job. When Jun'ichi was asked what he thought about Ōishi's method, he replied that he had been born the only son of a wealthy family, and that it had been his fortune never to have to work for his bread. Ōishi laughed and told him that in that case, if he could go through life without having to struggle with the difficulties of making a living, he would be able to make a conspicuous savings of effort. The downside is that there would be very little stimulation, and he would probably miss the road of success if he weren't careful. Jun'ichi thought this was evasive talk, and he lost hope somewhat.[22]

Jun'ichi will eventually reject Ōishi's view of art, but he begins to have misgivings about his own lack of experience. A short time after his second visit with Ōishi, he reads an article in a French magazine about the Italian landscape artist, Giovanni Segantini (1858–1899):

> Covering the magazine, Jun'ichi thought about it. Was this really the way to achieve art? The mountain in the Alps he himself had to paint was contemporary society. The vortex of the great city he had dreamed about

when he was in the provinces was now tossing him about. No, it would be nice if it were tossing him about. Although he ought to be tossed about, wasn't he still clinging to the ivy vines on the shore? Wasn't it true that he was not living in the real sense of the word? If Segantini had never opened his window or gone out of his door, what would have happened? If he had never done those things, living on top of the mountain would have been useless.[23]

Here we see how much Jun'ichi is tempted by the naturalist view that in order to write the artist must seek out all sorts of experience, especially sexual experience. Experience, it is argued, will provide the "means and material" to write a confession: that is, to write about the interior life and to create a literary identity. But for Jun'ichi, art should triumph over the mediocrity of life. He is uncomfortable with the naturalist conception of the artistic self and must continue his search elsewhere.

Jun'ichi encounters a different view of the artistic self when he goes to hear a lecture on Ibsen by the writer Hirata Fuseki. Fuseki is modeled on Sōseki, and his lecture recapitulates the essence of Sōseki's views on Japan's modernization.[24] Fuseki warns of the cliquishness that comes with following modern fads, and uses the way Ibsen is read in Japan as an example:

Originally Ibsen was the small [i.e., parochial] Ibsen of Norway. After he put his hand to social plays, he became the great Ibsen of Europe. It was the great Ibsen who was brought to Japan and who once again became the small Ibsen. Whatever is brought to Japan becomes small. Nietzsche becomes small. Tolstoy becomes small. I remember Nietzsche's words. "The world became small at that moment. Then, on top of it, the last human beings, who made everything small, are dancing around. Saying they have discovered happiness, the last human beings blink their eyes." The Japanese people have imported various doctrines and beliefs; they play with them and they blink their eyes. Because whatever comes into the hands of the Japanese becomes a small toy, it no longer has the power to frighten, even if it were originally a frightening thing. There is no need to bring Yamaga Sokō, the forty-seven rōnin, or Mito Rōshi back to earth and have them confront an Ibsen or Tolstoy who have been made so small.[25]

By reducing the ideas of great men, by making them familiar and accessible, the Japanese have condemned themselves to conformism—or worse, to a trivial, faddish kind of cultural consumerism that they mistake for modernity (or even for happiness). They have cut themselves off from those ideals that would make it possible to discover self-identity. Fuseki, whose tone of speech calls to mind the character Hirota, cites *Peer Gynt* and *Brand* as examples of a more heroic if nonetheless problematic concept of the self—a concept that contains a worldly facet and an otherworldly facet. He goes on to remark, "for what reason did Ibsen cut and discard the rotting cords of custom? It wasn't just to gain the freedom to throw his body in the mud. It was to spread strong wings to the wind and to try to soar high and far away."[26]

The two visions of art and of selfhood expressed by Ōishi and Fuseki represent the extremes that typically confront the young protagonist in a *Bildungsroman*. To put his choice in Lukács's terminology, Jun'ichi is confronted with the action of abstract idealism and the reflection or contemplation of Romanticism. Ōishi represents a view of the artist as a man who, seeing that received forms of rhetoric are no longer relevant, resolves to draw upon a private rhetoric, the record of his experiences, to translate his life into art. Fuseki sees that view as a devastating reduction. He sees the condition of the modern individual as a kind of continual searching, a spiritual homelessness, and calls for the individual to seek out his own way, to confront the greatness of the world.

Through his contact with these two men, Jun'ichi grasps the central problem of his own search and feels torn and restless. In terms of the plot, Fuseki's lecture marks an important turn in the protagonist's quest, for it not only intensifies his doubts, but also sets up the two crucial incidents that eventually bring about a reconciliation of these views for Jun'ichi. The first of these incidents is his meeting with Ōmura Shōnosuke at the lecture. The second is his decision to go see Ibsen's play *John Gabriel Borkmann*, where, by coincidence, he meets Sakai Reiko, an attractive widow whose late husband came from Jun'ichi's home province.

To understand the role given to Ōmura Shōnosuke in the narrative, it is necessary to return to the very beginning of *Seinen*, where Ōgai plays a little joke, by having his young hero, on one of his explorations of the unfamiliar terrain of the city, walk by the house of a writer named Mōri Ōson.[27] The humorous, self-mocking description of Ōson as a dyspeptic, frightening old man who writes tediously accurate novels and plays actually has an important function early in *Seinen*. As the story opens, Jun'ichi goes off to meet Ōishi Roka for the first time, but arrives only to find Ōishi still asleep. Apart from the satiric jab at the unwholesome lifestyle of certain types of literati, Ōishi's sleeping habits serve as a pretext to send Jun'ichi off on a perambulation around Tokyo. As noted above, walks through Tokyo were a staple of late Meiji fiction, and there is a clear symbolic connection between wandering through a modern metropolis, experiencing the sensation of urban space as a flow of people and objects, and the rootless state of the modern individual. In this particular case, Ōson's house acts as a signpost for Jun'ichi, who begins his search for literary selfhood by wandering, and even though the passage in question is obviously meant as a joke, the cityscape through which Jun'ichi moves in his quest is from the very beginning set in a metaphorical relationship with the literary landscape of modern Japan.

Ōgai initially inserts himself into the narrative as a joke, but he makes his presence felt more seriously in the discussions between Jun'ichi and Ōmura about literature and the artist. Through these discussions, Ōmura plays a crucial role as the guide Jun'ichi needs to succeed in his quest for artistic selfhood. In fact, the personal details of Ōmura's life make it clear that he is meant to serve as Ōgai's narrative alter ego. Ōmura is studying to be a doctor, but he is interested in literature and is especially well versed in German literature, criticism, and philosophy. Assigning to a specific character the role of authorial mouthpiece is usually a terribly limiting strategy for reading, but in this case, it is justified by virtue of the narrative form. In a *Bildungsroman* like *Seinen*, which deals with the education of the hero almost entirely in terms of intellectual experience and artistic growth, there is a need to reduce the characters to ideological types or mouthpieces for ethical positions. With the exception of the characterization of Jun'ichi, who is forced to evaluate the different motives and positions of the people he meets, most of the characters in *Seinen* tend for the most part to stand in for particular ideas and attitudes that are more abstract than psychologically realistic. This includes the portrait of Ōmura, who presents a view of the self that will provide the key lesson in the hero's educational growth and thus the resolution to the quest narrative.

Overcoming the Self

Discussions between the two young men about individualism and modern identity take place at several points in the narrative, but the central scene occurs in chapters 20 and 21, when Jun'ichi goes to visit Ōmura and they spend the day exchanging ideas. At one point, after they have discussed, among other topics, *The Blue Bird* by Maurice Maeterlinck (1862–1949), Ōmura gives a summary of his own philosophy, which also happens to summarize the Meiji discourse on the ethics of identity that frames the story of Jun'ichi's education. Ōmura argues that the happiness of the blue bird is nothing more than finding a balance between reflection and action. In Meiji Japan, he asserts, there are people who seek to achieve that balance through the ethics of Neo-Confucianism, but Ōmura criticizes this approach for lacking a transcendental aspect and for ignoring the autonomy of the individual. Even if Neo-Confucianism is supplemented by other Asian transcendental systems, such as the teachings of Lao-tzu or of Buddhism, the result is nothing new, merely warmed-over Wang Yang-ming Confucianism.

Ōmura then turns to survey the situation in the West. He sees the ethics of ancient Greece becoming transcendental around the time of Plato, and he points to Christianity as an extremely potent exploitation of that idea. However, Christianity went through a period when it became excessively otherworldly, and in the end, he believes that the ideal of the Buddhist hermit and the Christian hermit represent the same stage of cultural development. From that point on, according to Ōmura, further development occurred only in the West. The East, which had no Renaissance, stagnated, while the West developed the technologies of exploration and the natural sciences. Art and industry flourished in the West, but now progress was being made at the expense of excessive secularization. Schopenhauer, arguing that blind will is at the source of human life, tried to emphasize the transcendent world, but ended with a profound pessimism.

Ōmura contrasts this with Nietzsche, who argued that life and suffering are never separated, and so mankind must affirm life and take hold of it as it is, even with its suffering. Ōmura essentially agrees with Nietzsche's argument. He rejects Rousseau's call for a return to nature as impossible, he rejects the teachings of the scholars of Ancient Learning and National Learning in Japan as mere revivals of the past, he rejects the impulse of Romanticism to chase after impossible ideals, and he rejects Tolstoy's idealism, which turns its back on the world. He then presents his central point, which is his understanding of individualism:

> Individualism has two paths: egotism and altruism. Egotism represents
> the evil aspects of Nietzsche. It is the so-called will to power, a philosophy

in which the self is made greater by knocking down people. When people do that sort of thing to each other, it becomes anarchy. If you take that to be individualism, it goes without saying that individualism is evil. But the same is not true of altruism. Stoutly defending this citadel called the self, without giving an inch, altruism embraces all human things. I give loyalty to my leader. Yet as a citizen I am not the servant of that age long ago when everything was in disorder. I am filial to my parents, but I am not the slave of that age long ago when it was possible to sell or kill children. Loyalty, filial piety. These are nothing more than the values of humanity I can embrace. The whole of daily life is the values of humanity I continue to embrace. That being the case, how can I throw away that which I call myself? Can I sacrifice it? Yes, I can. Just as the greatest affirmation of love is double suicide, so the greatest affirmation of loyalty is death in battle. When life embraces all things, then the individual will die. Individualism becomes universalism. This is different from denying life and dying by turning your back on the world.[28]

Ōmura's breathless summary of the history of philosophy recapitulates a key issue in the discourse on the ethics of identity, by trying to find a balance between the conflicting appeals of autonomy and authenticity. More important, his attitude toward individualism is crucial to the design of the *Bildungsroman*. Ōmura provides a passionate defense of both personal freedom and the ethical admonitions of the Imperial Rescript on Education, and the detailed argumentation by which he makes his defense typifies the reflective, interior quality of the novel as a whole. This kind of discursive narrative, which dominates *Seinen*, is crucial not only for creating interiority but also for grounding the story in the authority of other universally valid, authentic texts as a way to authorize the interior self. His ideas fit squarely within the discourse on the ethics of identity, by presenting a catalogue of virtues as the grounds for modern selfhood and by identifying the problem of individual egotism that haunted Japanese intellectuals—an idea that by the 1930s came to dominate discussions of Japanese modernity. The naturalist view of the artist presented by Ōishi is revealed to be the wrong kind of individualism; it is nothing more than a reckless egotism that asserts the value of the self over all other ethical considerations. The appeal to high ideals, to turning one's back on the fashions of the day, expressed by Fuseki is likewise shown to be not only impractical but also irresponsible, in that it is a monastic denial of the self.

Ōmura's alternative, his altruistic individualism, is an appeal to a middle way—a naively hopeful version of Kantian subjective universality. This appeal is extremely charged as ideology, however, since it directs the self toward politically powerful ideals such as loyalty and filial piety. Ōmura dresses up his position as both a practical way to engage the world and as a Romantic vision of selflessness—a protofascist vision that just a few years later a battle-weary Wilfred Owen would dismiss as "The old lie / dulce et decorum est / Pro patria mori." But in narrative terms, the ethical merits of the argument are irrelevant, because what Ōgai is suggesting through Ōmura's position is the reconciliation of the aspirations of the individual with accepted social norms. The very notion of self is abstracted beyond private experience and given universal, public significance. Thus according to Ōmura it is possible for the individual to define and express the self even as that self is extinguished in the service of a larger ideal—the nation, the folk, the empire.

The intellectual quest for selfhood is fused with the quest for manly virtue immediately after the young men's discussion. They realize that they do not have the kind of life experience that would allow them to fully understand their philosophical arguments, and they are able to laugh at their own pretensions. More important, their discussion draws them together emotionally as friends. Indeed, at one point Ōmura wonders if what he feels toward Jun'ichi is a type of homoerotic love.[29] The bond that attaches the two young men is portrayed ambivalently, and Ōmura is forced to exercise a degree of self-control in his feelings toward his friend. In spite of this ambivalence, the friendship is presented as genuine and pure, and it becomes the emotional equivalent of the intellectual argument for altruistic selfhood. Jun'ichi and Ōmura in a sense discover themselves in their love for another individual. Jun'ichi in particular senses that the definition of selfhood must come through a control or reduction of the self according to socially sanctioned values, which give external meaning and order to the individual. Ōmura's ideas thus have as much emotional, figurative appeal as intellectual, ideological content—an appeal that in this context may be described quite properly as protofascist, since it idealizes the notion of binding the individual to a mythic racial/national whole. It is this pure, manly love that will serve Jun'ichi well in the challenge he faces immediately after leaving Ōmura—for he has agreed to go to Hakone to visit Sakai Reiko, and his education will be tested by the temptation the trip presents him.

The political dimensions of Ōgai's novel are, in a strange way, most obvious at this particularly intimate moment. A narrative of the process of acculturation that brings the individual into contact with his own humanity—that is, with those values that give him a sense of worth and identity—must be grounded in a specific historical space and time. Ōmura's paradoxical discovery of self in a socially defined identity external to the individual places his monologue squarely in the discourse that defined identity in terms of duties to society and the state. The *Bildungsroman*, as ideological formation and literary representation, is inseparable from the consciousness of history. As David Lloyd puts it, "the individual narrative of self-formation is subsumed in the larger narrative of the civilizing process, the passage from savagery to civility, which is the master narrative of modernity."[30] This historical consciousness helps to explain the apparent contradictions in Ōgai's own political views. He often lent support to marginalized writers and political figures, and was sharply critical of the government's handling of the Great Treason Incident of 1911, which led to the conviction and execution of the Socialist leader Kōtoku Shusui. At the same time, Ōgai was no liberal in the classical sense of the term, because what he favored as a means of promoting progress toward civilization and personal autonomy was not unbridled individualism but justice, which would assure social stability. Ōmura's call for sacrifice to the state is a reflection of the author's political stance, and is in line with the dominant discourse on the ethics of identity.

Throughout *Seinen*, the most obvious holdover of the quest for manly virtue is the story of Jun'ichi's coming of age sexually, which runs parallel to the story of his intellectual and artistic development. The feelings of compatibility that lead Ōmura to wonder if he is homosexually attracted to Jun'ichi are in fact not purely sexual, and they symbolize the higher plane upon which their relationship exists. The pure friendship of the young men, which has its basis in their intellectual pursuits, serves as a counterpoint to the pressures on Jun'ichi to become sexually experienced for the sake of discovering his artistic identity. The urge to seek out this type of experience is an expression of the unbridled individualism he must avoid. Although the ideological terms used to describe the constituent qualities of manly virtue have been shifted from Neo-Confucian to Western-based notions of individualism, the connection Ōgai draws for us between the realization of selfhood and the practice of ethical values has a clear parallel with the narrative treatment of the quest for manly virtue found in Akinari's story "Jasei no in."

This is not to claim any direct influence from Akinari on Ōgai. It is quite obvious from the numerous literary references in *Seinen* that Ōgai drew most heavily upon Western sources. Still, the comparison between *Seinen* and "Jasei no in" suggests the persistence of the divided ethical consciousness that emerged from the eighteenth-century discovery of a lost unitary language and ethnic identity.

As with Akinari's story, a central recurring element in *Seinen* is the protagonist's efforts to overcome sexual temptation that would cause him to lose his way on the road to authoring his identity. Jun'ichi encounters a number of tempting women along the way, including Oyuki, who lives next door to his boarding house, and Ochara, a geisha he meets at a banquet and who shows undisguised interest in him. Ochara is in some ways the more obvious (and thus perhaps less dangerous) threat, and she is even described as "the enemy." His feelings toward her at the banquet are explained to us as follows:

> Within Jun'ichi's heart there were indications of the usual enmity he felt toward women. Then he had the feeling that she was trifling with him even without their exchanging words. Of course this feeling was a little like making her his target, and he thought that perhaps he was falsely accusing her. But even that consideration was not enough to extinguish his feelings of enmity.
>
> Fortunately, because the seductive power she was using on Jun'ichi was not very strong, and because there had not been any direct collision between the two of them, Jun'ichi possessed enough autonomy to be able to retreat from before this charming enemy.[31]

In contrast, Jun'ichi's feelings for Oyuki are much more confused, in part because she is as naive and innocent as he. In certain respects, Oyuki brings out the more chivalrous aspects of his character, but, as he tries to figure out if she is being calculating in her interactions with him, there is an uncertainty in his attitude toward her. During one encounter, the narrative shifts to Jun'ichi's perspective:

> As he listened to her talk, Jun'ichi looked at Oyuki's face. Little waves of expression were constantly arising on her charming face, as though a light breeze was crossing over the surface of a foot-wide basin of water. He had lost count of how many times Oyuki had come to visit him, but rather

than looking at the girl, it was Jun'ichi who was always being looked at. Today was the first time he had gazed intently at her face.

Then he noticed it. He noticed that Oyuki was conscious of the fact that she was being looked at. It was a natural thing, but for Jun'ichi the moment it occurred to him he was struck by the feeling that he had made a great discovery. This was because his feeling that this girl would let a person look as he pleased was at the same time a feeling that she would let a person do as he pleased. To say that she would let a person do as he pleased was still not saying enough. It was more accurate to say it was as if she were waiting for a person to act, encouraging a person to act. However, if he took a step toward her, would she move a step toward him? Or would she retreat a step? Or would she take a defensive posture and hold her ground? He didn't know. Maybe she didn't know either. In any case, she had a strong desire for knowledge. That was made apparent in her waiting, encouraging attitude.

At the same time Jun'ichi thought that this girl was a breakable, fragile, endangered object, and he felt he must protect her. If the person in his present position were someone else, he thought that Oyuki's peril would truly be great. Then the unsettling, impulsive feeling that floated up within him the moment Oyuki had entered his room disappeared as though swept away.[32]

In his encounters with Ochara and Oyuki, Jun'ichi is tempted as much by the siren's call of artistic experience as by their physical charms. Yet in both cases he reveals a moral intuition that shows concern not only for his own moral well-being, but also, in an altruistic sense, for the moral well-being of these women, especially Oyuki. This revelation is crucial, for it helps to set off the far more important story of his association with Sakai Reiko, who is a truly dangerous temptress.

Although Sakai is situated in realistic settings, she is still a type, a femme fatale, who shares a number of important characteristics with her literary antecedent Manago. When she first meets Jun'ichi at the Ibsen play, it is clear that she is sexually attracted to the young man. At the same time, she is a rather mysterious figure who, in Jun'ichi's imagination, seems like a heroine from some interesting novel.[33] As a widow, she embodies the male fantasy of a woman who is sexually experienced but, by virtue of the calamity of her husband's death, no longer constrained by social convention. Sakai Reiko is in some ways a foil for the protagonist, since the source of her potential danger is not so much her allure as it is the inexperience of Jun'ichi. In "Jasei no in," Akinari shows us that the real evil lies within, by taking us inside the privileged perspective of Toyoo's mind through the narrative trick of revealing his erotic dreams to us. Similarly, Ōgai takes us inside Jun'ichi's mind by allowing us a brief glimpse into his diary and by shifting the perspective of the novel into the first person. Jun'ichi describes a visit to Sakai's home, telling us again that the situation felt "novelistic," as though he were in a dream.

> "Please come in. It has been a very long time, hasn't it," she said, pushing aside a movable *kotatsu* on which a faded red quilt in a broad pattern was spread. She stirred up the fire in a round brazier of paulownia wood, and set it in front of purple crepe cushions, which were laid out in the middle of the tatami room, looking as though they were for young ladies to sit upon.
>
> I sensed in her attitude an unexpected seriousness, an unexpected calm. There was nothing more than the faint shadow of a smile flickering within her eyes, which were, as always, a mystery. I was unable to imagine clearly just what her attitude toward me was. However, I soon sensed that it was an unexpected one. And then there arose in the depths of my consciousness both an emotion like a kind of dissatisfaction, and a budding spirit of resistance. I think it was at that moment that I first looked at her as an "enemy."[34]

It is worth noting that Jun'ichi's diary entry is opened to us right after his important encounter with Oyuki, and so the contrast between these women is stark. The diary form itself becomes a way to fully meld the protagonist's interior disposition with the external events of the narrative. The text of the diary makes it clear at a number of points that Sakai seems to have some sort of interest in Jun'ichi, but that interest is never made explicit, partly to convey to us the sense of mystery that tempts the young hero, and partly to indicate his own confusion and lack of experience. His description of the room, for example, reveals Ōgai's narrative strategy. The furnishings, which are both sensual and yet slightly tattered, are stereotypical images suggesting we are in the lair of some seductress.[35] The very conventional nature of the description in Jun'ichi's diary also suggests the fevered imagination of a passive young man whose experience with women, like his experience with the language of Tokyo, has been limited to the strictly literary.[36] To understand the interior development of his education, we must to a certain extent be kept guessing along with him about Sakai's motives. Ethical values act to define him as an individual capable of self-control and as a social being, but his sexual desire may mislead him, and if he loses his moral bearings, he will lose his manhood. Consequently, his view of Sakai as his enemy merely reflects the misogyny that, like the ambivalent feelings of homoeroticism and homophobia experienced by Ōmura, is an inescapable aspect of the ideal of manly virtue or machismo.

The moral development of the protagonist reaches its climax—or its anticlimax, if we describe the end of the story in terms of his sexual development—when Jun'ichi agrees to go off to Hakone to visit Sakai. Although part of him has been calculating how to find a way to go to Hakone out of the hope that he will have an affair with the widow, another part of him is irritated that he has given in this much to his curiosity, especially since there is nothing between him and the woman. While waiting at the station buffet, where he takes breakfast before leaving for Hakone, he wonders if he will become depraved like Seto. Then, just as he begins eating his ham and eggs, a strange, ugly woman comes in and sits at his table. She reminds him of a ghost, and he takes her appearance as a bad omen for his trip.[37] Although the narrative quest does not take Jun'ichi literally into the realm of the supernatural, the ghostly appearance of this strange woman has an allegorical quality that, reminiscent of "Jasei no in," stands in for the terra incognita both external and internal that the protagonist is about to enter. Later, in a clear echo of *Sanshirō*, Jun'ichi has to wait overnight for a train on his way to Hakone, and ends up sharing a room at a bizarre inn with a woman he does not know. Her strange behavior suggests she is a prostitute who works for the inn, and so Jun'ichi ends up being confronted with sexual temptation one final time before his encounter with Sakai, heightening his sense of uncertainty and foreboding. Unlike Sanshirō, however, Jun'ichi is no coward, and in many ways Ōgai's novel is in an almost petulant competition with Sōseki's.

When Jun'ichi finally arrives in Hakone, he is surprised to find Sakai with an older man, a painter named Okamura, and he senses at once that he is an intruder. The key scene is a dinner during which the narrative again blurs Sakai's attitude toward the young man. Is she really interested in him, or does she merely view him as a feckless youth? There is no answer for Jun'ichi, but at this important point, the narrative fuses the story of his sexual inexperience with the story of his literary aspirations. During dinner, Okamura talks on and on about gossip he has heard concerning young writers, and he mentions two recent books that caused a sensation: *Futon* (1907), by Tayama Katai (1872–1930), and *Baien* (*Soot*, 1909), by Morita Sōhei (1881–1949). As it turns out, Okamura has not actually read either book, but then, perhaps the point is that he does not have to read them so long as he knows the real-life stories, the gossip, upon which they are based. This exchange implies a strong criticism of self-centered narrative forms, such as the I-novel, naturalism, and confessional literature, suggesting that they are not art because they do not embody aesthetic or moral principles. Rather, they rely for their affective appeal on the expectations of the reader.

Going beyond the satiric jab at naturalism that Okamura's nonliterary interests imply, the choice of these two texts is significant. First, both are naturalist works that practice Ōishi's view that literature must be based on experience. Both works are confessions of sexual experience—*Baien* relates the story of the author's real-life affair with Hiratsuka Haruko (1886–1971; pen-name, Raichō), and *Futon* tells of the unfulfilled yearnings of a frustrated, middle-aged writer for a young woman who comes to study with him as a boarder. Second, both works make heavy use of allusion and reference to other literary texts as a way to create characters, explain motives, and establish a claim to seriousness. The reference to *Futon* and *Baien* contextualizes the dual nature, literary and sexual, of Jun'ichi's education. More important, it is an example of a general tendency in Meiji literature to define characters not so much by individuating them through circumstantial detail per se as by basing them on a literary model.

Okamura brings the two strands of Jun'ichi's development even closer together by asking him if he has come to Hakone to write something. When Jun'ichi replies straightforwardly that he has not, Sakai jumps in almost as if she is defending the young man, saying that because he is still young there is no need for him to hurry his writing.[38] When Jun'ichi asks Okamura if he has come to paint, Sakai again jumps in, mentioning that Okamura completed most of two works when he was in Hakone the previous summer. Her response suggests an intimacy with Okamura, and Jun'ichi realizes that this is not the first time they have come here together. He feels humiliated, betrayed, and a little foolish, but this revelation is the catalyst that brings about the resolution of his quest.

The authoring of Jun'ichi's sense of identity comes about not so much through experience as through narrative revelations that are directly conveyed by other texts. Ōgai carries the contextualization of Jun'ichi's education to an extreme to force the reader to share in the progress of that education. This narrative strategy is most apparent in the frequent use of foreign words throughout *Seinen*, especially words from French, which is the language Jun'ichi is studying. The use of foreign words is a radical experiment that gives the novel a highly unusual visual appearance and makes no concessions to the reader, who must learn how to read anew by learning with Jun'ichi the various texts and languages Ōgai brings to bear on the story. This is certainly no easy task, for the range of allusions is very broad (recent paperback editions of *Seinen*, with their extensive footnotes, resemble Eliot's "The Waste Land"). There is no attempt to translate these words—they are plunked down amidst the flow of Japanese, and their meanings may or may not be apparent from their contexts. The radical defamiliarization of both Japanese and Western languages is visually arresting—that is, it literally gives the reader pause—and the strange print landscape created by foreign words and alien literary allusions, the textual analogue to the visual chaos of the modern urban space Jun'ichi must navigate, forces the reader to actively share in the education of the protagonist and to arrive at a discovery of identity delineated in the text by broad assumptions about the nature of the individual and of art.

Following the dinner scene, Jun'ichi chooses to stay in a separate inn away from Sakai and Okamura. That evening, on his own, he decides that he must not see Sakai any more, thinking, in German no less, that the devil can take her ("Der Teufel hole sie!")[39] Overcoming his confusion, he decides to return to Tokyo on his own, and at that moment, he achieves the authorship of his identity and comes to know at last what he wants to write about:

> Jun'ichi kicked off the bedclothes, got up, and forgetting that there was no fire in the brazier, sat cross-legged on the bedding and thought. The more he thought about what he would write, the more his present surroundings and the things he had examined in the past lost all their value, and he had the feeling that he did not care about the beautiful lump of flesh that was lying down in the detached room of the lodging close by. The blood rose to his cheeks and his large eyes glittered. Jun'ichi had occasionally felt this kind of excitement before when he set out to write something, but he had never sensed the fullness of emotion as now, like a cloud before an evening rain bursting to full with electricity.
>
> The things Jun'ichi thought he would write would take a little different direction from current fashions. The subject of his work would be the leg-

ends he had heard from his late grandmother back in his home province. Earlier he had, from time to time, planned to write out those legends. He had thought variously about the form he would use, whether to write in verse or in prose. He had thought about studying the epic style like that in a certain story in *Three Tales* by Flaubert, and he had also considered taking the short scripts of Maeterlinck as his sourcebook.[40]

Jun'ichi's choice of literary subject reflects Ōgai's own feelings of ambivalence about the value of fiction—sentiments that would lead him in the last decade of his career, starting in 1912, to focus on stories from Japan's past as the source for his own writings. By rejecting personal experience as his literary subject matter, Jun'ichi begins a process by which he can overcome the self and achieve the transformation of individualism into universalism that Ōmura had talked about earlier. He discovers his literary identity not by writing of himself or his own experience, but by choosing, like Yanagita Kunio (1875–1962), to recover the folklore of his native land. It is in these authentic narrative traditions that he believes he can achieve an integration of his individual identity with nation and folk, with social norms and literary conventions. This ideal literary form for Jun'ichi is a complex, highly abstract figural representation of the ideological aim of the *Bildungsroman*.

Once he has made his decision, Jun'ichi is capable of a more charitable view of Sakai, and wonders if he might have a Platonic relationship with her. He also thinks that, like Ōmura, he too may be able to separate from a woman without feelings of obligations or hatred. Yet in spite of his resolution, he feels an overpowering loneliness, and hopes that at least some story might come out of his feelings.[41] The regrets that remain from his quest for selfhood, a narrative postpartum depression, are echoed in the final image of the novel. As Jun'ichi leaves Hakone, he looks over at the rooms where Sakai is staying, and sees that the sliding doors are shut and that the interior is still and deserted.[42] This image is one of a world of experience and possibilities now closed off, of mysteries left unexplored, and, potentially, of a hell not entered. This image demonstrates his moral growth and the stripping away of his youthful illusions, which includes the rejection of an overly literary imagination—the kind of book learning that spurred his interest in Sakai in the first place. His emotions at the end of the novel suggest the ambivalent nature of his growth as an individual. Jun'ichi's development is indeed open-ended and ongoing, and the achievement of his quest is not a final narrative closure. He has reached the point where he can write; that is, he has authored himself as a literary artist. But his achievement has been bought at the expense of his private desires. His loneliness suggests that he has not yet answered all the challenges presented by either Fuseki's view of the life of the literary artist or the naturalist claim for the necessity of personal experience.

Seinen closes without fully resolving the underlying problem of the representation of identity. As noted above, there can be no closure in the narrative of a life in progress, and so the final image Jun'ichi sees as he leaves Hakone is merely a convenient place to stop. Ōgai is fully aware of the willfulness of his narrative choice, and ends by acknowledging the lack of contingency in fiction.

> Ōgai speaks. For now, this is where I'll end my work, *Seinen*. Having written only a small portion of what I planned, the number of days covered in the story comes to only sixty or seventy. Beginning with the season when the frost begins to settle, I finally managed to write as far as the early winter season, before the snow begins to fall heavily. Two years have passed while writing that small amount. In any case, this is where I'll end for now.[43]

This ending demonstrates that Ōgai was aware of the ambiguities involved in writing realistically about the self. He recognizes that the modern artist must to some extent rely on personal experience, and Jun'ichi's education, his progress, makes it clear that the problem of modern self-identity is open-ended. This recognition points the way for Ōgai's increasing interest in history as narrative, in which social memories and personal memories, a private modern voice and a public rhetoric, are merged. But his eventual turn toward historical fiction and biography during the final decade of his life was not a rejection of fictional narrative as a representational mode. Rather, it was an expression of his desire to find a more authentic grounding for narratives of self-realization. His decision to abandon fiction and locate identity in history is an extension of his own search for artistic selfhood—a search possessing all the ambiguities of the quest for identity that shape the narrative form of the *Bildungsroman*.

4
Real Images

M ANY POSTWAR HISTORIES present the two decades from 1912 through
the 1920s as a liberal interlude between Meiji authoritarianism and
the quasi-fascist militarism of the 1930s.[1] This revisionist, almost wistful
narrative attempts to deflect guilt for World War II onto the militarists
alone, by suggesting an alternative path that could have avoided war and
domestic oppression. A more accurate characterization of the period is that
it was exceptional (that is, liberal) only in the sense that it witnessed an
acceleration of late Meiji tendencies to question the cultural synthesis that
had emerged out of the discourse on the ethics of identity.

The great transformation of the Meiji period, the process of sweeping
economic, cultural, and military modernization that initiated Japan's march
to great power status, was in some respects already a thing of the past by the
1920s. Many intellectuals no longer pictured Japan as modernizing but as
modern, and that national self-image stirred feelings of confidence that Japan was very much a power on the rise. Such feelings, which were reflected
in the intense burst of literary and artistic innovation that occurred at the
time, may explain why in retrospect the political atmosphere of Taishō-era
Japan (1912–1926) seems to have been more open and tolerant. The liberating sense of possibility that characterized the age, however illusory it may
have been, was a source of the brilliant efflorescence of the arts, literature,
philosophy, and film that marks the worldly culture of Taishō.

If Taishō culture was sophisticated, however, it was also edgy and self-
conscious, for the ongoing process of modernization had brought about
economic and social dislocations that opened deep fissures in society. In
particular, Taishō Japan was haunted by the original sin of Meiji—the decision to resist the power and cultural hegemony of the West by emulating

Western material culture, by embarking on its own empire-building project in Asia, by acquiescing in the racial ideology that supported colonialism, and by constructing a modern myth of Japanese cultural uniqueness. For many in the 1920s, the progress promised by modernization was ephemeral, since disparities in wealth and status seemed to be growing, foreign threats appeared to be looming everywhere, and the identity and mission of the nation remained contested and unsettled.

The Meiji cultural synthesis—that strange hybrid of Western modernity grafted onto a newly created imperial ideology of an essential, timeless Japan—appeared incapable of holding its center in a culture that was increasingly skeptical. A widespread anxiety over the perceived condition of spiritual homelessness and cultural drift was as common as the sense of confidence in Japan's potential, and it inspired an equally large variety of creative responses. Some artists reveled in the breakdown of a sense of order, and they looked to new forms and media, especially the cinema, as a means to escape the stultifying Meiji legacy. Others followed the example set by some Western modernists and experimented with ways to pick up the pieces of a fractured tradition. Still others sought to escape through the selfless objectivity promised by the utopian dreams of socialism or the mythic visions of nationalism.

Considering the broad ideological forces that shaped literary developments in the 1920s and 1930s, it is clear that the period was characterized not only by a sense that the culture was opening up, but also by a continuation of the struggle begun in the nineteenth century between the appeal of a modern universal culture, which took the will of the individual as a crucial component in ethical judgment, and the desire for a parochial culture, which provided a stable center to conceptions of personal and national identity. As we have seen, this struggle, largely played out between the boundaries set by the notions of autonomy and authenticity, created a sense of hybridity, emphasized the process of cultural translation as constitutive of modernity, established a new spatial imaginary that projected Japan as a cultural unity, and eventually collapsed the temporal imaginary, compressing or flattening the historical past onto the ideological plane of imperial origins.

Given the degree of continuity in the discourse on identity, are there reasons to think of the sense of freedom attributed to the atmosphere of 1920s Japan as a break or at least a detour in the historical course of modernization? Even though the source of the rhetoric of one of the dominant critical voices of the period, Kobayashi Hideo, may be located in the earlier discourse on identity, his recognition of the essentially fictive nature of the language of values exposed the emptiness of that discourse. Recognizing the disconnect between language and values created an anxious sense of the emptiness of modern culture, but it did not lead to an abandonment of the concept of an ontological core, a sense of selfhood. Rather, it intensified the belief that the core could be recovered only if the Japanese could pare back the surplus of thought produced by the workings of the rational mind—a surplus that characterizes both capitalist social organization and the condition of the individual in modern society. The Meiji-period discourse on identity was not abandoned in the 1920s and 1930s—after all, misgivings about the disconnect between language and values, as well as skepticism about the existence of pure, essential Japanese values, had been forcefully expressed by Meiji intellectuals. Rather, what seems most characteristic of the Taishō period was this intensification of anxiety and skepticism as the discourse itself was brought under greater scrutiny. Many artists and intellectuals came to believe that the ambiguities of the language of identity and the complex structure of thought that sustained them were more than just symptomatic of the predicament of modern Japanese identity—they were the cause.

The shift in attitudes that began to take place at the end of Meiji was exceptionally convoluted. The image of a unifying spatial and temporal origin of national identity, which was conveyed by the figure of the emperor, was never significantly displaced, but became for a time bleached out and attenuated. This occurred in large part because the physical and mental instability of the Taishō emperor robbed the state of an image of power that could be projected to counter challenges from both the right and left. The waning of the figure of the emperor as national paterfamilias weakened the claim that the inviolability of the imperial line justified and legitimated the institutional structure of the Meiji state. Because this claim had played such an important role in the discourse on identity, the result for Taishō Japan was the formation of a peculiar antinomy, as the belief in and longing for an authentic core of being continued in parallel with a growing awareness of the inauthentic nature of the rhetoric of authenticity itself.

How was it possible for this contradiction to remain unresolved for as long as it did? The answer lies in part in a deep ambivalence over the worth and desirability of the material forces that determine the conditions of modernity. The industrialization of production and the applications of scientific knowledge to technology had transformed the political economy of Japan, necessitating changes in social relations, work hours, market norms, and even family hierarchies that in turn brought about a change in consciousness of identity. Industrialization and the rise of new technologies also brought on immense demographic upheavals and explosive urban growth.[2] The flows of populations were paralleled by increasingly rapid and voluminous flows of information, political ideologies, and social movements through mass media. These flows were all in a symbiotic relationship with the fluctuating expansion of global capital markets, which simultaneously grew out of and sustained the material forces of modernity.

The sense of spatial flux that resulted from the physical remaking of the economy was compounded by one of temporal flux, as the linear, discrete notion of time imposed by capitalist modes of production disrupted the experience of time based on natural or agricultural cycles.[3] The experience of movement within newly defined social, political, and economic spaces, especially in urban areas, the fragmentation of social and family relationships, and the deluge of information through institutions of learning and a variety of media all fostered the compression of the experience of time and space, fundamentally altering their representation.

Because many of the profound effects of industrialization were cumulative over time, the sense that Japan had achieved its own form of modernity and a measure of progress was widespread by the Taishō era. The belief that progress toward modern civilization was inevitable in turn shaped the perception that the contradictory attitude of longing for authentic culture, while taking a worldly, skeptical view of it, was a temporary condition. Of course, the consciousness of being modern, of progressing, did not follow automatically from shifts in technology, and there was no single response to changed aspects of material life. As was the case in early Meiji, changes in attitude often preceded altered technology, in order to bring that technology into place and make people see the value of it, desire it, and even subject themselves to it. The ambivalence of attitudes toward modern culture was for that reason self-renewing and self-sustaining, until the economic crisis and dislocations of the 1920s forced a resolution. With the ascension of the young Shōwa emperor, Hirohito, nationalists and militarists once more had an ideological figure they believed provided an inviolable justification for achieving a resolution of the vexing question of identity, which they sought through the violent suppression of views skeptical of the authenticity of Japanese culture.

The strong reassertion of the myth of nation as an ideologically charged space was an effort to co-opt the conception of the rational, autonomous agent and make the individual both the subject and object of the myth. The concepts used to represent the modern experience of the compression of time and space, that of progress and of the nation, became even more deeply embedded in the discourse on the ethics of identity in the 1920s and 1930s. Human agency, subjectivity, and reason make progress appear to be the natural state of the world. This is the assumption that supported the claims of the early Meiji modernizers, who saw in scientific knowledge and rationalism the underpinnings of a universal human culture that was moving toward the perfection of institutions and societies. The myth of the nation acted as a counterweight to the globalizing, universalizing force of modernization. In this view, the nation, as both a geographical and ideological space, provides the literal and figurative ground of identity for the individual, conferring value to human agency and subjectivity, which is defined in terms of its relationship (its rights and responsibilities) to the nation.

The nationalist backlash in Japan speaks to the extent to which the intensification of both the material conditions of modernity and the consciousness of being modern had lured Taishō intellectuals and artists back to the assumption of a universal culture, which had so appealed to their early Meiji-period counterparts. Being modern, Japan could and did claim equal status with the cultures of the West, and that identification was, as Kobayashi recognized, liberating, in that it made Japanese artists more cosmopolitan. The anxiety over the created, fictive nature of the values and identity expressed by the rhetoric of authenticity was if anything more pronounced during this period, but the compensation was a blurring of the hierarchy of modern culture, which had previously made a sharp distinction between the original, European forms of modernity and their Japanese copies. As Yasushi Ishii puts it, the leveling of the hierarchy between Japan and Europe allowed Japanese artists to demand legitimation of their own practices:

> The political agendas of European avant-gardes receded into the background, and the Japanese avant-garde grew increasingly less concerned with *what* to produce than *how* to produce, and often converted avant-gardism into a set of techniques. Because Japanese avant-gardists were "cosmopolitan enough," they also stopped worrying about their origins or their genealogies.[4]

Japan may have been, in Kobayashi's phrase, a translation culture, but it at least shared the ontological emptiness of that condition with all modern cultures. In that respect, even though the period should not be viewed as an exceptional interlude, it did witness a temporary loosening of the connection between authenticity and the parochial origins of Japanese culture, the imperial line, that had been established during the late nineteenth century. The growing appeal of a universal, cosmopolitan culture created a break with the immediate past, and the violent, chauvinistic reassertion of imperial origins that dominated the 1930s was an attempt to close the void that had opened up. Even before political repression gained full momentum, however, artists and intellectuals were already seeking for ways to represent that void and to compensate for the loss it implied. Viewing Japan as part of a universal culture paradoxically strengthened the desire to find, if not authentic values and identity per se, then at least a place in which the authenticity of a parochial culture could be preserved, like some museum artifact.

In the closing years of Meiji, writers such as Sōseki and Ōgai conceived of nation and individual identity primarily in terms of spatial and temporal orders that were open-ended, developmental, and radically individuating. By the end of the Taishō period, these elements of rhetoric were being infused by a more performative conception that sought to experience communal identity, without mediation, as a phantom simultaneity: a fusion of past and present into a single essential culture. This shift in discursive practice was motivated by a desire to return to a pristine, preindustrial, communal notion of self—an almost orgiastic union of individual and nation within a boundless and timeless past. The language of the realistic novel was not fully adequate to narrate the experience of authentic identity as a timeless immediacy, since such an experience takes place all at once rather than in the developmental timeframe of formal realism. The mediating properties of the language of realism, which had been the discursive ground upon which modern conceptions of nation and individual had been engendered, had to be overcome. Consequently, identity came to be conceived increasingly in visual terms as well, that is, as an unmediated projection of real images—race, nation, and empire—that enabled perception of authentic cultural identity.

Visuality and Yokomitsu Riichi's New Sensation

Vision, as the constitutive sense of the spatial imagination, has been closely associated with the culture of modernity, and within the rhetoric of authenticity, visual representation has held an especially privileged position. Examples of that association were noted in the previous two chapters. Although the most obvious of these is the Western-style portrait of Mineko in *Sanshirō*, both Sōseki and Ōgai make frequent references to the new technologies of vision—film and photography, electric lights, the science of optics—that serve as metaphors for the allure and danger of progress, for the illumination of knowledge and the opening of one's eyes to the real world. Moreover, both Sōseki and Ōgai often resort to an imagistic representation of the spatial contexts and surfaces of their characters' lives. For example, the conceit of translating Mount Fuji to values of character suggests, in the sense Hirota presents it, a spatialization of identity. The physical movement and perambulations of the characters in and around Tokyo further develop this notion. Ōgai in particular organizes the narrative of *Seinen* around those public and private spatial nodes that define a student's life—a boarding house room, a new theatre for showing Western plays, a young widow's drawing room, a lecture hall, an artist's studio—all of which are part of the exhilarating and bewildering flux of image and space in the modern cityscape.

When Japanese experiences of modernity are placed in a comparative framework, it is not surprising to find that visuality should assume such an important role. The claim that modernity is especially or uniquely ocularcentric, even for the literary arts, is certainly a debatable proposition, but what is beyond dispute is that the notion of vision as the master sense of modern culture has been widely held.[5] One possible explanation for the prominence of the visual sense in modern Japanese literature is that there were longstanding practices, perfected during the Tokugawa period, of publishing in formats that combined both image (that is, woodblock prints) and text.[6] This explanation, however, oversimplifies the matter. For one thing, the pre-Meiji economy of book production made allowance for a variety of forms. As we saw in the case of Akinari and the rise of the *yomihon*, a divide had opened up as early as the 1760s between formats that combined image and text and those that were primarily text. For another, asserting a direct link between the interest in visuality among Taishō artists and writers and Tokugawa conventions of printmaking and narrative suggests a degree of continuity that unduly diminishes both Meiji rejections of certain aspects of Tokugawa culture and the impact of nineteenth-century Western literature and art.

This is not to say that earlier practices did not matter for Taishō writers. They did have an influence, but in part through the roundabout medium of modernist movements in Europe and America. The late nineteenth-century Western fad for things Japanese, particularly prints and other visual artifacts, was the product of a confluence of circumstances: the opening of Japan, which made its material culture more widely available, and Western developments in science, literature, and art, which began to challenge previously dominant modes of representation. The irony of this confluence is that Western artists were discovering a spirit of authenticity in Japanese art that they found lacking in their own—the same art that was being displaced and in some cases actively rejected by the culture of modernity in Meiji Japan. Regardless of the historical twists involved, the urgent desire to represent true experiences of the world in art was a common motivation for writers in a range of movements, from Symbolism to Futurism, from Art Nouveau to Dada.

With the pronounced turn in Taishō toward international modernist movements, the privileged place accorded to visual modes of representation by some artists in the West became an important consideration for literary developments in Japan. Most accounts trace the rise of the dominance of the visual in the West to the art of the early Renaissance in Europe. As the techniques of linear perspective evolved, the notion of light as a property of the divine, a legacy of medieval metaphysics, survived in the belief that the mathematical order of optics was a sign of God's will. Even though the theological associations of the early Renaissance conception of optics eventually weakened, the illusion of objectivity, mathematical precision, accuracy, and reality represented by linear perspective remained a potent and appealing effect.

Although linear perspective may be considered the dominant visual mode in the West from the late Renaissance well into the nineteenth century, Martin Jay argues that it was only one of several possible visual modes or, to use his term, scopic regimes of modernity. He identifies two alternatives, classifying one as a Baconian descriptivist model of vision and the other as a baroque model.[7] In setting out his overview, Jay describes what he calls Cartesian perspectivalism as the mode of surveillance, characterized by a monocular gaze occupying a privileged position (the eye atop a pyramid), while descriptive vision may be characterized as a mirror of nature, a fragmentary mode that draws attention to the articulated surface of the world in a way that prefigures the experience of vision created by photographic technology. He likens the third mode, the baroque, to the spectacle, in that it rejects the monocular, rational geometry of Cartesian perspectivalism, with its illusion of an objectified, three-dimensional space, in favor of a surplus of images that establish a disorienting and open visual field.

Jay proposes this scheme not to deny the historical importance of Cartesian perspectivalism, but to give a fuller account of the complexities of the history of the visual modes of modernity. By noting the continuing presence of alternative modes, he establishes the context in which challenges to claims for the accuracy and objectivity of linear perspective could arise. His account is based not only on the critique that the idealized vision of Cartesian perspectivalism was disconnected from history and the world, but also on internal tensions he identifies within the mode itself. Beyond the fact that actual practices of linear perspective did not always match the ideals of the model, the notion of a single, universal perspective, which implied a transcendental subject, drew attention to the contingency of perspective—the idea that perspective depends on the individual vision of separate viewers. If all viewers had an objective, transcendental view, then no one did, raising the problems of relativism and the potential separation of the perspective of the producing artist from that of the consuming viewer.[8]

The assumption of the objectivity of linear perspective, which was sustained first by its associations with theology and then by its connection with science and rationalism, never had the field all to itself, and came to be strongly contested, especially during the latter half of the nineteenth century.[9] This contestation was not limited to the purely visual arts, but had a major impact on literary developments, especially the novel, which has been the representational form most closely associated with the formation of modern subjectivity. The illusion of verisimilitude created by formal realism is the product of a kind of narrative surveillance that provides detailed, particularistic descriptions of individual characters moving through specific, delineated spaces. The recognition that linear perspective was not privileged, that it represented neither a divine nor an objective point of view, is apparent, in the case of the literary arts, in challenges to the authority of linear narrative.

Of course, the prestige and authority of formal realism have never been utterly diminished or displaced. The linear narrative of the Western novel was recognized in the Meiji period as an innovation linked to modernity. Looking back at works like *Sanshirō* and *Seinen*, they may seem less radical now, because they employ realistic elements that were already being challenged by Western artists at the time of their composition. Nonetheless, the process of translating the techniques of linear narrative and bringing them into some form of congruence with the conventions of pre-Meiji fiction provided its own challenge, by exposing the illusion of verisimilitude. The ways in which perspective is contested in Japan may parallel developments in the West, but Japanese literature is not simply derivative, and it must be evaluated within the context of particular literary experiments.

By the Taishō period, many writers were moving in new directions, and if Japan had already become modern, then the same was thought to be true for its literature. The gradual process of the vernacularization of style and the standardization of orthography and printing formats had coincided with the translation of Western narrative forms, bringing the economy of publishing and literary standards more in line with those of the capitalist cultures of the West.[10] Writers continued to be aware of their belated position vis-à-vis the West, and were deeply anxious about the impact of foreign cultures on the essence of Japanese identity, but in one respect, they were more accepting of that condition than their Meiji counterparts. The belief that their generation was truly modern, that for better or worse they were now cosmopolitan, put them on a more equal footing with their peers in the West,[11] and that attitude helped determine the course of literary developments.

A notable example of the effect of this attitude is the work of Yokomitsu Riichi (1898–1947), a central figure in the generation of writers who rose to prominence in Taishō. Yokomitsu played an active role in the intellectual and artistic crosscurrents of the time, and he was a dominating presence in literary circles for more than two decades. Beginning in 1920, he became more and more deeply involved and prominent in the Tokyo literary scene. His peers included some of the most powerful and influential figures of pre-war Japanese literature: the writer and publisher Kikuchi Kan, the polemicist Yasuda Yojūrō, and the writers Kawabata Yasunari, Kataoka Teppei, and Akutagawa Ryūnosuke. For the next twenty years, his peers would discuss Yokomitsu's work on equal terms with the most important writers and critics, such as Kawabata and Kobayashi.[12] Indeed, during this time he shared with the novelist Shiga Naoya the divine status conferred by the breathless epithet *bungaku no kamisama*, "a god of literature."[13]

Yokomitsu founded a literary magazine, *Tō* (*Tower*), in 1922, and over the next three years published a number of short stories, essays, and theoretical pieces in a variety of journals. His early period of intense activity culminated in 1924, when he joined with Kataoka and Kawabata to establish a new magazine, *Bungei jidai* (*Literary Age*). Criticism of the experimental work that

appeared in this journal was often harsh, and in response Kataoka, Kawabata, and Yokomitsu defended their project by trying to systematize their
aesthetic principles. The result was the creation of the *Shinkankaku-ha*, the
New Sensation School, for which Yokomitsu served as chief theorist.

As a founding member of the New Sensation School, Yokomitsu's call for
a new sensibility—literally a new sensory capacity to perceive the world in
an unmediated way—was initially motivated by his opposition to the narrow realism of the first-person narratives that characterized the work of
the White Birch School. He was also strongly opposed to the narrow ideological aims of the Proletarian School of writers, but he espoused neither a
simplistic anti-Marxism nor a return to traditional aesthetic values. Instead,
he gave voice to a particular version of the widespread if often ill-defined
concern over the influence of the West in the formation of modern culture
in Japan. He described his own career as moving through several phases:
from "a period of insubordination and absolutely desperate battle with the
Japanese language, through a period of combat with Marxism, arriving now
at a period of submission and obedience to the national language."[14] These
remarks have led some commentators to read into his early work a revolt
against the linear narrative of realist fiction common to many modernist
literary movements around the world at the time. Yokomitsu, however, cannot be described simply as an antirealist. His aesthetics were motivated by
the aspiration to create a culture that was modern and Asian, and through
that cultural project to somehow overcome the modernity of the West.
What Yokomitsu longed for was a culture that was at once parochial and
universal, which subsumed the West under an all but impossible synthesis
of the national and the cosmopolitan.

This desire for synthesis is manifested in the formation of his theory of
New Sensation. For example, near the end of his tract "Shinkankakuron" ("A
Theory of the New Sensation," 1925), he writes: "Futurism, Three-dimen-
sionalism, Expressionism, Dadaism, Structuralism, Surrealism—all of these
I recognize as belonging to the New Sensation school." This is an audacious
statement: the sheer inclusiveness of the definition makes the New Sensation School so universal in its reach that its practices are all but impossible to isolate or distinguish. Indeed, when the diverse membership of the
school is taken into consideration,[15] it is impossible to discern any elements
that gave it a sense of common purpose, especially when contrasted with
the Marxist aims that drove the Proletarian School. However, to focus on
the apparently mixed aims of Yokomitsu is to miss the one vital element of

his program, which is to create an overarching synthesis of literary praxis. Whatever problems arise in the formulation of his theory, the aims of his project of cultural renewal are unambiguous.

For Yokomitsu, the term "New Sensation" was a broad marker intended to strip away ideology and modern historical consciousness from art (an idea that Kobayashi would echo a few years later) and achieve unmediated apprehension of reality through the senses. Here is his definition of the term:

> The general concept I call Sensation [*kankaku*] refers to the surface signs [or symbols, *hyōchō*] of perception; it refers to the intuitive triggering mechanism [*shokuhatsubutsu*] of subjectivity, which strips away external aspects of nature and merges with an object. This definition is a bit extravagant and still does not quite get at the newness of the New Sensation. That is why we must acknowledge the importance of subjectivity. By subjectivity I refer here to the capacity for actions [*katsudō nōryoku*] by which an object may be perceived as itself, as it really is. Such perception is of course a synthesis of intellect and emotion. But at the moment subjectivity arises, when the intellect and emotion that create the capacity to perceive an object merge with the object itself, then either the intellect or the emotion will take on a dynamic form as the dominant trigger of sensation. It is very important to take this into account to explain the fundamental concept of the New Sensation. The representation [or signification, *hyōshō*] of an action that affects the capacity to perceive external, pure objectivity [*junsui kyakkan*] is Sensation. The concept of Sensation as it is used in literature is, to simplify, perception transformed to a surface sign.[16]

Yokomitsu's aim is the achievement of unmediated sensation—a state where perception and language are unified, which would situate him nowhere, in no particular place or time, and allow him access to the authentic without losing his modern, individual consciousness. His effort to co-opt realism, Symbolism, Futurism, and other styles suggests that he was aware of the synthetic nature of his project, which strove for the creation of an aesthetics of authenticity. In Yokomitsu's formulation, Sensation (*kankaku*), the representation of consciousness through surface signs, infuses mediating language with an unmediated ethical consciousness. Sensation in this sense provides hope for resolving the underlying paradox of modern subjectivity, which is the self-consciousness that blocks the ability to apprehend the real.

The efforts of so many intellectuals in the 1920s and 1930s—men such as Kūki Shūzō, Yanagi Soctsu, and Yasuda Yojūrō—to explode the limits imposed by historical consciousness are apparent in the obsessive search for cultural origins and for essential cultural characteristics. In order to erase the temporal sense of belatedness vis-à-vis the West or to contract the spatial distance from a mythic past, the focus turned to an exploration of the parochial elements of Japanese culture. For Yokomitsu, however, this parochialism was not quite enough: his conception of modernity was shaped by the desire to fuse the subjective, parochial qualities embodied by Japanese nationalism with the internationalist aspirations of modernist aesthetic movements.[17] In order to resolve his contradictory cultural aims, Yokomitsu had to enunciate his own version of the objective correlative that would contain the longed-for fusion of subjective experience and objective perception.

Yokomitsu explicitly addressed the problem of self-consciousness a decade after "Shinkankakuron," in another manifesto titled "Junsui shōsetsu ron" ("Theory of the Pure Novel," 1935):

> I have looked at various assertions that advocate a revival of the literary arts, but I have yet to see any concrete theory. The spirit [seishin] needed to bring about such a revival is a problem I will have to leave for another occasion. However, we must recognize here the numerous underlying sources of the spirit of activism [nōdō seishin] and romanticism [romanshugi] that have flourished since the start of this year. The specific assertions of these movements are issues that should be taken up after we have formulated a theory of the pure novel, for if we neglect the pure novel then neither activism nor romanticism have significance for literature. This is due to the excessive self-consciousness [jiishikikajō] of the intellectual class, which is the contemporary [gendaiteki] characteristic I mentioned earlier. Yet of the people involved in romanticism and activism [nōdōshugi], I have seen no one who can deal with the problem of self-consciousness, which is the most difficult to resolve.[18]

Yokomitsu goes to great pains in this essay to distinguish his term "pure novel" from the term junbungaku, pure literature, which gained currency in the 1920s. The distinction arises from his concern with the self-consciousness of modern intellectuals, exemplified by the notion of pure literature (junbungaku), which he sees as abstract and cut off from authentic aesthetic experience. His concept borrows from Kikuchi Kan's notion of content literature that is not simply popular literature but literature accessible to the masses by virtue of its contact with the essential characteristics of Japanese culture.[19] For Yokomitsu, modern intellectuals are faced with a nearly intractable problem, which is that emphasis on the subject and on individual autonomy creates the critical distance and epistemological skepticism that are the defining features of modern consciousness (what he calls the modern spirit). However, the heightened awareness of modern intellectuals of their belated historical position in an ongoing cultural tradition brings with it the realization that cultural values are relative and that the notion of personal autonomy, the constitutive element of the modern subject, is a fiction—nothing more than an ideological commodity in a cultural marketplace that the individual is powerless to control.

The search for a resolution to the conflicted consciousness of modernity was the prime motivation behind the formulation of his aesthetic principles. The emphasis Yokomitsu placed on achieving a kind of synesthetic immediacy in literature, an effect he tried to describe with the term Sensation, was itself highly abstract and did not single out vision as the dominant sense. Even so, many of his earliest stories are highly imagistic, and Yokomitsu's theories were put into practices that emphasized visual modes of perception. One of the most striking qualities of his developing style, for example, is the scopic, camera-like framing of the narrative perspective, which is best exemplified by the use of apparently objective catalogues of physical elements and surface details in a setting, a technique Yokomitsu employed in some of his early short works like "Hae" ("Flies," 1923) and "Haru wa, basha ni notte" ("Spring Rides in on a Carriage," 1926). This visual style is a marker of his ideological agenda, his desire to resolve the problem of modern identity by an aesthetics of authenticity that demanded the production of real images in art. Yokomitsu's pursuit of that dream is the common thread that ties together the various projects he undertook over the course of his career, and it was that dream that brought him to the city of Shanghai, which provided the setting and title for one of his most influential and sustained literary experiments.

Shanghai and *Shanghai*

Akutagawa, just before his suicide in 1927, had urged Yokomitsu to visit China to broaden his experience and political outlook. For a young Japanese writer driven by the belief that he had to know more of the world in order to sharpen his capacity to feel, the allure of the city was apparent. As a colonized city, it was Asian. As an exotic space where many cultures and races mixed, it was cosmopolitan. It was the creation of Western imperialism and a marketplace of secular materialism. It was a repository of the energy of an Asian modernity that exposed the parochialism of the West and challenged its claim to universality. Because it was both West and East and not wholly either one, Shanghai became for Yokomitsu a space onto which he could project a new image of Japanese identity—Japan as both colonialist power and liberator of Asia—that offered a means to overcome the divided ethical consciousness of modern culture.

The outlines of this vision can be traced to Yokomitsu's one-month sojourn in Shanghai in April 1928. The inspiration provided by this short visit led him to try to clarify and reconcile his political beliefs and aesthetic practices. He noted the political turn in his understanding of Japanese modernity in an essay titled "Kūki sonota" ("The Atmosphere, Etc."), which he wrote soon after his return from China. In jotting down his initial impressions, he remarks with considerable puzzlement that even though the people who are most cruel to the Chinese are the Americans, the Americans are nonetheless the people with whom the Chinese most want to associate. His puzzlement is expressed in strong terms when he writes, "for all that, if Japan does not cooperate with these Chinese, then East Asia will be able to do nothing on the world stage." A few sentences later, he adds that "only Japanese militarism possesses sufficient power to rescue the subjugated East."[20]

The ideological foundation of Yokomitsu's theory of New Sensation was a belief in the epiphanic power of art to put the individual in contact with authentic feelings that could remake ethical consciousness. As a result of his brief experience in China, his views extended in a more overtly political direction. He was convinced that only active intervention by Japan's modern culture could remake historical consciousness as well as allow all of Asia to escape the problem of identity imposed upon it by Western modernity. Thus the conception of both the form and content of Yokomitsu's novel *Shanghai* grew out of the ideological tensions revealed in the terms of the discourse on identity: the struggle between authenticity and autonomy, between universal civilization and national essence. To fully appreciate the ideological conception of the novel, we must keep in mind not only the aesthetic practices that defined Yokomitsu's modernism, but also the economic conditions and political circumstances that the novel references.

Because the story of the personal lives of a group of Japanese expatriates is set against the backdrop of the May Thirtieth Movement of 1925, a brief overview of the situation in Shanghai in the spring of that year is in order.

In November 1924, when Sun Yat-sen declared to Japanese reporters in Shanghai that "Shanghai is China," his words shocked the foreign community and gave comfort to radical Chinese elements in the city. Though the proclamation now seems a statement of the obvious, sovereignty was a hotly contested issue complicated by the city's colonial origins. In the eyes of most foreigners at the time, Shanghai was a unique place, where the intermingling of cultures and economies had created a genuinely international city that was in China but not of China.

Sun's death the following March left unresolved the question of his successor and exacerbated the general uncertainty over the issue of sovereignty in China at large. The atmosphere of unrest and the increasing radicalism of the antiforeign movement, which was directed primarily at the British and the Japanese in Shanghai, resulted in a series of strikes against Japanese textile mills that began in February 1925 and continued throughout much of the spring. The Japanese complained to the Municipal Police, but since most Japanese factories were on Chinese territory, the response of the authorities in the International Settlement was limited. The situation grew more heated in April, when the Municipal Council proposed a number of new bylaws that included measures to increase wharfage dues, reduce child labor, and license Shanghai's stock markets. These measures irritated large sections of Chinese Shanghai and were opposed by the General Chamber of Commerce, which claimed that foreigners had no right to impose such laws. The result was that for the first time in the city a common bond was created between the radicalism of certain groups of workers and students and the financial interests of Chinese businesses and property owners.

This volatile atmosphere exploded on May 15, 1925, when several Japanese mills were struck again. Foremen opened fire on a crowd of rioters, killing one worker and wounding five others. In reaction to this violence, the strikes widened, and a number of groups began to organize resistance against the Municipal Council. On May 30, a group of student protesters was sent into the International Settlement. The protest turned violent in the afternoon, and the Louza Police Station was overrun. At that point, the police opened fire, killing eleven and wounding twenty. The crowd fled, but the event galvanized Chinese opposition. A general strike that included students, workers, and merchants brought Shanghai to a halt. Violence and

looting erupted sporadically throughout the city and spread to other parts of China.

The foreign powers, Britain in particular, eventually restored control over the course of a long summer of disturbances, but the May Thirtieth Movement was a watershed event that undercut the political, economic, and moral arguments used to support foreign domination and privilege. The movement also coincided with the beginning of the civil war in China—a war that the Japanese government eventually used to justify its full-scale invasion and that ended only after the defeat of Japan and the ascension to power of the Communists in 1949.[21]

Yokomitsu uses Shanghai and the historical backdrop of the events of 1925 as a narrative machine that propels the plot of his story. Out of the physical realities of the city, he constructs an ideological dreamscape onto which his characters project their personal desires, emotions, and beliefs. By enmeshing the lives of his fictional characters in historical conditions and events, Yokomitsu attempts to reconcile his aesthetic aim of getting at unmediated experience with the moral aim of resolving the conflicted consciousness of modern culture. In *Shanghai*, the connection between these aims is established not simply by having the characters act as mouthpieces for particular ideological positions—though it must be noted that a number of the characters are delineated mainly by their political beliefs—but also by using the personal conflicts depicted in *Shanghai* as an analogue to the political conflicts that racked Japan and China in the 1920s and 1930s. The structure of the novel reflects these dual aims, in that the first part of the book is a series of sketches that sets out the backstory of the characters and connects them to particular spaces in the city. Once the backstory is filled in for us, the second half of the book shifts to the events surrounding the May Thirtieth Movement and its aftermath, which engulf, almost like a force of nature, the individuals Yokomitsu imagines for us.

The main character in the novel is a young man named Sanki, an expatriate who, unable to make his way in his homeland, left his mother behind in rural Japan ten years earlier. As the story opens, he is working at a Japanese bank, where he spends a good deal of time covering up the crooked dealings of his boss. He is world-weary in part because of his job and in part because he was unable to marry the woman he loves, Kyoko. He is also depicted as an ineffectual dreamer, an idealist whose romanticism is responsible for his failure in the world. His scruples eventually cost him his job and cast him adrift in the swirling vortex of Shanghai at this critical historical juncture.

The second major character is Kōya, Sanki's friend since childhood and Kyoko's brother. Kōya is the opposite of Sanki in almost every respect. He is aggressive, selfish, and unscrupulous, and he is determined to become a material success in life. As the story begins, he has just returned to Shanghai from his posting in a lumber exporting business in Singapore. He has two immediate goals in life: to help his company best the competition from the Philippines and to find a wife.

The narrative sets the stage for the depiction of the city in crisis by taking us through the spaces where these two young friends, Sanki and Kōya, interact with their fellow expatriates and other foreigners—the banks, companies, factories, and stock exchanges where they work, and the dance halls, sex parlors, and bars where they play. The other characters—their beliefs, attitudes, and even their physical appearance—are defined and identified for us by their association with specific places.[22] For example, the outsized, macabre figure of Yamaguchi, a businessman who makes his living preparing and exporting skeletons for medical research, is depicted vividly by way of his connection with the sexual playgrounds of the city and with the dark, rat-infested basement where he makes his living. The duality of his position in Shanghai is made even more explicit by his strong but incoherent support for both pan-Asian solidarity and Japanese militarism.[23] Takashige, Kōya's older brother and the foreman at a Japanese textile factory, is one of the most tangible connections between the Japanese colonial ideology and the events of May 1925. In his case, the space of the factory, which identifies his function in the narrative, is closely tied to fervent nationalism.[24]

There are numerous other instances in *Shanghai* where Yokomitsu uses a particular urban space, national identity, or political ideology to create or elaborate upon a character. However, the identifying function of urban spaces is especially noticeable in the depiction of the main female characters: Miyako, who works at one of Shanghai's dance halls, and who is especially popular with Western men; Osugi, a young woman whose straitened family circumstances have forced her to work at a Turkish bath in order to survive; Qiu-lan, a beautiful Chinese woman who is in reality a Communist agitator and spy; Oryū, the mistress of a Chinese businessman and madam of the Turkish bath where Osugi works; and Olga, a refugee from the Russian Revolution who has become a prostitute and a sex slave sold and traded among a number of Japanese men, including Yamaguchi.

The relationships between the two young men and these women are complicated, to say the least. Sanki is fond of Osugi. He, like a number of

other men, is attracted to her because of her innocence, a quality that stems directly from her helplessness. In spite of her job, her passivity represents a premodern ideal of pure Japanese womanhood to him. Because of his sentimentality, he does not realize that what he sees in her is a projection of his own longings for a return to his idealized dream of a pure Japan, which he associates throughout the novel with his rural hometown, the *furusato* where his mother waits for him. Sanki is unable to act on his desires, however, because of his scruples and his lingering attachment to Kyoko, who has married and returned to Japan. In this respect, he is similar to Sanshirō, in that he is caught between idealized worlds, one represented by his longing for the down-to-earth Osugi and the other by his modern romantic love for Kyoko.

Sanki's idealistic bent is responsible for the crisis that sets the plot in motion. On a visit to the Turkish bath, he rebuffs the advances of Oryū, who then spitefully fires Osugi, condemning her to the life of a streetwalker. Despite his feelings for Osugi, he cannot bring himself to intervene on her behalf or even to look after her. He all but abandons her for much of the time covered in the narrative, especially after he falls in love with Qiu-lan, a hopeless desire he knows he cannot satisfy. His actions are reprehensible, but the narrative treats him in a sympathetic manner by presenting his inner reflections on his motives, showing that he at least has a conscience.

In contrast, Kōya, who for the most part shows only flickers of self-reflection, has no romantic qualms about using the women he meets. He has an ongoing affair with Oryū, even though it means cheating on her patron. On the night Osugi is dismissed, he lets her into the apartment he shares with Sanki but then rapes her during the night. He feels almost no remorse over any of these actions, and though he is defensive when Sanki confronts him about Osugi, he refuses to admit any wrongdoing, seeing his actions as nothing that a little money cannot fix. Kōya carries on in this manner even as he pursues Miyako, who in his eyes would be the ideal wife. Miyako, however, wants nothing to do with him. On the surface, she is interested in Western men, who can better provide for her materially, but in reality, she is attracted to the classically handsome dreamer Sanki. For his part, Sanki is physically attracted to Miyako, but rejects her as a shallow temptress.

As if all of this were not enough, both Sanki and Kōya become entangled with Olga. After Sanki loses his job, Yamaguchi takes the opportunity to foist Olga on him, paying him to be her keeper for a few days. Kōya, after Miyako has rejected him and the turmoil in the city has frustrated his business prospects, is also forced to look after her in return for favors from Yamagu-chi. When he learns of her past and witnesses her vulnerability (she is not only cast adrift but also suffers from epileptic-like seizures), he undergoes a change and begins to see in her a soulmate and a possible wife.

If this brief synopsis makes *Shanghai* sound like a potboiler, then it is be-cause the novel is in part a potboiler. Following Kikuchi Kan's arguments for the value of content in literature and his own interest in the artistic possibil-ities offered by the new popular media of the cinema, Yokomitsu wanted to reach a larger readership, by employing a more accessible style and writing about subjects with mass appeal. To return to his own politically charged evaluation of his career, Yokomitsu had reached a point where he wanted his writing to obediently submit to the national language. In 1929, as he was in the midst of serializing *Shanghai*, he wrote of his aspirations in an essay titled "Mazu nagasa o" ("First, the Length"), where he claimed that "I have once again returned to realism, and think that I would like to settle in this mode for a while."[25] The word I have rendered as realism, *shajitsu*, refers to exact, objective description, to representing things as they really are. It also carries a secondary nuance of visual representation, in the sense of copying or projecting reality, a significant connotation in light of Yokomitsu's efforts to infuse language with unmediated sense perceptions. The idea of realism conveyed by the word *shajitsu* thus gives us some guidance in interpreting the aims of Yokomitsu's novelistic experiment.

Yokomitsu employed a number of the conventions of formal realism, which are sometimes easy to overlook because of the experimental ele-ments of *Shanghai*. A neutral narrative voice and perspective frequently provide exposition and background information, describe actions, and set up conversations between characters. The story Olga tells Kōya of her fam-ily's escape from Russia is an example of how the novel at times follows a decidedly linear narrative arc.[26]

Nevertheless, despite the use of recognizably realistic techniques, the fragmented, episodic plotline, the flattened psychological profiles of the characters, and the intense visual focus on the surface details of the urban landscape suggest that realism for Yokomitsu did not mean simply a lin-ear narrative that tries to conceal its own artifice under the pretense of an objective perspective. *Shanghai* is not a realistic novel in any conventional sense, but a hybrid form distinguished by two key features. The first is a fluid, shifting mix of narrative perspectives, the components of which may be described in terms of the visual modes of modernity—linear, descriptivist, baroque—discussed above. The second is the close association of each character with specific spatial and ideological positions represented by sections of the city, objects, nationality, and political movements. His characters are projected images of a historical consciousness that, at least from the standpoint of Yokomitsu's ideology, is more realistic than any depiction of the inner perceptions and attitudes of individuals.

Carnivalesque Realism

The mix of perspectives in *Shanghai* reflects the influence of the visual arts, particularly the cinema and modernist movements such as surrealism and expressionism, on the ways in which Yokomitsu conceived the narrative structure. This is perhaps best exemplified by the descriptivist technique of using word-images to depict detailed surfaces of the cityscape. This method is sometimes used to establish the point of view of a particular character, but quite often it creates a perspectival effect that may be likened to a camera's eye, not unlike the technique employed by Dos Passos in his 1930s trilogy *U.S.A.* Yokomitsu's descriptivist technique pares away the surplus of language, leaving a representation of concrete objects and spaces that resists the mediation of thought in order to bring about genuine sensation, in the programmatic sense in which he defined that term. Catalogues of objects, lists of shipping notices and telegrams, broken phrases and clauses that describe a physical setting—the presence in the text of this kind of imagistic language creates a photographic effect, by breaking the imagined visual field of the narrative (an illusion created by language) into its constituent parts, which the reader can apprehend only in fragments and at a glance. Yokomitsu's descriptivist techniques disrupt the gaze, the controlling surveillance, of linear narrative, and this effect carries over even to the physical appearance of the text, where dashes visually break up almost every page, setting off the internal thoughts of characters in order to allow the narrative to shift between their perspectives and the imagistic representation of urban settings.

Yokomitsu frequently uses his descriptivist technique for establishing shots, to borrow a cinematic term, allowing him to represent Shanghai as if the reader were looking at a filmed image. The following passages display this particular function. The first excerpt is the opening two paragraphs of the novel, which introduce both the city and the main character.

At high tide the river swelled and flowed backward. Prows of darkened motorboats lined up in a wave pattern. A row of rudders drawn up. Mountains of off-loaded cargo. The black legs of a wharf bound in chains. A signal showing calm winds raised atop a weather station tower. A customs house spire dimly visible through evening fog. Coolies on barrels stacked on the embankment, becoming soaked in the damp air. A black sail, torn and tilted, creaking along, adrift on brackish waves.

Sanki, a man with the fair skin and intelligent face of some medieval hero, walked around the street and returned to the Bund. A group of exhausted Russian prostitutes was sitting on a bench along the strand. The blue lamp of a sampan moving against the current rotated interminably before their silent eyes.[27]

The following passage is the opening paragraph of chapter 2.

A district of crumbling brick buildings. Chinese wearing long-sleeved black robes, swollen and stagnant like kelp in the depths of the ocean, crowded together on a narrow street. A beggar groveled on the pebble-covered road. In a shop window above him hung fish bladders and bloody torsos of carp. In the fruit stand next door piles of bananas and mangos spilled out onto the pavement. And next to that a pork butcher. Skinned carcasses, suspended hoof-down, formed a flesh-colored grotto with a vague, dark recess from which the white point of a clock face sparkled like an eye.[28]

In the first passage, the camera-eye description of the harbor is initially free-floating, unattached to the perspective of any character. The word-images are fragmentary but concrete, and we are not permitted to linger over or survey the scene to establish a single point of reference. Instead, we follow the flow of language as we skim over the disparate objects and images whose order and relationships are not explained. The initial effect of immediacy and wonder changes with the introduction of Sanki, who provides a set of eyes for the reader to make sense of the scene—we do not understand the significance of the word-images, but we at least understand that someone is looking at them and that they help establish his point of view. For that reason, it is appropriate to describe the effect in this case as cinematic.

The second passage creates an even stronger effect of immediacy, because it is presented in the novel without any possibility of assigning the scene to the perspective of a character. The closest character happens to be inside Oryū's Turkish bath, which is located between the pork butcher and the fruit stand, and thus cannot see the setting that the word-images represent. The effect of immediacy, wonder, and even disorientation over how to interpret the significance of the objects in the scene is heightened by the strange, nearly surrealistic juxtaposition of images that make the everyday strange, exotic, and even foreboding.

Yokomitsu's descriptivism, when it is employed in isolation as in the passages above, is one of the most distinctive and memorable elements of *Shanghai*. However, this technique more often appears in combination with others to help create a fluid perspective. To fully capture a sense of the overpowering stimuli provided by the experience of force and motion in the modern city, Yokomitsu developed a narrative mode that may be described as carnivalesque, allowing him to connect his descriptivist imagery with the moods and frames of mind of his characters. Although I am drawing on Martin Jay's terminology (the baroque visual mode), I have chosen the word carnivalesque because the term "baroque" has connotations that are not relevant to *Shanghai*. In addition, the novel itself suggests that "carnivalesque" is a more appropriate term, for whenever Sanki is sad he goes out "to observe the near-desperate revelry of the teeming crowds of all nationalities. It was like watching a carnival."[29]

A few examples will illustrate the narrative qualities of carnivalesque realism. The following scene sets up the initial explosion of violence at Takashige's factory.

In the depths of the rainy season rails were distorted by evening mist. A hooded carriage on the verge of breaking down crept like a shadow through a valley of brick buildings. A Eurasian prostitute rested against the wall of an arched gate, staring into the rainy street. Acacia flowers placed around the cover of the gas lamp in front of her were rotting and oozing. Headlights spouting fog between narrow buildings passed by carrying a drunken man who was asleep, his mouth agape.

Sanki walked by the prostitute and into the alley. At a soot-blackened bar near the back the sweetbreads he favored were simmering in a pot. The place was almost deserted. The bar's Madam stood by a miniature lamp cleaning her eyes with gauze soaked in boric acid and listening to the sound of the rain. Sanki ordered samshu and decided he would drink until Takashige arrived. Then the two were scheduled to check on the night shift at the factory. The shaved head of a Chinese man on the other side of the pot with the simmering sweetbreads remained motionless, emitting a dull sheen like a piece of Seto porcelain. The watery sound flowing from the gauze pressed against the Madam's eyes, together with the liquor, sent a chill up Sanki's spine. In front of the bar a Chinese man leaned on a brick pillar smoking a pipe with his eyes closed. On the tip of the needle of the pipe a toffee-colored bulb of opium trembled and gave off a sizzling sound. Pigs' feet with coarse hairs here and there thrust out cloven hooves.[30]

The first paragraph is another example of an eerily atmospheric establishing shot, but the description is complicated by the interaction between the setting and the feelings of the protagonist. Sanki is one of the objects in the scene, but he is also an observer who reacts physically to the stimuli around him. How we read the significance of the scene remains indeterminate and open, though certainly Sanki's mood, his unease at the violence he and Takashige are likely to confront at the factory, inflects the scene, turning the overabundant surface of objects and details into a partly comic, partly hellish atmosphere foreshadowing the chaos to come. In many ways, this technique exemplifies Yokomitsu's literary modernism.

The use of a carnivalesque realism to represent sensation, that is, to capture perceptions of the materiality of Shanghai, not only contributes to the fluid perspective of the novel but also serves as one of the primary means to create mood and delineate character. It also performs an ideological function, in that word-images are deliberately and rigidly patterned so that different spaces in the city are equated with specific characters and political positions.[31] The Chinese sections of the city are associated with natural images, such as flowers, vegetables, and birds, suggesting that the people there are more grounded in their native land than the foreigners in the International Settlement.[32] In contrast, the harbor, business, and pleasure districts are associated with the flow of water and light.

Sanki went out with Kōya, leaving Osugi at his place. It was rush hour and rickshaws filled the streets, flowing like a river. Riding atop their rickshaws, the two drifted along with the crowd. As if by mutual understanding they kept their silence about Osugi. In fact, Sanki was certain that Kōya had brought Osugi home, and Kōya was sure that Sanki had called her over to his place.

Other streams of rickshaws flowed out from between buildings. When those streams combined at street crossings, the figures of the rickshaw-men disappeared as their cars squeezed ever more tightly together. The passengers formed a silent throng, their upper bodies floating on waves that slid past all at the same speed. To Sanki it didn't seem there could be rickshawmen hidden beneath that crowd. Running along the walls of brick buildings, he gazed on this lively flood tide of people of all nationalities, and searched for faces of acquaintances. At that moment Kōya, who had been drifting behind Sanki, pulled alongside.[33]

The absolute identification between place and inhabitants, the physical experience of being caught up in the speed and movement of the modern metropolis, which is likened to the sensation of flowing water, is extended to include the flow of capital, the image that identifies the economic character of Shanghai.

[Kōya] decided to drop in at the nearby gold exchange and have a peek before going to the Muramatsu Steamship Company. At that moment the exchange was in the midst of its trading hours, and a human whirl-pool, spinning about with a roar, was squeezed into the middle of the hall. A wall of telephones slightly darkened the interior of the hall. The throng of people, smeared in oily sweat, chests pressed together, flowed back and forth between the two centers of buying and selling. The swirl continued round and round, back to front, left to right, amid a constant careening and shouting. It folded back on itself and then moved again, inscribing a circle and colliding with the wall. Repelled, it surged back. Spectators sitting on rows of chairs along the walls that surrounded and looked down on the trading pit silently cast glances toward the center of the whirlpool.[34]

The carnivalesque experience of spatial and visual flux is presented as potentially bewildering and exhilarating, but it is also identified with the desires and inner life of Kōya. The image of water and the sensation of flowing are transposed onto the different levels of imagined spaces in the novel: the carnival-like space of the city, which is the compressed space of economic transactions, where movement initiated in Shanghai has almost immediate effects in London or New York; and the space of Kōya's desires, which are provided an object and a stimulus in the whirl of the market.

The repetitive use of word-images gives the novel a tight internal co-
herence, by creating leitmotifs of sensation for different zones in the city
and for individual characters. As we can see from the passages above, the
overwhelming number of word-images are related to water, which conveys
sensations of flowing, dampness, fecundity, and decay; of shaking, swelling,
rising, sliding. These effects are reinforced in the language of the novel,
by the extreme repetition of certain grammatical forms: the subordinate
conjunction *to*, which marks a conditional temporal state; the conjunction
nagara, which expresses simultaneity of action; the adverb *futo*, which suggests sudden, unexpected action; the conjunction *shikashi*, which is primarily used by Yokomitsu as a visual bridge to run sentences together. All of
these elements combine to create a visceral sense of movement in language
that conjures the experience of space in a modern city.

Carnivalesque realism captures the surplus of goods that is the city even
when, as in the passage immediately above, we are presented a scene through
the eyes of a single character. The result is a fragmentation or fluidity of
perspective that helps to represent both the sense of physical disorientation
produced by Shanghai and the unsettling social and economic disruptions
that are an important part of the reality of the city. This reality is made visible to us most clearly by the depiction of back streets and slums, which are
associated invariably with images of stagnant water, human waste, and the
maze of dilapidated buildings. They are also identified with Osugi, who by
this time has been abandoned by Sanki and Kōya. In a desperate situation,
with nothing to eat and no support, she considers becoming a prostitute.
She takes to the streets, but the looks she gets from men are not at all what
she was expecting. She is pursued by a man, and in trying to get away, she
is drawn deeper into the slums.

> "You've got me wrong. I'm not like that."
>   In a panic, she ducked into an alley and anxiously turned corner af-
> ter corner. In the recesses of that alley she spied a swollen naked back
> through a hole of sharp, broken glass. She came to a halt. She had lost
> the way out. Above her head laundry was hanging in a row like fish blad-
> ders soaking the walls. A woman leaning against a pillar was coughing,
> her bony shoulders twitching. On the floor behind her a naked man and
> woman with diseased eyes were squatting around a single red candle.
> Osugi glanced up and saw silent faces peering out from each of the win-
> dows in the walls that pressed in on her from all sides. She stumbled

like a trembling stick across the paving stones and got lost farther and
farther in the labyrinth of walls. Lights gradually disappeared. And in the
darkness a mountain of countless rags she assumed was a pile of rubbish
began to creep from the corners of the walls. She was suddenly stopped
short by a wall, and her legs would not move. A pile of those black rags,
stuffed between the narrow walls, swept over her like a thick wave. In an
instant Osugi saw human nostrils lined up like dots before her eyes. As
she fainted she was sucked into a hardened wave of rag-covered backs
and disappeared.[35]

As in the passage where Kōya observes the gold exchange, Yokomitsu's
depiction of Osugi's plight conflates image, the black turgid water of the
slums, character, her tragic mix of naiveté and confusion, and the space of
the horrifying freak show of the backstreets of Shanghai as a way to represent the economic dislocations of modernity.

Yokomitsu's fluid perspective, the visual quality of his descriptivist style,
and his carnivalesque realism are perhaps used to best effect in the novel
after the historical events of May 1925 overtake the individual stories of the
characters. For example, the following passage appears about two-thirds of
the way into the novel, after the critical moment when some striking workers were shot and killed at Takashige's factory. A series of protests and riots
have led to a general strike. Sanki, who has fallen for the beautiful Fang
Qiu-lan, a leader of a Communist cell, takes a risk by going out in the streets
during the disturbances in hopes of seeing her again. He gets his wish during the fateful riot at the police station on May 30.

Sanki was forced back into the sunken entrance of a shop and could see
only a pivoting transom opened horizontally above his head. The rioting
crowd was reflected upside down in the transom glass. It was like being
on the floor of an ocean that had lost its watery sky. Countless heads
beneath shoulders, shoulders beneath feet. They described a weird, suspended canopy on the verge of falling, swaying like seaweed that drifted
out, then drew back and drifted out again. As the riot continued swirling about, Sanki searched for the face of Fang Qiu-lan in the crowd suspended over him. Then he heard more shots. He felt a tremor. He tried
to reach out into the crowd on the ground, as if he were springing up. He
disregarded his own equilibrium, which floated up into the confusion of
the external world. His desire to fight that external world, which rose up

irresistibly in him, was like a sudden attack of a chronic disease. Simultaneously, he began to struggle to steal back his composure. He tried to watch intently the velocity of the bullets. A river made of waves of human beings sped past in front of him. These waves collided and rose up like spray. Banners fell, covering the waves. The cloth of the banners caught on the feet of the flowing crowd and seemed to be swallowed up into the buildings. Then, at that moment, he saw Qiu-lan. A Chinese patrolman attached to the Municipal Police had grabbed her arms and restrained her near one of the banners. Sanki's line of sight was blocked suddenly, so he fought his way through the wave and ran to the side of a building. He could still see Qiu-lan in the clutches of the policeman as she silently watched the riot swirling around her. Then she saw him. She smiled. He sensed death.[36]

Yokomitsu's handling of scenes of crowds and rioting demonstrates the same kind of visual movement from a wide external perspective to an internal one employed in the opening scene of the novel. However, the passage above struggles against the conventional language of realism. For all its circumstantial detail, the scene achieves a surrealistic quality in its juxtaposition of the inverted images in the glass and the visualization of the velocity of the bullets. The mode of carnivalesque realism permits Yokomitsu to reveal to us the struggle of Sanki not to lose the consciousness of himself in the mob. There is a powerful tension between the unconscious tide of political revolution and the observing consciousness of the individual, and for Sanki, the politically charged scene before him momentarily dissolves to an image of sexual desire and death. The representation of a particular historical site and moment collapses to an ostensibly nonideological vision that erases historical time and place and creates a visual field onto which the sensation of individual desire may be projected.

Yokomitsu's hybrid form of realism creates a close association between each character and particular spatial and ideological positions. This feature was noted above in connection with the descriptivist mode used in the novel, but Yokomitsu is not after the affect of imagistic writing only. He goes to great lengths to represent the carnival that is Shanghai in order to create a historical space into which he can project his characters. This is most problematic aspect of the novel, because the projection of the characters onto historical events flattens out their psychological profiles, giving the reader little sense of their interior lives. Many of the characters are either assigned stock cultural traits or rendered as mere conduits for particular political viewpoints, and in that respect, *Shanghai* flies in the face of the expectations usually brought by a reader to a work of formal realism. However, even if the flatness of many of the characters is taken to be a flaw of the novel, that judgment is tempered by the aims of Yokomitsu's return to realism. The creation of realistic characters in this case has less to do with conjuring the illusion of interiority, of a developing individual consciousness at work below the outer appearance and actions of a character, and more to do with establishing a close identification between the characters and the swirl of historical realities.

In projecting his characters as images or embodiments of certain traits that define the identities of the Japanese in Shanghai, Yokomitsu relies on synechdochic descriptions in which a distinguishing physical feature stands in for the whole personality. Komori Yoichi has described this feature of the text as the reification of the bodies of the characters, especially Sanki.[37] The loss of humanity that comes with the capitalist transformation of the individual into an economic commodity is reflected in Yokomitsu's method of representing his characters. As commodities, the individual lives in *Shanghai* exemplify the circularity of projecting an identity whose idealized form is devoid of real content. As observers of the spectacle of Shanghai and as participants in that spectacle, they become the very embodiment of autonomy without content. Their physical appearances are like advertising copy, good in displaying or stimulating desires but ultimately empty of meaning until projected upon the space of historical consciousness.

Throughout the novel, the commodification of the characters is almost obsessively tied to physical appearance. This is most apparent for the women, whose bodies are explicitly marked as commodities. Oryū has a tattoo of a large gold spider on her back, an over-the-top sign of her predatory nature. Olga is marked by her Russian features, especially her white skin; her racial difference is the source of her market value. Osugi's value, in contrast, derives from the desire stimulated by her dark skin, which marks her as the daughter of a lower-class family but provides her with an aura of authenticity and innocence. Miyako, in contrast, is depicted as a *moga*, a modern girl, whose long legs, Westernized looks, extravagant tastes, and sexual liberation give her value as a hybrid—a product of global modernity whose appeal derives from a mix of exotic and familiar features.

Even Qiu-lan, who ostensibly represents a cause beyond herself, is depicted as an ideological commodity. In her role as worker, spy, and agitator, her physical appearance changes according to circumstances: a beautiful femme fatale when she appears at Miyako's dance hall or goes out with San-ki, a revolutionary in worker's garb, a spy disguised as a man when she has to escape the authorities. Near the end of the novel, we learn that she has been killed by her own comrades, perhaps because her relationship with the Japanese Sanki has compromised her. Her fate underscores how her bodily identities were simply markers that pointed to the emptiness of her individual character. This void was apparently filled by her ideology, but as it turns out, her beliefs were a mere gesture of autonomy, as her exploitation as an ideological commodity makes clear.

The commodification of the bodies of the male characters is given a similar degree of prominence. In the case of Kōya, he perceives his own identity as a businessman in terms of surfaces, keeping "his collars spotless, a sharp crease in his trousers, and a smile on his face, hiding the anxieties of the home office beneath a smoothly knotted tie."[38] He believes that his appearance, a mark of his economic prowess, will also make him a desirable husband. As the novel progresses, however, his perception of his identity as a desirable economic and sexual object comes to be linked to his body in terms of race. This linkage becomes clear to him the moment Miyako rejects him.

Kōya stared at the retreating figure. He knew instinctively that the sturdy long-legged foreigners who gathered around her were attracted to her legs. *Why should a Japanese man be scorned in this way?* Lamenting his own short legs, Kōya strolled up to the front of the park gate. It was too much of a bother for him to ask why the only legs not permitted to enter the park from this gate were Chinese.

Flickering in the light of the gas lamps, Miyako waited for Kōya under the fresh leaves of the pruned linden trees.

"You and I can always be good friends in a place where there are gas lights," she said.

Her triumphant smile made its way through a tunnel of green leaves that continued on into the distance. A road shining like a flat whetstone. A hedge of roses. Cars sliding by, their bellies reflected in the light. An alphabet of signs marching on toward this citadel of illumination. When he reached this point, Kōya had to admire the manners of the foreigners who continually gave him trouble, even if it was only because his admiration showed that he, at least, was not Chinese.[39]

At the beginning of the story, Kōya lacks the imagination or self-aware-ness to understand that he is not entirely in control of his fate and cannot impose his desires. The fact that his body is marked by his racial features suggests the nature of his personal dilemma, which he gradually becomes aware of over the course of the story. For example, in a later scene he argues about the economic and political situation of Asia with Oryū's patron, the Chinese businessman Qian, and ends up justifying Japan's policies and the need for Chinese-Japanese cooperation entirely on the basis of a crude the-ory of race. However, as a consequence of Qian's challenge to the ideologi-cal sources of his identity as a businessman, Kōya suddenly becomes aware that, despite his disdain for Qian and the Chinese, he too is a yellow man.[40] By the end of the novel, it seems that he gains some sense of reconciliation with his racial identity, at least insofar as he can feel desire and empathy for Olga. Even so, the impetus for the development of Kōya's character is his gradual awakening to the ideologically determined value of his body, which is often described in racial terms.

Whereas Kōya is a figurative embodiment of the ideology of race, Sanki's character is a projection of the ideology of nation. From the very beginning, he is equated with the conflicted consciousness of modern Japan. After the opening paragraphs of the novel, Sanki speaks with the Russian prostitutes and shares a cigarette with them.

> The prostitutes stood and sauntered away one by one along an iron rail-ing. A young woman at the end of the procession glanced back furtively at Sanki with her pallid eyes. Then, with a cigarette still between his lips, Sanki felt overwhelmed by a dream-like sadness. When Kyōko had an-nounced that she would leave, she had looked back at him in the same way as this young woman now.
>
> Stepping over the black ropes that moored the boats, the hookers disappeared among the barrels. All they left behind was a banana peel, which had been stepped on and crushed, and some damp feathers. A pair of booted feet was sticking out from the entrance of the patrolman's tower at the end of the wharf.
>
> As soon as Sanki was alone he leaned back against the bench and re-called his mother back in his home village.[41]

The introduction of Sanki and the Russian prostitutes brings alternative perspectives to the scene, which gradually becomes more subjective as these characters turn their gazes on one another, first as sexual commodities and then as empathetic figures, since all of them are strangers in a strange land. This scopic movement ends with the internal visualization by Sanki of the culturally potent image of his mother back in Japan. This move from external visualization, which situates the narrative in a murky alien setting colored in misty blues, grays, and blacks, to Sanki's internal visualization, the perspective of an outsider who expresses the rootless expatriate's longing for the familiar, equates desire with nostalgia and an awareness of loss from the very outset of the novel.

The only way Sanki can fill this void is to cling to his Japanese identity, and of all the characters, he is the one who is most directly linked to the idea of nation. On the day he loses his job, he takes Osugi to a restaurant. Having no way to support himself, he knows that he will have to abandon her, and he mulls over their circumstances.

> With the exception of the Russians, an individual—even if they were idle or unemployed or simply aimless—could be seen as an expression of patriotism simply by being here. Sanki laughed at the thought. The truth is, if he were in Japan the only thing he would be good for is reducing Japan's food supply. But because he was in Shanghai, the space his body took up was always a territory of Japan.
>
> *My body is a territory. This body of mine. Osugi's body.*[42]

Sanki is acutely aware of the irony of the sources of his sense of self, and, unlike the other characters, he better understands the implications of being reduced to a physical commodity in Shanghai. By thinking of his body as Japanese territory, his identification with his home country becomes absolute, but that identification exposes the emptiness of his sense of identity. Over the course of the novel, Sanki's self-understanding becomes paralyzing, as he becomes increasingly attracted to a nihilistic view of the world. Going out one night, he and Kōya discover the body of a murder victim. They leave the scene quickly and go their separate ways. Kōya heads for the Turkish bath, and Sanki decides to look in on a peepshow of naked Russian dancers.

> Sanki now saw in the twilight corner of this street a new aspect in the development of human degradation. These people no longer felt carnal desire. They laughed in high spirits in order to train for a new life as

humans who would be habitually depraved. An architecture of skin. A dance of nihilism. Our precursors. Weren't they truly emitting a bright, living light? *Banzai!* Sanki involuntarily raised his glass to toast them. The factory of skin extended and contracted, then transformed into an arched tunnel. A Chinaman with a shaved head covered in oil stuck out his tongue and started to crawl inside the tunnel like a camel. A flower garden filled with figs was reflected at a slant on the bluish skin of his head, which glistened from the oil. If you didn't look up at the world and everything in it from below, then its beautiful cinematic spectacle would be lost. The tunnel started to collapse. Sanki glanced behind him. He saw a beast stuck hard like the suckers of an octopus on the faces of a crowd of onlookers clustered together. From among the wave of clothing that buoyed up that huge beast, he came to appreciate the architecture of a barbarous civilization.[43]

Sanki is depicted from the beginning as a man attracted by death, but the reasons for his dark thoughts are initially attributed to his personal unhappiness at having had his dreams of love thwarted. As the story progresses, however, it is clear that the greater problem is that he is a man out of place and time. He is increasingly attracted to a self-denying nihilism, as he becomes more aware that he cannot escape the trap of modern consciousness. This awareness is liberating in that it completely cuts him adrift, a condition apparent in the fact that he is the only character who moves freely across all the different spaces of Shanghai. Yet for all his mobility, he cannot escape his own self-conscious desires, and thus resists the projection of his identity into a state where the self is overcome. Once the city falls into near anarchy, his fate is to be caught up in a history that he knows is profoundly alienating. He tries walking the streets disguised as a Chinese, but each time he witnesses an act of violence, he realizes he can never pass.

> He became aware again of the fact that he was Japanese. How many times had he been informed of that fact? Because of the danger posed by his being a flesh-and-blood embodiment of Japan, he felt that the crowd pressing in on him was a beast with fangs. He pictured simultaneously in his mind the spectacle before him now and the spectacle of his own body flowing from his mother's flesh. His own time, the flow marked by the interval between these two spectacles, was undoubtedly also the time

of Japan's flesh and blood. And perhaps from this point on as well they would be one. So what could he do to liberate his heart from his body and freely forget his mother country? His flesh could not resist the simple fact that the external world forced him to be Japanese. It wasn't his heart that resisted. It was his skin that had to take on the world. And so his heart, in obedience to his skin, began to resist.[44]

There is no possibility for a resolution of Sanki's dilemma. He feels that he has a responsibility to his mother country, that he needs to confront the violence on the streets, and yet wonders if his suicidal actions show that he is willing to die of his own volition. Were his ideas his own, or ideas he has been made to think for the sake of his nation? "Now he wanted to think for himself. But that would be to think of nothing at all—it would be to kill himself. *Right, so everything is empty.* In his isolation he was depressed right to the very pit of his belly."[45]

The indeterminacy of his fate and that of the other characters is represented in the structure of the narrative, which leaves the story suspended at a moment before the colonial and capitalist orders of Shanghai are restored. At the very end of the book, Sanki is finally reunited with Osugi. He has narrowly escaped death at the hands of a mob, and, having no food and no place to stay, he searches out the house where he has heard she now works as a prostitute. The electricity has been cut off, and when he finds her, her rooms are completely dark. She does not light any candles because she is ashamed for him to see the squalor and degradation of her life. The perspective of the novel's final scene shifts back and forth, revealing first Sanki's remorse.

> At that time he had nothing but words as a means of rescuing Osugi. If it were wrong to keep a woman who can no longer make a living in your house until she can, then what else could he do? The only thing he could be faulted for was not embracing Osugi and loving her. Sanki thought that of all his sins that was the worst.
>
> To make love with her.... What was wrong with that? It would be better for Osugi than not embracing her at all. In spite of that, until he came to embrace Osugi, he would think of ever so many things.
>
> And yet he had to admit that all his many thoughts came down to the same thing. How long could he go on mistreating Osugi?
>
> "Osugi? Come here. Don't think about anything. Just come here."

Sanki stretched his arms out to her. Her body fell heavily into them. At that moment Qiu-lan, in her aquamarine dress, vividly filled his arms.

Shortly after this moment, the narrative concludes with Osugi's desperate memories.

Osugi recalled the loneliness that followed the day Sanki left her behind in his house and did not return—a time she spent alone gazing absently at the surface of the water in the canal. On those occasions oil constantly floated beneath the fog like some design on the water. The bluish-green growing on the sides of the crumbling mortar lapped up the oil on the surface. Beside it floated the yellowish corpse of a chick that drew toward it scraps of greens, socks, mango peels, and straw rubbish. Together with pitch-black bubbles that welled up from the depths, these items formed a little island in the middle of the canal. Osugi did nothing for two or three days but gaze at that little island and wait intently for Sanki to come home. If tomorrow the naval brigade landed and restored order to the city, wouldn't she once again have to continue on blankly, just as in those days. Then once more the men—their coarse, shark-like skin, their mouths reeking of garlic, the sticky oil plastered to their hair, the long fingernails, the sharp irregular teeth. Reflecting on these things, she stretched out like a patient who has given up and stared into the darkness spread across the ceiling.[46]

The most remarkable aspect of the closing pages of the novel is that the vivid imagistic descriptions of the city continue to appear prominently even though this scene is played out in utter darkness. Shanghai has been wholly internalized, with Sanki and Osugi projecting their own desires as images of the city. Of course, the differences between the visions they project into the dark are enormous. Sanki's is an idealized desire to possess Qiu-lan, a vision of exotic sexuality that effaces not only cultural and historical differences but also his own moral responsibility for the fates of both Qiu-lan and Osugi.

Osugi's vision focuses on the social and economic inequities, embodied by the squalor of Shanghai, that are the causes of her terrible predicament. The early death of her father, who was a soldier, and the suicide of her mother, who was forced by the Japanese government to repay the pension she mistakenly received after the death of her husband, left Osugi adrift and in a precarious position. The cause of her degradation is thus tied explicitly to circumstances that arose as a consequence of Japan's pursuit of empire. Her gaze into a blank future suggests the costs of modernity, and the closing image of an utterly powerless woman, a common figure in the popular arts of this period, gives full expression to desperation associated with the modern city.

The Wrong Side of History

Almost a decade after the composition of *Shanghai*, Yokomitsu returned to the subject of the link between the city and his political and aesthetic ideas. In a miscellaneous essay written in 1939 called "Shinakai" ("The China Sea"), Yokomitsu tells of his second brief trip to Shanghai, which was by then occupied by the Imperial Army. On the way, he made a brief stopover in Kyushu to see Mt. Aso. This diversion provided him with a native site to contrast with Shanghai. Although he notes that most foreigners think there is nothing manmade worth seeing in Japan, he stresses love of nature as the essential trait of Japanese culture, in which only spiritual beauty exists. Authentic Japanese identity lacks the self-consciousness that defines urban—and urbane—culture.

> I no longer think that there are any cities in Japan. It is hard to call Tokyo or Osaka a city. They are simply collections of country villages that have been raked together, doing away with any formal need for a city. Put another way, we could say that the national entity [*kokuzentai*] is a single city. For the sake of nature the national entity maintains the form of a single city.
>
> Considering the current state of affairs, with the Japanese army spilling out over the continent, it seems to me that what is happening is that the one city that is Japan is gushing up and flowing out over the wilderness [*gen'ya*].[47]

Yokomitsu intentionally employs the language of paradox in what now seems a wishful, almost desperate attempt to assert that the spirit of Japan has overcome the conflicted identity of modern culture. The war, it appears, forced a resolution of Japan's divided ethical consciousness. The essence of the nation was always embodied in the premodern, authentic space of the village, not the modern city, but the tension represented by the spatial divide between rural and urban no longer seems such a pressing problem for Yokomitsu, who concludes there are no cities in Japan. The spirit of the nation, which *is* nature, which is ultimately beyond the control of human reason and the reach of language, takes the form of a universal city. And if the city is everywhere, then it is also nowhere, and the problem of identity dissolves.

The description of Japanese cities in this essay imagines a space where parochial identities can exist within the boundaries of empire. Indeed, Yokomitsu's essay invokes the language of imperial destiny, where nature, that pure, unmediated source of Japanese culture, is equated with the political will that has led to war. The image of a flood moving across the landscape of China is disturbingly apt and morally reprehensible in the context of Yokomitsu's beliefs, because it seeks to conceal the violence of war by the metaphor of the processes of nature, which burst asunder the temporal and spatial boundaries of human history. "Nature knows nothing at all of war. In that case, then, what does it know? Certainly the battlefront has flowed through, and continues to flow on to distant Changsha. I gaze after it, thinking about it after the fact. Goethe once said that everything becomes complicated when we consider it after the fact."[48]

Yokomitsu continues his essay by arguing that we are all within the flow of history, and he tries to overcome the problem of modern consciousness by reducing it to the sorts of recurring patterns he sees in the unconscious processes of nature. Here the significance of Shanghai is revealed in its boldest form, because he sees the city, especially the International Settlement, as "the birthplace [*kokyō*] of the problem that ever occupies my thoughts." He writes:

> The problem of the International Settlement is one of the most perplexing in the world. At the same time this location also represents the problem of the future only. To some extent it is a very simple thing, but there is no other place on earth that so manifests the quality [*seishitsu*] that constitutes the modern [*kindai*]. What is more, there exists nowhere in the world except the Settlement a site where all nations have created a common city. To think about this place is to think about the world in microcosm.[49]

Yokomitsu focuses on the future the city represents, which allows him to imagine a resolution of the dilemmas of modernity without having to deal with the inconvenient facts of the international political situation of his day. The essay is thus a return to the political and aesthetic ideology expressed by both the form and content of *Shanghai*. The intense focus of the novel on Japanese expatriates reflects not so much literary parochialism as the reality of Shanghai culture, which was born of imperialist desires and nurtured by colonial regimes. The book's depiction of the racial and political attitudes that were current at the time of its composition is deeply disturbing, because these attitudes are so thoroughly aestheticized and eroticized. *Shanghai* is a stylistic tour de force that, by vividly depicting a richly complex mix of politics and aesthetics, gives us a feel for the contours of the imaginary landscape of nation and empire in 1930s Japan.

During the composition of *Shanghai*, Yokomitsu explicitly stated that his aim was to create a new realism as a counterweight to the Marxist literature of the Proletarian School of the 1920s. The end result was a historically informed, sharply ideological literature that longed for the erasure of the consciousness that sustains political ideology. Yokomitsu's aim reflects the warring elements of his political beliefs, which eventually settled into an uneasy mix of pan-Asianism and antileftist nationalism, and his aesthetics, which embraced cosmopolitan culture as an object of desire while trying to maintain a central place for authentic Japanese/Asian culture. Yokomitsu's project was riven by a fault line along which his essentialist politics and his radical aesthetics, the tectonic plates of his modernism, shifted.

The desire to resolve conflicted identity and move beyond Western modernity to a broader cosmopolitanism was a powerful ideological justification for Japan's colonial and military policies in the 1930s. In the long run, the association of pan-Asian cosmopolitanism with the militarist dream that culminated in the Co-Prosperity Sphere was impossible to sustain. With military defeat came the collapse of that dream and of the dreams of men like Yokomitsu.

5
Toward a View from Nowhere

B Y THE TIME THE Japanese government broadcast the recording of Emperor Hirohito announcing Japan's surrender at noon on August 15, 1945, at least three million Japanese had died in the war. Millions more were sick, wounded, malnourished, and homeless. The material culture and the economic infrastructure of the country, especially the industrialized zones of urban areas, had been nearly obliterated.

Accompanying the physical destruction was a shattering of spirit that produced widespread malaise and demoralization. Guilt over the murderous conduct of the Japanese military was compounded by a sense of victimization. The devastating emotions fueled by remorse and the humiliation of defeat were made even more bitter by the awareness that Japan's losses had been in vain. Veterans were often treated with disdain, and some victims at home—war widows, orphans, and even survivors of the atomic bombings—faced indifference and discrimination. Many Japanese never had the opportunity to properly mourn their losses, either because loved ones did not return or because the sheer effort to survive took priority.

The realities and the perceptions of social upheaval were reinforced by the legal and economic reforms imposed by the American occupation authorities. These changes fundamentally challenged not just the accepted norms of the prewar period, but also the disciplining institutions that had sustained those norms. The system of primogeniture that determined inheritance and the laws governing property rights were amended; the legal status of women was altered with the constitutional conferral of a range of political, legal, and human rights; the military and the governmental structures that supported it were abolished; rights to assemble, to organize trade unions and political organizations, and to exercise free speech were extended; and the practices and structures of many of the largest business firms were brought under regulatory control. The effect of these changes went well beyond the primary aims of the American conquerors to demilitarize and democratize Japan. They radically altered prewar understandings of the basic categories of self-identity, family, and nation.

The occupation reforms were disruptive of received values and social institutions and their aims were often contradictory and incoherent, but their impact on the economy and on the legal and political status of individuals made palpable a sense of change and potential even amid the uncertainty. For most Japanese in 1945, the age just ended had ultimately proved tragic, but it was a period that could be read in hindsight as a coherent if simplistic narrative. Beginning in the mid nineteenth century with the forced abandonment of the policy of self-imposed isolation, Japan had reimagined itself as a nation, emerging at the turn of the twentieth century as a global military and colonial power. Ultimately, its dream of empire in Asia was destroyed by the reckless pursuit of war and conquest.

Because the new age that began with surrender loomed as a void presenting at best a chaotic prospect, most Japanese were forced to reconsider the meaning and sources of their values. As a result, despite the chaos, the late 1940s marked the beginning of one of the most radically transformative periods both culturally and economically in recent Japanese history—a cultural re-creation that was chronicled and exemplified by the remarkable output and achievements of literary artists.

Of all the talents who emerged during the unsettled atmosphere of the decade following the end of the war, Ōoka Shōhei (1909–1988) authored some of the most compelling representations of the ethical and spiritual crises confronting his age.[1] His career had begun as soon as he graduated from the Department of French at Kyoto Imperial University in 1932. With the support of Kobayashi Hideo, Ōoka tried his hand at fiction, but most of his output during the 1930s consisted of critical studies and translations. In 1933, he read *The Charterhouse of Parma* by Stendhal (Marie-Henri Beyle), and from that point on, he immersed himself in the study of Stendhal's works. Over the next decade, his interests expanded to include the works of André Gide, Raymond Radiguet, and Natsume Sōseki.

Several characteristics shared by the writings of Stendhal and Sōseki proved to be especially attractive to Ōoka: their irony and skeptical distance, their sensitivity to class distinctions, and their anxiety about the place of the individual in modern society. As a member of an important literary coterie centered on Kobayashi, Ōoka worked in an intellectual climate that viewed the ethical consciousness of Western modernity as a form of unbridled egoism. His early career thus coincided with a period when many of his older contemporaries, such as Yokomitsu, felt pressured to find a way out of the trap of individualism and return to an essential, authentic culture.

Ōoka was not able to support himself solely by his writing, and for several years he worked at jobs in companies where he could use his knowledge of French. In early 1944, he was drafted into the Army and eventually shipped out to Mindoro Island in the Philippines. Following the American invasion on December 15, he was taken prisoner in January 1945. Ill from malaria and traumatized by combat, Ōoka spent several months in a POW camp before being repatriated in December 1945.

The traumatic experience of war and defeat, which reduced the lives of soldiers to such basic instincts of human nature that it called into question the relevance of any system of moral, political, or religious values, tempered his early literary propensities and gave them a harder edge. Like many other writers of his generation, Ōoka was interested in exploring in his art the struggle between the individual's desire for self-realization, for personal autonomy and freedom, and the constraints of social conventions, which achieve their force by appealing to a belief that there is something real beyond the self. As a result of the war, however, Ōoka became preoccupied with the limits of human perspective, knowledge, and judgment, a tendency that led some contemporary critics such as Fukuda Tsuneari to label him a cynic.[2]

A high degree of skepticism about the sincerity of human intentions and the possibility of achieving moral certainty is a prominent element in Ōoka's writings, but to label this attitude a form of cynicism misleadingly implies that Ōoka is not searching for the ground of right action but already assumes it does not exist. Isoda Kōichi suggested that it might be more accurate to see in Ōoka's literary method a kind of stoicism. He argues that beyond Ōoka's reputed cynicism there is a hidden longing for purity or immaculateness (mukō).

Ōoka's stoicism is stoicism toward desires. Looking back over his literary career...I recall the following words recorded quietly in his journal of October 1946: "The descending order of my literary dream. Rimbaud—Lafcadio—Fabrice. An unsullied dream. A dream averse to reality" [from Sokai nikki].

Of course, if an untainted dream were easily achieved, then any literary youth could write about it. But isn't literature only ever born out of "dreams that have been killed?"[3]

Isoda points out the gap between the subjectivity of desires and intents and the purity and universal detachment of ideals that preoccupied Ōoka.[4] Expressions of doubt about the sincerity of human intentions and motives and the possibility of achieving moral certainty are a recurring element in Ōoka's fiction, which draws its power from the ambivalent attitudes it strikes toward the war in particular and the experience of modernity in general. There is a sense that the evil caused by human stupidity and desires is inescapable, but that apparent cynicism is softened by the artistic quest for a subtler language that can express something meaningful beyond the self. Ōoka creates a critical consciousness that strives for a total integration of the subjective motivations and actions of his characters with external historical and social realities.

Finding a Place in Postwar Japan

The novels *A Wife in Musashino* (*Musashino fujin*) and *Fires on the Plain* (*Nobi*) provide the most fully realized examples of Ōoka's critical consciousness. *A Wife in Musashino*, which was first published serially in the literary journal *Gunzō* from January to September 1950, was composed simultaneously with portions of Ōoka's great war novel. Ōoka had begun serializing *Fires on the Plain* in the journal *Buntai* from December 1948 to July 1949, but when the magazine folded before he could finish it, he decided to rewrite the novel even as he began preparing *A Wife in Musashino* for publication. Although the two novels stand alone, they are nonetheless linked to each other in theme and style, as obverse and reverse, by their depiction of the effects of war and defeat at home and overseas.

A Wife in Musashino was a critical and commercial success, quickly adapted to film by Mizoguchi Kenji and released in 1951.[5] The popular appeal of the novel may be attributed to a number of factors. First, it is in many respects a conventional narrative that softens its sharply critical view of the decadence of postwar Japanese society with elements of romantic melodrama. The story depicts the doomed love between Michiko, a beautiful young wife whose old-fashioned upbringing and values are now out of place in postwar Japan, and her cousin Tsutomu, a troubled young man recently returned from the war. Second, beyond the love story itself, Michiko is a variant of a popular archetype, the young woman whose life had been disrupted in some way by the war. This sentimentalized figure, whose beauty and potential as lover and mother have been sacrificed for the nation, dominated postwar film and fiction by artists whose views ran the whole of the ideological spectrum. This dominance was partly the effect of occupation censorship of portrayals of military themes and heroes, but the power of the archetype, which was most famously embodied by a number of actresses—Hara Setsuko, Tanaka Kinuyo (who portrayed Michiko in Mizoguchi's film version), and Takamine Hideko—was able to bear the weight of postwar aspirations, longing, and regret. Third, the romantic melodrama and the figure of Michiko contribute to a sense of nostalgia for spaces and values that maintain a connection, however tenuous, to traditions and ways of life that were perceived as authentic but fading amidst all the destruction and reconstruction.

The source of the popular appeal of *A Wife in Musashino* is the degree to which Ōoka enmeshes the story of Michiko and Tsutomu in postwar conditions. This feature of the novel may be traced back to his early engagement with Stendhal. Erich Auerbach has observed that what made Stendhal's fiction a significant literary phenomenon was its ability to logically and systematically situate the imagined lives of his characters "within the most concrete kind of contemporary history."[6] The influence of Stendhal's fiction was decisive, though it was also inflected, as noted above, by Ōoka's personal experience of war, which nurtured a deeper understanding of the nature of suffering. Ōoka's critical consciousness enabled him to write with logical precision and at times acerbity, without his voice becoming cold, abstract, or attenuated.

Ōoka so fully situates the motives and attitudes of his characters within contemporary history that his novel almost incidentally provides a snapshot of the state of Japan in 1947, when most of the action takes place. The subcultures of the black market, of decadent college students, and of the *panpan*, the prostitutes who show up in the areas around Koganei Station and Tsutomu's apartment in Gotanda, provide the backdrop to the story. This kind of closely observed detail helps convey the postwar atmosphere of license and desperation that sets off the tragedy of Michiko and Tsutomu.

Ōoka pays close attention as well to the settings in which the relationships among his characters play out. Many of these spaces provide evidence of the ongoing presence of war and defeat in 1947: the burnt-out ruins around Ebara, the deforested fields near Michiko's home at Hake, the abandoned factory and airfield that Tsutomu explores on one of his many hikes around Musashino, the untended and overgrown park near Gotanda, and the shabby hotels at Sayama ruined by the wartime economy. These spaces give a vivid sense of contemporary history not only by their specificity but also by their relationship to the most important space in the novel, the topography of the Musashino plateau.[7] Local spaces in the novel are explicitly linked to recent history, but they are grounded in a landscape that possesses both deep-rooted cultural and mythic associations and a material reality that is indifferent to the transience of human history.

Ōoka's imagined landscape simultaneously represents contemporary history and mythic memory. The depiction of the main characters—their personalities, habits of mind, and even their physical appearance—draws heavily on the deeply rooted cultural associations evoked by place. Eudora Welty has famously noted the importance of place to the literary arts, and has argued that skillful evocation of place through words has everything to do with making characters real: "Place in fiction is the named, identified, concrete, exact and exacting, and therefore credible, gathering spot of all that has been felt, is about to be experienced, in the novel's progress. Location pertains to feeling; feeling profoundly pertains to place; place in history partakes of feeling, as feeling about history partakes of place."[8] Welty presents not a romanticized glorification of space but a practical element in the rhetoric of fiction that sheds light on Ōoka's techniques.

Ōoka goes to considerable lengths to evoke the multiple planes of space that give specificity and depth to his characters and enable the reader to imagine their consciousness and motivations. Take, for example, the opening lines of the novel, which presents the backstory for the main characters in terms of their relation to place, especially Michiko's home in Hake.

People who live in the area aren't sure why the place is called Hake. But mention the name of Ogino Chōsaku, whose family is one of the oldest of the many Ogino households among the farmers of this region, and they assume that Hake is the elevation where Chōsaku's house is located.

There is a road that runs from the tracks midway between the Kokubunji and Koganei stations on the Chūō line. If you walk south along that road for about two blocks, crossing some level fields, the terrain suddenly descends and opens out onto the basin of a small river called the Nogawa. The slope of the narrow current is relatively steep because it is one of the oldest terraces created when the ancient Tamagawa River shifted to the southwest. In an earlier geological age the Tamagawa flowed out from the Kantō highlands, producing the sedimentation that shaped the broad Musashino plateau. This plateau is now bounded on the north by the rivers Irumagawa and Arakawa, on the east by Tokyo Bay, and on the south by the present-day Tamagawa.[9]

The effect of this kind of deep description, which is used throughout the novel, creates a sense that the story emerges out of the very landscape. The grounding of Michiko's family in this particular place also throws into greater relief the disjuncture between the suburban space of Hake and the new realities of postwar Japan.

Whenever people from the city, weary with concerns about money and food, visited these two houses, they went home either amazed or dejected that such a relaxed realm could exist in this harsh world. The houses commanded a view from the hillside of the greening Tama basin. Looking out at the clustered groves, in which a pale green seemed to be permanently fixed, people wondered if even the trees at Hake preserved the new colors of spring. Hearing that the pale green was chestnut blossoms, they felt even more amazed or dejected. Chestnuts were a profitable crop for the farmers of this area, so close to the city, and groves thickly covered the ground wherever you looked.[10]

The distance between Hake, the site of traditional values, and contemporary society is a motif running through the depiction of the incident that drives the plot: the adulterous affair between Michiko's husband Akiyama and Tomiko, the wife of Michiko's cousin Ōno. Akiyama and Tomiko are shallow, selfish, and morally reprehensible, but their motives are not incomprehensible. Neither feels at home in the worlds they inhabit, and their psychological and cultural displacement brings them together, even though they are not in love.

Akiyama is a descendant of peasants who marries Michiko, a descendant of *hatamoto* (samurai who once served the shogun), in order to climb the social ladder. He escaped his native village by becoming a scholar of French literature, and though he lacks imagination, his translations of Stendhal bring him a measure of wealth as a result of the publishing boom that occurred right after the war. His life is a variation of the near-mythic story of a young man coming from the provinces and making his way in Tokyo. The geographical poles of traditional village and modern metropolis consistently define the narrative parameters of this myth and create an inherently dramatic tension. Success in the modern world of Tokyo is desired, but even when it is achieved, it always comes at the cost of spiritual displacement and loss of identity.

Following the pattern of this modern myth, Akiyama overcomes the disadvantages of his birthplace and family past, but his newfound status as an intellectual and literati is not enough to satisfy the desire and ambition that drove him to seek a new life in Tokyo. The very emblem of his success, his marriage to Michiko, serves as a constant reminder of his former inferior status. Akiyama feels that he does not belong to Hake, and he does everything to avoid living there until his own home is destroyed by the American bombing campaign. Once he has moved to Hake, Akiyama's resentment grows until he is driven to take revenge.

Akiyama's resentments are not entirely without justification. His personal appearance constantly reminds him of his native place. Wiry and dark-skinned, he is self-conscious of his peasant heritage because of the caste discrimination he suffers at the hands of Michiko's brothers and her father.[11] The evocation of place establishes the character of Akiyama, who, though frighteningly vindictive, is not entirely beyond understanding. Akiyama's self-identification with characters like Stendhal's Julien Sorel, an ambitious social climber he misreads as a sophisticated romantic hero, suggests his lack of a moral center, and his displacement is an analogue to the complex, confused mix of yearning and ambition that propels the plot to its tragic end.

Tomiko is also an outsider trapped in a loveless, cynical, and abusive marriage. If Akiyama typifies the myth of the young man on the rise, Tomiko represents another cultural type, the *moga*, or modern girl. Like the character Miyako in *Shanghai*, Tomiko is a variation of a stereotype that first appeared in the 1920s whose Westernized beauty, vivaciousness, and sexual license suggested the simultaneous lure and danger of modern urban culture. Tomiko's milieu is the metropolis, and she is perhaps the most rootless of all the characters in the novel. Her father was a corporate executive who moved his family from place to place during her childhood. She picked up customs and manners from Tokyo, Osaka, and Nagoya, but was never grounded anywhere. The fact that she is so adept at performing her roles implies a woman who is essentially formless and empty.

Tomiko seems less developed than the other characters for much of the novel. Ōoka describes her initially in stereotypical terms—the coquette, the flirt. Tomiko is all fashion and show, all body and appetite; like Akiyama, she is resentful of her place in society. Being so rootless and restless, she is also capricious and headstrong, and those traits create the impression that her motivations verge on the irrational. By the end of the novel, however, Tomiko develops into a fully realized character. Nurtured in the culture of the modern metropolis, her identity is tied not to inner qualities but to outer surface. Her consciousness is drawn not from a spiritual core but from the gaze of others, especially men. Tomiko tries to satisfy her longings and desires through the only power—the only capital—she has, which is her body. She is empowered and victimized by her looks, though she lacks the moral consciousness to understand completely why she is trapped. Nonetheless, her motivations, the causes of her resentment, are not fully revealed to us until we learn that her brother-in-law made sexual advances to her when she was just fourteen.[12]

This revelation by itself does not explain everything, but the act of self-reflection that calls forth the memory of her childhood trauma gives a depth and interior reality to Tomiko that helps us understand the full force of her destructiveness. It is important to note that this moment of memory and self-reflection occurs at a hostess bar, the kind of place where male eyes and hands turn women into commodities. This identification with the demimonde of the Tokyo bar scene endows Tomiko with a conflicted identity as manipulative coquette and victim who is always a sexual object.

Ōoka's evocation of place to depict the subtle nuances of social and class distinctions is also brought to bear in the creation of the character of Tomiko's husband, Ōno. He is a hustler whose shady and reckless business dealings call to mind all the excesses of wartime profiteering and the postwar black market. His desire to keep up the appearance of high social status is materialized in his showiest possessions—his liberated wife and his modern-style home. Driven and superficial, he is every bit as egotistical and selfish as Akiyama and Tomiko. However, he is also connected to Hake in a way that they are not, and that connection gives his character a grounding that Akiyama in particular lacks.

Ōno is not a major figure in the novel, but he is identified with concrete spaces of home and garden that reveal his tastes, status, and weaknesses.

He turns his back on the more traditional aspects of Hake to pursue his fancies, though his identity is more firmly fixed than the others, because it is rooted in the place that evokes his family history. His class consciousness is the source of his prejudices, perverse mischievousness, lack of self-awareness, and pretentiousness. Yet he retains some sense of his responsibilities as a husband and father—a basic if unsophisticated core of moral awareness that enables him to forgive his wife and to recognize the horror of Tsutomu's final transformation at the end of the story.

Michiko, who feels at home in Hake, is the only character identified with a single place. She is accustomed to the area around Musashino, implying her connection to traditional culture. Her upbringing and family history, as the last direct descendant of the Miyaji family, is another important marker of her connection to the past. The cultural associations of Hake and Musashino and the history of her family are the sources of her identity. Because she has so fully internalized her role as wife, her sense of self is unassailable, and because she has so fully internalized the virtues that come with her role, she seems to instinctively know what is right and good, and is not driven by the desires, resentments, longings, or delusions that destabilize the lives of Akiyama, Tomiko, and Ōno.

Michiko's rootedness, the source of her moral strength, becomes in the particular context of postwar society the cause of her tragedy. Although she is not displaced at the beginning of her married life with Akiyama, she slowly comes to see herself as a kind of anachronism. Ōoka draws this aspect of her character to the reader's attention by the epigraph to the novel that sets up a comparison between Michiko and Radiguet's heroine, the Countess d'Orgel: "Are feelings such as those that stirred the heart of the Countess d'Orgel out of fashion?" Ōoka later explained that he appended the epigraph in order to be fair to the reader and indicate his debt to Radiguet. More important, he insisted that one of his aims was to defend the old-fashioned modesty (*kofū na teishuku*) of his heroine.[13] The word *teishuku* conveys more than just modesty. It refers to a range of wifely virtues, including devotion and chastity. Ōoka's phrase "old-fashioned modesty" neatly captures the two key aspects of Michiko's life: her role and status as traditional wife and the anachronism of that role in 1947.

The novel generally shows Michiko in a favorable light, but the narrative also stresses the inflexibility of her character and the precariousness of her situation. Her tragedy unfolds when she is confronted with two crises. The first arises when she falls in love with her cousin, Tsutomu. *A Wife in Musashino* was marketed as a *ren'ai shōsetsu*, a love novel, and it certainly owed its popular reception to its narrative mix of lurid adultery and doomed romance. Even so, the depiction of Michiko's love may be the most difficult aspect of the novel for contemporary readers to comprehend. This is in part because the notion of romantic love carried negative connotations for a woman like Michiko. As pleasant and natural as her feelings for Tsutomu are, she has been trained since childhood to view love as a potentially dangerous passion, an expression of willfulness and emotional autonomy unbefitting a wife. In the case of her love for Tsutomu, which is both adulterous and incestuous, the emotion is destructive of all the things that create and sustain her identity. Michiko's confused response to her emotional autonomy is not just psychologically credible, but crucial to the design of the narrative, which identifies character so closely with the spaces of the novel. It is therefore significant that Michiko confronts her feelings for Tsutomu at the very geographical heart of Musashino, in a place called Koigakubo ("Lovers' Ravine"), where the source of the Nogawa River that runs in front of Hake is located. Musashino is the source of identity for Michiko, but it contains a place associated with a legend of tragic love and suicide that stirs her consciousness of her own conflicted emotions.

Michiko's personal turmoil is a threat to her socially defined sense of her identity, but so long as she remains in the place that provides her with spiritual stability she can defend her old-fashioned modesty. Her ability to protect herself crumbles away, however, when the second crisis arises. Akiyama, Tomiko, and Ōno conspire in different ways to take Hake away from Michiko. All their actions—the disposition of the Miyaji estate that gave Akiyama partial control, the way Akiyama and Tomiko flaunt their adultery, Ōno's misuse of Michiko's land as collateral for his business dealings, Akiyama's demand for a divorce under conditions set by the new legal code—take advantage of the changing realities of postwar society and effectively diminish the value of Michiko's status.

> Now that [Akiyama] had left, memories came drifting back to Michiko as she sat at the desk. She had stopped loving him long ago, but at least he was someone she protected as part of the household at Hake. He had made his way honorably in society as a scholar, and he had given to her the title most becoming to a woman of her age—the title of *wife*. She realized, now that he was gone, just how accustomed she had grown to the ease conferred by that title.

Hereafter she would go by the designation of *abandoned wife*. It would be difficult to endure such wretchedness. It made her angry to think of her state as wretched. She felt that somehow she had to break the spell that held her.[14]

The sympathy of the novel toward Michiko's loss of status is more than a little nostalgic, but it credibly explains her reasons for resolving the crisis by deciding to kill herself. Michiko's suicide redeems her identity as wife, balances the moral scales, and shows her love for Tsutomu.

As she comes to her decision to commit suicide, the house at Hake loses its meaning for her. Visiting her family's grave in Tama cemetery, she asks the spirit of her father what she should do. Remembering a statement he once made that suicide was the moral course of action when there was a purpose to death, she determines to die.

Muttering the word "action," Michiko suddenly revised her thinking. *That's right. I have to stop Akiyama from disposing of the house as he wishes.* Her lingering attachment to Ōno and Yukiko was a mistake.

The vision of living happily with Tsutomu floated before her again. She dispelled that vision as well. *If I lived with him, I'd fall into the same brutish condition as Akiyama and Tomiko. Besides, Tsutomu is the kind of young man who can put his arm across the shoulder of a woman like Tomiko. That's right, isn't it? If I leave him my estate, perhaps he'll come to understand. It's best for me to die.* With that, Michiko made her decision and left her father's grave.

The natural world of autumn in the cemetery was transformed. She felt as though nature was pressing in on her, burning with the single color of red. Her eyes saw almost nothing.[15]

Once again the evocation of place serves, to borrow Welty's phrase, as the gathering spot of all that has been experienced in the novel. Michiko is immersed in a world suffused with the classical poetic image of *momiji* in autumn, but the traditional significance of image is inverted, suggesting annihilation rather than affirmation of identity.

As he stands by her bedside watching her die from an overdose of sleeping pills, Akiyama misreads his wife's motives as badly as he misreads Stendhal. In order to deflect blame from himself, he has to read her death as a romantic tragedy in which she has sacrificed herself for Tsutomu. He knows that his reputation will be ruined, and he hates her for what she has done. He even thinks that because she died for Tsutomu her suicide is "none of my business."[16] With no moral center, he cannot understand that her motive for death is inextricably bound to her identity as wife.

Michiko is the dominating presence in the novel, but Tsutomu is in many ways the most disturbing of all the characters. Displaced as a boy by his parents' divorce, then as a young man by the war, Tsutomu is described by a bewildering range of contradictory traits: decadent and amoral, quiet and sensitive. He needs to be spiritually healed and emotionally comforted, but his experience in the military has made him cynical and selfish. His impassive reaction to the news of his father's suicide at the end of the war shocks Michiko and prompts the narrative to remark that his lack of feeling might make him seem inhuman.[17] Having witnessed so many acts of depravity, he can no longer abide by the conventional rules of society.

Tsutomu is anti-intellectual and antidemocratic, but his powers of introspection make him the most self-reflective character in the novel. He knows that he is out of place when he finally returns to Japan, because he carries within himself the alien landscape of Burma that he still experiences as frightening moments of dissociation.

> Once in a while, whenever he was absorbed in some serious thought, he would go for a walk. Suddenly he would be caught up in the illusion that the green fields of Burma had sprung open around him. The center of these fields was always the spot on the ground before him where he fixed his eyes. Cannons would roar and people would groan. Afraid that his hallucination would turn into reality, he could not look up. Although he would eventually come to his senses and realize that he was simply on a street corner in a large city in Japan, the hallucination inevitably disrupted his thoughts.[18]

Because of these feelings of dissociation, Tsutomu is consciously obsessed with place and is absorbed in studying the topography of Musashino, which he explores in order to find himself.

> Memories of the mountains in Burma flooded back to him. Tropical jungles drop their leaves with no regard to season, and the forest paths are narrow. When he was in Burma, Tsutomu often recalled the forests of Musashino. Now, in this June forest of Musashino, he thought of the lush jungles of Burma.

Tsutomu sat down on the grass. Except for the singing of a bird hidden in the upper branches far above, there was no sound. He took a deep breath.

"One lives freely in the mountains and forests." He recalled this line of a Meiji-era poet. Tsutomu, who had wandered solitary in the tropical wilds, knew how frightening freedom could be. The harmony of the pleasant green of the oaks that had played the muse for the Meiji poet now looked to Tsutomu like nothing more than firewood. He could not imagine that an oak could grow so luxuriantly without the aid of human beings.[19]

The evocation of place as a way to put the reader in touch with deeper spiritual and aesthetic values has a long history in Japanese poetics.[20] However, these walks through the landscape are therapeutic for Tsutomu only to the extent that they make him aware that his heart is wounded.[21] In the process of exploring the land, of seeking out authentic meaning and identity in the ancient ground of Japanese culture, he discovers that Michiko is what he wants to be—a person rooted in a place, virtuous because grounded in an identity and in values that are authentic. The love he feels for her and she for him springs from this intense identification. As cousins, their love is already incestuous, but the identification goes further, in that they look like each other, like brother and sister.[22] Their mutual passion amounts to a kind of self-love, in that they recognize in each other a Platonic ideal of themselves.

The sense of belonging Tsutomu feels when he is at Hake has been denied to him by the circumstances of his childhood and by the war. He is driven to reconnect with society, and he believes that his love for Michiko will bring him closer to obtaining peace. His dream is blocked, however, by Michiko's moral qualms. She almost gives in to him, but the dire consequences that would ensue leave her no choice but to insist that they separate. Her decision so wounds him that he comes to hate society, which he blames for the rigidity of Michiko's ethical consciousness. He eventually expresses that hatred in a violent fantasy of murdering every citizen of Tokyo by poisoning the water supply. Appalled by his own thoughts, his illusion of finding himself by studying the topography of Musashino and reconnecting with the ontological ground of culture is wholly shattered.

I could never view the Musashino plateau, even though I climbed Sayama several times. So that's just a fantasy as well, isn't it? What does the delta of the ancient Tamagawa have to do with me? That river existed long

*before I was born. Even the forests of Musashino that people talk about
so much? Weren't they all planted just to protect generations of peasants
from the wind? Factories, schools, airports, the sprawling residences of the
citizens of Tokyo. These things are Musashino now.*[23]

In the collapse of this fantasy, we are presented with a devastating critique of the spatial imaginary of identity that had so sustained artists of the prewar period. When Ōno informs him of Michiko's death at the very end of the novel, Tsutomu undergoes a final displacement, a total exile, which is such a total destruction of feeling and identity that Tsutomu no longer remains human.

> Just as he was stepping out of the apartment, Ōno realized that he had not told Tsutomu that Michiko was dead. He hastily pulled Tomiko back inside.
>
> The human heart is a strange thing. Ōno tried to put on a brave front, but his heart was already strained by this setting, where he had quietly taken back his faithless wife. He lacked the imagination to be able to recognize the nature of the love between Tsutomu and Michiko, but he was able to sense, at that moment, that the news of Michiko's death had transformed Tsutomu into a kind of monster. And he was afraid.[24]

Ōoka does not treat either the death of Michiko or Tsutomu's metamorphosis in the language of a love novel. His style throughout the work is distant and unsentimental. In this respect, Ōoka openly acknowledged his debt to Stendhal and Radiguet, whose language, he noted, had been compared to the dry reverberation of ivory on ivory that occurs when chess pieces move across the board.[25] The rarefied elegance suggested by this image may apply in some degree to Ōoka's language, but that does not mean the novel is aloof and emotionally detached. By questioning motives and foregrounding the historical and personal forces acting on his characters, Ōoka's method gives them depth and thereby brings the reader closer to the sources of the tragedy of Michiko and Tsutomu.

Narrative Mode and the Morality of Thought

A Wife in Musashino presents a complex, ironic picture of the unintended or unforeseen consequences of the collapse of the old moral order that

came with the lifting of wartime repressions and the reform of laws governing adultery, inheritance, women's rights, and divorce. Though the narrative
expresses sympathy for the aims of the reformers, it is also skeptical about
the value of autonomy, since Tomiko, Tsutomu, Ōno, and Akiyama all mistake freedom for license. However, the novel is hardly advocating a return
to the moral authoritarianism of the prewar and wartime state. Michiko's
struggle to live according to the dictates of an older ethical consciousness
is self-destructive, and the novel does not naively valorize her actions. Her
suicide is a performance not of authentic values and moral valor, but of
an aestheticized anachronism, and in the end, her death is judged an accident.[26] Tsutomu, longing to see her, but afraid that showing up at Hake
without Michiko's consent will further harden her heart toward him, spies
on her. He sees her taking what looks like medicine, but because he does
not understand what she is doing, he does not act to stop her. The contingency of circumstances, then, means her death is nothing like the actions
of the old warrior class her father extolled. Instead, it is tinged with irony,
exposing the illusion that she was in control and the emptiness of her devotion to traditional values. As the narrative puts it: "If her death had not been
an accident, then no tragedy could be said to have taken place. That's the
way tragedy is in the twentieth century."[27]

The character who understands the nature of modern tragedy and must
live with its consequences is Tsutomu. He has stood on the precipice of
moral nihilism throughout the novel, having rejected every political and
ethical philosophy he has encountered in his studies. In the end, he is transformed into "a kind of monster" because he has received confirmation of the
terrible lesson that freedom and the inviolability of values are an illusion,
which he learned at the front in Burma. He realizes that chance governs life,
not necessity, and that human beings have no real control, but are subject to
the whim of their own desires and impulses, or to those of others.

This revelation comes to him just before his illusions about the topography of Musashino collapse and he fantasizes about murdering all the people
in Tokyo. On the way to Sayama Heights, the place that holds his most
important memories of Michiko, he observes the students around him on
the train.

They all had the same social status as he. They were poor and weary.
Many of them believed in Marxism. These students justified their weariness as a necessity. They seemed comical to him. They reasoned that the

war had also been a necessity. But Tsutomu, who had experienced the reality of war, knew that in war there was a madness and a disorder that cannot be gauged by the word *necessity*.

Could he explain his love for Michiko on the basis of necessity? There were many things about the actions people took that could not be judged on such a basis. So wasn't it a mistake to insist on necessity as an explanation? He could see nothing but madness behind the necessity these students invoked.[28]

Tsutomu sees through the fictive, random nature of the values, justifications, and identity that society uses to construct a sense of order, but he clings to one last hope, which is the vow he made to love Michiko. He knows that the vow is an empty performance. Yet the very act of believing that they might find happiness and meaning in nothing more than their feelings for each other offers a way to live in a world where belief in something genuine is otherwise impossible. Michiko's death, of course, puts an end to even that small hope, and as he loses all sources of belief, his nihilism makes him monstrous in the eyes of conventional society.

The consequences of disillusionment and the dissolution of ethical consciousness at the heart of Tsutomu's story are explored in even greater depth in *Fires on the Plain*. The narrator/protagonist, Private First-Class Tamura, has witnessed the breakdown of moral order that accompanies defeat on the battlefield, and like Tsutomu, he too comes to understand the fictive nature of values. Consequently, the only meaningful thing left for Tamura is to perform his story as a way to reconnect with his past and, possibly, with reliable sources of value and identity. By focusing events solely through the perspective of Tamura, Ōoka raises broad, disturbing questions about the ability to make moral judgments of actions taken under the duress of extreme situations. How does one narrate the past, or judge it, when the reliability of memory is uncertain? Is it possible to write intelligibly about extreme experiences that break the bounds of normative values? And to the extent that a narrative succeeds in capturing the essence of such experiences, does their reduction to literary language render them abstract and inauthentic?

These questions are not resolved in *Fires on the Plain* because of the circular manner in which they are raised. The narrative consists of Tamura's remembering and authoring his wartime self, and his ethical consciousness emerges out of the performance of his story. However, the narrative is disrupted by a jarring disjuncture between Tamura's remembrance of the universe of battle, murder, deprivation, and cannibalism in the Philippines, part of which has been lost to amnesia, and the scene of writing, six years after the war in a psychiatric hospital in Japan, where he explains his wartime autobiography as a type of therapy aimed at recovering and disclosing the past. By revealing this explanation of the origin and production of the text in the novel's final section, "A Madman's Diary," the narrative twists back onto itself, and its inconclusive, indeterminate ending forces the reader to reconsider the meaning of everything that has been told up to that point.[29]

The fracture that runs through Tamura's account, which attempts to deal directly with both the experience of war and the circumstances of the story's composition, creates the effect of multiple perspectives, even though there is but a single narrator. Compared to *A Wife in Musashino*, which on the whole is more conventional in the sense that the narrative is temporally linear, *Fires on the Plain* disrupts linearity. There is the remembering Tamura of the mental hospital, a critical persona who provides a retrospective interpretation of his earlier motives and values—a critical metanarrative of his life—and there is the remembered Tamura of the battlefield, a persona that in turn recalls the past and speculates on his condition. These multiple perspectives arise because, as Tamura attempts to view his situation more objectively by moving deeper into his memory, he becomes conscious of the gap between his subjectively recalled account and an objective point of view from which he could evaluate the ethical meaning of his experience. The dialectical tension produced by his growing awareness of this gap approaches what Adorno called "the morality of thought"—a process of ethical evaluation that is neither wholly detached nor wholly subjective, but one in which the narrator tries to be "at every moment both within things and outside them."[30]

The dialectical breach in the narrative that gives the effect of multiple first-person perspectives largely determines our interpretation and evaluation of Tamura's actions. Tamura's probing analysis of his remembered self is an attempt to restore the sense of autonomy that was stripped away when the Imperial Army compelled him, in spite of his moral beliefs, to fight and kill. It is an effort to ascend to a perspective beyond the particular and subjective—to what Thomas Nagel has termed "the view from nowhere." I am adapting Nagel's phrase here to suggest both the importance to Tamura's ability to make ethical judgments of assuming an objective view and the risk of alienation that accompanies a truly detached perspective on the world.[31] To find some ground for judging his actions, Tamura tries to evaluate his experiences on the basis of the most complete view of the circumstances and, by extension, of the most complete view of himself that he can achieve. Under normal circumstances, such self-analysis would be unexceptional. Although we cannot achieve absolute detachment, in the everyday world we can achieve sufficient objectivity to make judgments of right and wrong or good and bad with reasonable confidence. However, this kind of "common sense" breaks down in extraordinary situations, and the radical break that is the crucial feature of Tamura's account of his actions and experiences—his crime of murder, his resorting to cannibalism, his amnesia—points to the irreconcilable divide between the inherent limits of human perspective and the desire to get beyond the self to an objective view that would enable him to know the truth and recover his spiritual and psychic wholeness.

In order for Tamura to heal the split in his psyche, he believes he must somehow recover the missing part of his memory. To do that, he writes his wartime account with a view to looking at himself objectively, for only a view from "nowhere" holds the promise of achieving the kind of autonomy or narrative control that would enable him to discover the truth about himself. The predicament he confronts is that this objective view must start from the subjective experience that constitutes his divided sense of self; otherwise, he would have nothing to go on in his judgment of his actions and, more important, no reason for trying to move to a more detached perspective in the first place. An objective point of view holds out the promise of autonomy and self-knowledge, but the more knowledge of himself Tamura recovers, the more he realizes that he lacks complete knowledge and autonomy. As Tamura becomes aware of the chance, created nature of his subjective self, his search for ethical meaning, prompted by the desire for wholeness, blocks the satisfaction of that desire.[32] His obsession with his own story traps Tamura in the process of thought and ethical evaluation, leaving him uncertain and divided.

The paradox posed by Tamura's struggle with the problem of perspective reverberates throughout the text. In the final section of the novel, Tamura describes himself as a madman, but his so-called madness, which is a form of dissociation, is also the source of his most profound insights into the arbitrary nature of the moral values that most of us take to be normative, since his awareness of the presence of multiple selves within makes him skeptical and arouses the desire for a more complete view of the world. The fact that Tamura's psychological condition is complicated by retrograde amnesia provides a plausible reason for his inability to absolutely judge his actions, and it also provides the motive to examine his life through autobiographical journals. The amnesiac blank at the heart of his story, however, serves as more than just motive. It is a kind of narrative supplement that stands in for what is otherwise impossible to get at through the process of self-evaluation: complete knowledge of the self.

The fact that particular circumstances rob Tamura of his ethical autonomy and prevent him from achieving an objective view and getting at the whole truth in turn raises the important role that chance plays in his story. Chance is crucial to Tamura's evaluation of his motives, especially since the notion of chance could potentially be exculpatory. Unfortunately, explaining his actions as a matter of moral luck undermines the basis for believing in any value. His concern with the role chance has played in his life leads him on an obsessive quest for the detached perspective that would restore a sense of necessity or inevitability to his experiences.

The conception of chance and necessity is more complex and fully developed in Tamura's narrative than in Tsutomu's. Tsutomu, motivated by his desire for Michiko, rejects the idea of necessity, preferring to see human life as subject to chance because it provides him with a justification for destroying society's moral conventions. Tamura, on the other hand, wants to elevate the principle of chance to a matter of necessity. This obsession with objectivity and necessity is reflected throughout the text in Tamura's metaphysical speculations on the connections among his observations of the repetitious patterns of nature, the sense of the continuity of identity, and the origins of his religious sentiments. Tamura's outward projection of himself toward a view from nowhere exposes his lack of true autonomy and accounts for the concern with God and with Christian theology in particular that is so pivotal to the story. Tamura's desire to find something beyond himself suggests that the divine is an emanation of his own preoccupations—something that emerges from the process of critical self-analysis.

The treatment of the problem of narration in the novel emphasizes the metanarrative question of how to talk about extreme circumstances. This may seem to abstract from their historical context the terrible realities on which *Fires on the Plain* is based, but Tamura's story equates the problem of determining his own guilt with the metaethical problem of how he can talk about his guilt at all. The mediating presence of the self-conscious, questioning narrator is so strong in *Fires on the Plain* that the work cannot be read without considering the questions of epistemology posed by the narrative perspective. A representation of differing perspectives, even the multiple perspectives of a narrator such as Tamura, does not necessarily constitute an objective point of view. It can, however, create a convergence of perspectives out of which a more complete view of experience emerges. That convergence toward the point where an individual can be at every moment within things and outside them is always incomplete, but it makes the process of ethical judgment possible.

Dissociation, Amnesia, and the Created Self

Fires on the Plain begins *in medias res*, with Tamura being slapped by his squadron leader, as though he were being slapped into an awareness of his situation. This awakening begins the dialectical process by which the narrator reaches into his memory as far as he can go before he reaches its final limit: "Assuredly that forgotten period remains within me like a bright streak in the darkness. When my recollection reaches this point, what might be called a total reflection occurs, and I can go no further inward from the moment of the rain-spattered breechblock of the rifle I was holding."[33] The predicament for Tamura is that his intense scrutiny of the past does not lead to reintegration, but to a state of extreme dissociation signified by the empty "bright streak" of amnesia.

Tamura suffers from several kinds of memory loss: physiological amnesia, brought on by a wound to his head; repressed memory, the intentional forgetfulness that allowed him to get on with his life for five years immediately following the war; and, during his time in the Philippines, cultural amnesia—the loss of a sense of identity and humanity caused by his separation from the customs and institutions that defined him as an individual. In addition, the physical and psychological stresses of the fight for survival undercut the familiar view of the world that was the source of his belief system, and the loss of the ethical order that defined his identity leads to a growing awareness of his own mortality.

> My growing fascination with the natural beauty of the Philippines was itself a symptom of my abnormal state of mind. A successful infantryman must look at nature only from the standpoint of necessity. A gentle hollow in the ground is nothing but a shelter from artillery fire, the beautiful

green fields simply dangerous terrain that must be crossed on the double. Indeed to the foot soldier, as he is shoved around from place to place, depending on the particular tactics of the day, nature in all her sundry aspects is essentially meaningless. It is this very lack of meaning that supports his existence and provides the wellspring of his courage. Now if, as a result of cowardice or of introspection, this solid carapace of meaninglessness should crack, what is revealed beneath is something even more meaningless for living men: it is, in fine, a premonition of death.[34]

Tamura's dissociation begins with the loss of autonomy that occurs when he is conscripted, and his unexceptional view of the world and the things he takes for granted, such as the beauty of nature, are so radically challenged that his former way of thinking becomes as strange and alien as the landscape he traverses. The most basic assumptions and feelings that gave his life order, including the necessity of his own existence, are exposed as empty and superfluous. His resulting "madness" and insight are marked by a subtle but clear shifting in the perspective of the passage cited above. At the beginning, we are in a remembered moment of experience, which then shifts to the moment of retrospective evaluation that is the moment of writing—the only time Tamura can judge that his intimations were in fact a symptom of an "abnormal state of mind." This kind of modal shift in perspective is deeply embedded in the narrative and employed throughout the story.

Tamura's dissociated perspective is like an expanding series of concentric circles of interpretation created by the movement of stepping into and then back out of his remembered self, all the time questioning the authenticity and reliability of the personal memory that enables him to tell his story. Tamura's self-questioning is necessary to the process of regaining a sense of autonomy, but it creates other problems for him. It is when Tamura accepts his wartime responsibility and guilt—when he willfully chooses not to forget and to fully acknowledge all that he does remember—that he appears insane to others. During the years following his repatriation up to the time that he voluntarily entered the psychiatric hospital, he had been able to live a "normal" life reintegrated into Japanese society only by repressing his memories and denying his autonomy. After he returns to Japan, the strangeness of his experience continues to alienate him, and there is no way out of that condition. His wife could not share the memories that constituted his sense of self-identity, and "it was those memories that now, to use the lame metaphor, 'came between us.'"[35]

The most visible symptoms of Tamura's dissociating memories are his rituals of bowing and apologizing to his food, and his habit of grasping his right hand with his left to stop him from doing something he should not do. We learn in the wartime account that these rituals originated at a moment of temptation, when he wanted to eat the flesh of an officer whose death he witnessed. It was at that moment that his left hand tightly grabbed his right wrist and stopped the right hand from using a bayonet to cut away the dead man's flesh. This action became habituated, so that it no longer seemed mysterious to him, even though "at the time I felt that this living left hand of mine was not my own."[36] Upon returning to Japan, he gave up these habits, not because other people considered him insane, but because what had become important to him "was to hide my feelings [or intentions, *kokoro*] from others."[37] Then, five years after ceasing these actions, he resumed them.

> I did not feel like repressing and denying all my true thoughts. When, five years after my return, I resumed the ceremony of bowing in front of the dining table, and once more began to refuse all sorts of food, I was not inclined to regard this behavior as strange or to give it up. Nor could I help the fact that now my left hand would again stretch out to grasp my right hand; for I was being impelled by something outside myself—by God, perhaps. Certainly, were I not being moved from the outside, I should never have resumed these habits.[38]

This information about his repression of memories, provided to us in "A Madman's Diary," leads us to a radical reconsideration of the ethical meaning of Tamura's actions. If Tamura is compelled from without to resume his strange rituals, which are an expression of his guilt and thus signs of his ethical consciousness, then how are we to read his wartime account, which is also an expression of his deepest moral sentiments? Do we interpret his words as a truly critical, detached analysis of his intentions, or should we read them as a kind of passive revelation, the truth being channeled through the memories of a "madman" who lacks moral autonomy? The answer to this is not at all clear, for in both the wartime account and the diary Tamura wavers between his desire for autonomy (for narrative control) and his belief that there is something outside of him that controls his actions and militates against self-control. Even though he blames the return of his symptoms of dissociation on an outside force, he also resists that conclusion, since it would mean he is no longer responsible for his actions, and his resistance to the exculpatory feeling that he is being controlled from without, while suggesting the strength of his conscience, actually deepens his dissociation. This dilemma is especially noticeable at those points in the story of his wartime experience where Tamura tells us that he had the sensation of being watched and where his descriptions of his own actions shift into a divided first-person perspective. For example, at the crucial moment when he decides against eating the flesh of the Japanese officer whose death he observed, Tamura seems to be standing outside of himself, as he describes the most minute details of his own movements.

> As I stood there in my strange pose I once again felt that I was being watched. Until the eyes left me I knew that I must not change my position.
>
> "Let not thy left hand know what thy right hand doeth!"
>
> The voice, when it came, did not particularly surprise me. Since there was someone watching me, it was not at all strange that I should hear a voice as well.
>
> It was not the beast-like voice of the woman I had killed. No, it was that great hollow voice that had called to me in the village church.
>
> "Arise, I say unto thee, arise!" the voice chanted.
>
> I stood up. This was the first time I was driven by another being. I slowly moved away from the body. As I moved away step by step the fingers of my left hand, one by one, loosened their grip on my right hand—first the middle finger, then the ring finger, then the little finger, finally the thumb and the index finger together.[39]

Tamura, who is assailed by the feelings of both shame and guilt in this passage, is never wholly demoralized, and his most alienating, inhuman desires are always accompanied by a heightened awareness of his moral sentiments. Tamura describes his dissociation as being "split into many parts" and asserts that it is a universal human condition.[40] This observation does not, however, help him connect with the humanity of others. In fact, his condition becomes dehumanizing when he turns his gaze outward. Because of the awareness of the isolation of his existence and the loss of his autonomy, brought about by the threat of starvation, Tamura views the world with a peculiar sense of detachment. He rarely describes others as whole individuals, and his story becomes a catalogue of body parts: the lips of the officer who slaps him at the very beginning of the story; the open sore on Yasuda's leg and the image of his head and flesh when he dies; Nagamatsu's eyes and his mouth; the swollen, dismembered bodies of slain soldiers in the village; the arm of the dying officer; and the arms, feet, and buttocks of cannibalized soldiers.

This recurring use of body imagery visually dismembers all the people Tamura encounters, suggesting that cannibalism becomes possible only if the dictates of conscience are assuaged by turning humans into objects. Yet even in this extreme situation, where cannibalism might at least be morally excused, Tamura strives to assert his moral autonomy over the temptations that arise from the desire to survive. It is no wonder, then, that once he is back in Japan, in a "normal" social setting that denies the extreme and unfamiliar, his conscience takes control of his life—like God moving him from the outside—forcing him to confront the ethical meaning of his actions. The paradox is that, in order to make a determination of his responsibility, he must undertake an act of remembering that reenacts dismembering.

The outer signs of Tamura's dissociation—the rituals and the dehumanizing objectification of others—are obviously disturbing. However, it is not only what he remembers that alienates him from his humanity, but also what he forgets. Traumatic events open up a discontinuity that disrupts the received pattern of the remembered self,[41] and when that trauma is complicated by an amnesiac blank, the effort to reconstruct the past self in order to fully disclose it is intensified. This effect is apparent when Tamura appears to be standing outside of himself observing his own actions.

> It is once more the image of myself walking between the hills and the plains with a rifle on my shoulder. My green uniform has faded to a light brown and there are holes in the sleeves and shoulders. The figure is barefoot. Yes, from the indentations of his emaciated neck as he walks a few paces ahead of me, I can tell that this is certainly I, Private First-Class Tamura.
>
> But then who can be this "I" who is now looking at the figure? It also is I. After all, who is to say that "I" cannot consist of two people?[42]

The coexistence of a "narrated I" and a "narrating I" makes possible Tamura's insights into his condition, but this narrative dissociation is also a breakdown of identity. Moreover, this breakdown is compounded by the loss of memory of the last ten days of his war experience, when he apparently became a self-styled avenging angel. The gap in his memory that produces an unknown, unknowable self exacerbates his dissociation, by calling into question the reliability of the memories he still retains, since he no longer has a complete picture of himself. This is not to say that Tamura doubts the authenticity of all his memories. He asserts that his remembrances may be "nothing but illusion, but I cannot doubt all my feelings. Recollection is a type of experience, and who can say that I am not alive? Even though I can believe no one else, I still have faith in myself."[43] The experience of remembering is of course different from the remembered experience, but it is no less real. In the same way, the experience of the amnesiac blank is real for Tamura. However, the fact that he cannot completely know the self that lies beyond the limits imposed by his amnesia undermines the relationship of his memory to objective reality, blocks his free will or autonomy, and makes final judgment of his responsibility impossible.

Chance, Necessity, and the Problem of Autonomy

Amnesia is one source of Tamura's moral dilemma, since it represents a loss of control over his remembered self. However, even without memory loss, autobiographical memory presents an obstacle to Tamura in his attempt to regain a sense of autonomy. Such memory is never pristine; it is always being restructured, and the intentional aspect of its formation, its synthetic nature, gives rise to doubts about its reliability.[44] The formation of memory is the constitutive element of the sense of self and, though based on actual experience, is as contingent as the formation of any narrative. Amnesia is therefore not the only factor placing limits on Tamura's ability to know himself, since the very mode of representation he uses to depict his extreme experiences also works against attaining a sufficiently detached perspective.

Autobiographical memory in particular enables us to know the world, but it carries within itself a blind spot: the limit of human perspective that blocks complete knowledge. Our view of the remembered self, in order to move toward an objective perspective, must, as with any other conception of the world, "include some acknowledgment of its own incompleteness: at a minimum it will admit the existence of things or events we don't know about now."[45] That acknowledgment, however, also highlights the fact that the only position from where we cannot view ourselves in the world objectively and in its entirety is the place behind our eyes, and it is this paradox of human consciousness that prevents Tamura from realizing an objectively grounded sense of identity and values.

This paradox operates on some level in all of Ōoka's wartime writings, which are accounts of his real-life experience. The crucial difference for *Fires on the Plain* is that it overtly fictionalizes that experience by making the trustworthiness of autobiographical memory a key narrative element.[46] An autobiography, based as it is on past actuality, is felt to possess a kind of narrative necessity or inevitability, in that at least the material facts of the story appear to be settled independently of the will of the author prior to the moment of writing and interpretation. Simultaneously, autobiography, like historical narrative, strives to mask that sense of inevitability by insisting on the contingency of the events being narrated. Fiction, by way of contrast, is felt to be arbitrary from the standpoint of the raw facts of the story, which depend upon the willful choices of the author, and yet the emotional effects of fictional narrative rest on the illusion that what happens in a narrative seems not just plausible but somehow inevitable.

While the circumstances of the war determined the form and content of *Fires on the Plain*, like any narrative, the novel attempts to achieve a sense of inevitability by trying to conjure the illusion of the indissolubility of the objective world and its representation of that world—that is, the illusion that what we are getting is immediate, authentic experience. This illusion of the apparent congruence of words and the world operates as much in the testament of a real-life witness as in a fictional novel. The most daring aspect of *Fires on the Plain* is the way in which "A Madman's Diary" overtly calls that congruence into question, even as the longer opening account of Tamura's wartime experience, with its detailed, realistic descriptions of the narrator's life and state of mind, has seemingly sustained it. Just as Tamura resists a return to familiar, "normal" values, in order to recover his moral autonomy and give voice to his experience, so the mode of the novel resists the common-sense assumption of a deep, unbreakable connection between memory, language, and reality.

It may be just as well that reality and representation are not indissoluble—that the effect of immediate experience of reality in a narrative is a recognizable illusion—for it is the distinction between subject and object, between experience and representation, that enables the individual to use reality to explain reasons for acting and to make evaluations.[47] Thus, memory is essential to ethical evaluation, since recollection engenders the sense of personal continuity that permits an ordering and discrimination of values and enables (though does not ensure) critical analysis. The awareness of self provides a subjective reference point that allows us to move to a more detached perspective to judge our circumstances. This means that some types of memory and the formation of self-identity are intentionally organized—an intentionality manifested in the desire for autonomy.[48] Because we are limited by the blind spot of human perspective, we need both continuity and distance to establish our identity and values, and consequently, there is an ambivalence to the connection between memory and judgment, in that it seems at once natural to the way we think and also intentionally drawn or rhetorical.

Tamura acknowledges the limits of his consciousness, and he accounts for or at least includes in his self-analysis the silent blank of his amnesia, which he has no means of entering. Tamura has to negotiate the issues of identity and ethical behavior across a divided self within the constraints of an autobiographical narrative. The process of narrating his experience gives him some control, by holding out the promises of narrative autonomy and self-knowledge, but that same process exposes the fact that he can never get all the way inside himself. Tamura's amnesia is first and foremost a practical physiological deficiency, but it also comes to represent for Tamura the loss of control and identity. The madness of his moral insight forces him and the reader to confront the contingency of the remembered self.

Tamura's skeptical attitude about self-knowledge is a natural response to the problem of evaluating his actions during the days lost to his memory. He is keenly aware that his search for meaning is inextricably tied to his search for survival. The heightened self-awareness that produces the dialectic of the narrative emerges from the desperate desire to live that drives the plot. Because he is ill, Tamura moves from his base camp to the field hospital, and would likely die of starvation there were it not for the attack on the compound by the Americans, which he survives by sheer luck. He wanders through the jungle for several days and is on the verge of collapse when he is saved by the chance discovery of an abandoned plantation and its potato vines. Once he gains the provisions to sustain life, the desire for human companionship drives him down to a Filipino village, where he ends up murdering a young woman.

His act of murder seems almost accidental, and even though he feels morally responsible, the randomness of the deed destroys the illusion of autonomy that is the source of his sense of responsibility. Tamura tells us that from that moment "both the state and the act of free will [nin'i] were forbidden to me. I myself, by an act of free will, had stolen the inevitability [or necessity, *hitsuzen*] by which one life lived and had condemned myself ever after to a life in which everything is based on inevitability—the inevitability of having to live a life turned toward death."[49] Tamura's guilt forces him to accept the inevitability of his own life in order to find some meaning in the randomness of his crime. The concept of inevitability holds out the promise of a coherent view of the past, imparting a sense of continuity and duration. Yet Tamura is also forced to insist that the inevitability of his life was the product of an act of his own free will—for to locate the source of his sense of inevitability anywhere beyond himself would close off the dialectical process that allows him to disclose and interpret his past.

Tamura recognizes the principle of chance by which he has survived. More importantly, he comes to understand that the story of his life, the narrative form in which he has cast himself, is equally dependent on the principle of chance. This recognition, which occurs in "A Madman's Diary," links the performative narrative of *Fires on the Plain* to the ethical content of its story.

> People seem unable to admit this principle of chance. Our spirits are not strong enough to stand the idea of life being a mere succession of chances—the idea, that is, of infinity. Each of us in his individual existence, which is contained between the chance of his birth and the chance of his death, identifies those few incidents that have arisen through what he styles his "will"; and the thing that emerges consistently from this he calls his "character" or again his "life." Thus we contrive to comfort ourselves; there is, in fact, no other way for us to think.[50]

Tamura survives by luck, not by necessity. However, the implication that his life is all merely a matter of chance, even if that conclusion seems true when looked at from a detached, objective viewpoint, is not acceptable, because it undermines the subjective values on which his self-analysis depends. The sense that life has meaning and that existence is necessary or inevitable is exposed as false when examined from a more objective point of view. Yet it is not easy (which is to say, not human) to give up the sense that life is meaningful and necessary, for even if we concede that the sense of necessity is an illusion created by our desire for meaning and value, it is nonetheless constitutive of human consciousness, of the means to evaluate our condition. As Tamura succinctly puts it, there is "no other way for us to think." In the same way that remembering creates a concept of the past and a sense of identity, the dialectic between the inner remembered self and the outer remembering self, with its insistence on normative values, is simply the form human life takes.[51]

Tamura's skepticism brings him to an understanding of the chance nature of human life, but this understanding resolves nothing, since it does not bring the process of critical reflection to a halt. Having observed that we must hold on to the illusion that our lives are necessary and have meaning, Tamura at once dismisses his thoughts as "nonsense" (*tawagoto*).[52] He realizes that normative judgments derive from a sense of autonomy, a sense that we are free to reflect upon our own thoughts and beliefs, and that his difficulties in disclosing his past would simply go away if he stopped thinking about them—that is, if he could somehow return to an unconditioned state: "In reality my life in this mental home is spent gazing at the movements of the heavenly bodies, and day after day it is interrupted by sleep. My doctor has allotted me a daily assignment of cleaning and tidying my room; and this is not a bad thing, for while I am engaged in it I can forget the principle of chance."[53]

Tamura knows that his predicament disappears when he is no longer aware of himself, when he lives in a way that resembles the regimented life of the military, but he is unable to live in a permanently unreflective state. Nor can he embrace anti-intellectualism to relieve his obsession, since the self-consciousness of that approach would not permit him to forget himself. The process of thought and evaluation defines his identity, and his self-awareness forces him to cling to the sense that his life is governed by necessity, even though he recognizes that sense to be illusory. Tamura undertakes his narrative to find a resolution to this paradox: "If there is a technique for transforming the chance [*gūzen*] that dominates my present life into necessity [or inevitability, *hitsuzen*], then it is being able to connect my present life with my past life in which chance was forced on me by authority. It is for this reason that I am writing these notes."[54]

Writing becomes at this moment a highly charged act of political resistance: an assertion of individual autonomy over the political and military authorities that thrust the narrator into an extreme situation in which he was forced to act against his most deeply ingrained moral sentiments and ultimately to break one of society's most stringent taboos. Writing imposes form in order to restore to Tamura the illusion that his life story is governed by necessity. For Tamura, testing his own motives through this act of resistance is not a way of looking for something else (for example, the good or the right), but it *is* the good, which is another way of saying that the search for normative values is intrinsic to the way human beings are, the only way we can think. The effort to turn chance into necessity thus centers the narrative on the problem of autonomy and intention. If Tamura was reduced to murder and cannibalism by forces outside himself—the necessities of war, the hand of God—is he not morally responsible for his actions? To be able to answer the question of intentionality, the narrator realizes that he must reliably disclose his past, even though a crucial period of it is blotted out. The narrator's retrograde amnesia drives the narrative as the motive for writing and marks out the central mystery of the story. Without complete disclosure, however, that story cannot be finished, and we are left in an ethical gray zone.

Repetition and the Search for Meaning

The guilt Tamura feels is a powerful motive for determining if his crimes were the result of accident or intention. As his self-conscious pursuit of physical survival and existential meaning proceeds, he understands the limits of his perspective, and his search is directed increasingly toward a concept of the divine as a way to get beyond the ethical gray zone. The desire for the certainty of a divine order is manifested in his metaphysics, which is based on the discovery of apparent patterns in the repetitions of nature.[55] He comes to believe that repetition establishes a form or pattern that provides a sense of duration or continuity in the face of events that break apart received narratives of personal and cultural identity. Repetition not only gives meaning to the past in the present, by transforming what has been into something that is in the process of becoming, but it also opens up the possibility of control over the future, by suggesting that what is now will once again be.[56] Metaphysical speculation on the patterns of repetition occurs throughout the story and is explicitly tied to Tamura's "presentiment of death," which came to him because he could no longer maintain "the inherent assumption that we can repeat indefinitely what we are doing at the moment."[57] Later, when he considers his murder of the young woman in the village, the concept of repetition is tied to more than just the good of his physical survival. It is forever linked with his sense of guilt and responsibility. Fleeing the scene of his crime, he pauses at a river on the way back to the plantation.

The recurrent motion of the eddies fascinated me. I realized that it was yet another example of that repetition that had played so important a part in my thoughts since I had been on my own.

Just as repetition was inherent in nature, so, I now realized, should it exist in human life. My life in the mountains had fit into a regular cycle [*junkan*], but when I had come down to the village I had broken that cycle. As a result, I had killed an innocent Filipino woman. To be sure, it had been an accident; yet if the accident had arisen from my breaking a cycle, then I could hardly disclaim responsibility.[58]

Tamura looks for a reason for his crime in the breaking of repetition and pattern, but he has no certain answer as to why the repetitious cycle of his life in the mountains was broken in the first place. Was the murder a random event beyond his control or the outcome of his own will? Even when Tamura seems to find an excuse for his actions in the concept of repetition, his skeptical frame of mind pulls back from the refuge such reasoning offers. Accident or not, Tamura cannot escape the pangs of conscience. In response to the difficulty he faces in reaching a determination of his responsibility, he links the desire for repetition in life—the desire for the control over time repetition holds out to him—to the difficulties he encounters in disclosing the past. The clearest example of this link is provided by Tamura's speculations about his illusory remembrance of having once walked through the Philippine jungles and mountains, even though he had never been there before. He is puzzled by these "false memories" and explains them as the product of the need for a sense of repetition that emerges in life-or-death struggles.

The fact that "false memories" appear at moments of fatigue or prostration is not because life ceases its forward progress, but because on those occasions, once there is no more concern with mundane matters, the desire for repetition inherent to life is laid bare.

I did not consider my own improvised metaphysics particularly well grounded, but in any case this discovery gave me satisfaction. It made me feel a kind of pride in that it affirmed that I was living now.[59]

Tamura's observations on his false memories are noteworthy in that they suggest that there is a created element in all memory. The key for him is that the performance of memory, false or not, proves his existence, his sense of duration, by demonstrating his ability to reflect on his situation, even though he is highly skeptical of the reliability of those reflections. The process of thought is identified with Tamura's sense of himself, and so we must evaluate his circumstances from within that self-enclosed perspective.

The déjà vu experienced by the narrator connects his desire for survival to his self-consciously reflective nature, and it is a further manifestation of the central problem of the narrative, which is the problem of how to turn chance into inevitability. Is the central memory gap in *Fires on the Plain* the result of a wound only, or is it the result of repression? Is there something intentional in Tamura's failure to remember parts of his past, or is his forgetfulness the consequence of a random event? The book does not permit a definitive reading, because we can neither dismiss the crucial information that there is a physiological cause for the amnesia nor ignore the narrator's admission that for five years he repressed the wartime self that threatened his assimilation back into "normal" society. Moreover, the concept of repetition, like the form of Ōoka's novel itself, precludes a final resolution of these questions. On the one hand, the concept provides pattern and meaning by situating the open-ended narrative of the self within a larger, detached order. On the other hand, it fails to provide an explanation for the subjective causes of particular actions. For the narrator to get outside himself he must first somehow get all the way in, achieving the impossible state of being at once reflective and unconditioned, and the concept of repetition can bring him only part of the way toward that ideal state.

The cultural strangeness of the settings and situations Tamura encounters disrupts his sense of repetition and continuity and gives rise to his premonitions of death: "Again, was it not this same presentiment of death that made it seem so strange to me now that I should never again walk along this path in the Philippine forest? In our own country, even in the most distant or inaccessible province we are never assailed by this feeling of strangeness because subconsciously we know that there is always a possibility of our returning there in the future."[60] This observation of the desire for the possibility of a return, which provides a sense of order and familiarity, is a response to the unsettling effect of the foreign landscape.

Tamura's state of mind exhibits the dynamics of an outsider's encounter with the foreign, where the indigenous culture seems to disappear behind a landscape of unfamiliar signs. After Tamura stumbles across the abandoned plantation where he finds enough food to sustain him, he discovers a cross on a church in the distance while exploring the area around his newfound "paradise." He is drawn to that symbol as he contemplates the various meanings it has for him and for the "invisible" Filipinos.

> I felt not the slightest hatred for them. But because the country to which I belonged happened to be fighting the country to which they belonged, there could never be any human relationship between us, including the cross. We were in what might be called a condition of material crisis. Insofar as the international symbol of love, the cross, was in the hands of my enemies, it was for me no more than a symbol of danger.[61]

For Tamura, signs of the indigenous culture such as the cross and, most especially, the ominous signal fires are dangerously ambiguous, in that they stir the desire to connect once again with the cultural institutions that define his individuality and remind him of the inaccessibility of the native population, which, because unseen, is a mysterious and menacing presence. In spite of the dangers represented by these signs, Tamura is so physically and psychologically isolated that he is attracted to any system of values that can reintegrate his existence into a larger order in the world.

> As a result I arrived at a principle that was rational toward society and hedonistic where the self was concerned. In my status as a petit bourgeois, that principle certainly did not fully satisfy all my desires, but in any case I maintained my pride and felt no regrets.
>
> Because I had continued to hold onto this principle for living right up to the time it was stripped bare by the isolation of a defeated soldier, I did not expect to be attracted once more to the delusions of my childhood. I should not have been troubled to the point that I could not take my eyes off the cross I saw in the distance.[62]

Tamura's need for a "principle for living" is driven by a desire to hold onto a sense of continuity and self-identity. His attraction to Christianity is not a leap of faith, because that desire never totally overwhelms his skeptical, critical frame of mind. In a sense, his ethical awareness is at odds with the survival instinct, which is the source of his fascination with and longing for a foreign religious system. The struggle between his unspeakable desires and his self-conscious reflection is expressed through the conflation of cannibalism and the image of Jesus sacrificing his body and blood.

The use of Christian imagery in the novel highlights the extreme nature of the search for survival and meaning. Christian symbols provide a tentative language to express the instinctive desire for life and order, even though they actually intensify the narrator's awareness of his isolation. Tamura longs for the divine state of true detachment and complete autonomy and self-knowledge, but the impenetrable alienness of the Christian God reveals that the absolute is beyond his reach. The tension between the desire for union with God and the critical self-awareness that blocks the leap of faith needed to make that union possible comes to a crisis near the end of the wartime narrative, when Tamura tries to provide a justification for his murder of Nagamatsu. This justification suggests a profound transformation of his moral and religious sentiments—a transformation marked in the following passage by a radical shift from a retrospective point of view, in which the moments of experience and of remembering/writing are distinct, to a perspective in which the moments of experience and writing, of remembrance and expectation, are collapsed into a narrative present.

> I felt great anger: if as a result of hunger it is inevitable [*hitsuzen*] that human beings would eat each other, then this world of ours is no more than the result of God's wrath.
>
> And if at this moment I could vomit forth anger, then I am no longer human. I am an angel. I must carry out God's wrath.[63]

This momentary fusion of Tamura's selves, and the illusion that he has transcended the human realm, mark the passage to ethical insight, which is represented as a form of madness. As it turns out, the illusion of transcendence is conditional and short-lived. The reassertion of a critical, questioning self in the madman's diary that immediately follows this transformation resituates the story squarely within the human realm and the sphere of ethical concerns. Tamura cites God as the ultimate reason for his actions, but because the days that follow his transformation are lost to amnesia, he is not really certain how to interpret his own story. He remembers that he killed people, but insists he did not eat them.[64] A few pages later he wonders if, during his days of wandering, he had been under the illusion that he had ascended to a divine state as an avenging angel. Without a clear answer, Tamura cannot be sure he did not descend into a state of total alienation by killing other humans to eat their flesh. He seems confident he did not kill for human flesh, but his effort to recover his memory leads him to consider all of the possibilities, and that questioning works against a simple, intuitive acceptance of Christian myth as an ultimate system for him. The narrator is at last forced to conclude that "there is no such thing as God. His is an existence so tenuous that it depends entirely on people's disposition to believe in it. The problem is whether or not I was hallucinating [that I was an agent of God]."[65]

Tamura's dismissal of God is an important stage in his moral quest, but it does not end his search, since his rejection of God brings him back to the problem of the synthetic nature of his memories and his understanding of the order of the world. His rejection of God leaves unsatisfied his hunger for an order beyond himself. God as first cause, God as sacrifice, and God as avenger are all manifestations of Tamura's inner moral sentiments—fundamental desires for justice, freedom, and mercy that he continues to struggle with in the face of his uncertainty and guilt.[66] The recognition that God's existence is a matter of belief directly challenges the authority of his own moral sentiments. Nonetheless, it is precisely because he views the divine in a critical, analytical way, because he cannot make a leap of faith and close off the issue of subjective responsibility, that his quest is an ethical one. Even if the voice of God is nothing more than the sound of his own conscience, it speaks to him in recompense for the silence of his memory. God is the state of unconditioned wholeness that Tamura longs for and resists. His struggle with God is an internal ethical struggle, a projection of the critical dialogue Tamura has with himself that he can neither escape nor resolve because he cannot achieve complete autonomy and self-knowledge.

Tamura's account of his experiences pushes him deeper inside himself as a way to achieve an objective, autonomous view of the world and thus turn chance into necessity. The self-analysis that constitutes his story, however, is inherently open-ended, and formal closure can be achieved only by resort to a rhetorical sleight of hand. At the end of the book's penultimate chapter, "Once More to the Fires on the Plain," Tamura writes that he seems to hear the sound of drums, which conjures up for him the image of the signal fires. He returns to his room and, as the sound continues, begins to recover his lost memories, though not completely. He thinks that by writing more notes all of his memories will come back to him. At this point, the diary of the madman merges back into the wartime memoir, but now the wartime account is transformed. The final section, titled "A Dead Man's Writings," strives to overcome the limits of knowledge exposed by skeptical self-awareness through the device of assuming a supernatural perspective.

This final shift in perspective places Tamura in a transcendent realm of myth. His transcendence is of course an illusion of language—*Fires on the Plain* seems to revel in its exploitation of the illusion of autobiographical narrative, which is that the narrator is able to tell us everything about his inner life. The importance of this step to ethical judgment is that it momentarily permits Tamura to assert that it was not his will but circumstances that were responsible for his actions. Even though we are supposedly in the realm of the dead, Tamura is compelled to assert that the circumstances of his war experience, and his view of himself as the instrument of justice, absolve him of his guilt.

> On the deserted plain the grass continues to sway round about me with that same eternal motion I saw when I was alive. In the dark sky the sun glows still darker, like obsidian. But it is too late.
>
> Through the grass the people approach. They seem to glide forward, sweeping aside the grass with their feet. They are the people who now inhabit the same world as I, the people I have killed—the Filipino woman, Yasuda, Nagamatsu.
>
> The dead people are laughing. If this is indeed celestial laughter, how awesome a thing it is!
>
> At this moment a painful joy enters my body from above. Like a five-inch nail, it slowly pierces my skull and reaches to the base of my brain.
>
> I remember. They are laughing because I have not eaten them. I killed them but did not eat them. I have killed them because of war, God, chance—forces outside of myself; but it was assuredly because of my own will that I did not eat them. This is why in their company I can now gaze at that dark sun in this country of the dead.
>
> Yet perhaps while I was still alive as a fallen angel armed with a rifle I really wanted to eat them in order to chastise humanity. Perhaps my secret desire, when I saw those fires on the plain and set out in search of the people who must be beneath them, was to eat them.[67]

The figurative state of death at the end of the novel is a rhetorical move toward an imagined state of reintegration, a mythic memory that is a curious amalgam of images from ancient imperial mythology and Christianity. However, adopting the voice of a dead man brings us into the presence of relative language only, not of absolute truth. The mythic closure of the text cannot hold; it is too far removed from the subjective human values and ethical sentiments that permit the judgment of right and wrong. Even writing from the perspective of the dead, Tamura is unable to suspend his questioning state of mind, because such a move is so obviously self-serving on the matter of his guilt.

The moment he experiences the laughter that signals the expiation of his crime, his critical self-awareness returns, and the reassertion of his living

self with its "secret desire" makes him question the meaning of his mythic memory. If the reason he murdered lies outside himself, then how can
there be any meaning or value to human life? Ethically, the narrative cannot
have it both ways—Tamura recognizes that he cannot excuse himself by
virtue of both his will and chance. He wants inevitability and contingency
to somehow coexist. He wants to reassert his autonomy and yet somehow
be absolved of responsibility. Tamura's memory loss and his guilt cannot be
transcended, except through an imaginative act of expiation and forgive-
ness. The mythic language of the closure of the novel is a formal effort to
vanquish dissociation, to resolve the dialectical tension of the narrative and
achieve a sense of ethical wholeness that reveals some larger meaning and
order in Tamura's experience. This imaginative vision of ethical reintegration, however, does not resolve the question of responsibility. All the narrator can do at the very end is intone an invocation to God, a prayer consist-
ing of a string of conditionals conveying more ambivalence than faith.

In his postwar novels, Ōoka struck an agnostic attitude toward the possibility of belief in culture-defining values. His skepticism arose from his
recognition of the irreconcilability of desires for an objectively grounded
morality and for self-realization. In a society where ethical consciousness
is fractured by these conflicting desires, grounds for belief in values can no
longer be located in universal principles, but only in the process of reflective judgment itself.[68] Ōoka sought to achieve a meaningful sense of identity through the act of confronting the modern apprehension of a divide
between normative values and self-realization. The only apparent means
of bridging that divide is to act as if personal autonomy and freedom are
the ultimate sources not only for authentic values and meaning but also for
authentic memories and an authentic past.

The ambivalence Ōoka expresses in his writing should not be confused
with hackneyed notions of the ambiguity of traditional Japanese aesthetics.
His is a powerfully ethical literature that describes not just the war and its
aftermath, Japan's nearly apocalyptic struggle with modernity, but also the
inner search for meaning and identity in a world where received moral categories have been utterly shattered. The "untainted dream" that so impressed
Isoda as the heart of Ōoka's literary method is expressed not by a systematic
statement of abstract principles, but through a narrative perspective that,
by its divided, skeptical nature, strives for an autonomous view from no
particular place.

6

Kitsch, Nihilism, and the Inauthentic

C HARLES JENCKS, in an acerbic account of developments in twentieth-century architectural style, has asserted that "happily, we can date the death of modern architecture to a precise moment in time," which he claims was "July 15, 1972 at 3:32 p.m. (or thereabouts)."[1] At that moment, several blocks of the Pruitt-Igoe housing complex in St. Louis, Missouri, which had been built from an award-winning design based on the ideals of the Congress of International Modern Architects, were dynamited. Hailed at the time of its construction as the model of a machine for living, the complex proved to be uninhabitable. Its failure was so complete that it not only called into question the viability of large-scale urban planning, but also, for some, discredited architectural modernism altogether. The demise of an aesthetic movement that had represented the hopes of so many for creating a humane urban environment would normally elicit more sober reflection, and yet Jencks's undisguised glee is perhaps understandable when we consider the cold abstraction of so many modernist projects—not to mention the rarity of an event that allows a historian of aesthetics to periodize with uncompromising precision.

Those engaged in the study of Japanese literary history can be grateful to have the same rare good fortune as their counterparts in architectural history, since the death of literary modernism in Japan may also be traced to a more or less precise moment in time: November 25, 1970, at around 12:15 p.m. At that moment, in Tokyo, the writer Mishima Yukio thrust a sword into his abdomen and ended his life in ritual suicide. Although the passing of modernism in Japan was marked by the psychological implosion of a single individual, it was still a spectacular event, one reported around the world. Mishima's suicide commanded interest not only because of the lurid personal tragedy of an internationally famous writer, but also because of the various interpretations of the meaning of it all, which often took the form of essentialist reflections on the conflict in Japan between modernity and tradition.[2]

The imploding contradictions of Mishima's life remain compelling now only because the author was so audaciously self-conscious about them, inviting us to read them as the contradictions of modernity itself. He was among the first Japanese writers to gain an international audience in the postwar years, and he converted his commercial and critical success into celebrity status, which gave him the freedom to assume a variety of other public roles. Starting out as a literary aesthete, he transformed himself into a boxer, a bodybuilder, and devotee of martial arts. He acted in tough-guy films and was a walk-on in revues and plays. He bought a kitschy dream house—a faux Italianate "villa" that could have served as the setting for a scene from a Suzuki Seijun film. He took on the role of a cultural critic lamenting the state of postwar Japanese society, and he eventually played the part of a political ideologue, creating his own private military group devoted to a return to rule by the emperor.

Given his idiosyncratic right-wing views and his penchant for publicity stunts, it is hardly surprising that judgments of his literature have been colored by the suspicion that as a writer Mishima is also just playing a role—a suspicion that forces the reader to take pause when considering the seriousness of the work. There is something of the poseur about Mishima, an attitude that creates the impression of an emptiness at the core of his art and of his being. He eagerly cultivated a reputation as a serious artist, but at the same time, his commercial instincts, thirst for international recognition, exhibitionism, and comic-opera emperorism all waged a self-conscious war against that reputation. He was a prolific fabulist, but he seemed to have sensed that all of his narratives, including the narrative of his life, were little more than empty structures. His skepticism made him a sharp critic of postwar culture, and yet throughout his life, Mishima's critique of the sterility of that culture coexisted uneasily with his crass exploitation of it. Mishima was an artist in revolt against modern culture, and his struggle led him to embrace an aesthetics of the inauthentic, an artistry of kitsch.

Few things illustrate the brazen nature of Mishima's conflicted ambitions better than the way his novels were marketed in England in the 1970s. Following his suicide, Penguin Books reissued paperback versions of many of his translated works with a common cover image, featuring the famous

photograph of a nearly naked and very buff Mishima brandishing his samurai sword. On the back were blurbs that usually promised stories about sex,
violence, and death, and they ended with the hook, "Here is Mishima. Here
is Japan." This tagline, perhaps like the fashions of the day, seems a bit excessive, but there can be little doubt that Mishima would have approved of the
absurdity of the total identification. For even if we resist Mishima's strategies to get us to read him as *the* representative of Japan's modern identity,
the particular contradictions in his work remain an expression of the more
widespread, fundamental paradox associated with the culture of modernity
discussed throughout the essays above. Both the embrace of modernity and
the revolt against it is grounded in a preoccupation with origins and authenticity, and the paradox of modernity arises from the presence of two
opposing but equally compelling responses to that preoccupation. One is
an effort to return to or regain origins, which necessitates a rejection of the
present. The other is an attempt to obliterate origins, to make everything
start with the now, which necessitates a rejection of the past.

The impossibility of ever completely reconciling these responses results
in a sense of loss for the modern artist, who either denies the value of individual autonomy by rejecting the present, or who alienates the individual
from social institutions that impose meaning and order from without by
rejecting the past. Zygmunt Bauman locates the origin of this loss in what
he describes as the twisted dialectics of inextricable contradictions that
characterize modernity:

> The absolute manifesting itself only in the particularity of individuals
> and their encounters; the permanent hiding behind fleeting episodes, the
> normal behind the unique. Above all, the drama of modernity derives
> from the "tragedy of culture," the human inability to assimilate cultural
> products, over abundant because of the unbound creativity of the human
> spirit. Once set in motion, cultural processes acquire their own momen-
> tum, develop their own logic, and spawn new multiple realities confront-
> ing individuals as an outside, objective world, too powerful and distant to
> be "resubjectivized." The richness of objective culture results therefore in
> the cultural poverty of individual human beings...[3]

As we have seen in many of the works cited in the essays above, the sense
of loss Bauman discusses is expressed as a temporal or spatial disloca-
tion. The tragedy of culture is a recognition of the lack of duration in

both human and narrative time, which forces a turning inward, a reliance on the subjective consciousness and autonomy of the individual to give significance to human experience. This turn inward is accompanied by skepticism toward the act of narration, an embrace of relativism, and gestures toward nihilism. Concurrently, there is a reaction against this loss of absolute values and a displacement outward, a reenactment of traditional values without belief, a decentering of the self reflected in antimodern obsessions with finding in the heroic, in nostalgic visions of the past, or in death itself substitutes or simulacra for absolute values, beliefs, or identity. Mishima reveled in the bind of modern consciousness but was also aware to an almost hypersensitive degree of the personal and artistic costs involved. He was driven to celebrate the transcendent and the ideal even as he mocked the futility of the effort to fix his present time and place in an eternal form.

Nihilism, Kitsch, and the Authentic Image

There is a close relationship between the aesthetics of loss and two important manifestations of modern culture: nihilism and kitsch. Nihilism, as an ethical position, is an extreme reduction of the paradox of modernity, in that it accepts the notion that there can never be irreducible or absolute grounds for justifying belief in any value. To the nihilist, truth is impossible to achieve in a world fragmented and made relative by the subjective consciousness of modern identity. Though we may intuitively sense that we need to know what is true in order to know how to act—that is, to perform what we believe is right—as soon as the relative nature of moral and aesthetic values is recognized, their constructed nature becomes apparent.[4] This recognition apparently leaves no alternatives other than acceptance of the task of creating arbitrary meaning out of a world of appearances, or despair at the loss of absolute values, meaning, and identity.[5]

The nihilist position embraces what George Steiner argues is the defining feature of modernity, which is the "break in the covenant between word and world." He defines that covenant as the presumption that being is "sayable" and that the "raw material of existentiality has its analogue in the structure of narrative."[6] A preoccupation with the incommensurability between language and reality undermines the ability to do what is right based on knowledge of what is true.

Kitsch is one possible aesthetic response to nihilism that tries to be both a reaction against despair and an acceptance of the world of appearances. It is a self-conscious stylization, a willful performance of authenticity that announces itself as fake. Kitsch art is inauthentic because it seeks to replicate art that is viewed as timeless or sublime, in order to mask or compensate for the loss of what is felt to be authentic. Matei Calinescu notes that "the great psychological discovery on which kitsch is founded lies in the fact that nearly everything directly or indirectly associated with artistic culture can be turned into something fit for immediate 'consumption,' like any ordinary commodity."[7] The connection of kitsch to nihilism is apparent in the kind of aesthetic response elicited by kitsch art.

> Kitsch is the direct artistic result of an important ethical mutation for which the peculiar time awareness created by capitalist modes of production has been responsible. By and large, kitsch may be viewed as a reaction against the terror of change and the artifice of a chronological time no longer based on natural cycles that flows from an unreal, created past into an equally unreal, created future. Under such conditions, the surplus of time, the very idea of spare time, socially increases and comes to be thought of as a strange burden, the burden of emptiness. Kitsch experiences are an easy way of killing time, a pleasurable escape from the banality of both work and leisure. The fun of kitsch is just the other side of terrible and incomprehensible boredom.[8]

The distinguishing feature of kitsch aesthetics is its knowing embrace of the inauthentic in an attempt to find a substitute for the real. By stressing the knowingness or self-consciousness involved in determining when the term may be applicable, this definition of kitsch is close to the notion of "camp" in Pop Art. However, this definition does not provide by itself a standard by which to judge whether or not a work of art is kitsch. Indeed, it is impossible to offer such a standard without willfully effacing the relativism that engenders the contradictions and anxieties of the culture of modernity. In a relativistic culture, beauty really is in the eye of the beholder, and so a watercolor of Elvis on black velvet or a plastic dashboard Jesus may be kitsch to some but objects of veneration to others. The crucial point is that kitsch can be an operative concept only to those who are conscious of a disjuncture between the authentic and the fake, between high, pure culture and popular, vulgar culture.

This qualification of the meaning of the phrase "kitsch aesthetics" is important in that it enables us to discuss kitsch art in general and Mishima's art in particular. The knowing embrace of the inauthentic typical of kitsch aesthetics reveals behind its campy attitude and surface the need to overcome or avoid, if not actually to resolve, the modern's sense of loss. Kitsch art wears its counterfeit nature on its sleeve. The aesthetic lie at the heart of kitsch is not so much a function of its pretense of uniqueness or originality as its pretense that, because of the self-consciousness of the artist, the forgery (or simulacrum) somehow reproduces the aesthetic value of the work or style being copied. The aesthetic lie of kitsch may result in the same kind of bad faith that Walter Benjamin argued comes with the mass production of art. For Benjamin "the presence of the original is the prerequisite to the concept of authenticity." He goes on to famously remark:

> That which withers in the age of mechanical reproduction is the aura of the work of art. This is a symptomatic process whose significance points beyond the realm of art. One might generalize by saying: the technique of reproduction detaches the reproduced object from the domain of tradition. By making many reproductions it substitutes a plurality of copies for a unique existence. And in permitting the reproduction to meet the beholder or listener in his own particular situation, it reactivates the object produced. These two processes lead to a tremendous shattering of tradition which is the obverse of the contemporary crisis and renewal of mankind.[9]

Kitsch and nihilism replicate the contradictory responses to the preoccupation with origins at the heart of the paradox of modernity. The covalence of kitsch and nihilism may be observed in figures used to represent the loss of meaning. For example, widely recognized character types, such as the blasé sophisticate who commits suicide out of boredom, the spurned lover who seeks death on the battlefield, or the tortured genius whose blinding Nietzschean insights into the emptiness of existence leads to despair and self-destruction, are stylized representations of the nihilist problematic. However, these representations create a strange incongruity by virtue of their connection with the authentic experience of death.

An example of the kind of effect this type of representation may produce is the morbid sentimentality associated with death (or memorial) photography, especially the memorial photographs of dead children that was a widespread custom in late nineteenth- and early twentieth-century America.[10] The incongruity in the photographs arises from the denial of death by the use of cute, innocent clothing and by the pious poses of the dead children. This denial was both an expression of authentic grief and an effort to assuage that grief through the production of a stylized, contrived, quasi-religious authenticity. The spread of memorial photography, made possible by the mass-reproduction technology of the camera, is a testament to the emotional and psychological effectiveness of these images, and the original owners, the bereaved families, certainly did not think of these photographs as kitsch, if for no other reason than that they lacked the self-consciousness to perceive them as such—that is, the meaning and associations called forth by the photographs were grounded in authentic emotions. However, now that the original owners are gone, and with them their authentic grief, the photographs, which were mementos meant to comfort and serve the purpose of denial, have lost their "aura," and the resulting incongruity—the subjects are, after all, little corpses—creates a distance from the viewer that makes the photographs eerily kitschy.

Saul Friedlander has remarked on the incongruity, what he calls the "frisson," between kitsch and death, which arises from the fact that on the level of individual experience, death creates "authentic" feelings of dread and loneliness. Moreover, he argues that the juxtaposition of kitsch and death is the bedrock of fascist aesthetics: a point that, as will be observed below, has relevance to Mishima's work.[11] Although the incongruity of kitsch treatments of death in American funeral customs may seem at first glance far removed from the kitsch of fascist aesthetics, the use of modern technologies in the service of antimodern impulses is emblematic of the "twisted contradiction" that characterizes responses to the material culture of modernity. The religious sentimentality that informs the contrived photographs of dead children is no different from the fascist sentimentality that revolts against the loss of moral certitude and tradition. Insofar as these photographs serve as reminders of death, their sentimentality inevitably loses spiritual authenticity the moment they are severed from their origins, the genuine feelings of grief that gave the photographs their "aura" in the first place.

Similarly, the quasi-religious, mystical sentimentality that accompanies fascist revolt carries as a precondition an awareness of the nihilist problematic, and so is doomed to fail in its effort to overcome the modern. Fascist aesthetics are obsessed with the moment of simultaneous creation and destruction, and the emblematic hero of fascism is the beautiful youth destined to die young. The very appeal of such a doomed hero derives from the subliminal realization that the mythmaking of fascist aesthetics is an empty structure, a mask that represents only a single, contingent possibility in a relative universe. As Friedlander notes:

> The young hero destined for death is surrounded by a nimbus of complex emotions; he is the carrier of either one of two banners, one proclaiming an implicit [Christian] religious tradition, the other that of a cult of primitive and archaic values. He confronts that which denies them: the abject world of modernity, the obscure weight of material powers, the revolting inanity of nonhuman factors. Unvanquished unto death, the hero takes on an almost supernatural incandescence.[12]

Mishima recognized that the power of such figures was their appeal to transcendent, authentic ideals. He also understood the lie operating beneath the surface of those figures. The difficulty that arises when trying to describe the source of Mishima's aesthetics is due to his willingness to be simultaneously critical of and seduced by kitsch. This ambiguous attitude is suggested in remarks he made on the art of photography:

> It seems to me that before the photograph can exist as art it must, by its very nature, choose whether it is to be a record or a testimony. Whatever special lenses are used, and however the subject is thereby distorted, the camera only knows how to relate things directly. However abstract the composition, therefore, the individual meaning of the objects related inevitably remains as a kind of indispersible precipitate. The photographer's whole job is to filter this off by one of two methods. It is a choice between record and testimony.[13]

Mishima's reduction of the essence of photographic art to a choice between record and testimony derives from a distinction between what he calls the "absolute authority" of an object recorded on film and the distortion of an object that expresses the subjective judgment of an artist whose testimony is, in Mishima's words, "everything." In his account, a struggle arises between the overt willfulness of the camera—expressed by the choice and contextualization of subject—and the sheer physicality (or foundness) of the subject, which survives even in the most radically performative, presentational modes.

Mishima's view of photographic art reflects his own peculiar preoccupation with the nature and meaning of authenticity. This preoccupation is on full display in his short film *The Rites of Love and Death*, based on his short story "Yūkoku" ("Patriotism"), where scenes of lovemaking and ritual suicide are carried out beneath a large scroll painting of two Chinese characters meaning "the attainment of sincerity." This word-image, which dominates the camera frame, creates both a textual and photographic space onto which Mishima can transfer his obsession with authenticity, with finding the genuine and sincere expression of cultural meaning and identity, and through that transference experience a state that normally lies beyond the individual in a timeless realm, which is the realm of ideology, art, and myth.

The aesthetic tension embodied in the calligraphic slogan that is the visual ground of *The Rites of Love and Death* is a clear and perhaps heavy-handed expression of the tortured dialectic characteristic of that strain of modern aesthetics marked by the impulse toward creative dissolution. Mishima's observations on the nature of photographic art raise an indisputable point, though one that is hardly original with him, about the distorting process of an art form that depends upon the mass-production technology of the camera: a distortion that casts serious doubts about whether a photographic image, which can be widely copied and distributed, can ever be considered authentic art. Technologically reproduced images, in order to be art, depend on something extraneous, that is, the willfulness or self-consciousness of the artist who confers aesthetic meaning and form on them. If the aesthetics of photography is determined by the attitude of the artist, then it may be rejected as false or fake art due to its subjectively grounded, created nature. The predicament that photography makes evident, which Mishima describes as a dialectic choice between record and testimony, is that the consciousness necessary to make art possible is aesthetically and epistemologically unstable. The recognition of this instability, moreover, envelops not just the way we experience photography, but also the way we experience the world.

Like other antimodern aesthetics—fascism, primitivism, postmodernism—kitsch is a reaction against the perceived bad faith of modernity. It is therefore hardly surprising to find elements of kitsch, especially the incongruity between the authentic experience of the violence of death and inauthentic kitsch representations of it, throughout the works of an artist as conflicted as Mishima. Accordingly, an analysis of his aesthetics, his modernism, may properly begin with his suicide. This does not mean we should read his works solely through the prism of that violent act. Nevertheless, in order to be able to engage his aesthetics, we must at least recognize the powerful impulse that drove him to try to exert a kind of absolute control over the texts of his art and his life.[14]

Violence and the Aesthetics of the Inauthentic

The culture of modernity is distinguished by the ritualistic impulse to transgress against established order, even when that transgression is self-consciously recognized as nothing more than a prelude to immolation. The effort to make everything new, to make everything begin now by the process of creative dissolution, is an effort to free the artist by exploding the temporal and spatial constraints imposed by established norms.[15] In the logic of this form of transgression, transcendence depends upon an annihilating gesture toward the authentic.

The idea of violence as sacred and aesthetic originates in the destructive/creative impulse that has haunted modern culture.[16] Violence motivated by the desire for values believed to be genuine can only realize that motivation by an act that is inherently finite and temporal. This is best illustrated in the fascist imagination of order, where violence is depicted as a kind of cleansing or purging of the body politic in response to the malaise of modern civilization.[17] The imaginary temporal and spatial orders of bourgeois culture are represented both as the supreme achievement in the teleology of progress and as an alienating site where the expression of genuine feeling and identity are suppressed. Consequently, there is an ongoing struggle between submitting to the modern order and longing to transgress it. As noted above, Friedlander locates one instance of that struggle within fascist ideology. "Submission nourishes fury, fury clears its conscience in the submission. To these opposing needs, Nazism—in the constant duality of its representations—offers an outlet: in fact, Nazism found itself to be the expression of these opposing needs."[18]

Fascist violence aimed for a resolution of the contradictions of modern culture by obliterating the present and reconfiguring it as space on which authentic origins could be projected. The fascist aesthetics of violent purification and suppression of the body is, however, only one manifestation of the modern ideology of violence, which invariably purports to be an expression of freedom, even in its leftist variants. The aesthetic potential of violent transgression may be expressed in very different ways: as a desire to liberate from social rules and customs, imagined as a return to an original, ordered state of nature; or as a desire to liberate by imposing social constraints and a sense of order—a desire best captured in the chilling slogan "work will make you free."[19] Either way, violence is justified as an effort to assert control in order to alleviate the anxiety created by the spare time that modern urban, technological communities have made possible and by the crumbling of affective ties that governed traditional notions of human relationships. At the core of the modern experience of individuality is an emphasis on self-realization through activity or performance, rather than through inherited status or qualities, that has weakened both socially determined boundaries of self-definition and any stable center of the personality.[20] Thus, aesthetic violence is justified by the need to suppress the heightened awareness of the contingency and createdness of the modern sense of self, and by the desire for authentic culture.[21]

The recourse to violence and its justifications as political act or aesthetic expression can never be more than a temporary escape from the awareness of time and from the self-consciousness of language and thought that mark modern culture. The spatial and temporal orders of the present give way to a cyclical, mythic time that, in its constant return, runs counter to the longing for the transcendent experience that elevates the present to an eternal moment. For that reason, fascism in particular among modern political ideologies made violence routine, systematic, and institutional.

Because of the actual violence inscribed upon the body in certain modernist ideologies, care must be taken when discussing the expressive function of violence. There is the danger of abstraction that can aestheticize the effects of physical violence on individuals, transforming violence into a cultural fetish.[22] Such a transformation is readily apparent in Mishima's writings, and the phenomenon became widespread in the 1960s and 1970s when, for example, the works of Sade were treated as liberating texts, or when aspects of the Nazi regime were eroticized in films such as *Seven Beauties* or *The Night Porter.* At the same time, it would also be ethically questionable and historically misleading to divorce violence from its expression in language and thereby fail to address the admittedly uncomfortable nature of its aesthetic appeal.

The aesthetics of violent transgression figures over and over in the rites of twentieth-century literary and cinematic narratives, and has resulted in the modernist canonization of mad poets, outcast ideologues, or charismatic criminals.[23] Pound, Lewis, and Genet come most immediately to mind when considering this aspect of modern culture. The mythopoeic impulse that dominates their art, with its breaking and recasting of worlds, is undoubtedly the defining attitude of what is now sometimes referred to as high modernism, and it is an impulse that has clear political ramifications. The archetypes of myth destroy both the sense of present time and space, conflating the past and present and sweeping away historical consciousness, which, by always striving to account for the contingent in human affairs, blocks the achievement of feeling without ideology. The collapsing of historical depth that results from myth-making permits the individual to escape into the unconditioned realm of organic or natural culture, or to submerge identity in a collective that rejects the claims of individualism.

The desire to get beyond language and thought and return to an authentic culture has played an important role in the formation of cultural identity in Japan. Modern Japanese identity is profoundly alienated because it is so heavily tied to modes of production and representation that have been perceived as failing to embody the true values or spirit of Japan. As a result, the nation has been wracked by spasms of individual violence and by the violence of coercive social control.

Mishima's embrace of the alienation caused by modern culture, which he took as the source of his art, was apparent to his contemporaries. Isoda Kōichi saw Mishima as a man appalled by the weakness and collaboration of Japanese intellectuals with postwar politics, and at their inability to assume individual responsibility. Isoda thought this weakness was the result of the efforts of postwar modernists who rejected the prewar ideology of the *Roman-ha* (Romanticists), but continued to cling to totalizing concepts of perfectibility that ironically made them "legitimate offspring of the Japanese *Roman-ha*." According to Isoda, when Mishima is compared to most of his contemporaries,

his radical modernism is self-evident. The will that seeks for the sympathy and understanding of another person, and that tries to place the masses under its control was nothing at all to Mishima. Even if we assume that all individuals possess autonomy, it turned out that absolute self-autonomy was achieved not by some left-wing intellectual but, ironically, by Mishima Yukio. There are various opinions about the content and political meaning of his thought. However, I think its actual meaning is supported by an extreme ultra-modernity that utterly rejects the collusion of Japanese community. If Yasuda Yojūrō embodied the character of Japanese community, then what separates him from Mishima is in fact nothing more than this modernity. And isn't this modernity the logic of achieving independent responsibility, which is close to Western individualism, and which is heterogeneous with the concept of modernism? The ethics of *Hagakure* is here linked to the most radical modernism as the ethics of achieving independent responsibility.[24]

Isoda's characterization of the difference between Mishima and Yasuda as a difference in emphasis between the individual and the community is justified in terms of the appeal of their work. Mishima's violent antimodernism clearly owed a debt to the *Roman-ha*, but that is where the connection to the movement ends for him. Yasuda's communalism was a vision of an idealized past, and in that respect is an antimodern swerve, but his postwar denials of the power of his own writings broke the covenant with authentic culture inspired by that vision. Mishima was, in contrast, a radical modernist insofar as his nostalgia and his contempt for the sterility of postwar Japanese society were turned inward. His critique of modern Japan took a fascist swerve toward a martial code, but he knew that turn was a performance, that the code was anachronistic and inauthentic because it was self-consciously revived.

In the end, what distinguishes Mishima's modernism from that of the *Roman-ha* is his attitude of knowingness toward the inauthenticity of modern culture, which he recognized but accepted as a way to make the present moment meaningful through the performance of a return to Japan's martial past. In a late autobiographical piece, *Taiyō to tetsu* (*Sun and Steel*, 1968), Mishima states his understanding of the problem of the ethics of modern identity.

Wielding both the sword and the pen is to hold at the same time a flower that falls and a flower that does not; it is to hold at the same time the two most contradictory desires of human nature, and the two dreams of the realization of those desires....

The destruction of these ultimate dreams occurs upon learning the secret that the flower that dreams of the sword is nothing more than an artificial flower, while learning the other secret that death supported by the lie that dreams of the pen is not death with any special grace. In short, all salvation is cut off to the dual way of the pen and the sword, and its dual secrets, whose fundamental essences must never be revealed to one another, mutually see through the other's mask. [The dual way] must be self-composed, possessing in a single form the final destruction of the principle of death and the final destruction of the principle of life.

Is it possible for humans to live this kind of ideal? Fortunately, it is extremely rare for the dual way of the pen and the sword to assume that absolute form. And even when the ideal is realized, it is over in an instant. Because even if there is always an awareness and premonition [of the end], which takes the form of a sense of unease, this final pair of secrets, which mutually assault one another, has no chance to prove itself until the moment of death.[25]

Mishima's idealized vision of the moment of death as the point when the problem of identity is resolved in the fusion of the literary and the martial leads inevitably to the realization that outside such an ideal both the pen and the sword, words and world, are inauthentic, empty structures. Mishima understands that the realization of nihilism can never exist in real life except, perhaps, at that fleeting moment when the subjective consciousness slips, like an object falling into a black hole, beyond the horizon of the singularity of death:

To devote death to one's heart each day, and to converge moment by moment on death, which must come to us, is to place the power to imagine the worst possible outcome in the same location as the power to imagine glory.... In that case, [that devotion] is sufficient to be able to transfer things carried out in the world of the spirit to the world of the flesh. As I have stated before, in order to receive this kind of violent transformation, even in the world of the flesh, I thoroughly prepared myself and readied an attitude to be able to receive it any time. Thus the theory that everything had the potential to be reclaimed was born within me. Because it had been proven to me that even the flesh, which ought to be a prisoner by virtue of growing and decaying moment by moment with time, had the potential to be reclaimed. It is therefore not strange at all that the thought that even time itself could be reclaimed should have come to life within me.

> For me, the fact that time could be reclaimed, at once meant that the beautiful death I had been unable to achieve previously had become a possibility.[26]

Mishima is convinced that he can overcome time, break through his self-awareness, and achieve the dream of reconciling the momentary with the eternal by returning to the violence epitomized by the self-less warrior, who accepted the inevitability of death.

Because *Sun and Steel* is a late autobiographical piece, the statement of his aesthetic purpose is based on a retrospective look at his life experiences. Mishima's aesthetics are inseparable from the context of his critical self-interpretation, and thus it would be a mistake to indiscriminately project this statement back onto his earlier works of fiction as a guide for reading. However, if we separate the self-destructive purpose for which he put his principles to work late in his career, we find a remarkably consistent presentation of the sources of his ideas about art and beauty. The presence of this common element in his work is significant in that it suggests the problem of identity is a developing theme, not a retrospective interpretation imposed on the reader by the author.

In *Kinkakuji* (*Temple of the Golden Pavilion*, 1956), for example, Mishima finds a metaphor in the burning of the famous Zen temple in 1950 for the creative/destructive duality that marks nihilist aesthetics. The young acolyte, Mizoguchi, the narrating I who commits the infamous act of arson, is a stutterer who is utterly incapable of connecting his words with the world. The weariness and impotence that come over him as he contemplates the beauty of the Kinkakuji, which has been an object of veneration for him since his childhood, are the result of his unceasing struggle to reconcile reality with his perceptions of it. He had hoped that the war would provide a way out of his predicament either through his death or through the destruction of the Kinkakuji by American bombs. Because neither happened, he resolves to break through that weariness by the nihilistic acts of arson and suicide. By planning to destroy the barrier between his vision of beauty and the reality of the temple, Mizoguchi hopes to resolve the modernist paradox.

In the buildup to the climax of the novel, Mizoguchi ponders the beauty of the temple one last time. That beauty has so enthralled him that it is now as much a product of his memory as it is the product of his direct experience of it. Therein lies the discovery of the true nature of the temple's beauty. Unable to make out the details of the building in the darkness of the night on which he sets the fire, he closes his eyes and relies on his inner vision to determine what it is that has such a hold on him:

> However, as my memory of its beauty grew ever stronger, the darkness became the ground onto which I could self-indulgently draw my visions. Within this dark, crouching shape, every aspect of what I thought of as beauty lay concealed. Through the power of memory, the details of beauty came sparkling one by one out of the darkness, and, as the sparkling diffused, at last the Kinkakuji gradually became visible beneath the light of a mysterious time that was neither day nor night. Never before had the Kinkakuji appeared to me in such a completely detailed form, glittering in every corner. It was as though I had gained the powers of vision of a blind man.[27]

The beauty of the temple is the creation of the young acolyte's memory of it. It is no longer connected to the real presence of the temple but arises out of a synthesis between the form of the temple and the individual mind contemplating it. The worlds of art and experience are completely sundered for Mizoguchi, who is forced to create an architecture of the mind. And in that architecture he finds that it was

> beauty that not only unified the struggles, the contradictions, all the discordances of the various parts, but actually controlled them! Like a scripture that has been copied painstakingly, letter by letter, with gold dust on dark-blue parchment, the temple was a structure built out of gold dust in the long, dark night. However, I did not know if beauty was the Kinkakuji itself, or something identical to the empty night that surrounded it. Perhaps beauty was both. It was the particulars, it was the whole structure, it was the temple, it was the night that enveloped the temple. Thinking about it in that way, I felt that the enigma of the beauty of the Kinkakuji, which had heretofore tormented me, was halfway solved. The reason was that when I examined the beauty of each detail ... in no way did the beauty end in or be completed by them. Instead, a foreshadowing of the beauty of the succeeding detail was contained in every part. The beauty of each detail was filled with an uneasiness in itself. While dreaming of perfection, it was drawn toward the next beauty, the unknown beauty, never knowing completion. Foreshadowing was linked to foreshadowing, and each foreshadowing of beauty, *which did not exist here*, became, as it were, the theme of

the Kinkakuji. Those foreshadowings were the signs of emptiness. Emptiness was the structure of this beauty. Thus, naturally the foreshadowings of emptiness were contained in the incompleteness of the details; and this delicate construction of fine timber, like a devotional necklace swaying in the breeze, was trembling in the foreshadowing of emptiness.[28]

This idea of the nature of beauty plays upon the Buddhist notion of the emptiness of reality. The existence of beauty depends not on any absolute, but on the relationship of individual details, images, or memories. The creation of beauty requires the totalizing power of the imagination, but the subjective ordering of those relationships in turn requires an acceptance of the relative nature of aesthetic values.

Mizoguchi's aesthetic discovery, then, is double-edged. The recognition of the beauty of the Kinkakuji, which is nothing more than the recognition of his own concept of the temple, gives him the freedom to control the reading of the temple's beauty, but in his understanding of that beauty, he also feels an uneasiness that foretells the emptiness of his own aesthetic concepts. Mizoguchi, of course, cannot resolve the nihilist/relativist problematic. He is limited to making a gesture toward nihilism by destroying himself along with the temple: an act that would at least conjure the sense of authenticity that comes with death. Mizoguchi's failure is an explicit critique of the inauthentic; Mizoguchi is a kitsch aesthete. He is at last capable of destroying the object he believes blocks the expression of himself, but his self-awareness causes him to lose nerve, and he is incapable of completing his vision of self-immolation. Having committed arson, he retreats to a nearby hill and watches the blaze, casually smoking a cigarette. By failing to extinguish the self, Mizoguchi fails to destroy the subjective, inner vision of the Kinkakuji that is the source of his dilemma.

Identity and the False Confession

Temple of the Golden Pavilion gives a vivid critique of counterfeit aesthetics, but it is neither the earliest nor the most original formal expression of that critique. In Mishima's first major novel, *Confessions of a Mask* (*Kamen no kokuhaku*, 1948), he achieves a technical innovation by reversing the formula of the naturalist confession that art is life. For the narrator, life is art; its essence is observable only through a subjective, relative perspective, and thus, like beauty, is an empty structure. The complexity of the narrative arises from the tricky nature of the confessional form. As the title suggests, it is not clear if the narrative is a "true confession" or a "false confession," and the lack of clarity is important to the conception of the work.[29]

The term false confession is intended to point to the playful aspects of the work, and the parody implied by the term is an accurate description not only of Mishima's technique in this novel, but also of the narrator's self image. Even so, to speak of *Confessions of a Mask* as a false confession is perhaps a little redundant, since a confession by nature exposes its own artifice. There is in any confession some ulterior motive—the desire for truth and sincerity, for absolution, for idealizing an individual life, for defining a new identity, or for simply generating interest in a story that exposes the narrator's secrets—that threatens to make the narrative insincere and thus false. The narrator of *Confessions of a Mask* actively manipulates the possibility of ulterior motives at those points in his story where he professes fear at his abnormality and uniqueness, while confirming his abnormality by pointing out that fear.

The novel is the account of a young man who, tormented by his growing awareness of his homosexuality, strives to mask the genuine self that makes him different and isolated. However, the narrator is so self-aware and so critical of his own stratagems to hide his identity that he cannot tolerate those self-delusions. The endlessly regressive self-exposure of the narrative, which reduces identity to a mask, is the insoluble problem that the narrator must confront, but rather than try to overcome this dilemma, the narrator identifies what he takes to be his true nature not only in his homoerotic longings but also in the unstable act of self-exposure, in which the real presence of identity always slips away. The narrator compares his method of self-analysis to a Möbius strip, with internal and external surfaces twisted together to make a one-sided perspective that gives the illusion of being multidimensional:

> My powers of introspection had a structure that defied one's imagination, just like those circles made by twisting a long narrow piece of paper once, and then pasting the ends together. What you think is the outer surface turns out to be the inner. And what you take to be the inner surface is really the outer. In later years I slowed down a little, but when I was twenty-one I did nothing but run blindly around the track of my youthful emotions; and the speed of my rotations became dizzyingly fast

due to the frenzied apocalyptic feelings that arose with the final stages of the war. I was allowed no time to go one by one into causes, effects, contradictions, or confrontations. The contradictions continued, just as they were, to rub against each other at a speed so great that they were not discernible.[30]

The narrator gains credibility by his self-questioning, but at the same time, he forces himself and the reader to see that credibility as just another pose or mask. The mere utterance of the dilemma of an individual who cannot speak his true identity does nothing to resolve that dilemma. If confessing is no different from donning a mask, then all efforts to define the self—or indeed all human experience and memory—are empty and illusory. When the exercise of will and self-awareness become ends unto themselves, then all human activity, like the narrative structure of *Confessions of a Mask*, spirals forever inward, blocking genuine knowledge of the self.

At one point, the narrator claims to desire death in order to conceal his difference from others. The appeal of death is its promise of nothingness in the face of the inability to resolve the divide between the narrator's perception of his "abnormal" self and the "normal" reality of the world. Yet when he has the chance to seek out death at the time he is drafted into the army, he receives a medical discharge on the basis of a misdiagnosis of a lung inflammation as tuberculosis. By accepting what he knows to be false, he rules out the possibility of death in war. In reflecting upon his actions, he writes,

> then suddenly my other voice spoke up, saying that not once had I ever really wanted to die. These words allowed me to loosen the knots of my shame. It was a difficult thing to say, but I understood that my wish to go into the army only to die had been a lie, and that instead I had been embracing some carnal expectations of army life. And I understood that the power that let me persist in this expectation was the primitive, mystical belief all humans hold, the belief that I, at least, would not die... .
>
> Nevertheless, this thought was extremely disagreeable to me. So I preferred to feel that I was a man who had been forsaken by death. I preferred to concentrate my delicate nerves, like a surgeon operating on an internal organ, to look dispassionately upon the strange agony of a person who desired death, but who had been repudiated. I felt that the degree of my pleasure in this thought was wicked.[31]

The narrator, who fails to take the step toward death, is a clear literary antecedent of Mizoguchi. The predicament in *Confessions of a Mask* is, however, more complicated, in that the narrator first universalizes his experience by noting that everyone fears and denies death, then stresses the uniqueness of his situation by adopting the rationalization that he alone has been refused by death. He admits the falsehood of his sense of uniqueness—his sense of immortality—but even the honesty with which he confesses his self-serving actions does not render them authentic.

Mishima pushes the autobiographical confession, with its interior perspective, to a radically new use. There is of course no doubt that the story is based on the facts of Mishima's life, but this simple equation of art and life is of little help in resolving the predicament of the narrator. The disbelief of some readers regarding Mishima's homosexuality at the time of the novel's publication, far from being a complete misreading of the text, points out the difficulty at the heart of *Confessions of a Mask*. The skepticism toward his credibility, which the narrator invites by constantly pointing out the underlying motives for his confession, extends in a peculiar way to include the question about whether or not Mishima is telling the truth about his real life. A crucial part of his confession is the revelation of his impulse to write or narrate himself—to play, if you will, with the text of his life. This proclivity is illustrated early on, when the narrator rewrites a Hungarian fairy tale that tells of a beautiful prince who, like all the other noble heroes who attract the narrator, is fated to die young. In the tale, the prince undergoes numerous horrible deaths, only to revive each time and gain victory. The narrator is fascinated in particular by the prince's gory death by a dragon, but he is dissatisfied with the part of the story that tells of the prince coming back to life. As a result, he takes to covering up that part with his hand and reading the story according to his own preference. He writes: "Adults would have perhaps read as absurd the sentence that resulted from that method of cutting. However, this young, arrogant censor, who was so easily addicted to his own whims, while clearly discerning the contradiction in the two phrases 'he was torn to pieces' and 'he fell to the ground,' could not discard either."[32]

The urge to rewrite, to represent death in a consciously contrived form, reveals the incongruity between words and death and thus puts the narrator's edited tale in the realm of kitsch. This belated urge to rewrite and reinterpret is turned upon the narrator's own life, when the problem of his sexuality becomes more pronounced. At the beginning of chapter 3, he tells us that the idea that life is a stage, a kind of dramatic performance, became an obsession with him, and that he came to believe that life was nothing more than an assumption of roles. Accordingly, when he begins to be troubled by what he sees as his different sexuality, he looks for models to define himself as a "normal" boy. At this point in his life, his early tendency to define himself in terms of the literature he has read becomes even more pronounced:

> The time was nearing when one way or another I would start out in life. The preliminary knowledge I had for this journey came first of all from my numerous novels, a one-volume dictionary of sex, the dirty books that had circulated among my friends, and the many innocent, lewd conversations I heard each night that we went on outdoor exercises. My burning curiosity was a more faithful traveling companion than all of these. For my attitude on my departure, I decided it was best to be a "machine of deceit."[33]

The narrator's dissociation and his inability to connect with others are thus explicitly related to the literary quality of his life, and he relies on fiction to learn about normal behavior. He pretends to be the same as the other boys, but the desires that drive them, especially their sexual desire for women, is beyond the vocabulary of his self-created identity, since he suffers from what he calls a deficiency in the power of his mental associations.

When the narrator confesses that he is being untrue to himself by donning a narrative mask to define his persona, he is also assuming the paradoxical pose that he is giving a true portrait of himself. This twisted confession makes it nearly impossible to judge the truthfulness of the story. Are we to doubt him when he exposes the self-deceptions he has used to justify his actions? Conversely, are we to believe him when he makes claims for the truthfulness of his story? Throughout the text, these questions are complicated again and again by the narrator's awareness of them. The novel opens with the narrator discussing the trustworthiness of his memory, the faculty that makes his memoir possible. The problem of credibility with his memory arises because it is apparently too good to be true. He claims to be able to remember scenes from his birth, a claim that both amuses the adults around him and threatens them, since they see the claim as a childish trick to get them to talk about sex. The narrator, however, assures us that there was no such ruse behind his memory, which is of a light striking the basin where he was first bathed. Whatever explanations there might have been for this false memory—that it was suggested to him later or that he made it up—the narrator insists that he clearly saw the light:

> The refutation that had the most power against this memory was the fact that I was not born in the daytime. I was born at nine in the evening. There could have been no sunlight streaming in. Even when teased with suggestions that perhaps it was an electric light, I was still able to walk with no trouble at all into the absurdity of thinking confidently that, even though it was nighttime, a ray of sun shone down on that one spot on the basin. The brim of the basin on which the light flickered somehow lingered in my memory as being something I definitely saw at the time of my first bath.[34]

The significance of this memory is twofold. First, the image of light, with its extraordinary implication of an almost preternatural self-awareness on the part of the narrator, is a recurring motif. Indeed, the story ends with an image of reflected sunlight described as both alluring and menacing, because it confirms by arousing the narrator's different sexuality and because it calls to mind the emptiness of his confession, which is a presentiment of his death. Second, it creates confusion over the good faith and credibility of the confession. The danger of this confusion is apparent to the narrator, for he is careful to completely assure the reader that the next earliest memory he talks about is true.[35] This memory, of a handsome young night-soil man who worked in the neighborhood, is important to the narrator, because it marked his first feelings of sexual desire. The dual scatological and eschatological associations of this memory, which also seems neatly contrived, create the confusion of sexuality and the sense of difference that force the narrator into a life of assuming one mask after another in order to connect himself with normal human experience.

The problem of his sexual identity is overpowering for the narrator, and his early propensities are established by the homoerotic images of his earliest memories and of the first storybooks he read as a child—images that eventually evolve into graphic, violent adolescent fantasies. As noted above, he is particularly drawn to stories of beautiful young princes who die bloody deaths. Moreover, he is a sickly child, and when he is finally allowed out to play with a cousin named Sugiko, he finds that he must go against the image of himself he has created and act in a manner that conforms to the expectations of others. He tells us that in Sugiko's house,

I was required, without anything being said and without being told, to be a boy. The masquerade so uncongenial to my heart had begun. From about this time I began to vaguely comprehend the mechanism by which the thing reflected in the eyes of others as my acting was a manifestation of the need for me to return to my true nature, and that what was reflected as my natural self in the eyes of others was my acting.[36]

The narrator's homosexuality is demonstrated to us and to the narrator himself many times. His first orgasm is achieved while he stares at a picture of the martyring of St. Sebastian—an image that explicitly conveys for the narrator associations of sexual desire and death; his first pangs of love are felt for a male classmate; and, near the end of the novel, the narrator gains what he takes to be absolute proof when he fails to be sexually aroused during an encounter with a prostitute. However, the narrator presents such proof not simply to convince the reader of his true nature, but also to convince himself. The need to convince himself arises from his uneasy conviction that his true nature and identity, the things that make him an individual, are what separates him from the rest of humanity.

This predicament is most clearly portrayed in his relationship with a young woman, Sonoko. She represents for him the ideal described in the passage from *The Brothers Karamazov* that prefaces the novel:

Ah, Beauty! The thing I cannot stand at all is that even splendid people who possess a pure heart and surpassing reason often start out embracing the ideal of the Madonna and end up with the ideal of Sodom. There is something even worse. Namely, those people who embrace in their hearts the ideal of Sodom while at the same time not denying the ideal of the Madonna, and who keep aflame in their hearts the longing for a beautiful ideal from the depths of their soul, as in the pure days of their youth.[37]

The story of the relationship with Sonoko takes up much of the second half of *Confessions of a Mask*. He seeks her out in part to confirm the suspicions he has about himself, and in part as an ideal of beauty that will provide him an image of permanence through which he can assuage the anguish caused by concealing his identity. Although there is always a distance between them—a distance created by the narrator observing the ways Sonoko assumes his normality and thus misreads him—she nonetheless represents, like death, a possible resolution to his conflicted consciousness. The problem is that the attainment of the ideal of either beauty or death remains beyond the reach of his confession. Almost from the moment he first sees Sonoko, he tells us, he felt purified by the sight of her beauty. He then abruptly stops his account to address the reader directly.

> Having written this, those who have read to this point will probably not believe me. This is because it may seem there is nothing to distinguish between the artificial first pangs of love I felt toward Nukada's younger sister, and the throbbing of my heart on this occasion. Because there was no reason why the ruthless analysis of the earlier instance should have been disregarded this time only. If that is the case, then my act of writing has been meaningless from the beginning. For it will be thought that what I am writing is nothing more than the product of the desire to write in this manner. Because, for the sake of this desire, anything I write is acceptable so long as it is coherent and accords with reason. However, an accurate part of my memory recalls one point of difference with what I felt now and what I had felt earlier. That difference was a feeling of remorse.[38]

He claims his feeling of remorse is genuine and not part of his masquerade, because her beauty strikes him as ideal and asexual. He also tells us that he was confused by his feeling of remorse and did not understand its origins. He then explicitly connects these feelings with the problem of the credibility of his feelings and of his memory. The connection between his confused emotions and the problem of confession is important to the design of the narrative as a whole, because he feels that his remorse may have been a presentiment of sin. His confession confirms his abnormality, his sin, over and over, but it never allows him to establish absolutely his identity, and it prevents him from ever connecting with his ideal of beauty, Sonoko. To the very end she presumes his heterosexuality, and he is thereby forced to continue to lie and to hide his identity from her. Confirming the reality of his homosexuality cannot stop the masquerade, because his confession lacks the power to become real. He is in the same situation as when he first met Sonoko:

> The usual "act" had been transformed into a part of my personality. It was no longer an act. The consciousness that I was masquerading as a normal person had corroded the original normality within me, and I was finally forced to persuade myself each time that this consciousness was noth-

ing more than a feigned normality. Put another way, I became a person who believes only in the counterfeit. That being the case, this feeling in my mind that I wanted to regard the attraction of my heart for Sonoko as counterfeit perhaps in reality revealed a masked desire that wanted to think of that feeling as true love.[39]

The maddening circularity of the narrator's self-analysis is not a sign of indecision, but it signifies an irreparable breach between reality and the ability to represent it. The instant the narrator became aware that the narrative of his life, his identity, is a pose, his "true" identity and his ideal of beauty became as insubstantial and intangible as a ghost, and the confessional narrative is reduced to a series of paradoxes. There is the paradox of his identity. He wants to confess his difference and assert his uniqueness, and yet he fears the isolation that would result. To resolve this paradox, he confesses his tendency to masquerade, but in the end, the mask becomes the image of himself, suggesting once again that he cannot connect with his genuine identity. The confession of a mask is by nature an empty narrative, and the narrator's self-conscious acceptance of that condition makes him a kitsch aesthete.

The emptiness of narrative is related in *Confessions of a Mask* to the specific predicaments of identity and credibility, but it has wider implications for the ethics of identity. The narrator touches on those implications when he describes the ravages of war he witnessed with Sonoko upon their return to Tokyo following the great air raids of the spring of 1945. The fire bombings destroyed everything that served as evidence of human existence. Not only did property go up in flames, but so did the primary relationships that held civilization together. In a desperate effort to stay alive, women killed their lovers and children murdered their mothers.[40] Like the beauty of the Kinkakuji when it comes under the gaze of Mizoguchi's inner vision, when the very fabric of human relationships and social values is subjected to the intense scrutiny the narrator of *Confessions of a Mask* turns on himself, it is exposed as relative, contingent, and empty.

Structures of Emptiness

The obsession with surfaces and false appearances, which dominates *Confessions of a Mask*, became the most important recurring element in

Mishima's writing. That persistent obsession raises the question of how seriously Mishima's work is to be taken. Is it possible to distinguish between inauthentic art and art that is about (that critiques) the inauthentic? In the case of Mishima, the answer is a qualified yes, since he plays upon the modernist paradox to brilliant formal and psychological effect in both *Confessions of a Mask* and *Kinkakuji*. The tragedy of Mishima's career is that his aesthetic discovery imprisoned him. Mishima found himself trapped by the realization that what he had become as an artist and an individual was an identity of his own construction, and thus one that held no absolute meaning. This could not have been a satisfying situation for an ambitious, self-absorbed artist driven by a preoccupation with authenticity. By the time he wrote *Sun and Steel*, his critique of the inauthentic had played itself out, and he was becoming a kitsch artist. Did Mishima recognize what was happening? No matter how much he may have enjoyed the masquerade, his knowledge about himself was surely a burden heavy enough to make him long for the presumed authenticity of violent death.

The attempt by Mishima to impose a final, authoritative reading on his life grew out of a lifelong project of narrating and renarrating his literary self in a struggle to achieve some degree of reintegration of language or text into the experience of the material world. Mark Freeman has observed that the narrative imagination, in the project of rewriting the self, performs an articulation of the world that would not otherwise have existed without the act of writing.

> In this sense, life histories are indeed artifacts of writing; they are the upsurge of the narrative imagination. This, however, is hardly reason to fault them or to relegate them to the status of mere fictions. We too, *as selves*, are artifacts of the narrative imagination. *We*, again literally, would not exist, save as bodies, without imagining who and what we have been and are: kill the imagination and you kill the self. Who, after all is said and done, would want to die such a death?[41]

Who but Mishima Yukio? His suicide was a response to the irreconcilable loss of values and meaning in modern culture. And unlike his fictional characters, the narrator of *Confessions of a Mask* or Mizoguchi in *Kinkakuji*, who were objects of his critique of the inauthentic, Mishima sought to resolve the problem of the inauthentic, to make whole again the breach between his words and his world, and to reclaim time itself by consciously opting to overcome the problem of identity in the only way he thought possible.

The irony of his death is that it can be interpreted as just another expression of the inauthentic. His suicide, with its counterfeit political motives, possesses a disturbingly contrived, literary quality.[42] Through his death, he in effect rewrote all of his works, by making his career seem teleological and thereby resituating the source of his art in something genuine. He imposed an interpretation of his life and art as inseparable, as leading inexorably toward that final moment when what Steiner calls the "compulsion to freedom," the "agonistic attempt to repossess, to achieve mastery over the forms and meanings" of one's own being,[43] coincided with an absurd, excruciating act of self-immolation. Mishima's suicide thus makes a claim on us by highlighting the contradiction at the heart of his explorations of the problem of identity. The horror of the event is grounded in Mishima's drive to give his life some sense of formal closure, but the overt staging of his death seems out of proportion with the finality of the event. For all of its horrible reality, his suicide, his *seppuku*, was also just another piece of writing: a forgery, a simulacrum, a work of kitsch art.

EPILOGUE

A LTHOUGH MISHIMA killed himself by committing *seppuku*, the ritual disembowelment practiced by the military class as a way to save face or demonstrate authentic loyalty, his death is now often characterized as *jiketsu*.[1] *Jiketsu* is a synonym for the more general term for suicide, *jisatsu*, but it carries with it the notion of committing suicide with a purpose. In fact, the primary meaning of *jiketsu* is "self-determination," literally, deciding on one's own. The distinction is a crucial one: it signifies a suicide committed not as a last resort or act of hopelessness but as an expression of individual will. It implies an autonomous moral choice.

What, then, was Mishima choosing? This question is pregnant with implications that continue to haunt Japanese artists even as memories of Mishima's life fade to ghostlier shades. The common response in the days immediately following his death was that he was choosing literally nothing, that he was a disturbed nutcase who had thrown away his life and accomplishments. Yet if it can be said he was mad, then it seems he was crazy like a fox. For in spite of all the careful planning that went into his final performance, he knew that his call for an overthrow of the government and a return to an authentic Japanese society under imperial rule would not be heeded, and that he was simply planning the spectacle of his own death.

The apparent nihilism of the act opened a frightening void that had to be filled—not so much to explain away or give significance to Mishima's motives as to reassure others in the significance of their own. Thus, the right-wing polemicist Yasuda Yojūrō, who had always viewed Mishima with suspicion and taken him for a fake ideologue, praised his *jiketsu* as an apotheosis, a critique of abject modernity that served as the ultimate expression of cultural authenticity.[2] On the other side of the political spectrum,

Ōe Kenzaburō was spurred to confront the unsettled and unsettling regrets and resentments that lingered in postwar Japanese society in the novellas *The Day He Himself Shall Wipe My Tears Away* and *Teach Us to Outgrow Our Madness*. In the context of the discourse of these works, Mishima's *jiketsu* can be interpreted as an eruption of a submerged cultural pathology, the disfiguring ambiguity of Japanese identity.

All of these responses—that Mishima was mad, that he was a cultural hero, that he represented an unresolved and dangerously reactionary element in Japanese culture—are equally plausible. But because they are self-serving, they are also all equally misguided. They are self-serving because they fail to confront the uncomfortable implication that Mishima's *jiketsu* was a performance of belief that laid bare once and for all the constructed nature of values. Despite their sharp political differences, Yasuda and Ōe shared the assumption that grounds for justifying belief can be found. When Mishima turned his back on that assumption, when he rejected the discourse and quit the field, he raised the possibility that belief is a simulacrum and that the sources of belief can be performed without conviction in anything but the performance itself.

Mishima made the effort to convince others that his conversion to militarism and to emperorism was sincere, but his ideology remained vague and inchoate because his attitude of sincerity was directed toward the performance rather than the contents of belief. Long before his death, he had come to the realization that the discourse on the ethics of identity was a dead end, a game rigged so that it could never be resolved but would always re-create itself in an infinite regress. Having recognized that the sources of all ethical values were constructed and relative, the only possibility left to him was belief without conviction. Mishima chose to resolve the contradictory appeals of autonomy and authenticity by consciously and willfully performing the culturally essential role of the warrior-artist who dies for a set of principles he knows to be arbitrary and illusory.

Mishima's *jiketsu* of course did nothing to resolve the contradictions that lie at the heart of the discourse on the ethics of identity. What his *jiketsu* revealed, however, was an attitude, the willfulness behind the performance of belief, that could offer a way to escape or at least sidestep the problem of modern identity. That attitude has established a clear line of demarcation in the recent history of Japanese literature, and artists who came of age in the 1970s and 1980s have since exploited it in various ways. Kitano (Beat) Takeshi, for example, has made a number of films over the past fifteen years, including *Sonatine* and *Hanabi*, that treat willful, intended acts of violence as an affirmation of values the protagonists know are empty. In *Hanabi*, he even brings the word *jiketsu* itself to the foreground, as an element in one of the paintings that play a prominent visual role in the film. The insertion of this word makes it clear that the violent actions and double suicide performed by the corrupted cop (portrayed by Kitano) are intended to set right a moral universe that has ceased to have meaning to him. All that matters is the role itself, the simulacrum of moral and aesthetic goods.

Another perhaps even more striking example of the attitude revealed in *jiketsu* is provided by the fiction of Murakami Haruki. Murakami begins his 1982 novel *A Wild Sheep Chase* (*Hitsuji o meguru bōken*) with a direct reference to Mishima's suicide. The opening chapter, "November 25, 1970,"[3] begins in 1978, with the narrator learning about the death of a former girlfriend whose name he had forgotten. After attending her funeral, he provides a flashback to the time when, as a twenty-year-old college student, he first met her in the fall of 1969. They have a brief and utterly casual relationship for a short time. They drift apart and he does not see her again until the fall of 1970, when they begin to sleep together every week on Tuesday nights, going out the following day for what she calls their "Wednesday picnics."

On Wednesday, November 25, they are out for their usual walk, but it is clear that their relationship is in deep trouble. The narrator is incapable of emotional intimacy and commitment. They try to talk it out, but get nowhere.

> We walked through the woods to the ICU campus, sat down as usual in the lounge, and nibbled on some hot dogs. It was two in the afternoon, and the image of Mishima Yukio kept flashing over and over on the lounge TV. The volume control was broken, so we could hardly hear anything being said. It made no difference to us one way or the other. When we finished our hot dogs we each drank another cup of coffee. Some student got up on a chair and fiddled with the volume for a while, but he gave up, got off the chair, and disappeared.
>
> "I want you," I said.
>
> "Sure," she said, smiling.[4]

They go back to his apartment, but when he wakes up he finds her sobbing. She asks if he ever thought of killing her, and when he brushes aside the question with a joke she laughs, but then adds that she will die when she is twenty-five. As it turns out, she dies at the age of twenty-six.

The narrator who is relating these memories is the prototype of the detached, occasionally naïve, coolly skeptical young man who appears so frequently in Murakami's fiction. The news of the death of his old girlfriend coincides with a turning point in his life. Nearing thirty at the start of the novel, his marriage has fallen apart and he has grown cynical about his business, a small public relations firm that works on translations and advertising. The narrator tells his business partner, "whether it's some inconspicuous translation job or some sham ad copy for margarine, it's all basically the same thing. We've spread around our share of insubstantial words, that's for sure. But then again, where do you find words with any substance? You see? There's no honest work anywhere. It's like there's no honest breathing or pissing."[5]

The narrator is strangely disconnected from the world around him, mainly because he recognizes that in contemporary life everything is equivalent to advertising copy and that the media can create an aura whose presence allows the consumer to experience a virtual world as real. The power of this aura and its disjunctive effects is at work in the reference to Mishima's *jiketsu*, which is given prominent mention at the very beginning of the novel but then treated as an insignificant event, as mere background to the setting. Mishima, whose death was at once a reaction against and an embrace of this aura, is reduced to a media image reproduced in an infinite loop of television replays that diminish the aura of significance surrounding his act. Moreover, because the volume control on the TV set doesn't work, he is robbed of the words that should have been the substance of his art and of his final performance. The allusion is thus offhand, diffident, and almost stripped of any meaning other than its power to suggest a particular moment in the life of the narrator.

Although the spectacle of Mishima's performance is diminished, reduced to fit the size of a TV screen, the date of his death still holds importance to the narrator, who gives his personal experience of loss some degree of significance by connecting it to a more famous historical event. Even though the narrator treats the death offhandedly, it serves as a crucial point of reference, signifying the ill-defined sense of loss and aimlessness that plagues the narrator (and his generation). Although he is passively drawn into a fantastic, utterly contrived search to find the eponymous sheep, his condition of loss and aimlessness, symbolized by Mishima's death, ensures that he gets drawn into the quest. As it turns out, there is no grand moral to be drawn from the narrator's quest, no ideological payoff. All that matters in the novel is the performance of the quest, the performance of self-discovery, in which history and politics are reduced to the immediate experience of the surface of modern consumer society.

The narrator is after performance without ideology or conviction, but he is trying to get to this ideal without appearing to be conscious that he is performing. Willfully striving for that ideal would simply recirculate all the contradictions of the discourse of the ethics of identity. Conscious disengagement, the reduction of history to nothing more than markers of individual experience, exemplified by the treatment of Mishima's death in *A Wild Sheep Chase*, is required to avoid that trap, and this attitude is a recurring element in Murakami's fiction. It even becomes the topic of a short story, "Fall of the Roman Empire; The Indian Uprising of 1881; Hitler's Invasion of Poland; And the World of High Winds."

The story begins when the narrator notices that a powerful wind is blowing outside his apartment: "Just at that moment, as I always do—that is, as I always do on Sunday afternoons—I was sitting at the table and writing down a week's worth of entries in my diary while playing some easy-listening music. It's my custom to jot down simple memos to record each day's events, and then, on Sunday, to put them all together in proper sentences."[6] As soon as he sees the wind blowing wildly, he goes out onto his veranda to bring in the laundry. After folding the clothes, he checks the weather map in the newspaper and is puzzled to read that the chance of wind is zero percent; the day should be as calm as the age of the Pax Romana.

He returns to his diary and records a series of minor events from the past week. On Thursday, his girlfriend came over carrying an airline overnight bag and a cloth blindfold. She enjoys wearing the blindfold when they make love, and though the narrator is not into such things, he notes that everyone has some strange proclivities. He also remarks that his method of writing is always like the Thursday entry: 80 percent fact and 20 percent observation. On Friday, he went to a bookstore in Ginza to meet a friend, who happened to be wearing a strange tie with phone numbers on it. The instant he writes this fact his phone rings, but when he picks it up, the sound of the wind in the receiver is so loud that he cannot hear anything. The noise reminds him of an American Indian uprising in 1881, which he then confuses with the Candice Bergen film *The Wind and the Lion* (a story set in Morocco). Giving up on the phone, he goes back to his diary to write his entry for Saturday. He went to see the movie *Sophie's Choice*, and records the depiction of Hitler's invasion of Poland, but then confuses this film with two other Meryl Streep movies: *Kramer Versus Kramer* and *Falling in Love*.

Eventually, the wind calms and his girlfriend shows up to make dinner. He asks her why the wind would start blowing and then stop so suddenly. She brushes off the question, saying there are lots of things people don't know. While she prepares dinner, he writes down three memos to use for the Sunday entry of his diary next week: fall of the Roman Empire, Indian uprising of 1881, Hitler's invasion of Poland. The story ends with the narrator explaining that

> because I write down things like this, I'm able to remember exactly and accurately what happened today by the time next week rolls around. By using this kind of careful, rigorous system, I have been able to continue my diary for these twenty years without ever missing a single day. All meaningful actions have their own systems. Whether the wind is blowing or not, I am living in that kind of condition [*sonna guai*].[7]

The narrator is not unreliable. The factual mistakes and confusions he makes seem unimportant to him. He is instead obsessed with details of time and place, and he claims to have a memory like the lid of a blast furnace. His method of writing reflects that obsession and gives him a way to bring order into a world literally blown about in a high wind of signifiers. His memos read like bookmarks on a web browser or like an evening's programming on the History Channel. The temporal and spatial horizons of the narrator's easy-listening world have been compressed to the point where the most trivial daily events become memorable (or at least rememberable) by virtue of their association with grand historical moments. In a consumerist, high-tech society that produces an overabundance of goods and knowledge, it seems that the only thing left to the individual is the illusion of choice. Murakami's narrator picks and chooses, and the willful, rigorous method he uses to keep his diary going is also the way he authors the conception of himself.

There is, of course, something slightly unsettling about this attitude and the subtle shift in the discourse on the ethics of identity it indicates. To give meaning to the smallest occurrences of everyday life by associating them with important historical events runs the risk of trivializing the moral and political significance of those events. The unease over this aspect of Murakami's fiction helps to account for the criticism that his work is all style and no substance, that it is a cynical exercise in consumerism lacking the commitment and vision that is the mark of great art.

This critique can seem at times too strident, a prescriptivism that stubbornly overlooks the playful performance of language that makes Murakami's characters so appealing. Yet the critique is not entirely without justification, and even serious fans of Murakami seem all too willing to revel (or wallow) in his play of words as the only value that matters. Both the critics and the fans have sold Murakami a little short, for his achievement has been in capturing the temper of his times. I know that phrase sounds hopelessly ponderous and out of date, but I believe it is an accurate statement. Murakami has managed to emanate the aura of art around himself and his fiction. That aura may be a virtual effect, the product of a refusal to get caught in the trap of modern identity, but it makes some form of an ethics of identity possible in a period where belief without conviction is the "condition" (*guai*) artists live in now.

Although Murakami's fiction provides evidence of a recalibration of the discourse on the ethics of identity since Mishima's death, it is important to keep in mind that even with its playful originality, it shares many of the concerns and employs the language and many of the same techniques as the works I have discussed throughout this study. His stories consistently represent individuals trying to come to some definition of selfhood, to find some way to translate the language and signs of value into a meaningful identity, even if the only signs of values are the flotsam and jetsam of contemporary consumer culture. The performative nature of the search for identity may suggest that the sources of selfhood are empty, but the apparent emptiness of the worlds created in Murakami's fiction is an effect of the very act of playing a role. The resulting aura of insubstantiality recalls the image of Miyake Setsurei's elusive phantom of identity, a phantom that expresses an impossible desire for simultaneous self-expression and self denial, for willfully choosing one's values or willfully associating personal identity with archetypal social roles and historical events. This aura is an important narrative element, which connects Murakami's work to the long history of literary experiments that have sought a way out of the paradox of modern identity.

NOTES

Preface

1. Jorge Luis Borges, "Pierre Menard, Author of the *Quixote*," in *Labyrinths: Selected Stories and Other Writings* (New York: New Directions Books, 1964), 39.

2. Ibid., 40.

3. Ibid., 43.

4. Ibid.

5. Ibid., 44.

6. Martha Nussbaum, *Love's Knowledge: Essays on Philosophy and Literature* (New York: Oxford University Press, 1990), 22.

Introduction. Real Identities

1. Ōe Kenzaburō, *Japan, the Ambiguous, and Myself: The Nobel Prize Speech and Other Lectures* (Tokyo: Kodansha International, 1995), 117–118.

2. Ibid., 42 and 65ff.

3. Ibid., 127–128.

4. Maeda Ai, "Gen'ei no Meiji," in *Maeda Ai chosaku shū* (Tokyo: Chikuma shobō, 1989), 4:434. Maeda goes on to discuss the work of Nishi Amane as a key example of this kind of ethical synthesis.

5. Miyake Setsurei, *Miyake Setsurei shū*, in *Nihon gendai bungaku zenshū* (Tokyo: Kōdansha, 1969), 2:310.

6. A number of scholars have criticized histories that depict the formation of national identity only from the viewpoint of intellectuals, who tend to stress the anxieties created by modernization. See Irokawa Daikichi, *The Culture of the Meiji Period*, ed. Marius Jansen (Princeton, N.J.: Princeton University Press, 1985), 74–75; and Isoda Kōichi, *Shisō to shite no Tōkyō* (Tokyo: Kōdansha, 1990), 36–38. While these views are a valuable corrective, the effect on the popular attitudes of

intellectuals was profound, and their power to mobilize the nation is an important fact that should not be discounted.

7. Fukuzawa Yukichi, *Fukuzawa Yukichi shū*, in *Nihon gendai bungaku zenshū* (Tokyo: Kōdansha, 1969), 2:8. See also Fukuzawa Yukichi, *An Encouragement of Learning*, trans. David Dilworth and Umeyo Hirano (Tokyo: Sophia University Press, 1969), 1. Hereafter I will cite this work by giving two sets of page numbers: the first from the Japanese version I consulted, the second from the Dilworth and Hirano translation.

8. Ibid., 2:8; 1. The language of the Enlightenment was a key source for Fukuzawa. However, this rhetoric has precedents in some rather unusual places, including the fiction of Shikitei Sanba. See, for example, the arch opening of Sanba's *Ukiyoburo* (*Bathhouse of the Floating World*). Shikitei Sanba, *Ukiyoburo*, in *Nihon koten bungaku taikei*, ed. Nakamura Michio (Tokyo, Iwanami shoten, 1957), 63:46–50. A fine translation of this work is available in Robert Leutner, *Shikitei Sanba and the Comic Tradition in Edo Fiction* (Cambridge, Mass.: Harvard University Press, 1985).

9. Fukuzawa, 2:14; 15.

10. Ibid., 2:14; 16.

11. Ibid., 2:20; 30.

12. Irokawa, *The Culture of the Meiji Period*, 65.

13. Thomas R. H. Havens, *Nishi Amane and Modern Japanese Thought* (Princeton, N.J.: Princeton University Press, 1970), 142.

14. Ibid., 148.

15. Douglas Howland writes: "Nishi's early translations attest to his idea that if he properly understood the origin of language, then he would be able to correctly translate Western knowledge into Japanese, and in effect, rewrite that knowledge as the new basis for Western civilization in Japan." Douglas Howland, "Nishi Amane's efforts to translate Western knowledge: Sound, written character, and meaning," *Semiotica* 83, no. 3/4 (1991): 285–286. For a catalogue of Nishi's translated terms, see Havens, *Nishi Amane*, 92–100.

16. Miyake, *Miyake Setsurei shū*, 313–316.

17. Ibid., 317. The connection between the notion of climate and race had an enormous influence on the discourse on identity. See the 1894 essay of Shiga Shigetaka, *Nihon fūkeiron* (Tokyo: Iwanami shoten, 1937); and Watsuji Tetsurō's 1935 essay, *Fūdo; ningengakuteki kōsatsu* (Tokyo: Iwanami shoten, 1940). See also Naoki Sakai, "Return to the West/Return to the East: Watsuji Tetsuro's Anthropology and Discussions of Authenticity," in *Japan in the World*, ed. Masao Miyoshi and H. D. Harootunian, 237–270 (Durham, N.C.: Duke University Press, 1993).

18. Miyake, *Miyake Setsurei shū*, 317.

19. Ibid., 316.

20. Ibid., 312, 314–315.

21. Ibid., 325.

22. Okakura Kakuzō, *The Awakening of Japan* (1904; repr. New York: The Japan Society, Inc., 1921), 5–6.

23. In an 1894 essay titled "Sei-Shin no shin igi," Tokutomi gives vent to his irritation at Westerners who showed racial contempt and dismissed modern Japanese culture as imitative. Cited in Kenneth Pyle, *The New Generation in Meiji Japan* (Stanford, Calif.: Stanford University Press, 1969), 176–178.

24. Okakura, *The Awakening of Japan*, 6–7.

25. Ibid., 194.

26. Ibid., 194–195. The phrase "the sadness of things" refers to the concept of *aware*, the sensitivity to change and mutability that was an aesthetic and moral concept in classical Japanese culture.

27. Ibid., 199–200.

28. Tokutomi Sohō, *The Future Japan* (Edmonton: University of Alberta Press, 1989), 157.

29. For a summary of the sources of the notion of purity, see John Dower, *War Without Mercy: Race and Power in the Pacific War* (New York: Pantheon Books, 1986), 203–233.

30. Kobayashi Hideo, *Literature of the Lost Home: Kobayashi Hideo—Literary Criticism 1924 1939*, trans. Paul Anderer (Stanford, Calif.: Stanford University Press, 1995), 53. See also my comments on Nakamura Mitsuo in Dennis Washburn, *The Dilemma of the Modern in Japanese Fiction* (New Haven, Conn.: Yale University Press, 1995), 6–7.

31. Kobayashi, *Literature of the Lost Home*, 54.

32. Ibid. Paul Anderer notes that the final sentence of the original essay was dropped when the piece was published in Kobayashi's collected works. This sentence is: "With the passing of time, history reveals in clearer outline to the writer certain objective facts, and presses on him a structure that he can in no way evade. And, as the writer matures, his character becomes more and more concrete and distinctive, and paradoxically becomes part of the content of the structure that presses upon him." Anderer is justified in restoring this sentence to his translation, even if only in a note, because it helps illustrate the circularity of Kobayashi's language.

33. Ibid., 38.

34. Ibid., 40.

35. See Charles Taylor, *Philosophy and the Human Sciences* (New York: Cambridge University Press, 1985), 2:258.

36. Charles Taylor, *The Ethics of Authenticity* (Cambridge, Mass.: Harvard University Press, 1991), 26–29.

37. Ibid., 69.

38. For a representative critique of Taylor, see Lydia Liu, *Translingual Practice: Literature, National Culture, and Translated Modernity—China 1900–1937* (Stanford, Calif.: Stanford University Press, 1995), 8–10.

39. Taylor, *The Ethics of Authenticity*, 22–23.

40. Ibid., 91.

41. Theodor Adorno, *The Jargon of Authenticity* (Evanston, Ill.: Northwestern University Press, 1973), 5–6.

42. Trent Shroyer, foreword to Adorno, *The Jargon of Authenticity*, xiv.

43. The following studies explore in depth examples of the language of authenticity. Leslie Pincus, "In a Labyrinth of Western Desire: Kuki Shuzo and the Discovery of Japanese Being," in *Japan in the World*, ed. Masao Miyoshi and H. D. Harootunian, 222–236 (Durham, N.C.: Duke University Press, 1993); Marilyn Ivy, *Discourses of the Vanishing: Modernity, Phantasm, Japan* (Chicago: Chicago University Press, 1995); Stephen Dodd, *Writing Home: Representations of the Native Place in Modern Japanese Literature* (Cambridge, Mass.: Harvard University Asia Center, 2004).

44. Shimomura Toratarō, "Nishida Kitarō and Some Aspects of His Philosophical Thought," in Nishida Kitarō, *A Study of Good* (Printing Bureau, Japanese Government, 1960), 192–195.

45. For fuller accounts of Maruyama's notion of autonomy, see Rikki Kersten, *Democracy in Postwar Japan: Maruyama Masao and the Search for Autonomy* (London: Routledge, 1996); and Victor J. Koschmann, "Maruyama Masao and the Incomplete Project of Modernity," in *Postmodernism and Japan*, ed. Masao Miyoshi and H. D. Harootunian, 123–141 (Durham, N.C.: Duke University Press, 1989).

46. Maruyama Masao, *Nihon no shisō* (Tokyo: Iwanami shoten, 1961), 155–156.

47. Ibid., 156.

48. Ibid., 159.

49. Ibid., 158.

50. Ibid., 177–179.

51. See Maruyama's essay "Kindai Nihon no shisō to bungaku—hitotsu no keesu sutadi to shite" in Maruyama, *Nihon no shisō*, 67–122.

52. Kobayashi Hideo, *Gohho no tegami*, in *Kobayashi Hideo zenshū* (Tokyo: Shinchōsha, 1979), 10:20.

53. Stephen Vlastos, "Tradition: Past/Present Culture and Modern Japanese History," in *Mirror of Modernity: Invented Traditions of Modern Japan*, ed. Stephen Vlastos, 1–16 (Berkeley: University of California Press, 1998). See also Haruo Shirane and Tomi Suzuki, eds., *Inventing the Classics: Modernity, National Identity and Japanese Literature* (Stanford, Calif.: Stanford University Press, 2000); and my discussion of canon formation in Washburn, *The Dilemma of the Modern*, 80–93.

1. Ghostwriters and Literary Haunts

1. Naoki Sakai, *Voices of the Past: The Status of Language in Eighteenth-Century Japanese Discourse* (Ithaca, N.Y.: Cornell University Press, 1991), 311.

2. Maruyama Masao, *Studies in the Intellectual History of Tokugawa Japan*, trans. Mikiso Hanc (Princeton, N.J.: Princeton University Press, 1974), 177–185.

3. Sakai, *Voices of the Past*, 335–336. Sakai observes a gradual collapse of that sense of distance over the course of the nineteenth century, so that the unity of the Japanese people and individual subjectivity was equated with the existing language and community without mediation. Because of this distance, "eighteenth-century discourse did not totally degenerate into a version of cultural nationalism."

4. For an overview of the complicated history of the composition and publication of *Ugetsu monogatari*, see Asano Sanpei, *Ueda Akinari no kenkyū* (Tokyo: Ōfūsha, 1985), 156–157; and Shigetomo Ki, *Akinari no kenkyū* (Tokyo: Bunri shoin, 1971), 91.

5. It was not until after his death that Takizawa Bakin identified him as the author. See Shigetomo, *Akinari no kenkyū*, 86–87, 90–91. See also Asano, *Ueda Akinari no kenkyū*, 111.

6. Maruyama, *Studies in the Intellectual History of Tokugawa Japan*, 137–138, 173.

7. Ibid., 80–81.

8. Ibid., 107. The *Ken'en* was Sorai's school.

9. Norinaga Motoori, *Kinsei bungakuronshū*, in *Nihon koten bungaku taikei* (Tokyo: Iwanami shotcn, 1966), 94:101.

10. For a summary of Akinari's debates with Norinaga, see Blake Morgan Young, *Ueda Akinari* (Vancouver: University of British Columbia Press, 1982), 78–87.

11. Washiyama Jushin, *Ueda Akinari no bungeiteki kyōkai* (Kyoto: Hōzōkan, 1979), 117–118.

12. Ueda Akinari, *Ueda Akinari shū*, in *Nihon koten bungaku taikei* (Tokyo: Iwanami shoten, 1959), 56:312. Hereafter, I will cite this as *NKBT*, followed by the volume and page numbers. Akinari shows his skepticism about Japan's myths in his autobiographical miscellany. See Ueda Akinari, *Tandai shōshin roku*, in *Ueda Akinari zenshū* (Tokyo: Kokusho kankōkai, 1969), 1:351–422.

13. Ueda Akinari, *Akinari ibun*, ed. Fujii Otoo (Tokyo: Kokusho kankōkai, 1974), 101–102. Hereafter, I will cite this title as *Ibun*. For a discussion of the critical terminology in *Nubatama no maki*, see Tanaka Toshikazu, *Ueda Akinari bungei no sekai* (Tokyo: Ōfūsha, 1979), 7–18.

14. *Ibun*, 104.

15. *Ibun*, 108. An interlinear note in the text explains that "writings" (*fumi*) refers to the *Nihon shoki*. This is in line with Akinari's belief that the *Kojiki* was a faulty text.

16. *Ibun*, 109.

17. *NKBT*, 56:36.

18. These two senses of verisimilitude correspond to Western notions of realism. See Tzvetan Todorov, *The Poetics of Prose*, trans. Richard Howard (Ithaca, N.Y.: Cornell University Press, 1977), 82–83; and Ian Watt, *The Rise of the Novel* (Berkeley: University of California Press, 1957), 13.

19. Ōwa Yasuhiro, *Ueda Akinari bungaku no kenkyū* (Tokyo: Kasama shoin, 1976), 31.

20. Uzuki Hiroshi, *Ugetsu monogatari hyōshaku* (Tokyo: Kadokawa shoten, 1969), 11–12.

21. Ōwa, *Ueda Akinari bungaku no kenkyū*, 27–28.

22. Uzuki, *Ugetsu monogatari hyōshaku*, 707–712.

23. Ibid., 102–104. *Shiramine* is adapted from the Nō play *Matsuyama tengu*.

24. The work echoes the *jo-ha-kyū* structure of the Nō drama, and the collection as a whole follows the sequence of plays suggested for the Nō theater in *Hachijō kadensho*. C. Andrew Gerstle, *Circles of Fantasy: Convention in the Plays of Chikamatsu* (Cambridge, Mass.: Harvard University Press, 1986), 4–7.

25. *NKBT*, 56:38–39.

26. *NKBT*, 56:40.

27. *NKBT*, 56:40.

28. *NKBT*, 56:41.

29. *NKBT*, 56:41. Sutoku refers to the example of Wu Wang, a rebel who nonetheless received the mandate of Heaven and founded the Chou dynasty, which lasted for eight hundred years.

30. *NKBT*, 56:42.

31. *NKBT*, 56:46.

32. Uzuki, *Ugetsu monogatari hyōshaku*, 327. The Three Treasures are the Buddha (*butsu*), the Law (*hō*), and the Priesthood (*sō*). Another popular name for the bird was the *sanbōdori*. It is a species of owl called *konohazuku*.

33. *NKBT*, 56:79. The poem appears in volume 10 of *Seireishū* (c. 835), a collection of Kūkai's verse.

34. *NKBT*, 56:80. The poem appears in volume six of the *Shinsenrokujō*, under the topic "birds."

35. *NKBT*, 56:80.

36. *NKBT*, 56:82.

37. *NKBT*, 56:82. The poem appears in book 16, "Miscellaneous Poems."

38. *NKBT*, 56:83.

39. *NKBT*, 56:84.

40. *NKBT*, 56:85.

41. *NKBT*, 56:85. Hidetsugu was reborn in the *asuradō*, the realm of fighting demons. The *asuradō* is one of the six realms of existence—heaven, hell, and the realms of hungry ghosts, beasts, fighting demons, and humans. The angry spirits of men of power enter the realm of demons or become *tengu*.

42. *NKBT*, 56:85.

43. *NKBT*, 56:86.

44. Uzuki, *Ugetsu monogatari hyōshaku*, 635–636.

45. *NKBT*, 56:132.

46. *NKBT*, 56:138–139.

47. Robert E. Hegel, *The Novel in Seventeenth-Century China* (New York: Columbia University Press, 1981), 58.

48. Joseph Levenson, "The Amateur Ideal in Ming and Early Ch'ing Society: Evidence from Painting," in *Chinese Thought and Institutions*, ed. John K. Fairbank (Chicago: The University of Chicago Press, 1957), 338.

49. Hegel, *The Novel in Seventeenth-Century China*, 56–57.

50. Young, *Ueda Akinari*, 128.

51. Mark Morris, "Buson and Shiki: Part I," *Harvard Journal of Asiatic Studies* 44, no. 2 (December 1984): 389.

52. Ibid., 385.

53. Buson wrote a preface for *Yakanashō*, Akinari's study of *kireji*, in 1773. Two years later, Akinari contributed an epilogue and several poems for Buson's *haikai* collection *Zoku akegarasu*.

54. Yosa Buson, *Buson shū*, in *NKBT*, 58:290–291.

55. There are two main sources: story 24, *Hito no tsuma, shinite nochi, moto no otto ni aeru koto*, from volume 27 of *Konjaku monogatari*, *NKBT*, 25:510–512; and a Chinese story called *Ai-ching chuan* that appears in the *Chien-teng hsin-hua* (*New Tales for Trimming the Wick*, c. 1378), compiled by Ch'u Yu (1341–1427). See Uzuki, *Ugetsu monogatari hyōshaku*, 269–274.

56. Murasaki Shikibu, *Genji monogatari*, Nihon koten bungaku zenshū (Tokyo: Shōgakukan, 1972), 14:41. The poem was sent by the emperor, Genji's father, to Genji's grandmother, to express his grief over the loss of Genji's mother. The image of the desolate dwelling (*asajifu no yado*) is associated with yearning.

57. *NKBT*, 56:60.

58. *NKBT*, 56:61.

59. *NKBT*, 56:66. The poem is *Kokinshū* no. 747.

60. *NKBT*, 56:66.

61. *NKBT*, 56:70.

62. References to Tegona and the village of Mama appear in *Manyōshū* no. 431–433, no. 1807–1808, no. 3386–3387.

63. *NKBT*, 56:70.

64. *NKBT*, 56:71.

65. *NKBT*, 56:71.

66. *NKBT*, 56:76.

67. Uzuki, *Ugetsu monogatari hyōshaku*, 628–631.

68. *NKBT*, 56:127.

69. *NKBT*, 56:128.

70. *NKBT*, 56:129. These poems are drawn from the *Cheng tao ko* (no. 103 and 104), a T'ang collection by the Sōtō monk Hsuan Chueh (665–713). They also appear in the Nō play *Yoroboshi*.

71. *NKBT*, 56:130.

72. *NKBT*, 56:131. The temple is the Daichūji, on Taiheisan.

73. Shigetomo Ki, *Kinsei bungakushi no shomondai* (Tokyo: Meiji shoin, 1963), 226. Italics in the original.

74. Tsuga Teishō, *Nihon koten bungaku zenshū* (Tokyo: Shōgakukan, 1973), 48:74. For a discussion of the influence of Chinese models on Teishō's style, see Ōwa, *Ueda Akinari bungaku no kenkyū*, 207–208.

75. Akinari probably studied medicine under Teishō in the early 1770s, though there is little documentation about their relationship. Nakamura Yukihiko, *Kinsei sakka kenkyū* (Tokyo: San'ichi shobō, 1961), 161.

76. Andrew Plaks, *The Four Masterworks of the Ming Novel* (Princeton, N.J.: Princeton University Press, 1987), 45. On the growth of urban culture and popular literature, see Jaroslav Prusek, "Urban Centers: the Cradle of Popular Fiction," in *Studies in Chinese Literary Genres*, ed. Cyril Birch (Berkeley: University of California Press, 1974), 26off.

77. C. T. Hsia argues that the mixture of classical and vernacular elements is a common feature of a great deal of Ming fiction. C. T. Hsia, *The Classic Chinese Novel* (New York: Columbia University Press, 1968), 12–13.

78. For a discussion of the critical distinction between elegant (*ga*) and vulgar (*zoku*) styles in Japanese literature, see Nakamura, *Kinsei shōsetsushi no kenkyū*, 285–289.

79. This story is from volume 16 of the anthology *Yu-shih ming-yen*, compiled by Feng Meng-lung (1574–1646).

80. Uzuki, *Ugetsu monogatari hyōshaku*, 175.

81. *NKBT*, 56:47–48.

82. *NKBT*, 56:52–53.

83. *Ukiyo-zōshi* is a term that refers broadly to fiction written between the late seventeenth and late eighteenth centuries. Ihara Saikaku (1642–1693) and Ejima Kiseki (1667–1736) perfected the form, the character sketches of Kiseki being especially popular. Akinari composed two such works, *Shodō kikimimi sekenzaru* (*Worldly Monkeys Listening in All Directions*, 1766), and *Seken tekake katagi* (*Characters of Worldly Mistresses*, 1767).

84. *NKBT*, 56:53–54.

85. Uzuki, *Ugetsu monogatari hyōshaku*, 147.

86. *NKBT*, 56:57–58. Samon tells the story of Kung-shu Tso, chief adviser to Liang, the ruler of Wei during the Warring States period. When Tso falls ill, Liang asks him who should take his place. Tso recommends Shang Yang, but warns the king that if he chooses not to appoint him, then he should kill him. For if Shang Yang were to go to another state, he would pose a threat to Wei. When Tso realizes his recommendation will be ignored, he secretly alerts the young man to escape. Shang Yang later assists the kingdom of Ch'in in the conquest of Wei.

87. *NKBT*, 56:58.

88. Uzuki, *Ugetsu monogatari hyōshaku*, 458–462.

89. *NKBT*, 56:86. The *Wu tsa tsu* contains excerpts of classical texts and commentary. Compiled by Hsieh Chao-che in the early sixteenth century, it became available in Japan from the Kanbun era (1661–1673). The work survives because of these Japanese editions.

90. *NKBT*, 56:86.

91. *NKBT*, 56:93.

92. *NKBT*, 56:96–97.

93. *NKBT*, 56:98.

94. *NKBT*, 56:98.

95. Uzuki, *Ugetsu monogatari hyōshaku*, 518.

96. *NKBT*, 56:111.

97. Asō Isoji has made a study of the relative difficulty of the *yomihon* compared to the *ninjōbon*, the *sharebon*, and the *kokkeibon*, finding that on average, the *yomihon* contains more than twice the number of Chinese characters. Aso Isoji, *Edo bungaku to Chūgoku bungaku* (Tokyo: Sanseidō, 1957), 375ff. See also Robert Leutner, *Shikitei Sanba and the Comic Tradition in Edo Fiction* (Cambridge, Mass.: Harvard University Press, 1985), 6; and Nakamura Yukihiko, *Kinsei shōsetsushi no kenkyū*, 323–330.

98. Donald Keene, *World Within Walls: Japanese Literature of the Pre-Modern Era, 1600–1867* (New York: Holt, Rinehart, and Winston, 1976), 377; and Young, *Ueda Akinari*, 48.

99. Asō, *Edo bungaku to Chūgoku bungaku*, 538.

100. Ibid., 369.

101. Wm. Theodore de Bary, "Sagehood as a Secular and Spiritual Ideal in Tokugawa Neo-Confucianism," in *Principle and Practicality: Essays in Neo-Confucianism and Practical Learning*, ed. Wm. Theodore deBary and Irene Bloom (New York: Columbia University Press, 1979), 130.

102. Watt, *The Rise of the Novel*, 17–18.

103. Ibid., 14.

104. Maruyama, *Studies in the Intellectual History of Tokugawa Japan*, 178–179.

2. Translating Mount Fuji

1. Natsume Sōseki, *Sanshirō: A Novel*, trans. Jay Rubin (Seattle: University of Washington Press, 1977), 54–55. I will hereafter cite this work as *Sanshirō*. For purposes of citation, I have relied on Rubin's translation, which is one of the finest English translations of a work of Japanese fiction. In preparing this essay, I referred to the Japanese version in *Natsume Sōseki zenshū*, vol. 7 (Tokyo: Iwanami shoten, 1956).

2. Ibid., 45.

3. The novels that preceded the composition of *Sanshirō* should make us cautious about attempting any neat categorizations of Sōseki's novelistic practices. The hybrid quality of his writing remained a prominent feature throughout his career. For discussions of Sōseki's style see Edwin McClellan, *Two Japanese Novelists: Sōseki and Tōson* (Chicago: University of Chicago Press, 1969); Alan Turney, introduction to *The Three-Cornered World*, by Natsume Sōseki, trans. Alan Turney (London: Peter Owen, 1965); Minae Mizumura, "Resisting Women—Reading Sōseki's *Gubijinsō*," in *Studies in Modern Japanese Literature: Essays and Translations in Honor of Edwin McClellan*, ed. Dennis Washburn and Alan Tansman, 23–37 (Ann Arbor: Center for Japanese Studies, The University of Michigan, 1997); and Angela Yiu, *Chaos and Order in the Works of Natsume Sōseki* (Honolulu: University of Hawaii Press, 1998).

4. *Sanshirō*, 15.

5. Hirota's ambivalent attitude toward Mount Fuji indicates the conservative appeal of Shiga Shigetaka's *Nihon fūkeiron* (1894).

6. Marius Jansen, *Sakamoto Ryōma and the Meiji Restoration* (New York: Columbia University Press, 1994), 294–304; and H. D. Harootunian, "Late Tokugawa Culture and Thought," in *The Emergence of Meiji Japan*, ed. Marius Jansen (New York: Cambridge University Press, 1995), 116–137. For a discussion of the performative, ritual nature of the document, see John Breen, "The Imperial Oath of April 1868: Ritual, Politics, and Power in the Restoration," *Monumenta Nipponica* 51, no. 4 (Winter 1996): 407–429.

7. Sugimoto Tsutomu, *Edo no hon'yakukatachi* (Tokyo: Wasdea daigaku shuppanbu, 1995), 249–251.

8. *Sources of Japanese Tradition*, comp. Ryusaku Tsunoda et al. (New York: Columbia University Press), 2:139–140.

9. Okakura Kakuzō, *The Book of Tea* (New York: Dover, 1964), 19.

10. Paul de Man notes the connection between translation and metaphor in "The Epistemology of Metaphor," *Critical Inquiry* 5 (Autumn 1978): 21. He writes: "It is no mere play of words that 'translate' is translated in German as *übersetzen* which itself translates the Greek 'meta phorein' or metaphor. Metaphor gives itself the totality which it then claims to define, but it is in fact the tautology of its own position. The discourse of simple ideas is a figural discourse or translation and, as such, creates the fallacious illusion of definition."

11. Barbara Johnson, "Taking Fidelity Philosophically," in *Difference in Translation*, ed. Joseph F. Graham (Ithaca, N.Y.: Cornell University Press, 1985), 148.

12. Kenneth Gergen, following the work of Hans-Georg Gadamer, connects the problem of circularity in translation to a basic problem of hermeneutics. Understanding is primarily a product of localized horizons of understanding, not of immediate access to the author's inner intentions. Because we cannot presume an internal language that has to be located, "all we have at our disposal in the process of under-

standing is a domain of public discourse (or action). We imagine there is a domain of private discourse to which this must be attached. Yet, we possess access neither to the private discourse itself nor to the rules by which it is translated into the public domain." Consequently, "readings or translations can only be rendered true by definition." Kenneth Gergen, "Social Understanding and the Inscription of Self," in *Cultural Psychology: Essays on Comparative Human Development*, ed. James Stigler, Richard Shweder, and Gilbert Herdt (New York: Cambridge University Press, 1990), 579–580.

13. George Steiner, *After Babel: Aspects of Language and Translation* (New York: Oxford University Press, 1992), 246.

14. Lawrence Venuti, *The Translator's Invisibility: A History of Translation* (London and New York: Routledge, 1995), 4–9.

15. Octavio Paz, "Translation: Literature and Letters," in *Theories of Translation: An Anthology of Essays from Dryden to Derrida*, ed. Rainer Schulte and John Biguenet (Chicago: University of Chicago Press, 1992), 154–155.

16. The sheer volume of literary translations alone is staggering. For a survey of this type of translation activity, see Yanagida Izumi's groundbreaking studies *Meiji shoki hon'yaku bungaku kenkyū* (Tokyo: Shunjūsha, 1971) and *Seiyō bungaku no in'yū* (Tokyo: Shunjūsha, 1974).

17. There is a reference to that bias in Akinari's preface to *Ugetsu*, where he notes the belief that the immorality of the deceptive nature of fiction is proven by instances of karmic retribution.

18. Yanagida, *Meiji shoki hon'yaku bungaku kenkyū*, 13.

19. Niwa Jun'ichirō, *Ōshū kiji: Karyū shunwa, Meiji hon'yaku bungaku shū*, in *Meiji bungaku zenshū*, vol. 7 (Tokyo: Chikuma shobō, 1972), 109.

20. Katō Shūichi, Maruyama Masao, et al., eds., *Hon'yaku no shisō* in *Nihon kindai shisō taikei* (Tokyo: Iwanami shoten, 1991), 15:343–344.

21. From *Kaikoku zushi* by Wei yuan (1794–1857), cited in Katō Shūichi et al., *Hon'yaku no shisō*, 15:344.

22. Sugimoto Tsutomu, *Nihon hon'yakugoshi no kenkyū* (Tokyo: Yasaka shobō, 1983), 31.

23. Katō Shūichi et al., *Hon'yaku no shisō*, 15: 361–366.

24. Cited in Sugimoto, *Nihon hon'yakugoshi no kenkyū*, 45–46.

25. Katō Shūichi et al., *Hon'yaku no shisō*, 15:270–271.

26. Ibid., 15:284–287.

27. Ibid., 15:317.

28. *Sanshirō*, 15.

29. Ibid., 122–123.

30. Ibid., 60, 93.

31. Ibid., 193.

32. Ibid., 193–194.

33. Ibid., 195.

34. Ibid., 183–184.

35. Ibid., 101.

36. Ibid., 18.

37. Ibid., 9.

38. Ibid., 130.

39. Ibid., 63–64.

40. Ibid., 64.

41. Ibid.

42. Ibid., 76–77.

43. Ibid., 151–154.

44. Ibid., 107–109.

45. Ibid., 187.

46. Ibid., 93–94.

47. Ibid., 208.

48. Ibid., 209.

49. Ibid., 212.

3. Manly Virtue and Modern Identity

1. My definition of the *Bildungsroman* is based on a number of sources, but for a good summary of the key features of the form, see Marc Redfield, *Phantom Formations: Aesthetic Ideology and the Bildungsroman* (Ithaca, N.Y.: Cornell University Press, 1996), 38.

2. Ibid., 39.

3. Martin Swales, "Irony and the Novel: Reflections on the German Bildungsroman," in *Reflection and Action*, ed. James Hardin (Columbia: University of South Carolina Press, 1991), 63.

4. H. D. Harootunian, "America's Japan/Japan's Japan," in *Japan in the World*, ed. Masao Miyoshi and H. D. Harootunian, 196–221 (Durham, N.C.: Duke University Press, 1993).

5. Stephen Greenblatt, *Marvelous Possessions: The Wonder of the New World* (Chicago: University of Chicago Press, 1991), 3–4. Greenblatt argues that "representational practices are ideologically significant … but I think it is important to resist what we may call *a priori* ideological determinism, that is, the notion that particular modes of representation are inherently and necessarily bound to a culture or class or belief system, and that their effects are unidirectional."

6. Ian Watt, *The Rise of the Novel: Studies in Defoe, Richardson, and Fielding* (Berkeley: University of California Press, 1957), 11–19.

7. *Hōjōki* (*An Account of My Hut*, 1212), by Kamo no Chōmei (1155–1216) and *Oku no hosomichi* (*Narrow Road to the Deep North*, 1694), by Matsuo Bashō (1644–1694)

illustrate how private modes of representation can be fashioned out of a reimagining of the past.

8. William J. Bouwsma, *A Usable Past: Essays in European Cultural History* (Berkeley: University of California Press, 1990), 180.

9. Ibid., 182.

10. Ihab Hassan, *Selves at Risk: Patterns of Quest in Contemporary American Letters* (Madison: The University of Wisconsin Press, 1990), 30.

11. Georg Lukács, *The Theory of the Novel* (Cambridge, Mass.: The MIT Press, 1971), 135.

12. Ibid., 132.

13. Wulf Koepke, "*Bildung* and the Transformation of Society: Jean Paul's *Titan* and *Flegeljahre*," in *Reflection and Action*, ed. James Hardin (Columbia: University of South Carolina Press, 1991), 231.

14. James Hardin, introduction to *Reflection and Action*, ed. James Hardin (Columbia: University of South Carolina Press, 1991), xi–xii.

15. One of the earliest recorded usages of the hortatory sense of *masurao* is in a poem carved in a stone inscription, a *bussokusekika*. The work also appears in *Man'yōshū* in *Nihon no koten* (Tokyo: Shōgakukan, 1985), 5:176–177. See *MYS* #2758.

16. Ueda Akinari, *Ugetsu monogatari*, in *Nihon no koten* (Tokyo: Shōgakukan, 1983), 57:104–105.

17. Ibid., 85.

18. Ibid., 88.

19. Mori Ōgai, *Seinen*, in *Ōgai zenshū* (Tokyo: Iwanami shoten, 1972), 6:275. Hereafter I will cite the text with the abbreviation *ŌZ* followed by the volume and page numbers. The translations of the text are mine. A sensitively rendered translation is available in *Youth and Other Stories*, ed. J. Thomas Rimer (Honolulu: University of Hawaii Press, 1994).

20. *ŌZ*, 6:321.

21. Ibid., 6:287–288.

22. Ibid., 6:294.

23. Ibid., 6:299.

24. Richard Bowring, *Mori Ōgai and the Modernization of Japanese Culture* (Cambridge: Cambridge University Press, 1979), 142–143.

25. *OZ*, 6:313–314.

26. Ibid., 6:314.

27. Ibid., 6:278.

28. Ibid., 6:421–423.

29. Ibid., 6:429–430.

30. David Lloyd, *Anomalous States: Irish Writing and the Postcolonial Movement* (Durham, N.C.: Duke University Press, 1993), 134.

31. *ŌZ*, 6:407.

32. Ibid., 6:378–379.

33. Ibid., 6:330.

34. Ibid., 6:382–384.

35. Compare this with the description of Manago's furnishings. Ueda, *Ugetsu monogatari*, 89–90.

36. Uno Kōji, *Uno Kōji zenshū* (Tokyo: Chūō kōronsha, 1968), 10:152. Uno has noted that a characteristic element of Ōgai's work is his preference for passive characters. He writes that when the topic is love, "at the very least in *Gan* and *Seinen*, and even in *Vita Sexualis*, Ōgai wrote more cleverly about passive characters than about active characters. On the other hand, he became all too easily mediocre when he wrote about active characters in love."

37. *ŌZ*, 6:438–439.

38. Ibid., 6:458.

39. Ibid., 6:465.

40. Ibid., 6:465–466.

41. Ibid., 6:470.

42. Ibid., 6:471.

43. Ibid.

4. Real Images

1. Andrew Gordon has noted the prevalence of the idea of "Taishō democracy" in histories of modern Japan and as a corrective has substituted the phrase "imperial democracy." See Andrew Gordon, *A Modern History of Japan from Tokugawa Times to the Present* (New York: Oxford University Press, 2003), 161–181.

2. For a summary of these developments, see Gordon, *A Modern History of Japan*, 97–105 and 139–154.

3. Maeda Ai's reading of Higuchi Ichiyō's *Takekurabe* shows how the changes in modes of production affected the understanding and representation of time and space. His analysis focuses on the two festivals depicted in the story: the festival for the agricultural gods at Senzoku temple, which maintains a space for children's play; and the festival at the Ōtori shrine to the god of money, which was aimed at people who were not permanent residents of the area around the temple. Maeda situates Ichiyō's story in the process by which the latter festival, in which the movement of people in a modern capitalist society divorces them from agricultural time and space, overtakes the former. He sees the modern arising in the change from the agricultural space of play to an ethos of hard work and determination to succeed, and he calls this "our original sin" (*wareware no genzai*). See "Kodomo no jikan, *Takekurabe*," in *Maeda Ai chosakushū* (Tokyo: Chikuma shobō, 1989), 3:265–292.

4. Yasushi Ishii, "how ghostly were the 1920s in Japan? a projection without sources," *Stanford (Electronic) Humanities Review* 5: Supplement, *Cultural and*

Technological Incubations of Fascism (December 1996): 12. Available at: http://www. stanford.edu/group/SHR/5-supp/text/ishii.html. Gennifer Weisenfeld presents a similar picture of the avant-garde. See Gennifer Weisenfeld, introduction to *Mavo: Japanese Artists and the Avant-garde, 1905–1931* (Berkeley: University of California Press, 2002).

5. Martin Jay, "Scopic Regimes of Modernity," in *Vision and Visuality*, ed. Hal Foster (Seattle: Bay Press, 1988), 3. Jay notes what he calls the ubiquity of the idea that vision is the dominant sense by pointing to the works of Richard Rorty on the metaphor of the mirror of nature, Michel Foucault on the prevalence of surveillance in modern culture, and Guy Debord on modernity as the society of the spectacle. Jay takes these respective ideas as the basis for the terminology he uses to describe the principle scopic regimes of modernity. The connection between literature and visuality has long been a point of debate, starting at least with Joseph Frank's contention that modern literature was fundamentally spatial in its disruption of temporal continuity. See Joseph Frank, "Spatial Form in Modern Literature," *Sewanee Review* 53 (Spring, Summer, Autumn 1945).

6. Peter Kornicki, *The Book in Japan: A Cultural History from the Beginnings to the Nineteenth Century* (Honolulu: University of Hawaii Press, 2001), 169–190.

7. Jay, "Scopic Regimes of Modernity," 4. Jay is careful to qualify his scheme as one that draws on general, ideal characterizations and is not exhaustive.

8. Ibid., 10–11.

9. Roger Friedland and Deirdre Boden, "NowHere: An Introduction to Space, Time, and Modernity," in *NowHere: Space, Time and Modernity*, ed. Roger Friedland and Deirdre Boden (Berkeley: University of California Press, 1994), 2–3.

10. Edward Thomas Mack, *The Value of Literature: Cultural Authority in Interwar Japan*, Ph.D. diss., Harvard University (May 2002), 71–91.

11. Harry Harootunian has written a lively account of the perceptions of modern culture in everyday life in Harry Harootunian, *Overcome by Modernity: History, Culture, and Community in Interwar Japan* (Princeton, N.J.: Princeton University Press, 2000), 16–30.

12. *Bungei dokuhon: Yokomitsu Riichi*, (Tokyo: Kawade shobō, 1981), 273–278.

13. Asami Fukashi, "Yokomitsu Riichi nyūmon," *Yokomitsu Riichi shū* in *Nihon gendai bungaku zenshū* (Tokyo: Kōdansha, 1961), 65:484.

14. Yokomitsu Riichi, "Kakikata sōshi," in *Yokomitsu Riichi zenshū* (Tokyo: Kawade shobō, 1987), 16:369.

15. For a full treatment in English of the history of the *Shinkankaku-ha*, see chapters 3 and 4 of Dennis Keene, *Yokomitsu Riichi: Modernist* (New York: Columbia University Press, 1980).

16. Yokomitsu Riichi, *Ai no aisatsu, Basha, Junsui shōsetsu ron* (Tokyo: Kōdansha, 1993), 245–246.

17. Yamazaki Kuninori, *Yokomitsu Riichi ron* (Tokyo: Hokuyōsha, 1979), 164.

18. Ibid., 265.

19. For an overview of the main tenets of Kikuchi's critical theory, see Mack, *The Value of Literature*, 224–238.

20. Cited by Sugano Akimasa, "Samayou Shanghai no Nihonjin," in *Shanghai*, by Yokomitsu Riichi (Tokyo: Kōdansha, 1991), 292.

21. For a more complete account of the May Thirtieth Movement, see Nicholas R. Clifford, *Spoilt Children of Empire: Westerners in Shanghai and the Chinese Revolution of the 1920s* (Hanover, N.H.: University Press of New England, 1991).

22. Maeda Ai analyzed the connection of character to space in Maeda Ai, *Shanghai* in *Toshi kūkan no naka no bungaku*, in *Maeda Ai choshakushū*, vol. 5 (Tokyo: Chikuma shobō, 1989). A number of other critical works have taken a similar line of analysis. See Komori Yoichi, *Kōzō to shite no katari* (Tokyo: Shiyōsha, 1988); Gregory Golley, *Voices in the Machine: Technology and Japanese Literary Modernism*, Ph.D. diss., University of California at Los Angeles (2000); and Seiji Lippitt, *Topographies of Japanese Modernism* (New York: Columbia University Press, 2002). Lippitt (87–92) provides a sensitive overview and insightful critique of the readings of Maeda and Komori.

23. Yokomitsu Riichi, *Shanghai*, trans. Dennis Washburn (Ann Arbor: Center for Japanese Studies, The University of Michigan, 2001), 66. Hereafter cited as *Shanghai*.

24. Ibid., 27, 76.

25. Cited in Yamazaki, *Yokomitsu Riichi ron*, 162.

26. *Shanghai*, 193–199.

27. Ibid., 3.

28. Ibid., 7.

29. Ibid., 5.

30. Ibid., 88.

31. Maeda Ai, *Shanghai*, 260–268. Maeda's analysis of the novel's imagery is overly schematic and does not fully account for the ideological sources underlying Yokomitsu's methods.

32. *Shanghai*, 97.

33. Ibid., 32.

34. Ibid., 34–35.

35. Ibid., 63–64.

36. Ibid., 149–150.

37. Komori, *Kōzō to shite no katari*, 520.

38. *Shanghai*, 36–37.

39. Ibid., 52.

40. Ibid., 119.

41. Ibid., 4–5.

42. Ibid., 44–45.

43. Ibid., 110–111.

44. Ibid., 156–157.

45. Ibid., 157.

46. Ibid., 214–217.

47. Yokomitsu Riichi, *Yokomitsu Riichi zenshū* (Tokyo: Kawade shobō, 1956), 12:196.

48. Ibid., 197.

49. Ibid.

5. Toward a View from Nowhere

1. Ōe Kenzaburō, "On Modern and Contemporary Japanese Literature," in *Japan, the Ambiguous, and Myself* (Tokyo: Kōdansha International, 1995), 46–47.

2. Fukuda Tsuneari, *Sakkaron*, in *Fukuda Tsuneari hyōronshū* (Tokyo: Shinchōsha, 1966), 3:303–337. For other assessments of Ōoka's cynicism, see Kojima Nobuo, "Ōoka Shōhei to shinishizumu," in *Ōoka Shōhei, Fukunaga Takehiko*, ed. Nihon bungaku kenkyū shiryō kankōkai (Tokyo: Yūseidō, 1978), 50–56; and Nakano Kōji, *Zettai reido no bungaku* (Tokyo: Shūeisha, 1976), 100–117.

3. *Ōoka Shōhei, Fukunaga Takehiko*, 80. For *Sokai nikki*, see *Ōoka Shōhei shū* (Tokyo: Iwanami shoten, 1982), 15:24.

4. Ōe Kenzaburō has described Ōoka's art in similar terms. Cited in Ikeda Jun'ichi, *Ōoka Shōhei* (Tokyo: Tōjusha, 1979), 41.

5. Fukuda Tsuneari, who wrote the screenplay for Mizoguchi's film, believed *A Wife in Musashino* was a seminal work of postwar literature. See Fukuda Tsuneari, *Sakkaron*, 3:303–337.

6. Erich Auerbach, *Mimesis: The Representation of Reality in Western Literature*, trans. Willard R. Trask (Princeton, N.J.: Princeton University Press, 1968), 457–458.

7. Musashino is a city in the east-central area of the Tokyo metropolis, at the center of the Musashino plateau, a diluvial upland in the southwestern Kantō plain. The name means "the plains of Musashi," Musashi being one of the fifteen provinces of the Tōkaidō region of central Japan established by the Taika Reforms of 646. Because the province was administered by a succession of important military clans—the Minamoto, the Uesugi, the Tokugawa—Musashi conjures up images of Japan's martial history.

8. Eudora Welty, "Place in Fiction," in *On Writing* (New York: Modern Library, 2002), 46–47. Welty's comments are pertinent to Yokomitsu Riichi's methods as well.

9. Ōoka Shōhei, *A Wife in Musashino*, trans. Dennis Washburn (Ann Arbor: Center for Japanese Studies, The University of Michigan, 2004), 3.

10. Ibid., 14.

11. Ibid., 94.

12. Ibid., 139. Ōoka made the moral and spiritual costs of turning women into sexual objects the subject of his 1961 novel *Kaei* (*The Shade of Blossoms*).

13. Ōoka Shōhei, "*Musashino fujin* no ito" ("My Intentions in *A Wife in Musashino*"), in *Ōoka Shōhei shū*, 15:439.

14. Ōoka Shōhei, *A Wife in Musashino*, 121–122.

15. Ibid., 125.

16. Ibid., 142.

17. Ibid., 19.

18. Ibid., 19–20.

19. Ibid., 35–36.

20. A work that influenced Ōoka's conception of cultural space is Kunikida Doppo's *Musashino*.

21. Ōoka Shōhei, *A Wife in Musashino*, 37.

22. Ibid., 38.

23. Ibid., 128–129. In preparing the translation of this novel, I decided to use italics to visually mark out the thoughts of the characters. No special emphasis is intended.

24. Ibid., 145.

25. Ōoka Shōhei, "*Musashino fujin* no ito," 439. The use of the image of chess pieces to describe Radiguet's style was suggested to Ōoka by Albert Thibaudet's 1938 study *Reflections on the Novel*, which Ōoka cites in "*Musashino fujin* no ito."

26. Ōoka Shōhei, *A Wife in Musashino*, 144.

27. Ibid., 24.

28. Ibid., 127.

29. Ōoka Shōhei, "*Nobi* no ito" in *Ōoka Shōhei shū*, 15:410. "A Madman's Diary" was originally a preface to the first version of the novel. The preface was omitted in the revised version, which appeared in *Tenbō* from January to August 1951, because Ōoka feared that informing the reader of Tamura's madness would undercut the appeal of the story. When the novel came out in 1952, Ōoka again changed his mind, placing "A Madman's Diary" at the end and altering the structure of the story.

30. Theodor Adorno, *Minima Moralia*, trans. E. F. N. Jephcott (New York: Verso, 1974), 74.

31. Thomas Nagel, *The View from Nowhere* (New York: Oxford University Press, 1986), 147. For Nagel, as for Adorno, the view from nowhere includes the subjective element of the appearance of value to individuals with particular perspectives: "To find out what the world is like from outside we have to approach it from within: it is no wonder that the same is true for ethics."

32. Nagel, *The View from Nowhere*, 117–119.

33. Ōoka Shōhei, *Fires on the Plain*, trans. Ivan Morris (Rutland, Vt.: Charles E. Tuttle Co., 1957), 236–237; 3:405. I have used the wording of the translation for the most part, but there are some passages where I have made minor changes where I

thought it was justified. My citations thus have two sets of page numbers: the first from the translation by Morris, the second from volume 3 of *Ōoka Shōhei shū*.

34. Ibid., 19–20; 3:240–241.

35. Ibid., 230; 3:339.

36. Ibid., 186–187; 3:365.

37. Ibid., 229; 3:398.

38. Ibid., 230; 3:399–400.

39. Ibid., 187–188; 3:364–365. Tamura's sensations mirror common experiences of shame and guilt. See Bernard Williams, *Shame and Necessity* (Berkeley: University of California Press, 1993), 88–95; and Richard Wollheim, *The Thread of Life* (Cambridge, Mass.: Harvard University Press, 1984), 219–221.

40. Ōoka Shōhei, *Fires on the Plain*, 231; 3:400. The word for "split," *bunretsu suru*, also means to dismember.

41. Jefferson Singer and Peter Salovey, *The Remembered Self* (New York: The Free Press, 1993), 67–80.

42. Ōoka Shōhei, *Fires on the Plain*, 241–242; 3:409.

43. Ibid., 240; 3:407–408. Tamura's assertion of his faith in himself is a direct echo of Bergson. Henri Bergson, *An Introduction to Metaphysics*, trans. T.E. Hulme (New York: Liberal Arts Press, 1949), 9.

44. For the notion of autobiographical memory, see Alan Baddeley, *Human Memory: Theory and Practice* (Boston: Allyn and Bacon, 1990); and Mark Freeman, *Rewriting the Self: History, Memory, Narrative* (New York: Routledge, 1993).

45. Nagel, *The View from Nowhere*, 108, 126–130.

46. Ōoka's experience with memory loss and his recognition of the chance nature of his survival are recounted in his short memoir "Tsukamaru made." David Stahl, *The Burdens of Survival: Ōoka Shōhei's Writings on the Pacific War* (Honolulu: University of Hawaii Press, 2003).

47. Richard Shweder, *Thinking Through Cultures: Expeditions in Cultural Psychology* (Cambridge, Mass.: Harvard University Press, 1991), 353–354.

48. In Western antiquity, the art of memory was closely linked to ethics. Frances A. Yates, *The Art of Memory* (Chicago: University of Chicago Press, 1966), 36–37.

49. Ōoka Shōhei, *Fires on the Plain*, 169–170; 3:352.

50. Ibid., 233–234; 3:401–402. For a discussion of the importance of chance and the illusion of inevitability to the sense of meaning in human life, see Nagel, *The View from Nowhere*, 211–214.

51. Christine Korsgaard, *The Sources of Normativity* (Cambridge: The Tanner Lectures on Human Values, Clare Hall, Cambridge University, November, 1992), 3:13–22.

52. Ōoka Shōhei, *Fires on the Plain*, 234; 3:402.

53. Ibid., 234; 3:402.

54. Ibid.

55. To find a way to live with this insight, Tsutomu also looks to the repetitious patterns of nature for meaning. Ōoka Shōhei, *A Wife in Musashino*, 34–35.

56. Paul Ricoeur, *Time and Narrative*, trans. Kathleen Blamey and David Pellauer (Chicago: University of Chicago Press, 1988), 3:76–77.

57. Ōoka Shōhei, *Fires on the Plain*, 18; 3:240.

58. Ibid., 118; 3:315.

59. Ibid., 93; 3:296–297. Tamura is responding directly to Bergson's theory that false memories appear whenever the sense of duration of consciousness is suspended. See Bergson, *An Introduction to Metaphysics*, 5–8.

60. Ōoka Shōhei, *Fires on the Plain*, 18; 3:239–240.

61. Ibid., 79–80; 3:285–286.

62. Ibid., 80–81; 3:286.

63. Ibid., 223; 3:396.

64. Ibid., 230; 3:399.

65. Ibid., 238; 3:406.

66. Ibid., 235; 3:403.

67. Ibid., 244–246; 3:411–412.

68. Alessandro Ferrara, *Modernity and Authenticity: A Study of the Social and Ethical Thought of Jean-Jacques Rousseau* (Albany: State University of New York Press, 1993), 86–91, 112–117, and 135–139.

6. Kitsch, Nihilism, and the Inauthentic

1. Charles Jencks, *The Language of Post-Modern Architecture* (New York: Rizzoli International Publications, Inc., 1984), 9.

2. For a representative response, see Henry Miller, *Reflections on the Death of Mishima* (Santa Barbara, Calif.: Capra Press, 1972). Miller's work is especially interesting in that it provides what seems now like an almost parodic catalogue of attitudes prevalent at the time, including an exotic view of the traditions of Japan that Mishima lamented.

3. Zygmunt Bauman, *Legislators and Interpreters* (Ithaca, N.Y.: Cornell University Press, 1987), 114–115.

4. Johan Goudsblom, *Nihilism and Culture* (Totowa, N.J.: Rowman and Littlefield, 1980), 87.

5. Bauman, *Legislators and Interpreters*, 125–126. Bauman writes, "Descartes's *malin génie* has always been with us, in one disguise or another, his presence confirmed by ever renewed desperate attempts to annihilate the threat of relativism, as if no such attempts had ever been undertaken in the past. Modernity was lived in a haunted house. Modernity was an age of certainty, but it had its inner demons.... Unlike the medieval certainty of the schoolmen, the certainty of modern philosophers constantly entailed the poignant awareness of the *problem* of relativism. It had to be an embattled, militant certainty."

6. George Steiner, *Real Presences* (Chicago: The University of Chicago Press, 1989), 90, 93. See also 132–133.

7. Matei Calinescu, *Five Faces of Modernity: Modernism, Avant-Garde, Decadence, Kitsch, Postmodernism* (Durham, N.C.: Duke University Press, 1987), 247.

8. Ibid., 248.

9. Walter Benjamin, "The Work of Art in the Age of Mechanical Reproduction," in *Illuminations* (New York: Schocken Books, 1969), 220–221. It is striking how Benjamin's language amplifies the jargon of authenticity even as he critiques it.

10. For examples of this custom see Stanley Burns, *Sleeping Beauty: Memorial Photography in America* (Altadena, Calif.: Twelvetrees Press, 1990).

11. Paul Friedlander, *Reflections of Nazism: An Essay on Kitsch and Death*, trans. Thomas Weyr (Bloomington: Indiana University Press, 1993), 27.

12. Ibid., 33–34.

13. Yukio Mishima, preface to *Ordeal by Roses: Photographs of Yukio Mishima by Eikoh Hosoe* (New York: Aperture, 1985).

14. Isaiah Berlin, "The Apotheosis of the Romantic Will" in *The Crooked Timber of Humanity: Chapters in the History of Ideas* (New York: Vintage Books, 1990), 228–229.

15. Hannah Arendt, *On Violence* (New York: Harcourt, Brace & World, 1969), 65–66. Arendt argues that historically the resistance to hypocrisy has been more often the cause of political violence and unrest than a sense of injustice.

16. Berlin, "The Apotheosis of the Romantic Will," 230–231.

17. David Forgacs, "Fascism, Violence, and Modernity," in *The Violent Muse: Violence and the Artistic Imagination in Europe, 1910–1939*, ed. Jana Howlett and Rod Mengham (Manchester: Manchester University Press, 1994), 20–21.

18. Friedlander, *Reflections of Nazism*, 135.

19. Michel Foucault, in *Madness and Civilization*, argues that the asylum that emerged in the eighteenth century was not a space of nature but a uniform domain of legislation: "Formerly, unreason was set outside of judgment, to be delivered, arbitrarily, to the powers of reason. Now it is judged, and not only upon entering the asylum, in order to be recognized, classified and made innocent forever; it is caught, on the contrary, in a perpetual judgment, which never ceases to pursue it and to apply sanctions, to proclaim its transgressions, to require honorable amends, to exclude, finally, those whose transgressions risk compromising the social order." Michel Foucault, *The Foucault Reader*, ed. Paul Rabinow (New York: Pantheon Books, 1984), 157–158.

20. William Bouwsma, *A Usable Past: Essays in European Cultural History* (Berkeley: University of California Press, 1990). I refer the reader again to this work, which is cited in the chapter on Ōgai, above.

21. Berlin, "The Apotheosis of the Romantic Will," 237.

22. The aesthetics of violence is a primary concern in the 1930s in the work of members of the Japanese Romanticists (the *Roman-ha*), especially the writings of

Yasuda Yojūrō. The influence of these writers on the generation coming of age during that time—that is, Mishima's generation—was enormous. See Alan Tansman, "Bridges to Nowhere: Yasuda Yojūrō's Language of Violence and Desire," *Harvard Journal of Asiatic Studies* 56, no. 1 (June 1996): 35–75.

23. René Girard, "The Founding Murder in the Philosophy of Nietzsche," in *Violence and Truth: On the Work of René Girard*, ed. Paul Dumouchel (Stanford, Calif.: Stanford University Press, 1988), 240.

24. Isoda Kōichi, "Mishima no kindaisei—jishu sekinin no ronri," in *Isoda Kōichi chosakushū* (Tokyo: Ozawa shoten, 1990), 1:303.

25. Mishima Yukio, *Mishima Yukio zenshū* (Tokyo: Shinchōsha, 1975), 32:96–97. Subsequent citations of Mishima's *zenshū* will use the abbreviation *MYZ* followed by the volume and page numbers. Mishima's use of the phrase "apprehension" (*zoruge*, written with the characters for *fuan*) suggestively echoes Akutagawa's explanation of his reasons for choosing to die. Akutagawa's unease stemmed from the paranoid delusions that shattered his psyche, but it also points to an artistic malaise: the paranoia that accompanies the inability to believe in the certainty of art and experience. See Bauman, *Legislators and Interpreters*, 114.

26. *MYZ*, 32:101–102.

27. Ibid., 10:265.

28. Ibid., 10:267.

29. Some critics have expressed puzzlement over the failure to understand this work as a "true confession," and they seek to set the record straight by emphasizing that *Confessions of a Mask* is a sincere autobiographical account of Mishima's early life, not a parody of a confession. Donald Keene, *Dawn to the West: Japanese Literature of the Modern Era* (New York: Holt, Rinehart, and Winston, 1984), 1:1183–1184.

30. *MYZ*, 3:291–292.

31. Ibid., 3:263.

32. Ibid., 3:180.

33. Ibid., 3:241.

34. Ibid., 3:164–165.

35. Ibid., 3:167.

36. Ibid., 3:182.

37. Ibid., 3:162.

38. Ibid., 3:265–266.

39. Ibid., 3:273.

40. Ibid., 3:278–279.

41. Mark Freeman, *Rewriting the Self: History, Memory, Narrative* (New York: Routledge, 1993), 223.

42. There is an important parallel here with the suicide of Akutagawa Ryūnosuke, whose death was also interpreted as evidence of the crisis of modern culture. Un-

der that interpretation, his death became a literary act, a way to take control over his identity by constructing an ending that turned his life into a work of art. For a brief summary of the interpretations of Akutagawa's suicide as a literary act, see Nakamura Shin'ichirō, "Akutagawa Ryunosuke nyumon," in *Nihon gendai bungaku zenshū*, vol. 56 (Tokyo: Kōdansha, 1960).

43. Steiner, *Real Presences*, 205.

Epilogue

1. *Jiketsu* seems to carry less of a stigma. For an example of how commonly it has come to be used, see the various contributions to *Mishima Yukio: Botsugo sanjūnen*, a special edition of *Shinchō* (November 2000).

2. Yasuda Yojūrō, "Mishima Yukio; sono risō to kōdō," in *Romanjin Mishima Yukio: Sono risō to kōdō*, ed. Hayashi Fusao, Muramatsu Takeshi, et al. (Tokyo: Roman, 1973), 69–120.

3. Murakami Haruki, *Hitsuji o meguru bōken* (Tokyo: Kōdansha bunko, 1985), 1:7. The translation by Alfred Birnbaum gives the title "Wednesday Afternoon Picnic" for the first chapter. See Murikami Haruki, *A Wild Sheep Chase* (New York: Kōdansha International, 1989), 3.

4. Murakami, *Hitsuji o meguru bōken*, 1:20.

5. Ibid., 1:84.

6. Murakami Haruki, *Pan'ya saishūgeki* (Tokyo: Bunshun bunko, 1989), 157.

7. Ibid., 168.

BIBLIOGRAPHY

Adorno, Theodor. *The Jargon of Authenticity*. Translated by Knut Tarnowski and Frederic Will. Evanston, Ill.: Northwestern University Press, 1973.

———. *Minima Moralia*. Translated by E. F. N. Jephcott. New York: Verso, 1974.

Anderson, Benedict. *Imagined Communities: Reflections on the Origins and Spread of Nationalism*. New York: Verso, 1983.

Arendt, Hannah. *On Violence*. New York: Harcourt, Brace & World, 1969.

Asami, Fukashi. "Yokomitsu Riichi nyūmon." *Yokomitsu Riichi shū* in *Nihon gendai bungaku zenshū*, vol. 65. Tokyo: Kōdansha, 1961.

Asano, Sanpei. *Ueda Akinari no kenkyū*. Tokyo: Ōfūsha, 1985.

Asō, Isoji. *Edo bungaku to Chūgoku bungaku*. Tokyo: Sanseidō, 1957.

Auerbach, Erich. *Mimesis: The Representation of Reality in Western Literature*. Translated by Willard R. Trask. Princeton, N.J.: Princeton University Press, 1968.

Baddeley, Alan. *Human Memory: Theory and Practice*. Boston: Allyn and Bacon, 1990.

Bargen, Doris G. "Spirit Possession in the Context of Dramatic Expressions of Gender Conflict: The Aoi Episode of the *Genji monogatari*." *Harvard Journal of Asiatic Studies* 48, no. 1 (June 1988): 95–130.

Barthes, Roland. *A Barthes Reader*. Edited by Susan Sontag. New York: Hill & Wang, 1982.

———. *Critical Essays*. Translated by Richard Howard. Evanston, Ill.: Northwestern University Press, 1972.

Bauman, Zygmunt. *Legislators and Interpreters*. Ithaca, N.Y.: Cornell University Press, 1987.

Bellah, Robert. *Tokugawa Religion: The Cultural Roots of Modern Japan*. New York: The Free Press, 1985.

Benjamin, Walter. *Illuminations*. Edited by Hannah Arendt. Translated by Harry Zohn. New York: Schocken Books, 1968.

Bergson, Henri. *An Introduction to Metaphysics*. Translated by T. E. Hulme. New York: Liberal Arts Press, 1949.

Berlin, Isaiah. *The Crooked Timber of Humanity: Chapters in the History of Ideas*. New York: Vintage Books, 1992.

Berman, Marshall. *All That Is Solid Melts Into Air: The Experience of Modernity*. New York: Simon and Schuster, 1982.

Bhabha, Homi, ed. *Nation and Narration*. New York: Routledge, 1990.

Blacker, Carmen. *The Japanese Enlightenment: A Study of the Writings of Fukuzawa Yukichi*. Cambridge: Cambridge University Press, 1964.

Booth, Wayne C. *The Rhetoric of Fiction*. Chicago: The University of Chicago Press, 1983.

Borges, Jorge Luis. *Labyrinths: Selected Stories and Other Writings*. Edited by Donald A. Yates and James E. Irby. New York: New Directions Books, 1964.

Bouwsma, William J. *A Usable Past: Essays in European Cultural History*. Berkeley: University of California Press, 1990.

Bowring, Richard. *Mori Ōgai and the Modernization of Japanese Culture*. Cambridge: Cambridge University Press, 1979.

Breen, John. "The Imperial Oath of April 1868: Ritual, Politics, and Power in the Restoration." *Monumenta Nipponica* 51, no. 4 (Winter 1996): 407–429.

Brower, Robert H. "Masaoka Shiki and Tanka Reform." In *Tradition and Modernization in Japanese Culture*, edited by Donald Shively, 379–418. Princeton, N.J.: Princeton University Press, 1971.

Budick, Sanford and Wolfgang Iser, eds. *The Translatability of Cultures: Figurations of the Space Between*. Stanford, Calif.: Stanford University Press, 1996.

Bungaku henshūbu, ed. *Hon'yaku*. Tokyo: Iwanami shoten, 1982.

Bungei dokuhon: Yokomitsu Riichi. Kawade shobō, 1981.

Burns, Stanley. *Sleeping Beauty: Memorial Photography in America*. Altadena, Calif.: Twelvetrees Press, 1990.

Burns, Susan L. *Before the Nation: Kokugaku and the Imagining of Community in Early Modern Japan*. Durham, N.C.: Duke University Press, 2003.

Bush, Susan. *The Chinese Literati on Painting: Su Shih (1037–1101) to Tung Chi-chang (1555–1636)*. Cambridge, Mass.: Harvard University Press, 1971.

Calinescu, Matei. *Five Faces of Modernity: Modernism, Avant-Garde, Decadence, Kitsch, Postmodernism*. Durham, N.C.: Duke University Press, 1987.

Chang, H. C., ed. *Tales of the Supernatural in Chinese Literature*. 3 vols. New York: Columbia University Press, 1984.

Clifford, Nicholas R. *Spoilt Children of Empire: Westerners in Shanghai and the Chinese Revolution of the 1920s*. Hanover, N.H.: University Press of New England, 1991.

Davidson, Donald. *Inquiries Into Truth and Interpretation*. Oxford: Clarendon Press, 1984.

de Bary, Wm. Theodore. *Learning for One's Self: Essays on the Individual in Neo-Confucian Thought*. New York: Columbia University Press, 1991.

——. *Neo-Confucian Orthodoxy and the Learning of the Mind-and-Heart*. New York: Columbia University Press, 1981.

——. "Sagehood as a Secular and Spiritual Ideal in Tokugawa Neo-Confucianism." In *Principle and Practicality: Essays in Neo-Confucianism and Practical Learning*, edited by Wm. Theodore de Bary and Irene Bloom, 127–188. New York: Columbia University Press, 1979.

Debord, Guy. *The Society of the Spectacle*. Translated by Donald Nicholson-Smith. New York: Zone Books, 1994.

de Man, Paul. *Blindness and Insight: Essays in the Rhetoric of Contemporary Criticism*. Minneapolis: University of Minnesota Press, 1983.

——. "The Epistemology of Metaphor." *Critical Inquiry* 5 (Autumn 1978): 13–30.

Doak, Kevin Michael. *Dreams of Difference: The Japan Romantic School and the Crisis of Modernity*. Berkeley: University of California Press, 1994.

Dodd, Stephen. *Writing Home: Representations of the Native Place in Modern Japanese Literature*. Cambridge, Mass.: Harvard University Asia Center, 2004.

Dower, John. *War Without Mercy: Race and Power in the Pacific War*. New York: Pantheon Books, 1986.

Ebara, Taizō. *Edo bungaku kenkyū*. Tokyo: Kadokawa shoten, 1958.

Etō, Jun. *Kindai izen*. Tokyo: Seikyōsha, 1985.

Ferrara, Alessandro. *Modernity and Authenticity: A Study of the Social and Ethical Thought of Jean-Jacques Rousseau*. Albany: State University of New York Press, 1993.

Forgacs, David. "Fascism, Violence, and Modernity." In *The Violent Muse: Violence and the Artistic Imagination in Europe, 1910–1939*, edited by Jana Howlett and Rod Mengham, 5–21. Manchester: Manchester University Press, 1994.

Foucault, Michel. *The Foucault Reader*. Edited by Paul Rabinow. New York: Pantheon Books, 1984.

Frank, Joseph. "Spatial Form in Modern Literature." *Sewanee Review* 53 (Spring, Summer, Autumn 1945): 221–240, 433–456, 643–653.

Freeman, Mark. *Rewriting the Self: History, Memory, Narrative*. New York: Routledge, 1993.

Friedland, Roger and Deirdre Boden, eds. *NowHere: Space, Time, and Modernity*. Berkeley: University of California Press, 1994.

Friedlander, Saul. *Reflections of Nazism: An Essay on Kitsch and Death*. Translated by Thomas Weyr. Bloomington: Indiana University Press, 1993.

Fujimura hakushi kōseki kinenkai, ed. *Kinsei bungaku no kenkyū*. Tokyo: Shibundō, 1936.

Fukuda, Tsuneari. *Sakkaron*. In *Fukuda Tsuneari hyōronshū*, vol. 3. Tokyo: Shinchōsha, 1966.

Fukuzawa, Yukichi. *An Encouragement of Learning*. Translated by David Dilworth and Umeyo Hirano. Tokyo: Sophia University Press, 1969.

———. *Fukuzawa Yukichi shū*. In *Nihon gendai bungaku zenshū*, vol. 2. Tokyo: Kōdansha, 1969.

Genette, Gerard. *Narrative Discourse: An Essay in Method*. Ithaca, N.Y.: Cornell University Press, 1980.

Gergen, Kenneth. "Social Understanding and the Inscription of Self." In *Cultural Psychology: Essays on Comparative Human Development*, edited by James Stigler, Richard Shweder, Gilbert Herdt, 569–606. New York: Cambridge University Press, 1990.

Gerstle, C. Andrew. *Circles of Fantasy: Convention in the Plays of Chikamatsu*. Cambridge, Mass.: Harvard University Press, 1986.

Giddens, Anthony. *The Consequences of Modernity*. Stanford, Calif.: Stanford University Press, 1990.

Girard, René. "The Founding Murder in the Philosophy of Nietzsche." In *Violence and Truth: On the Work of René Girard*, edited by Paul Dumouchel, 227–246. Stanford, Calif.: Stanford University Press, 1988.

Gluck, Carol. *Japan's Modern Myths: Ideology in the Late Meiji Period*. Princeton, N.J.: Princeton University Press, 1985.

Golley, Gregory. *Voices in the Machine: Technology and Japanese Literary Modernism*. Los Angeles: Ph. D. dissertation, University of California at Los Angeles, 2000.

Gordon, Andrew. *A Modern History of Japan: From Tokugawa Times to the Present*. New York: Oxford University Press, 2003.

Goudsblom, Johan. *Nihilism and Culture*. Totowa, N.J.: Rowman and Littlefield, 1980.

Greenblatt, Stephen. *Marvelous Possessions: The Wonder of the New World*. Chicago: University of Chicago Press, 1991.

Hanan, Patrick. *The Chinese Vernacular Story*. Cambridge, Mass.: Harvard University Press, 1981.

Hardin, James, ed. *Reflection and Action*. Columbia: University of South Carolina Press, 1991.

Harootunian, H. D. "America's Japan/Japan's Japan." In *Japan in the World*, edited by Masao Miyoshi and H. D. Harootunian, 196–221. Durham, N.C.: Duke University Press, 1993.

———. "Late Tokugawa Culture and Thought." In *The Emergence of Meiji Japan*, edited by Marius Jansen, 53–143. New York: Cambridge University Press, 1995.

———. *Overcome by Modernity: History, Culture, and Community in Interwar Japan*. Princeton, N.J.: Princeton University Press, 2000.

———. *Things Seen and Unseen: Discourse and Ideology in Tokugawa Nativism*. Chicago: The University of Chicago Press, 1988.

Harvey, David. *The Condition of Postmodernity.* Oxford: Basil Blackwell, 1989.

———. *Spaces of Capital: Towards a Critical Geography.* New York: Routledge, 2001.

Hassan, Ihab. *Selves at Risk: Patterns of Quest in Contemporary American Letters.* Madison: The University of Wisconsin Press, 1990.

Havens, Thomas R. H. *Nishi Amane and Modern Japanese Thought.* Princeton, N.J.: Princeton University Press, 1970.

Hegel, Robert E. *The Novel in Seventeenth-Century China.* New York: Columbia University Press, 1981.

Hegel, Robert E. and Richard C. Hessney, eds. *Expressions of Self in Chinese Literature.* New York: Columbia University Press, 1985.

Heisig, James W. and John C. Maraldo. *Rude Awakenings: Zen, the Kyoto School, and the Question of Nationalism.* Honolulu: University of Hawaii Press, 1994.

Hibbett, Howard. *The Floating World in Japanese Fiction.* New York: Oxford University Press, 1959.

Howland, Douglas. "Nishi Amane's Efforts to Translate Western Knowledge: Sound, Written Character, and Meaning." *Semiotica* 83, no. 3/4 (1991): 283–310.

Hsia, C. T. *The Classic Chinese Novel: A Critical Introduction.* New York: Columbia University Press, 1968.

Ikeda, Jun'ichi. *Ōoka Shōhei.* Tokyo: Tōjusha, 1979.

Irokawa, Daikichi. *The Culture of the Meiji Period.* Edited by Marius Jansen. Princeton, N.J.: Princeton University Press, 1985.

Ishii, Yasushi. "how ghostly were the 1920s in Japan? a projection without sources." *Stanford (Electronic) Humanities Review* 5. Supplement: *Cultural and Technological Incubations of Fascism* (December 1996). http://www.stanford. edu/group/ SHR/5-supp/text/ishii.html.

Isoda, Kōichi. "Mishima no kindaisei—jishu sekinin no ronri." In *Isoda Kōichi chōsaku shū*, vol. 1, 302–304. Tokyo: Ozawa shoten, 1990.

———. *Shisō to shite no Tōkyō.* Tokyo: Kōdansha, 1990.

Ivy, Marilyn. *Discourses of the Vanishing: Modernity, Phantasm, Japan.* Chicago: Chicago University Press, 1995.

Jansen, Marius. *Sakamoto Ryōma and the Meiji Restoration.* New York: Columbia University Press, 1994.

Jay, Martin. "Scopic Regimes of Modernity." In *Vision and Visuality*, edited by Hal Foster, 3–27. Seattle: Bay Press, 1988.

Jencks, Charles. *The Language of Post-Modern Architecture.* New York: Rizzoli International Publications, Inc., 1984.

Johnson, Barbara. "Taking Fidelity Philosophically." In *Difference in Translation*, edited by Joseph F. Graham, 142–148. Ithaca, N.Y.: Cornell University Press, 1985.

Johnson, Chalmers. "The People Who Invented the Mechanical Nightingale." In *Showa: The Japan of Hirohito*, edited by Carol Gluck and Stephen Graubard, 71–90. New York: W. W. Norton & Company, 1992.

Kao, Karl S. Y., ed. *Classical Chinese Tales of the Supernatural and the Fantastic.* Bloomington: Indiana University Press, 1985.

Karatani, Kōjin. *Origins of Modern Japanese Literature.* Edited by Brett de Bary. Durham, N.C.: Duke University Press, 1993.

Katō, Shūichi. *A History of Japanese Literature.* Vol. 2, *The Years of Isolation.* Translated by Don Sanderson. London: The Macmillan Press, Ltd., 1983.

Katō, Shūichi, Maruyama Masao, et al., eds. *Hon'yaku no shisō.* In *Nihon kindai shisō taikei,* vol. 15. Tokyo: Iwanami shoten, 1991.

Katsukura, Toshikazu. *Ugetsu monogatari kōsōron.* Tokyo: Kyōiku shuppan sentaa, 1977.

Katsura, Juichi. *Kindai shutaishugi no hatten to genkai.* Tokyo: Tōkyō daigaku shuppankai, 1974.

Kawamura, Minato. *Iyō no ryōiki.* Tokyo: Kokubunsha, 1983.

Kayanuma, Noriko. *Akinari bungaku no sekai.* Tokyo: Kasama shoin, 1979.

Keene, Dennis. *Yokomitsu Riichi: Modernist.* New York: Columbia University Press, 1980.

Keene, Donald. *Dawn to the West: Japanese Literature of the Modern Era.* New York: Holt, Rinehart, and Winston, 1984.

———. *World Within Walls: Japanese Literature of the Pre-Modern Era, 1600–1867.* New York: Holt, Rinehart, and Winston, 1976.

Kermode, Frank. *The Sense of an Ending: Studies in the Theory of Fiction.* New York: Oxford University Press, 1967.

Kersten, Rikki. *Democracy in Postwar Japan: Maruyama Masao and the Search for Autonomy.* London: Routledge, 1996.

Kobayashi, Hideo. *Gohho no tegami.* In *Kobayashi Hideo zenshū,* vol. 10. Tokyo: Shinchōsha, 1979.

———. *Literature of the Lost Home: Kobayashi Hideo—Literary Criticism 1924–1939.* Translated by Paul Anderer. Stanford, Calif.: Stanford University Press, 1995.

Koepke, Wulf. "*Bildung* and the Transformation of Society: Jean Paul's *Titan* and *Flegeljahre*." In *Reflection and Action,* edited by James Hardin, 228–253. Columbia: University of South Carolina Press, 1991.

Kojima, Nobuo. "Ōoka Shōhei to shinishizumu." In *Ōoka Shōhei, Fukunaga Takehiko,* edited by Nihon bungaku kenkyū shiryō kankōkai. Tokyo: Yūseidō, 1978.

Komori ,Yoichi. *Kōzō to shite no katari.* Tokyo: Shiyōsha, 1988.

Konishi, Jin'ichi. "The Genesis of the *Kokinshū* Style." Translated by Helen McCullough. *Harvard Journal of Asiatic Studies* 38, no. 1 (June 1978): 61–170.

Kornicki, Peter. *The Book in Japan: A Cultural History from the Beginnings to the Nineteenth Century.* Honolulu: University of Hawaii Press, 2001.

Korsgaard, Christine. *The Sources of Normativity.* Cambridge: The Tanner Lectures on Human Values, Clare Hall, Cambridge University, November, 1992.

Koschmann, Victor J. "Maruyama Masao and the Incomplete Project of Modernity." In *Postmodernism and Japan*, edited by Masao Miyoshi and H. D. Harootunian, 123–141. Durham, N.C.: Duke University Press, 1989.

Leutner, Robert W. *Shikitei Sanba and the Comic Tradition in Edo Fiction.* Cambridge, Mass.: Harvard University Press, 1985.

Levenson, Joseph. "The Amateur Ideal in Ming and Early Ch'ing Society: Evidence from Painting." In *Chinese Thought and Institutions*, edited by John K. Fairbank, 320–341. Chicago: The University of Chicago Press, 1957.

Levine, George. *The Realistic Imagination: English Fiction from Frankenstein to Lady Chatterley.* Chicago: The University of Chicago Press, 1981.

Lippitt, Seiji. *Topographies of Japanese Modernism.* New York: Columbia University Press, 2002.

Liu, Lydia. *Translingual Practice: Literature, National Culture and Translated Modernity—China 1900–1937.* Stanford, Calif.: Stanford University Press, 1995.

Lloyd, David. *Anomalous States: Irish Writing and the Postcolonial Movement.* Durham, N.C.: Duke University Press, 1993.

Lukács, Georg. *Essays on Realism.* Edited by Rodney Livingstone. Translated by David Fernbach. Cambridge, Mass.: The MIT Press, 1980.

——. *The Theory of the Novel.* Translated by Anna Bostock. Cambridge, Mass.: The MIT Press, 1971.

MacIntyre, Alasdair. "Incommensurability, Truth, and the Conversation between Confucians and Aristotelians about the Virtues." In *Culture and Modernity: East-West Philosophic Perspectives*, edited by Eliot Deutsch, 104–122. Honolulu: University of Hawaii Press, 1991.

——. *Whose Justice? Which Rationality?* South Bend, Ind.: University of Notre Dame Press, 1988.

Mack, Edward Thomas. *The Value of Literature: Cultural Authority in Interwar Japan.* Cambridge, Mass.: Ph. D. dissertation, Harvard University, May 2002.

Maeda, Ai. *Gen'ei no Meiji.* In *Maeda Ai chosakushū*, vol. 4. Tokyo: Chikuma shobō, 1989.

——. *Kindai dokusha no seiritsu.* In *Maeda Ai choshakushū*, vol. 2. Tokyo: Chikuma shobō, 1989.

——. "Kodomotachi no jikan, *Takekurabe*." In *Higuchi Ichiyō no sekai*. In *Maeda Ai chosakushū*, vol. 3, 265–292. Tokyo: Chikuma shobo, 1989.

——. *Toshi kūkan no naka no bungaku.* In *Maeda Ai choshakushū*, vol. 5. Tokyo: Chikuma shobō, 1989.

Man'yōshū, vol. 4. In *Nihon no koten*, vol. 5. Tokyo: Shōgakukan, 1985.

Maruyama, Masao. *Nihon no shisō.* Tokyo: Iwanami shoten, 1961.

——. *Studies in the Intellectual History of Tokugawa Japan.* Translated by Mikiso Hane. Princeton, N.J.: Princeton University Press and Tokyo: Tokyo University Press, 1974.

Matsuo, Yasuaki. *Kinsei no bungaku: Bashō, Saikaku, Akinari.* Tokyo: Bunka shobō, 1963.

McClellan, Edwin. *Two Japanese Novelists: Sōseki and Tōson.* Chicago: University of Chicago Press, 1969.

Miller, Henry. *Reflections on the Death of Mishima.* Santa Barbara, Calif.: Capra Press, 1972.

Mishima, Yukio. *Mishima Yukio zenshū.* Tokyo: Shinchōsha, 1975.

——. Preface to *Ordeal by Roses: Photographs of Yukio Mishima by Eikoh Hosoe.* New York: Aperture, 1985.

Miyake, Setsurei. "Miyake Setsurei shū." In *Nihon gendai bungaku zenshū*, vol. 2. Tokyo: Kōdansha, 1969.

Mizumura, Minae. "Resisting Women—Reading Sōseki's Gubijinsō." In *Studies in Modern Japanese Literature: Essays and Translations in Honor of Edwin McClellan*, edited by Dennis Washburn and Alan Tansman, 23–37. Ann Arbor: Center for Japanese Studies, The University of Michigan, 1997.

Mori, Ōgai. *Seinen.* In *Ōgai zenshū*, vol. 6. Tokyo: Iwanami shoten, 1972.

——. *Youth and Other Stories.* Edited by J. Thomas Rimer. Honolulu: University of Hawaii Press, 1994.

Morita, Kirō. *Ueda Akinari no kenkyū.* Tokyo: Kasama shoin, 1979.

Moriyama, Shigeo. *Genyō no bungaku: Ueda Akinari.* Tokyo: San'ichi shobō, 1982.

——. *Ueda Akinari: shiteki jōnen no sekai.* Tokyo: San'ichi shobō, 1986.

——. *Ueda Akinari shoki ukiyo-zōshi hyōshaku.* Tokyo: Kokusho kankōkai, 1977.

Morris, Ivan. Introduction to *Modern Japanese Stories: An Anthology.* Rutland, Vt.: Charles E. Tuttle Company, 1962.

Morris, Mark. "Buson and Shiki." *Harvard Journal of Asiatic Studies* 44, no. 2 (December 1984): 381–425 and *Harvard Journal of Asiatic Studies* 45, no. 1 (June 1985): 255–321.

Motoori, Norinaga. *Kinsei bungakuronshū.* In *Nihon koten bungaku taikei*, vol. 94. Tokyo: Iwanami shoten, 1966.

Murakami, Haruki. *Hitsuji o meguru bōken.* Tokyo: Kōdansha bunko, 1985.

——. *Pan'ya saishūgeki.* Tokyo: Bunshun bunko, 1989.

Murasaki Shikibu. *Genji monogatari.* In *Nihon koten bungaku zenshū*, vol. 14. Tokyo: Shōgakukan, 1972.

Nagel, Thomas. *The View from Nowhere.* New York: Oxford University Press, 1986.

Najita, Tetsuo. *Visions of Virtue in Tokugawa Japan.* Chicago: The University of Chicago Press, 1987.

Najita, Tetsuo and Irwin Scheiner, eds. *Japanese Thought in the Tokugawa Period: Methods and Metaphors.* Chicago: University of Chicago Press, 1978.

Nakamura, Shin'ichirō. "Akutagawa Ryūnosuke nyūmon." In *Nihon gendai bungaku zenshū*, vol. 56. Tokyo: Kōdansha, 1960.

Nakamura, Yukihiko. *Kinsei sakka kenkyū.* Tokyo: San'ichi shobō, 1961.

————. *Kinsei shōsetsushi no kenkyū.* Tokyo: Ōfūsha, 1961.

Nakamura, Yukihiko, ed. *Kinsei bungakuronshū.* In *Nihon koten bungaku taikei,* vol. 94. Tokyo: Iwanami shoten, 1966.

Nakano, Kōji. *Zettai reido no bungaku.* Tokyo: Shūeisha, 1976.

Natsume, Sōseki. *Natsume Sōseki zenshū.* 7 vols. Tokyo: Iwanami shoten, 1956.

————. *Sanshirō: A Novel.* Translated by Jay Rubin. Seattle: University of Washington Press, 1977.

Nicholls, Peter. *Modernisms.* Berkeley: University of California Press, 1995.

Nihon bungaku kenkyū shiryō kankōkai, ed. *Meiji no bungaku.* Tokyo: Yūseidō, 1981.

Nishi, Amane. *Nishi Amane tetsugaku chosakushū.* Edited by Asō Yoshiteru. Tokyo: Iwanami shoten, 1933.

————. *Nishi Amane zenshū.* Edited by Ōkubo Toshiaki. Tokyo: Munetake shobō, 1960.

Niwa, Jun'ichirō. *Ōshū kiji: Karyū shunwa. Meiji hon'yaku bungaku shū.* In *Meiji bungaku zenshū,* vol. 7. Tokyo: Chikuma shobō, 1972.

Nosco, Peter. *Remembering Paradise: Nativism and Nostalgia in Eighteenth-Century Japan.* Cambridge, Mass.: Council on East Asian Studies, Harvard University, 1990.

Nosco, Peter, ed. *Confucianism and Tokugawa Culture.* Princeton, N.J.: Princeton University Press, 1984.

Nussbaum, Martha. *Love's Knowledge: Essays on Philosophy and Literature.* New York: Oxford University Press, 1990.

Odaka, Toshirō. *Kinsei shoki bundan no kenkyū.* Tokyo: Meiji shoin, 1964.

Ōe, Kenzaburō. *Japan, the Ambiguous, and Myself: The Nobel Prize Speech and Other Lectures.* Tokyo: Kodansha, 1995.

Okakura, Kakuzō. *The Awakening of Japan.* New York: The Century Co., 1904. Reprint, New York: The Japan Society, Inc., 1921.

————. *The Book of Tea.* New York: Dover Publications, Inc., 1964.

Ōoka, Shōhei. *Fires on the Plain.* Translated by Ivan Morris. Rutland: Charles E. Tuttle Co., 1957.

————. "Musashino fujin no ito." In *Ōoka Shōhei shū,* vol. 15. Tokyo: Iwanami shoten, 1982.

————. "Nobi no ito." In *Ōoka Shōhei shū,* vol. 15. Tokyo: Iwanami shoten, 1982.

————. *A Wife in Musashino.* Translated by Dennis Washburn. Ann Arbor: Center for Japanese Studies, The University of Michigan, 2004.

Ooms, Herman. *Tokugawa Ideology: Early Constructs, 1570–1680.* Princeton, N.J.: Princeton University Press, 1985.

Ōwa, Yasuhiro. *Ueda Akinari bungaku no kenkyū.* Tokyo: Kasama shoin, 1976.

Parkin, Alan J. *Memory: Phenomena, Experiment, and Theory.* Cambridge, Mass.: Blackwell Publishers, 1993.

Paz, Octavio. "Translation: Literature and Letters." In *Theories of Translation: An Anthology of Essays from Dryden to Derrida*, edited by Rainer Schulte and John Biguenet, 152–162. Chicago: University of Chicago Press, 1992.

Pincus, Leslie. "In a Labyrinth of Western Desire: Kuki Shuzo and the Discovery of Japanese Being." In *Japan in the World*, edited by Masao Miyoshi and H. D. Harootunian, 222–236. Durham, N.C.: Duke University Press, 1993.

Plaks, Andrew H. *The Four Masterworks of the Ming Novel*. Princeton, N.J.: Princeton University Press, 1987.

Plaks, Andrew H., ed. *Chinese Narrative: Critical and Theoretical Essays*. Princeton, N.J.: Princeton University Press, 1977.

Prusek, Jaroslav. "Urban Centers: The Cradle of Popular Fiction." In *Studies in Chinese Literary Genres*, edited by Cyril Birch, 259–298. Berkeley: University of California Press, 1974.

Pyle, Kenneth B. *The New Generation in Meiji Japan: Problems of Cultural Identity, 1885–1895*. Stanford, Calif.: Stanford University Press, 1969.

Redfield, Marc. *Phantom Formations: Aesthetic Ideology and the Bildungsroman*. Ithaca, N.Y.: Cornell University Press, 1996.

Ricoeur, Paul. *Time and Narrative*. Translated by Kathleen Blamey and David Pellauer. Chicago: University of Chicago Press, 1988.

Rimer, J. Thomas, ed. *Culture and Identity: Japanese Intellectuals During the Interwar Years*. Princeton, N.J.: Princeton University Press, 1990.

Rorty, Richard. *Philosophy and the Mirror of Nature*. Princeton, N.J.: Princeton University Press, 1979.

Russell, Bertrand. *The Problem of China*. London: George Allen & Unwin Ltd., 1922.

Sakai, Naoki. "Return to the West/Return to the East: Watsuji Tetsuro's Anthropology and Discussions of Authenticity." In *Japan in the World*, edited by Masao Miyoshi and H. D. Harootunian, 237–270. Durham, N.C.: Duke University Press, 1993.

———. *Voices of the Past: The Status of Language in Eighteenth-Century Japanese Discourse*. Ithaca, N.Y.: Cornell University Press, 1991.

Sas, Miryam. *Fault Lines: Cultural Memory and Japanese Surrealism*. Stanford, Calif.: Stanford University Press, 1999.

Sharf, Robert. *Coming to Terms with Chinese Buddhism: A Reading of the Treasure Store Treatise*. Honolulu: University of Hawaii Press, 2002.

Shiga, Shigetaka. *Nihon fūkeiron*. Tokyo: Iwanami shoten, 1937.

Shigetomo, Ki. *Akinari no kenkyū*. Tokyo: Bunri shoin, 1971.

———. *Kinsei bungakushi no shomondai*. Tokyo: Meiji shoin, 1963.

Shikitei Sanba. *Ukiyoburo*. In *Nihon koten bungaku taikei*, vol. 63. Edited by Nakamura Michio. Tokyo: Iwanami shoten, 1957.

Shimomura, Toratarō. "Nishida Kitarō and Some Aspects of His Philosophical Thought." In *Nishida Kitarō. A Study of Good*, 191–217. Tokyo: Printing Bureau, Japanese Government, 1960.

Shirane, Haruo and Tomi Suzuki, eds. *Inventing the Classics: Modernity, National Identity and Japanese Literature.* Stanford, Calif.: Stanford University Press, 2000.

Shroyer, Trent. Foreword to *The Jargon of Authenticity.* By Theodor Adorno. Evanston, Ill.: Northwestern University Press, 1973.

Shweder, Richard. *Thinking Through Cultures: Expeditions in Cultural Psychology.* Cambridge, Mass.: Harvard University Press, 1991.

Singer, Jefferson and Peter Salovey. *The Remembered Self.* New York: The Free Press, 1993.

Sinnott-Armstrong, Walter and Mark Timmons, eds. *Moral Knowledge?: New Readings in Moral Epistemology.* New York: Oxford University Press, 1996.

Soja, Edward. *Postmodern Geographies: The Reassertion of Space in Critical Social Theory.* New York: Verso, 1989.

Stahl, David. *The Burdens of Survival: Ōoka Shōhei's Writings on the Pacific War.* Honolulu: University of Hawaii Press, 2003.

Steiner, George. *After Babel: Aspects of Language and Translation.* New York: Oxford University Press, 1992.

———. *Real Presences.* Chicago: The University of Chicago Press, 1989.

Sugano, Akimasa. "Samayou Shanghai no Nihonjin." In *Shanghai.* By Yokomitsu Riichi. Tokyo: Kōdansha, 1991.

Sugimoto, Tsutomu. *Edo no hon'yakukatachi.* Tokyo: Wasdea daigaku shuppanbu, 1995.

———. *Nihon hon'yakugoshi no kenkyū.* Tokyo: Yasaka shobō, 1983.

Swales, Martin. "Irony and the Novel: Reflections on the German Bildungsroman." In *Reflection and Action,* edited by James Hardin, 46–68. Columbia: University of South Carolina Press, 1991.

Tanaka, Toshikazu. *Ueda Akinari bungei no sekai.* Tokyo: Ōfūsha, 1979.

Tansman, Alan. "Bridges to Nowhere: Yasuda Yojūrō's Language of Violence and Desire." *Harvard Journal of Asiatic Studies* 56, no. 1 (June 1996): 35–75.

Taylor, Charles. *The Ethics of Authenticity.* Cambridge, Mass.: Harvard University Press, 1992.

———. *Philosophy and the Human Sciences.* New York: Cambridge University Press, 1985.

Todorov, Tzvetan. *The Fantastic: A Structural Approach to a Literary Genre.* Translated by Richard Howard. Cleveland: Case Western Reserve University Press, 1973.

———. *The Poetics of Prose.* Translated by Richard Howard. Ithaca, N.Y.: Cornell University Press, 1977.

Tokutomi, Sohō. *The Future Japan,* Edmonton: The University of Alberta Press, 1989.

Tsubouchi, Shōyō. *Shōyō senshū.* Edited by Shōyō kyōkai. Tokyo: Dai'ichi shobō, 1977.

Tsuga, Teishō. *Hanabusa sōshi*. In *Nihon koten bungaku zenshū*, vol. 48, edited by Nakamura Hiroyasu, Nakamura Yukihiko, and Takada Mamoru. Tokyo: Shōgakukan, 1973.

Tsunoda, Ryusaku, Wm. Theodore de Bary, and Donald Keene, eds. *Sources of the Japanese Tradition*. New York: Columbia University Press, 1958.

Turney, Alan. Introduction to *The Three-Cornered World*. By Natsume Sōseki. Translated by Alan Turney. London: Peter Owen, 1965.

Ueda, Akinari. *Akinari ibun*. Edited by Fujii Otoo. Tokyo: Kokusho kankōkai, 1974.

———. *Seken tekake katagi*. In *Ueda Akinari shoki ukiyo-zōshi hyōshaku*, by Moriyama Shigeo. Tokyo: Kokusho kankōkai, 1977.

———. *Tales of Moonlight and Rain*. Translated by Leon Zolbrod. Vancouver: University of British Columbia Press, 1974.

———. *Tandai shōshin roku*. In *Ueda Akinari zenshū*, vol. 1. Tokyo: Kokusho kankōkai, 1969

———. *Ueda Akinari shū*. In *Nihon koten bungaku taikei*, vol. 56, edited by Nakamura Yukihiko. Tokyo: Iwanami shoten, 1959.

———. *Ueda Akinari zenshū*. Edited by Suzuki Toshiya. Tokyo: Fuzambō, 1938.

———. *Ugetsu monogatari*. In *Nihon koten bungaku zenshū*, vol. 48, edited by Nakamura Hiroyasu, Nakamura Yukihiko, and Takada Mamoru. Tokyo: Shōgakukan, 1973.

Uno, Kōji. *Uno Kōji zenshū*, vol. 10. Tokyo: Chūō kōronsha, 1968.

Uzuki, Hiroshi. *Ugetsu monogatari hyōshaku*. Tokyo: Kadokawa shoten, 1969.

Venuti, Lawrence. *The Translator's Invisibility: A History of Translation*. London and New York: Routledge, 1995.

Vlastos, Stephen, ed. *Mirror of Modernity: Invented Traditions of Modern Japan*. Berkeley: University of California Press, 1998.

Washburn, Dennis. *The Dilemma of the Modern in Japanese Fiction*. New Haven, Conn.: Yale University Press, 1995.

Washiyama, Jushin. *Akinari bungaku no shisō*. Kyoto: Hōzōkan, 1979.

———. *Ueda Akinari no bungeiteki kyōkai*. Osaka: Izumi shoin, 1983.

Watsuji, Tetsurō. *A Climate: A Philosophical Study*. Translated by Geoffrey Bownas. Tokyo: Printing Bureau, Japanese Government, 1961.

———. *Fūdo; ningengakuteki kōsatsu*. Tokyo: Iwanami shoten, 1940.

Watt, Ian. *The Rise of the Novel: Studies in Defoe, Richardson, and Fielding*. Berkeley: University of California Press, 1957.

Weisenfeld, Gennifer. *Mavo: Japanese Artists and the Avant-Garde, 1905–1931*. Berkeley: University of California Press, 2002.

Welty, Eudora. *On Writing*. New York: Modern Library, 2002.

Williams, Bernard. *Shame and Necessity*. Berkeley: University of California Press, 1993.

Wilson, William Ritchie. "The Truth of *Haikai.*" *Monumenta Nipponica* 26, no. 1–2 (1971): 49–53.

Wollheim, Richard. *The Thread of Life.* Cambridge, Mass.: Harvard University Press, 1984.

Yamazaki, Kuninori. *Yokomitsu Riichi ron.* Tokyo: Hokuyōsha, 1979.

———. *Seiyō bungaku no in'yū.* Tokyo: Shunjūsha, 1974.

Yanagida, Izumi. *Meiji shoki hon'yaku bungaku kenkyū.* Tokyo: Shunjūsha, 1971.

Yang, Winston L. Y., and Curtis Adkins, eds. *Critical Essays on Chinese Fiction.* Hong Kong: The Chinese University Press, 1980.

Yang, Winston L. Y., Peter Li, and Nathan K. Mao, eds. *Classical Chinese Fiction.* Boston: G. K. Hall & Co., 1978.

Yates, Frances A. *The Art of Memory.* Chicago: University of Chicago Press, 1966.

Yiu, Angela. *Chaos and Order in the Works of Natsume Sōseki.* Honolulu: University of Hawaii Press, 1998.

Yokomitsu, Riichi. *Ai no aisatsu, Basha, Junsui shōsetsu ron.* Tokyo: Kōdansha, 1993.

———. *Shanghai.* Translated by Dennis Washburn. Ann Arbor: Center for Japanese Studies, The University of Michigan, 2001.

———. *Yokomitsu Riichi zenshū.* Kawade shobō, 1956.

———. *Yokomitsu Riichi zenshū.* Tokyo: Kawade shobō, 1987.

Yosa, Buson. *Buson shū.* In *Nihon koten bungaku taikei*, vol. 58, edited by Teruoka Yasutaka. Tokyo: Iwanami shoten, 1969.

Young, Blake Morgan. *Ueda Akinari.* Vancouver: University of British Columbia Press, 1982.

Index